Frontiers of Research in Intra-Industry Trade

Frontiers of Research in Intra-Industry Trade

Edited by

P. J. Lloyd
Ritchie Professor of Economics
University of Melbourne
Australia

and

Hyun-Hoon Lee
Professor of Economics, Division of Economics and International Trade
Kangwon National University
South Korea

First published 2002 by
PALGRAVE MACMILLAN
Houndmills, Basingstoke, Hampshire RG21 6XS and
175 Fifth Avenue, New York, N.Y. 10010
Companies and representatives throughout the world

PALGRAVE MACMILLAN is the global academic imprint of the Palgrave Macmillan division of St. Martin's Press, LLC and of Palgrave Macmillan Ltd. Macmillan® is a registered trademark in the United States, United Kingdom and other countries. Palgrave is a registered trademark in the European Union and other countries.

ISBN 0–333–97126–4

This book is printed on paper suitable for recycling and made from fully managed and sustained forest sources.

A catalogue record for this book is available from the British Library.

Library of Congress Cataloging-in-Publication Data
Frontiers of research in intra-industry trade / edited by
P. J. Lloyd and Hyun-Hoon Lee.
    p. cm.
  Papers from a conference on the Frontiers of research
in intra-industry trade held at the University of Colorado
at Boulder on Aug. 24–26, 2000.
  Includes bibliographical references and index.
  ISBN 0–333–97126–4
    1. Intra-industry trade—Congresses. 2. Intra-industry
trade—Econometric models—Congresses. I. Lloyd,
P. J. (Peter John) II. Lee, Hyon-Hoon, 1959–
HF1414.35 .F76 2002
382–dc21   2001058217

10 9 8 7 6 5 4 3 2 1
11 10 09 08 07 06 05 04 03 02

Printed and bound in Great Britain by
Antony Rowe Ltd, Chippenham and Eastbourne

Contents

List of Tables   vii

List of Figures   x

Acknowledgements   xi

Notes on the Contributors   xii

List of Abbreviations   xiv

1 Introduction
   P. J. Lloyd and Hyun-Hoon Lee   1

Part I   Development of Intra-Industry Theory and Measurement

2 Controversies Concerning Intra-Industry Trade
   P. J. Lloyd   13

Part II   Models of Intra-Industry Trade

3 Horizontal Intra-Industry Trade and the Growth of
   International Trade
   Nicolas Schmitt and Zhihao Yu   33

4 Intra-Industry Trade in Homogeneous Products
   Daniel M. Bernhofen   49

5 Fragmentation and Intra-Industry Trade
   Ronald W. Jones, Henryk Kierzkowski and Gregory Leonard   67

6 The Geography of Intra-Industry Trade
   Mary Amiti and Anthony J. Venables   87

**Part III   Empirical Studies and Policy Issues of
Intra-Industry Trade**

7 Marginal Intra-Industry Trade: Towards a Measure
   of Non-Disruptive Trade Expansion
   Marius Brülhart   109

8 Long-Term Trends in Intra-Industry Trade
Lionel Fontagné and Michael Freudenberg   131

9 Intra-Industry Trade in Services
Hyun-Hoon Lee and P. J. Lloyd   159

10 Intra-Industry Trade and the C–H–O Model:
evidence and Implications for Adjustments
David Greenaway and Chris Milner   180

Part IV Intra-Industry Trade, Affiliate Production and FDI

11 A Unified Approach to Intra-Industry Trade and
Foreign Direct Investment
James R. Markusen and Keith E. Maskus   199

12 Factor Endowments and Intra-Industry Affiliate Production
by Multinational Enterprises
Karolina Ekholm   220

13 Globalization and Intra-Firm Trade: Further Evidence
Kiichiro Fukasaku and Fukunari Kimura   237

14 Intra-Industry Trade in Assets
Herbert G. Grubel   273

Author Index   291

Subject Index   293

List of Tables

3.1 Trade liberalization in the standard model
for $\frac{d(T/P)}{T/P} = 3$ per cent   39

3.2 Trade liberalization and non-traded goods
for $\frac{d(T/P)}{T/P} = 3$ per cent   44

5.1 US imports of televisions and parts from Mexico and
exports to Mexico, 1992–9   75

5.2 Grubel-Lloyd measure of intra-industry trade in
televisions, USA–Mexico, 1992–9   76

5.3 Grubel-Lloyd measure of intra-industry trade in
automobiles, USA–Mexico, 1992–9   77

5.4 Grubel-Lloyd measure of intra-industry trade in aircraft,
USA–Canada, 1992–9   79

5.5 Grubel-Lloyd measure of intra-industry trade in
semiconductors, USA–Canada, 1992–9   79

6.1 Benchmark case: $\sigma_1 = \sigma_2 = \sigma_3$, $t_1 = t_2 = t_3$ 95

6.2 Transport costs and demand elasticities:
$\sigma_2 < \sigma_1 = \sigma_3$, $t_2 < t_1 = t_3$ 97

8.1 Trade patterns and economic policy concerns   133

8.2 Share of trade types in EU-15 trade, 1999   141

8.3 Determinants of the share of trade types in bilateral
trade between EU-12 member countries, panel of 14
industries and 11 countries, 1980–94   146

8.4 EU-15 members trade by price–quality range, 1999   149

9.1 Share of services trade, 1992–6   164

9.2 Intra-industry trade in services by country, 1992–96,
1-digit industries   165

9.3 Intra-industry trade in services by country, 1992–6,
comparison between 1-digit and 2-digit industries   166

9.4 Intra-industry trade in services by industry, 1992–6   167

9.5 Determinants of IIT in services   171

9.6 Trade imbalance factors, 1992–6   174

10.1 Summary of some econometric evidence on relationships
between share of intra-industry trade in bilateral trade
and per-capita income differences   184

10.2 Summary of cross-sectional tests of the C–H–O
model for US–OECD trade, 1962–83   186

10.3   Panel equation tests of C–H–O model for US–OECD
         trade, 1962–83   187
10.4   Shares of horizontal and vertical IIT in USA's bilateral
         trade in manufactures   188
10.5   Relative importance of vertical and horizontal IIT in
         UK's bilateral intra-industry trade, manufactured
         goods, 1988   189
10.6   Summary of cross-section and panel testing of vertical
         IIT model for USA–OECD trade, 1989–92   192
10.7   Average levels of bilateral intra-industry trade in Asia,
         1984   193
11.1   Grubel-Lloyd indices, 1987 and 1997   202
11.2   Changes in Grubel–Lloyd indices for affiliate sales
         and total trade, 1987–97   203
11.3   Intra-industry affiliate sales logit regressions   213
11.4   Intra-industry trade logit regressions   215
11.5   Ratio of intra-industry affiliate sales to intra- industry
         trade OLS regressions   217
12.1   Intra-industry affiliate production between Sweden
         and other OECD countries   226
12.2   Grubel–Lloyd indices of intra-industry trade between
         Sweden and other OECD countries   227
12.3   Non-linear estimations of logistic functions   229
12.4   Random effects estimation of transformed
         logistic functions   231
12.5   Estimated change unexplained by included variables,
         1986–98   232
13.1   Significance of foreign affiliates in manufacturing
         industry of selected OECD countries, 1996   240
13.2   Patterns of globalization of industry, eight surveyed
         industries   242
13.3   US intra-firm trade in goods, 1977–97   245
13.4   US exports and imports shipped to/by MOFAs by/to
         non-bank US parents, by country of affiliate and
         by product, 1977–94   247
13.5   Trade between parents and affiliates by country of
         parent and country of affiliate, 1989 and 1994   249
13.6   Intra-firm transactions in the *Basic Survey of Business
         Structure and Activity* (1994 F/Y) (1)   251
13.7   Intra-firm transactions in the *Basic Survey of Business
         Structure and Activity* (1994 F/Y) (2)   254

13.8	Microdata regression results: manufacturing and non-manufacturing	258
13.9	Microdata regression results: machinery industries	259
13A.1	US merchandise exports and imports associated with non-bank US MNCs, 1977–97	262
13A.2	US merchandise exports and imports associated with non-bank US affiliates of foreign MNCs, 1977–97	265
13A.3	Intra-firm trade data in the *Basic Survey of Business Structure and Activity* (1994 F/Y)	267
14.1	Financial accounts for Germany, 1998	275
14.2	Direct investment, 1998	279
14.3	Direct investment by major regions, 1992–8	281
14.4	Portfolio investment flows, 1998	283
14.5	Portfolio investment – equities, GL Index and ranking, 1998	284
14.6	Other investments, flows 1998	287

List of Figures

6.1	Country 8 trade in goods 1 and 3	94
6.2	The location of production	98
6.3	Intra-industry trade indices for country 8	98
6.4	The location of production	101
6.5	Intra-industry trade of countries 4, 10 and 16	101
6.6	The location of production	102
6.7	Intra-industry trade of countries 4, 10 and 16	103
7.1	Measures of IIT and quasi-MIIT	115
7.2	MIIT measures	119
7.3	Measures of MIIT and sectoral performance	124
7.4	Hypothetical map of adjustment costs and trade changes	126
8.1	Market structure, differentiation of products and the determinants of trade	136
8.2	Trade types in intra-EU-12 trade, 1980–99	142
8.3	Evolution of trade types in intra-EU-12 trade by country, 1980–99	144
8.4	Trade types in bilateral intra-EU-12 trade, 1999	145
8.5	Germany's and Italy's strengths and weaknesses by price–quality range in bilateral trade, 1999	150
8.6	Contribution to EU-15's trade balance, by industry and price–quality range, 1999	151
8.7	EU-15's strengths and weaknesses by price–quality range in bilateral trade with China and Hong Kong, 1999	152
10.1	Trade in vertically differentiated varieties	190
11.1	Intra-industry trade with no liberalization	206
11.2	Intra-industry trade with trade liberalization	206
11.3	Intra-industry trade with investment liberalization	207
11.4	Intra-industry trade with investment and trade liberalization	207
11.5	Intra-industry affiliate sales with investment liberalization	208
11.6	Intra-industry affiliate sales with investment liberalization, countries twice as big	208
13.1	Relationship between R&D intensity and other variables	256
14.1	Direct investment: Japan, France, Germany	279
14.2	Direct investment: Canada, US and UK	280
14.3	Direct investment by regions	281
14.4	Equities rank order: *GL* v. *X+M*	286

Acknowledgements

This volume emerged from a conference on the Frontiers of Research in Intra-Industry Trade held at the University of Colorado at Boulder on 24–26 August 2000. We would like to thank the many people involved in the organization and execution of the conference, especially Jim Markusen, who handled the arrangements at the University of Colorado end of the chain. Ellen Delano at the University of Colorado and Penelope Gouletsas at the University of Melbourne did a sterling job in dealing with many enquiries and all the paperwork. The conference was supported by the Carl McGuire Center for International Studies at the University of Colorado at Boulder, and by the Asian Studies Centre at the University of Melbourne.

The conference was organized by a committee comprising the two editors and Herbert Grubel and James Markusen. We wish to thank all the participants at the conference for generating such lively discussion on all aspects of intra-industry trade. This undoubtedly helped the authors of this book. The conference was a very happy occasion as well as a very productive one intellectually.

Finally, we thank Nicola Viinikka and other staff at Palgrave Macmillan who carried out all the tasks involved in editing the manuscript and bringing the book to publication.

P. J. LLOYD
HYUN-HOON LEE

Notes on the Contributors

Mary Amiti is Senior Lecturer, Department of Economics, University of Melbourne, Australia.

Daniel M. Bernhofen is Professor, Department of Economics, Clark University, Worcester, MA, USA.

Marius Brülhart is a teacher at the École des Hautes Études Commerciales, University of Lausanne, Lausanne, Switzerland.

Karolina Ekholm is a teacher at the Stockholm School of Economics, Sweden.

Lionel Fontagné is Director, Centre d'Études Prospectives et d'Informations Internationales (CEPII), Paris, France.

Michael Freudenberg works in the Directorate for Science, Technology and Industry (DSTI), Industry Division, Organization for Economic Cooperation and Development, Paris, France.

Kiichiro Fukasaku is Head of the Research Division, OECD Development Centre, Paris, France.

David Greenaway is Professor of Economics and Pro-Vice-Chancellor, University of Nottingham, Nottingham, UK.

Herbert Grubel is Professor of Economics (Emeritus) Simon Fraser University and Senior Fellow and David Somerville Chair in Taxation and Finance, Fraser Institute, Vancouver, BC, Canada.

Ronald W. Jones is Xerox Professor of Economics, Department of Economics, University of Rochester, USA.

Henryk Kierzkowski is Professor of Economics, Graduate Institute of International Studies, Geneva, Switzerland.

Fukunari Kimura is Associate Professor of Economics, Keio University, Tokyo, Japan.

Hyun-Hoon Lee is Professor of Economics, Kangwon National University, Chuncheon, Korea.

Gregory Leonard works for the The Brattle Group, Washington, DC, USA.

P. J. Lloyd is Ritchie Professor of Economics, Department of Economics, University of Melbourne, Australia.

James R. Markusen is Professor of Economics, Department of Economics, University of Colorado, Boulder, USA.

Keith E. Maskus is Professor of Economics, Department of Economics, University of Colorado, Boulder, USA.

Chris Milner is Professor, Department of Economics, University of Nottingham, Nottingham, UK.

Nicolas Schmitt is Professor, Department of Economics, Simon Fraser University, Vancouver, BC, Canada.

Anthony J. Venables is Professor of International Economics, London School of Economics, UK.

Zhihao Yu is a teacher at the Leverhulme Centre for Research on Globalization and Economic Policy, University of Nottingham, Nottingham, UK.

List of Abbreviations

CBERA	Caribbean Basin Economic Recovery Act
cge	computable general equilibrium
CES	constant elasticity of substitution
CN	Combined Nomenclature
EEC	European Economic Community
Eurostat	Statistical Office of the European Community
FATS	Foreign Affiliates Trade Statistics
FDI	foreign direct investment
GATS	General Agreement on Trade in Services
GATT	General Agreement on Tariffs and Trade
GDP	gross domestic product
GNP	gross national product
HTS PSP	US Production Sharing Provision of Harmonized Tariff Schedule Chapter 98
IIAP	intra-industry affiliate production
IIT	intra-industry trade
IMF	International Monetary Fund
IPT	inward processing trade
IRS	increasing returns to scale
ISIC	International Standard Industrial Classification
MNE	multinational enterprise
NAFTA	North Atlantic Free Trade Area
NIE	newly industrializing economy
OECD	Organization for Economic Co-operation and Development
PCGDP	per capita gross domestic product
R&D	research and development
RIIT	relative intra-industry trade
SAH	smooth adjustment hypothesis
SITC	Standard International Trade Classification
UN	United Nations
WTO	World Trade Organization

1
Introduction

P. J. Lloyd and Hyun-Hoon Lee

When intra-industry trade was first observed in the 1960s by Verdoorn (1960), Balassa (1963, 1966) and Grubel (1967), it was a new and exciting way of examining patterns of goods trade. These authors made the revolutionary observation that there was specialization within industries and two-way international trade in the multiple outputs of industries. Grubel and Lloyd (1975) developed the most widely used index for the measurement of intra-industry trade. Using this measure, they found that the unweighted mean share of intra-industry trade in the total goods trade of ten major OECD countries in 1967 was 50 per cent. Grubel and Lloyd and others attempted to develop a theoretical basis for the existence of intra-industry trade in both homogeneous and differentiated products. However, the underlying concept of an industry was rarely examined, and theorizing was, in the main, partial equilibrium analysis.

Starting with the work of Krugman (1979) and Lancaster (1980), a number of formal general equilibrium models which yielded intra-industry trade were developed. These models used different specifications of industries and international trade. Some yielded what became known as horizontal intra-industry trade in differentiated final products or in homogeneous products, some vertical intra-industry trade in different qualities of products, and some other forms of intra-industry trade such as fragmentation. New models continue to emerge.

New aspects of intra-industry trade have also been observed. The concept of intra-industry trade has expanded to incorporate marginal intra-industry trade, intra-firm trade, intra-industry trade in New Geography models, and intra-industry trade in services.

The world is becoming one global economy. In the second half of the twentieth century, the world economy witnessed many dramatic

1

changes in technology of information and transportation, and successive rounds of multilateral trade negotiations under GATT. As a consequence, international trade increased dramatically, outpacing income growth. Furthermore, in most developed countries and developing countries alike, a large portion of the volume of international goods traded is intra-industry trade. In services trade and in affiliate production the proportion of intra-industry trade is even higher than in goods trade. (See the chapters in this book by Lloyd and Lee, and by Markusen and Maskus, respectively.) This high level of intra-industry trade makes the subject more important than ever before.

The present book looks at the frontiers of research in intra-industry trade. It consists of four parts. Part I is a single chapter on some historical controversies in the development of the theory and empirical measurement of intra-industry trade. The chapters in Part II are concerned with further development of models of intra-industry trade, while those in Part III consider empirical patterns and trends, and some important policy issues associated with intra-industry trade. Part IV considers intra-industry trade associated with industries in which there are also intra-industry or two-way flows of FDI and assets. This is a new and increasingly important area of intra-industry analysis.

Development of intra-industry trade theory and measurement

Chapter 2 in Part I takes a retrospective view of three important controversies in the development of intra-industry analysis. They are the fundamental aggregation problem, the choice of measure in empirical studies, and the incorporation of intra-industry trade into analyses of the factor content of international trade.

The first raised the question of whether observed intra-industry trade was real, or the result of categorical aggregation of unrelated commodities into one group. This issue was resolved by the accumulation of empirical evidence and the development of models of international trade that yielded both intra- and inter-industry trade. These models also indicate the appropriate measure of intra-industry trade. For the purpose of explaining trade patterns and comparative advantage, the Grubel–Lloyd measure is appropriate. For the purposes of empirical studies that compare distributions of trade variables, the appropriate measure is an index of similarity. The related question of an adjustment to the measure for the trade imbalance is unresolved. The third question is a current issue that may become a new controversy. Recent empirical tests of factor proportions and differences in technologies or products as alternative hypotheses have been enriched by the addition of intra-industry to inter-industry trade flows.

Models of intra-industry trade

Part II consists of four chapters that focus on modelling intra-industry trade. The models relate to trade in goods with no associated FDI or international production.

In Chapter 3, Nicolas Schmitt and Zhihao Yu investigate further the properties of a model of intra-industry trade with horizontal differentiation. They argue that the standard model of intra-industry trade (that is, the Dixit–Stiglitz–Krugman model) is able to explain the significant gap between the growth rates of trade and of output, provided that it includes non-traded products. The post-Second World War period is characterized by a significantly higher growth rate in world manufactured trade than in world output. Roughly, world manufactured trade has grown on average by about 3 per cent per year faster than GDP since 1950. Over the same period, the share of intra-industry trade has increased significantly and represents today a significant proportion of overall trade. There is no well-accepted model explaining this gap in the growth rates. This chapter argues that there is a simple channel through which the gap between growth in trade and in output can be explained: non-traded horizontally differentiated products are becoming traded as barriers to trade decrease. Specifically, they find that in a model based on Krugman (1980), which includes both traded and non-traded goods, the effect of trade liberalization on the change in the share of export in total output almost doubles compared to the standard model, as some non-traded goods become traded when the cost of trade decreases. Furthermore, they also find that the change in the share of export is sensitive to higher degrees of scale economies.

Chapter 4, by Daniel Bernhofen, extends the theory of intra-industry trade in which product differentiation is not the driving force behind such trade. He divides the literature on intra-industry trade in homogeneous products into a 'competitive branch' and a 'strategic branch'. He provides a critical assessment of the recent theoretical and empirical contributions in these literatures, offers some suggestions for future research, and shows how relaxing the strict product homogeneity assumption in the strategic trade model yields some new results. Although intra-industry trade is a result of strategic interaction, relaxing the intensity of strategic interaction in the form of lowering the degree of product substitutability makes firms more eager to trade and thus leads to more two-way trade. This characteristic feature of the model also has some implications for anti-trust policy. Although a higher degree of product differentiation decreases firms' incentives to refrain from forming a collusive agreement not to sell into each other's national market, it also reduces the disciplining effect of foreign trade on domestic market power. Furthermore, he shows that – for a given degree of product substitutability – the incentives of international collusion are stronger in industries with a relatively low degree of market concentration.

The costs of outsourcing parts of previously vertically integrated production processes have been going down steadily, and as a consequence, there has been considerable international fragmentation of these processes. Lower real wages abroad have helped to induce labour-intensive fragments to move from advanced to less advanced countries. In some industries, such as autos and parts, the resulting trade is recorded as intra-industry trade. In others, it would be inter-industry trade that expands. In discussing the links between fragmentation and intra-industry trade, Chapter 5, by Ronald Jones, Henryk Kierzkowski and Gregory Leonard, looks more intensively at selected industries in US trade. These are the colour television industry, the automobile industry, and apparel manufacture, with particular attention to trade within the NAFTA area. In some industries, for example, the television industry in the USA and Mexico, intra-industry trade remains at a high level for the industry as a whole, but much less when trade is separated into fragments, such as cathode ray tubes or final assembled sets. For other industries, such as the automobile sector, the aggregate measure of intra-industry trade has been falling, but the measure in parts separately has experienced a rapid increase.

In Chapter 6, Mary Amiti and Anthony Venables explore the implications of new geography for intra-industry trade. This is a new area of research. One of the most robust empirical findings on intra-industry trade is that measures of intra-industry trade relative to inter-industry trade decline with distance. This chapter develops a model that has some geographic structure – a number of countries at different distances from each other. This yields a natural benchmark case in which intra-industry trade occurs, but relative intra-industry trade measures are independent of distance. This model explores a variety of deviations from this benchmark and how they create patterns of relative intra-industry trade that are correlated with distance.

The deviations include letting transport costs and demand elasticities vary across industries, and letting factor endowments vary systematically with geography. Spatial models create their own forces of industrial location. The overall conclusion is that the negative relationship between relative intra-industry trade and distance is explained more plausibly as a corollary of industrial location than as a consequence of trading technologies.

Empirical studies and policy issues of intra-industry trade

Part III comprises four chapters devoted to empirical and policy issues of intra-industry trade.

In Chapter 7, Marius Brülhart points out that the appropriate definition of intra-industry trade continues to be a matter of debate in the context of adjustment in factor markets to changes in international trade. In this context, economists assume conventionally that intra-industry trade entails relatively smooth factor-market adjustment to trade liberalization. A range of measures has been developed. These measures capture the degree of symmetry of *changes* in exports and imports at the sector level. Brülhart gives a critical overview of these measures. He concludes that a consensus is emerging that, in the context of adjustment, one should use measures that are based on *marginal* intra-industry trade.

Chapter 8, by Lionel Fontagné and Michael Freudenberg, examines European trade patterns over the period 1980–99, using data on values and unit values of bilateral trade flows at a very disaggregated level. European integration has proceeded in a manner that is both original and quite unexpected. Contrasting with the conclusions of *ex ante* studies, the share of intra-industry trade of varieties has remained remarkably stable over time, whereas the share of intra-industry trade of qualities has increased rapidly, and is now the most important trade type in intra-European trade. Thus the quality of goods and the positioning of the quality ladder are now playing a crucial role. They also address the determinants of shares of trade types in bilateral trade and show that R&D efforts, technological progress or the qualification of the labour force are determinants of the merging qualitative division of labour in Europe.

Hitherto, all empirical studies and analyses of intra-industry trade have been confined to trade in goods. Yet, for the analysis of trade flows and their effects on the allocation of resources and the welfare of national residents, there is no reason to separate trade in goods from trade in services. Chapter 9, by Hyun-Hoon Lee and P. J. Lloyd, seeks to remedy this gap in the study of intra-industry trade by using data compiled recently under an OECD classification of trade in services. It is found that the shares of intra-industry trade in services for most countries are high, and have remained very stable over the period 1992–6. They also carry out an empirical analysis of inter-country differences in intra-industry trade in services, and examine the effect that the inclusion of trade in services has on the observed levels of intra-industry trade in goods and services combined.

In Chapter 10, David Greenaway and Chris Milner consider the evidence from the tests of horizontally- versus vertically-differentiated intra-industry trade. New models developed in the 1980s allowed for inter-industry specialization in homogeneous goods, and for intra-industry specialization in horizontally differentiated goods. This is often referred to as the Chamberlin–Heckscher–Ohlin model of international trade, and it came to be accepted as the dominant explanation of observed intra-industry trade. This chapter argues that this view is largely misplaced. Evidence from North–North, North–South and South–South trade points to vertically differentiated goods as the dominant form of intra-industry trade.

The chapter then considers the implications of this shift in explanation of the analysis of labour market adjustments to changes in international trade. Evidence of substantial intra-industry variation in skills and wages modifies the smooth adjustment view of labour markets.

Intra-industry trade, affiliate production and FDI

Economic interactions among the high-income developed countries are characterized by high degrees of both intra-industry trade and intra-industry affiliate production and sales. Similar high-income countries both trade heavily with and invest into each other. Empirical estimation gives good support to the predictions of the theory of intra-industry affiliate sales, with somewhat weaker results for intra-industry trade. Chapter 11, by James Markusen and Keith Maskus, shows how the theory of direct investment can be integrated with the theory of international trade in goods. Building on their own recent work, they construct a general equilibrium model of trade in goods and affiliate production activity where the pattern of firm location, production and trade are simultaneously and endogenously determined. The model is tested empirically using data of US bilateral trade and affiliate production with ten countries or regions. This confirms that the intra-industry affiliate sales index rises relative to the intra-industry trade index as countries become richer and more similar in size and in relative endowments.

In Chapter 12, Karolina Ekholm examines hypotheses relating to intra-industry FDI and affiliate production in models of the type developed by Markusen and Maskus. She measures the extent of intra-industry affiliate production (IIAP), using Swedish data on affiliate activities to calculate Grubel–Lloyd indices. These measures are compared to the corresponding measures for intra-industry trade (IIT). She examines whether IIAP and IIT can be explained by dissimilarity in relative factor endowments, and whether IIT can be explained by the interaction between differences in GDP and differences in relative factor endowments, as suggested by theory. It is found that dissimilarity in relative endowments of overall capital affects both IIAP and IIT negatively. Furthermore, she estimates negative effects of dissimilarity in relative endowments of human capital. She also shows that the estimated changes over time unaccounted for by changes in the variables included in the analysis differ between IIAP and IIT in a way that is consistent with the prediction that decreases in trade costs would decrease IIAP, but not IIT.

One important aspect of recent international trade is trade between a parent company and its foreign affiliates, in which case products are traded internationally but stay within the ambit of a multinational enterprise (MNE). This type of trade is called *intra-firm* trade as opposed to trade among unrelated parties, known as *arm's-length* trade. Chapter 13, by Kiichiro Fukasaku and Fukunari Kimura, updates research on this phenomenon by analyzing the available data on intra-firm trade for two major OECD countries – the USA and Japan.

They argue that globalization may or may not enhance the weight of intra-firm trade within overall trade. On the one hand, globalization provides more room for firms to conduct global operations, which may result in greater intra-firm transactions, while, on the other, globalization reduces the *service costs* of linking remote locations together, which makes arm's-length trade easier and cheaper. The US case shows that the share of intra-firm trade to the overall trade has been relatively stable over time, while the Japanese case suggests that firms with higher R&D intensity do not necessarily have higher intra-firm transaction ratios in electronics industry. They also find that intra-firm trade has strong industry-specific and firm-specific characteristics. Intra-firm trade is mainly the result of upstream–downstream fragmentation across different locations. Fragmentation sometimes takes a form of splitting a production block into several sub-blocks and locating them in the most suitable places. In other cases, a firm produces in one location and conducts sales activities in another. This chapter highlights the importance and advantage of using micro data to analyze in more detail the intra-firm behaviour of MNEs.

Chapter 14, by Herbert Grubel, considers intra-industry trade in asset flows (rather than in affiliate production resulting from FDI, as in the chapters by Markusen and Maskus, and by Ekholm). This is a neglected area of research. He considers the capital account of Germany as a representative industrial country to indicate the relative importance of direct, portfolio and other investment, and the subcategories within these major aggregates. Using data from a number of OECD countries, intra-industry trade in all categories of asset flow is found to be substantial, especially in portfolio investments, though it differs across countries and time.

The second part of the chapter considers theoretical models that are capable of explaining intra-industry trade in assets. Existing models are adequate, though there remains much room for rigorous empirical testing. The chapter concludes with a discussion of the implications of intra-industry trade in assets for policies such as the liberalization of capital controls.

Concluding remarks

Intra-industry trade has become a part of the mainstream of international economics. Most models that go beyond 2×2 dimensions now incorporate some form of intra-industry trade. (The first number indicates the number of goods, the Second the number of factors.) Computable general equilibrium models of national economies or of the world economy usually incorporate intra-industry trade. Empirical studies usually relate to data that has both intra- and inter-industry trade. Thus, the concept of intra-industry trade continues to be a useful way of organizing the pattern of trade.

Some of the chapters overlap in their content and provide fascinating examples of the way research progresses by the interaction of ideas. Moreover, some of the modellers in Part II conduct their own empirical tests and some of the chapters in Part III that are primarily empirical extend the existing theory before conducting their tests. The same applies to the chapters in Part IV.

Much research remains to be done on intra-industry trade in goods, services and investment. The ideas and empirical findings in this book have advanced our knowledge of the causes of comparative advantage, the patterns of trade, and the effects that international trade has on the welfare of the residents of trading nations.

References

Balassa, B. (1963) 'An Empirical Demonstration of Classical Comparative Cost Theory', *Review of Economics and Statistics*, 45: 231–8.

Balassa, B. (1965) *Economic Development and Integration* (Mexico City: Centro De Estudios Monetarios Latinoamericanos).

Grubel, H. G. (1967) 'Intra-industry Specialization and the Pattern of Trade, *Canadian Journal of Economics and Political Science*, 33: 374–88.

Grubel, H. G. and P. J. Lloyd (1975) *Intra-Industry Trade: The Theory and Measurement of International Trade in Differentiated Products* (London: Macmillan).

Krugman, P. R. (1980) 'Scale Economies, Product Differentiation, and Pattern of Trade', *American Economic Review*, 70: 950–9.

Krugman, P. R. (1979) 'Increasing Returns, Monopolistic Competition and International Trade', *Journal of International Economics*, 9: 469–79.

Lancaster, K. (1980) 'Intra-Industry Trade under Perfect Monopolistic Competition', *Journal of International Economics*, 10: 151–75.

Verdoorn, P. J. (1960) 'The Intra-block Trade of Benelux,' in E. A. G. Robinson (ed.), *Economic Consequences of the Size of Nations* (London: Macmillan), pp. 291–329.

Part I

Development of Intra-Industry Theory and Measurement

2
Controversies Concerning Intra-Industry Trade*

P. J. Lloyd

There have been a number of fairly vigorous controversies in the literature on intra-industry trade. This chapter examines three. The first two date back to the beginning of the debates about the nature of intra-industry trade: namely, the fundamental aggregation problem and the choice of measure. The latter includes the question of whether an adjustment should be made for the trade imbalance. There are other controversies (Greenaway and Torstensson, 1997, review developments in intra-industry trade analysis over the 1990s), but the two chosen are persistent and important. The third issue is the incorporation of intra-industry trade into analyses of the factor content of international trade. This is an important current issue that may become a new controversy.

Controversy 1: Categorical aggregation

The most important controversy, without doubt, is that relating to the aggregation of international trade statistics into the exports and imports of 'industries'. It affects our measured levels of intra-industry trade, the empirical explanation of these flows, and their policy implications. It is fundamental to the progress of intra-industry analysis.

Early investigators of intra-industry trade had to choose some digit level of the Standard International Trade Classification (SITC) to define their industries. When intra-industry trade was measured in this way, there were sceptics who regarded the observed intra-industry trade, or the greater part of it, as spurious. For example, in his review of the book by Grubel and Lloyd (1975), Lipsey (1976, pp. 313–14) concluded that 'much, although not all, of intra-industry trade is a statistical phenomenon'. In order to distinguish between theoretical predictions and empirical observations, Finger (1975) insisted on calling the former

13

'intra-industry trade', and the latter 'trade overlap'. He went so far as to assert that the 'literature [on intra-industry trade] is valueless' and contended that 'A careful examination of the literature which attempts to explain this observation will cause the reader to be shocked by the liberties which have been taken with the scientific method.'[1] Similarly, Rayment (1983, p. 5) 'placed inverted commas around the industry of intra-"industry" trade as a reminder that this is a statistical construct'. These critics believed that trade in heterogeneous and unrelated products was grouped together in the Standard International Trade Classification. This phenomenon was labelled by Gray (1979) 'categorical aggregation', a term that seems to have stuck.

Within-group product heterogeneity was interpreted by these critics mainly as differences in factor intensities, although mention is also made of different production functions and markets. Rayment (1976) observed that intra-industry variation among factor intensities in UK manufacturing was almost as large as inter-industry variation. Similarly, for US manufacturing industries, Finger (1975) found that the intra-industry variation among measures of both physical capital intensity and human capital intensity accounted for 39 per cent of the total variation.

Finger then related his observations to trade theory by adapting the two-country, two-factor, many-commodity version of the Heckscher–Ohlin model that had been outlined by Jones (1956). In the Finger version of the model, the industry produces a number of varieties of a product. Under some assumptions, the costs of each variety in one country relative to that in the other can be ranked in the same order as the factor intensities of the commodities. Finger concludes that intra-industry trade is impossible in this model, as countries will export one group of commodities (varieties) and import the other, except possibly for the single borderline commodity.

We can see now that this reasoning is quite inadequate for the consideration of intra-industry trade. There can be no intra-industry trade in this model simply because every product is made by its own one-product industry. There are no multi-product industries and there is nothing to link industries apart from the economy-wide factor price equilibrium.

A few years later we had the advent of theories that predicted and explained intra-industry trade. The first of these were the models of Krugman (1979) and Lancaster (1980), followed closely by a number of other models. Many of these models have novel features other than intra-industry trade, such as the introduction of economies of scale, imperfect competition and strategic interdependence, and product varieties. Indeed, the modelling of intra-industry trade led to a revolution in international trade modelling and, as a side effect, in industry economics.

To construct such models one must first define an industry in an economically meaningful way. Industries are product groups that are directly linked in production and/or consumption. On the demand side, Krugman, and many others subsequently, have used the device of weak separability of the utility function to define the industry group. Such an industry is well-defined only if all consumers in the world economy have the same preferences, at least in respect to the groupings of commodities. On the supply side, the links may be a joint production technology of some kind. This includes the common use of an (industry-) specific factor or intermediate input relations, as both of these produce a type of jointness. The former was used in the intra-industry trade model of Falvey (1981) and the latter in the intra-industry trade model of Dixit and Grossman (1982). Again, the technologies must be the same across countries at least with respect to jointness.

When an analytically meaningful concept of the industries has been specified, the appropriate groupings in the SITC are also defined, which should be the groupings that correspond most closely to the specified industries.

With these definitions of industries, two-way or overlapping trade in the products of an industry will be explicable in terms of the models. For example, both the Falvey (1981) and the Dixit–Grossman (1982) models allow intra-industry exchange of products based on differences in capital–labour intensities, a result that Rayment and Finger had earlier denied. Indeed, the Falvey model is a model of product varieties similar to that proposed by Finger. Moreover, in the Falvey and the Dixit–Grossman models there are other industries or sectors outside that in which intra-industry trade occurs. These patterns of intra-industry trade and the existence of intra-industry variation in factor proportions are quite consistent with the Law of Comparative Advantage.

In the models with economies of scale in all industries developed by Krugman, Helpman, Lancaster and others, there is again both intra- and inter-industry trade. There is intra-industry trade in manufactured commodities that have the same factor intensity ratio, another result that Finger ruled out. The Law of Comparative Advantage does not hold, as there may be what Lancaster (1980, p. 167) called a 'false comparative advantage', and because identical countries with identical pre-trade prices gain from trade.

In many of the models, the number of industries is two, with one industry producing multiple products and the other a single homogeneous product. In a model with two industries and two factors, Helpman (1981) showed that the Heckscher–Ohlin theorem continues to apply to net (= inter-industry) trade in these models. Thus, again, there is no inconsistency between intra-industry trade and the factor proportions variation within industries. Helpman then derives propositions relating inter-industry trade and the share of intra-industry trade in the manufacturing industry to factor proportions in his model. Further, he proves that the factor price equalization theorem carries over, under specified conditions, from the 2×2 Heckscher–Ohlin model to his model with two factors and many products (strictly, infinitely many). In doing this, he effectively uses aggregate indices of output and prices in the continuum industry.

Lloyd (1994) extends these results by using formal aggregation theory. He shows that, in models with many commodities and both intra- and inter-industry trade, one can aggregate quantities and prices consistently to obtain aggregates in the industry or industries with many differentiated products provided certain homogeneity conditions are satisfied. In addition to the Helpman–Lancaster model, this can be done, for example, in the Dixit–Grossman model. If consistent aggregation is possible in both production and consumption, one can rewrite these high dimensional models in terms of a simpler model of greatly reduced dimensions. Using the terminology of intra-industry trade analysis, the value of trade in the low dimensional version of the model is the price times the quantity of the aggregate good, and this is equal to the value of inter-industry trade for all commodities in the high dimensional version of the model. This low dimensional model can be used to test whether propositions such as the Heckscher–Ohlin theorem, factor price equalization and univalence hold. One uses the full high dimensional version of the model to explain the share of intra-industry trade.

This aggregation does not apply to all models. For example, it does not apply to the Falvey model, because an aggregate industry-level production function does not exist in this model and it does not apply to the Helpman–Lancaster model if the symmetry conditions are relaxed.

These results have an implication for the way in which we build models, either in pure theory or cge models for policy simulations. Several of the many-commodity trade model that exhibit intra-industry trade were derived from the $2 \times 2 \times 2$ Heckscher–Ohlin model, or the $2 \times 3 \times 2$ Jones specific factor model. (The first number indicates the number of industries, the second the number of factors, and the third the number of countries.) One of the two industries is then disaggregated into a horizontally or vertically related group. I suggested in an earlier paper (Lloyd, 1994, p. 108) that this could be used as a general technique of model building:

> Plainly one could use the same device in a Heckscher–Ohlin or Jones model of any dimensions. One simply takes a set of industries and disaggregates each horizontally or vertically. Moreover, the method of disaggregation can and should vary among industries. Some industries are obviously of the sequential Dixit and Grossman type, some involve instead jointness in production and some have differentiated consumer products.

I might add that cge modelbuilding needs to catch up with these techniques. The great majority of cge models still use the Armington Assumption. Armington's (1969) model was in fact the first model to incorporate intra-industry trade, by using separability of the utility function in a way that anticipated the work of Krugman and several others. On the supply side, models based on the Armington assumption have maintained the traditional assumption that an industry produces only one good in one country under constant returns to scale. Assuming finally that the products of the national industries are differentiated final goods, there is intra-industry trade in a genuine cge model of the world economy, but there is nothing to explain the national differentiation. As with the differences in technology in the classical model, these are exogenous and atmospheric. Cge modelling needs to introduce explanations of national differentiation and intra-industry trade, and the explanations should differ realistically among industries.

Controversy 2: The choice of measure of intra-industry trade

The debate about the choice mainly concerns the choice of statistic but there is also an important question as to whether an adjustment should be made for the trade imbalance, and a question of the choice in practice of the level of aggregation in the SITC classification of goods traded.

The choice of statistic

The statistic used to measure intra-industry trade affects the measured levels of intra-industry trade substantially. A number of different measures were proposed early in the history of intra-industry trade; Kol (1988) reviews the measures proposed.

One measure has become standard. This is the measure known as the Grubel–Lloyd measure after its originators (Grubel and Lloyd, 1971; and Grubel and Lloyd, 1975, ch. 2). Suppose there are n industries in the economy that are indexed by $i = 1, \ldots n$. For a multiple-product industry, industry i, let X_i be the aggregate value of exports of industry i, and M_i be the value of imports of industry i. As Grubel and Lloyd (1975, p. 20) put it, 'Intra-industry trade is defined as the value of exports of an "industry" which is exactly matched by the imports of the same industry.' That is,[2]

$$R_i = (X_i + M_i) - |X_i - M_i| \tag{2.1}$$

The complement of intra-industry trade is called inter-industry trade:

$$S_i = |X_i - M_i| \tag{2.2}$$

The value of intra-industry trade is then normalized by dividing by $(X_i + M_i)$ to give:

$$B_i = (X_i + M_i) - |X_i - M_i|/(X_i + M_i) \tag{2.3}$$

This is simply the proportion of the total trade of the industry that is intra-industry trade as distinct from inter-industry trade.

The economy-wide measure of intra-industry trade can now be obtained by averaging each industry measure B_i across all n industries, using the relative shares of industry exports plus imports as weights:

$$
\begin{aligned}
B &= \sum_i B_i \bullet \left[(X_i + M_i) / \sum_i (X_i + M_i) \right] \\
&= \frac{\sum_i (X_i + M_i) - \sum_i (|X_i - M_i|)}{\sum_i (X_i + M_i)}
\end{aligned}
\tag{2.4}
$$

The first equation is the weighted mean of the proportions of intra-industry trade in each industry. The weights are all positive fractions and $B \in [0,1]$. The mean is equal to intra-industry trade summed across all industries as a proportion of the total trade.

There is an equivalent statement of the measure. R_i can also be written:

$$R_i = 2 \min (X_i, \ M_i) \tag{2.5}$$

as Grubel and Lloyd (1975, p. 20n) noted. Hence,

$$B = \frac{\sum_i 2 \min (X_i, \ M_i)}{\sum_i (X_i + M_i)} \tag{2.6}$$

The most basic feature of the measure is that it was derived by matching the value of exports and imports in each industry and then averaging these measures. Trade theory indicates that this is the appropriate definition in analyzing patterns of international trade. Helpman (1981) was the first to show the role of the Grubel–Lloyd measure rigorously in a trade model. He begins with an analysis of net (= inter-industry) trade. The measure of inter-industry trade is $|X_i - M_i|$. Before the recognition of intra-industry trade, this measure was used widely in the empirical study of trade patterns and comparative advantage. Then intra-industry trade is simply the complement of inter-industry trade $(X_i + M_i) - |X_i - M_i|$, as in Equation (2.1). As he seeks propositions concerning the share of intra-industry trade, Helpman uses the Grubel–Lloyd measure given in Equation (2.3).

There is an alternative concept. We could instead match the *proportions* of exports and imports in industry i. Following the same procedure as with the index above, we can define the match in each industry as:

$$F_i = \left[\frac{X_i}{\sum_i X_i} + \frac{M_i}{\sum_i M_i} - \left| \frac{X_i}{\sum_i X_i} - \frac{M_i}{\sum_i M_i} \right| \right] \Big/ \left[\frac{X_i}{\sum_i X_i} + \frac{M_i}{\sum_i M_i} \right]$$

If these industry measures are then weighted by the average share of the exports and imports of the industry in the total export and import trade respectively, we have:

$$F = \sum_i F_i \bullet \frac{1}{2} \left[\frac{X_i}{\sum_i X_i} + \frac{M_i}{\sum_i M_i} \right] \tag{2.7}$$

Expanding the F_i terms in the summation, this reduces to:

$$F = 1 - \frac{1}{2} \sum_i \left| \frac{X_i}{\sum_i X_i} - \frac{M_i}{\sum_i M_i} \right| \tag{2.8}$$

Or, equivalently, substituting Equation (2.5) in (2.7),

$$F = \sum_i \{2 \ \min([X_i / \sum_i X_i], [M_i / \sum_i M_i])\} / [X_i / \sum_i X_i + M_i / \sum_i M_i] \bullet D_i$$

$$D_i = \frac{1}{2} [X_i / \sum_i X_i + M_i / \sum_i M_i]$$

which reduces to

$$F = \sum_i \min\left(\left[X_i/\sum_i X_i\right], \left[M_i/\sum_i M_i\right]\right)$$ (2.9)

Of the three forms, that in Equation (2.9) is the simplest and easiest to calculate.[3]

This index is a measure of the extent to which industry exports as a proportion of total exports match industry imports as a proportion of total imports. It is in fact the same index as the Grubel–Lloyd Index B with the proportions of imports and exports replacing the values.

This alternative measure appears in a number of international trade contexts as a measure of similarity. Finger and Kreinen (1979) use Equation (2.9) to measure the similarity of the distributions of exports by commodity and imports by commodity. Glick and Rose (1998) derive Equation (2.7) independently once again to measure the similarity of the distribution by commodity of the exports of two countries to a third country or countries. Indeed, the measure in Equations (2.7) or (2.8) or (2.9) can be used to compare the similarity of any two discrete distributions. Even more broadly, it is an example of a family of similarity or matching indices used to measure the similarity or match between two objects (T_i, S_i) which take the form $\sum_i^n f(T_i, S_i) \bullet w_i$. Here, f is some index of similarity and the w_i are weights. These indices are widely used in psychology, spatial analysis and other areas of the social sciences (see Watson, 1997).

With these results, we can resolve the issue of the choice of measure. The choice depends on the purpose of the empirical study. For the purpose of explaining specialization and comparative advantage, a matching of values is appropriate. As noted in the previous section, the Grubel–Lloyd does this and provides a measure of inter- and intra-industry trade that predicts the pattern of trade specialization. This explains why the Grubel–Lloyd measure became the standard one in empirical studies of commodity trade. For the purpose of measuring similarity between two distributions, however, one needs to match the proportions rather than the values.

The Grubel–Lloyd measure can also be used for the analysis of two-way affiliate production (see Chapters 11 and 12 in this volume). Similarly, Greenaway, Lloyd and Milner (2001) have used the measure to analyze two-way market penetration by means of trade in goods and affiliate production combined.

There has been a parallel debate about the best measure of *changes* in intra-industry trade in time series analysis. This has given rise to a set of measures of 'marginal' intra-industry trade which are discussed in Chapter 7 in this volume. This is a major development which is proving useful in the analysis of adjustment problems.

Adjusting for the trade imbalance

The question of whether an adjustment should be made to the average measure for the aggregate trade imbalance has perplexed empirical researchers and is still unresolved.

Grubel and Lloyd (1975, p. 22) argued that the measure in Equation (2.4) had the undesirable feature that, when the aggregate goods trade was unbalanced, it could not attain a value of 1. It was, in their words, 'biased downwards'. Such biases will be particularly large when the measure is applied to bilateral rather than multilateral flows.

They recommended the adjusted measure:

$$C = \frac{\sum_i (X_i + M_i) - \sum_i (|X_i - M_i|)}{\sum_i (X_i + M_i) - \left|\sum_i X_i - \sum_i M_i\right|} \tag{2.10}$$

By simple manipulation,

$$C = B \bullet 1/(1-k) \tag{2.11}$$

where

$$k = \frac{\left|\sum_i X_i - \sum_i M_i\right|}{\sum_i (X_i + M_i)}$$

is the relative trade imbalance for all goods. Thus, the unadjusted measure 'captures both the trade imbalance and the strength of intra-industry trade' (Grubel and Lloyd, 1975, p. 497). Note that $C \in [0, 1]$, as desired, but C cannot be expressed as a weighted mean.

The need for some form of adjustment in the presence of a trade imbalance has been accepted generally. A number of authors have, however, criticized the method of adjustment in Equation (2.10) and offered alternative adjustments.

Aquino (1978, p. 280) objected that C applies to total trade only and does not have a counterpart at the individual commodity level to B_i.

Instead, Aquino believed that there should be an adjustment or correction to the value of B_i in every industry. He proposed an adjustment to provide 'an estimate of what the values of exports and imports of each commodity would have been if total exports had been equal to total imports' (Aquino, 1978, p. 280). By making the same equiproportionate adjustment in each industry,

$$X_i^e = X_i \bullet \frac{1}{2} \frac{\sum_i (X_i + M_i)}{\sum_i X_i} \quad \text{and} \quad M_i^e = M_i \bullet \frac{1}{2} \frac{\sum_i (X_i + M_i)}{\sum_i M_i}$$

he obtains the measure:

$$D = \frac{\sum_i (X_i^e + M_i^e) - \sum_i (|X_i^e - M_i^e|)}{\sum_i (X_i^e + M_i^e)} \tag{2.12}$$

Aquino made the adjustment to multilateral trade in manufactures only. Loertscher and Wolter (1980) applied the Aquino adjustment to bilateral trade in manufactures.

Balassa (1979, 1986) insisted that the adjustment be made only to intra-industry trade across all goods (and all countries). But he made the same proportionate adjustment for this as Aquino. Bergstrand (1983) made a proportionate adjustment to bilateral trade flows but argued that a multilateral adjustment factor should be used. Again, his adjustment is equiproportionate but it differs from that of Aquino by taking account of the imbalances in both countries.

Greenaway and Milner (1981) question the equiproportionate adjustment for all sub-industries in the Aquino adjustment. (They also object to Aquino's practice of adjusting for intra-industry trade in manufactures alone.) The implications of the equiproportionate adjustment are plain from the previous discussion of indices. Substituting the expressions for X_i^e and M_i^e into Equation (2.12), factoring and cancelling terms in the numerator and denominator, we see that the Aquino index is none other than the index defined in Equation (2.7). That is, the Aquino index is the Grubel–Lloyd weighted average index but using export and import proportions in place of the values of exports and imports. It is a different concept of intra-industry trade, not an adjustment of the Grubel–Lloyd concept.

Lee and Lee (1993) suggest that, when regressing the unadjusted index of intra-industry trade on explanatory variables, the set of explanatory variables should include a measure of the relative trade imbalance. This is because the unadjusted index is correlated negatively with the trade imbalance. This is equivalent to first regressing the unadjusted measures on the measures of trade imbalance and then using the estimated value of measure of intra-industry from the regression equation as an adjusted measure. The adjustment is made using observations from all countries in the sample.

Finger (1975, n. 4) stated that 'Any adjustment contains implicit assumptions about the effect on trade patterns of eliminating the phenomena being adjusted for, hence the "unadjusted" figures could be misleading because of the invalidity of these implicit assumptions.' This difficulty of deciding on the appropriate adjustment has led some authors, such as Kol (1988, ch. 4) and Greenaway and Milner (1981) to the pragmatic conclusion that it may be best not to make an adjustment.

One further comment should be made immediately. All empirical studies of intra-industry trade to date have ignored trade in services. The reason is no doubt that comparable statistics of intra-industry trade in services have not been available. From the point of view of specialization in international trade, however, there is no reason to distinguish between trade in goods and trade in services. One should, in principle, study intra-industry trade patterns in goods and services simultaneously. This would, of course, change the average levels but, in the present context, it will also generally change the trade imbalances as a proportion of total trade, the factor k in Equation (2.11). For some countries, this factor will be smaller when intra-industry trade in goods and services is measured. In such cases, the magnitude of the adjustment that might be made, and therefore the importance of adjustment, is reduced. Chapter 9 will examine this issue.

This brings us back to the question of whether any adjustment should be made to the index. Greenaway and Milner (1981) distinguish between 'equilibrium' and 'non-equilibrium' multilateral imbalances; the latter can be avoided or minimized by using averages over years, as recommended by Greenaway and Milner. This would best be done by summing the numerator and denominator of Equation (2.4) separately over the length of the borrowing cycle. However, in a world in which there is inter-country borrowing and lending, there may be 'equilibrium' imbalances on a nation's current account over many years. This is the nub of the problem.

It is still not clear to me how empirical researchers should treat persistent national trade imbalances. The answer may depend crucially on the purpose of the intra-industry trade analysis. Unfortunately, economic theory gives us little guidance as we do not have, to my knowledge, models of the world economy in which there is intra- and inter-industry trade and international lending and borrowing of the non-industry-specific type.

Choice of level of aggregation

Many empirical workers still regard the actual classification of goods traded in the SITC as a rough one based on technical properties of goods rather than a meaningful definition of industries. We are, however, lumbered with the SITC and unavoidable aggregation errors. It is therefore important to understand how observed intra-industry trade changes with the level of aggregation in this classification.

Suppose we accept some digit level of aggregation in the classification of goods traded. At this level, the groups are called 'industries'. The value of exports and imports of some industry, industry i, at this level are made of subgroups or sub-industries, $j \varepsilon S_i$, defined at some more disaggregated level. That is,

$$X_i = \sum_j X_{ij} \qquad j \varepsilon S_i. \qquad i = 1, \dots, n$$

$$M_i = \sum_j M_{ij} \qquad j \varepsilon S_i. \qquad i = 1, \dots, n$$

Substituting these expressions in the Grubel–Lloyd measure (see Equation (2.3) above), we have:

$$B_i = \sum_j X_{ij} + \sum_j M_{ij} - |\sum_j X_{ij} - \sum_j M_{ij}| / \sum_j (X_{ij} + M_{ij}) \qquad (2.13)$$

If, instead, we use the more disaggregated classification, the average level of intra-industry trade in the products within industry i is given by:

$$\bar{B}_{ij} = (\sum_j X_{ij} + \sum_j M_{ij}) - \sum_j |X_{ij}. - M_{ij}| / \sum_j (X_{ij} + M_{ij}) \qquad (2.14)$$

By the Triangle Inequality, $|\sum_j X_{ij} - \sum_j M_{ij}| \leq \sum_j |X_{ij} - M_{ij}|$. Hence, $\bar{B}_{ij} \leq B_i$. $\bar{B}_{ij} < B_i$ if there is at least one sub-industry with exports exceeding imports, and at least one with imports exceeding exports. Ignoring the special case in which exports exceed imports or vice versa for all j sub-industries, the measured level of intra-industry trade must decline as one goes to a more disaggregated level of the trade classification. *A fortiori*, the measured level of intra-industry trade across all industries must decline too.

This result is familiar, but one can say more. As Gray (1979) observed, the fall in the measured intra-industry trade with disaggregation is because there are sub-industries with inter-industry trade balances that are of opposite sign. Formally, at the higher level of aggregation, the term in the numerator of Equation (2.3) is

$$\sum_j X_{ij} + \sum_j M_{ij} - \left| \sum_j X_{ij} - \sum_j M_{ij} \right| = 2 \min \left(\sum_j X_{ij}, \sum_j M_{ij} \right)$$

$$= \sum_j 2 \min (X_{ij}, M_{ij}) + 2 \min (X'_i, M'_i)$$

$$(2.15)$$

where $X_i = X_I - \sum_j 2 \min (X_{ij}, M_{ij})$ and $M_i = M_i - \sum_j 2 \min (X_{ij}, M_{ij})$

This states that intra-industry trade in industry i at the more aggregated level consists of intra-group trade at the more disaggregated level plus the trade in products of the industry that is the matching of exports and imports across sub-industries. Hence, the extent to which disaggregation lowers measured intra-industry trade depends on whether the intra-industry trade at the aggregated level is matching within or across sub-industries.[4]

Controversy 3: Factor content of international trade

The development of models that yielded intra-industry trade and the accumulating evidence that intra-industry trade did not vanish with disaggregation led to the acceptance of intra-industry trade by all international economists as a real phenomenon.

A good example of recent empirical research that incorporates intra-industry trade is the literature on empirical test of trade theories. Vanek (1968) posed the test of comparative advantage of some country in terms of the factor content of its exports and imports. Suppose there are n industries and m primary inputs. The industries each produce a single output and the primary inputs are homogeneous (non-industry-specific). Vanek assumed that trade is free and therefore that all goods prices are equalized among the trading countries, and that the technology of production is the same in all trading countries. Consequently, factor prices are equalized and, in each industry, factor proportions are equalized across countries. Then the factor content is

$$F = Az \qquad (2.16)$$

where F is the vector of factor contents, A is the technology matrix that specifies the primary input requirements of producing the goods, and z is the vector of net trades (an element is positive if there are net exports and negative if there net imports). The model is sufficiently general to allow the use of intermediate inputs. In this case, A is a matrix of direct and indirect input requirements. If additional assumptions are made, tests can be made of Heckscher–Ohlin-type hypotheses. Vanek assumed that all consumers have identical homothetic preferences.

While this model is general in terms of the number of primary inputs and goods, it still makes a number of restrictive assumptions. Attention has focused on the assumption that the technologies are identical among the countries. If the technologies differ, the factor content should be respecified as

$$F = AX - A^*M \qquad (2.17)$$

where X and M are vectors of gross exports and imports respectively and A^* is the technology matrix of the foreign country. A number of methods have been used to determine A^*. (The model can be extended readily to multiple trading partners.) A and A^* will depend on the technologies and the equilibrium factor prices in the home and foreign countries, respectively. Attempts have been made to incorporate technology differences in empirical tests (see, for example, Trefler and Zhu, 2000, and references therein).

Recently, Davis and Weinstein (2000a and 2000b) have pointed out that the traditional tests using Equation (2.16) assumed implicitly that the factor content of matched intra-industry trade is zero; that is, they have ignored intra-industry trade. To see the role of intra-industry trade, we rewrite gross exports and imports as

$$\begin{aligned} X &= G + x \\ M &= G + m \end{aligned} \qquad (2.18)$$

where the symbol G stands for the vector of matching (intra-industry) trade in the industries. $G_i = \min(X_i, M_i)$ is the value of matching trade in industry i. (It is $1/2\, B_i$ in Equation (2.3).) With this convention, x and m are non-negative. The value of x_i (or m_i) will be strictly positive if the country is a net exporter (or importer) of the industry's products, and zero if it is a net importer (or exporter). Substituting Equation (2.18) in Equation (2.17), gives:

$$F = (A - A^*)G + Ax - A^*m \qquad (2.19)$$

The first component is the factor content of matching intra-industry trade. Its contribution to factor content depends on the value of matching trade and the differences in technology. The second component is the contribution of net exports and imports. If there is an integrated equilibrium and technologies are identical, $A = A^*$ and factor content reduces to Equation (2.17).

Davis and Weinstein (2000a) test the patterns of inter- and intra-industry trade in North–North trade. They assume that all technology differences are of the factor-augmenting type, and that consumer preferences are identical and homothetic. They find that for more than half of the countries in their sample intra-industry trade is a more important conduit for net factor service trade than is inter-industry trade.

To explain the contribution of intra-industry trade, we can apply the results noted in the section dealing with the first controversy. In the Lancaster–Helpman type of model with differentiated products within the manufacturing industry, homogeneous labour and capital, and identical technologies across countries, the Heckscher–Ohlin theorem continues to hold for net trade. In the present context, this means that the factor content can be defined solely in terms of the net trade vector, as in Equation (2.16). But this occurs precisely because all the products of the differentiated products industry are produced with exactly the same factor proportions, and therefore factor proportions do not affect intra-industry trade. This is a very special result. It will not hold for the Lancaster–Helpman model if the symmetry is relaxed, and it does not hold for other models yielding intra-industry trade. For example, it does not hold for the Dixit–Grossman and Falvey models, in which different products/varieties use different factor proportions. In these models, intra-industry trade has non-zero factor content.

Trefler and Zhu (2000) have pointed out that Equation (2.17) (or Equation (2.19)) does not measure the true factor content if there is international trade in intermediate inputs. This equation assumes that all intermediate inputs are supplied domestically. This is a strong assumption as more than a half of total world goods trade by value is trade in intermediate inputs. In effect, Davis and Weinstein have assumed that all intra-industry trade is trade in final products.

Recently, much has been written about the phenomenon of 'fragmentation', the separation of the stages in the value chain among nations. Fragmentation yields a type of intra-industry trade with trade in intermediate inputs. The model of Dixit and Grossman (1982) models this type of trade. One needs to make an adjustment for the import content of intermediate input usage.[5] This can be done by excluding imported intermediate inputs in the manner of Trefler and Zhu (2000).

This problem of measuring factor content is a good illustration of how intra-industry trade has now been mainstreamed and combined with inter-industry trade.

Notes

* I would like to acknowledge the helpful comments of Mary Amiti, Hyun-Hoon Lee and participants at the meeting in Boulder, Colorado.
1 Gray(1979, p. 87) described this as 'language that has a belligerence typical of a dissertation'.
2 The symbols used are as far as possible the same as those in Grubel and Lloyd. Grubel and Lloyd multiply the indices by 100 to express the results as a percentage. Here the index is expressed as a fraction.
3 This measure has a curious history. It has been discovered independently a number of times. The form in Equation (2.8) had been developed by Grubel and Lloyd (1975, Equation (2.14)) (though they rejected it as it provides a matching index of the proportions of exports and imports, not the values). The form in Equation (2.7) was developed by Kol and Mennes (1986). The form in Equation (2.9) was developed by Finger and Kreinen (1979) in a different context and applied to intra-industry trade by Kol and Mennes (1986). Kol and Mennes (1986) note the equivalence between all three forms of the measures when used in the one domain. Aquino (1978) used a fourth definition, in order to provide a measure that adjusted for the trade imbalance, not realising its equivalence to Equation (2.7). This form is given in Equation (2.12) in the text.
   It is ironic that Finger, the critic of Grubel and Lloyd and other writers on intra-industry trade, should (with Kreinen) apparently discover a Grubel–Lloyd index!
4 The result in Equation (2.15) has been used in a different context by Greenaway, Lloyd and Milner (2001) to relate intra-industry trade to intra-industry international production by multinational enterprises.
5 Alternatively, this is one of the models in which the products of an industry may be aggregated consistently in production and consumption to produce new measures of aggregate output and consumption (see Lloyd, 1994, p. 104). This produces some sharp results. With the assumptions of free trade and identical technologies, net exports or imports can be combined once again with a technology matrix to yield the factor content of international trade. The technology matrix is, however, a world technology matrix for the production of the final vertically integrated product of the industry.

References

Aquino, A. (1978) 'Intra-Industry Trade and Inter-Industry Trade Specialization as Concurrent Sources of International Trade in Manufactures', *Weltwirtschaftliches Archiv*, 114: 275–96.

Armington, P. (1969) 'A Theory of Demand for Products Differentiated by Place of Production', *IMF Staff Papers*, 16: 159–78.

Balassa, B. (1979) 'Intra-Industry Trade and the Integration of Developing Countries in the World Economy', in H. Giersch (ed.), *On the Economics of Intra-Industry Trade* (Tübingen: J. C. B. Mohr).

Balassa, B. (1986) 'Intra-Industry Specialization: A Cross-country Analysis', *European Economic Review*, 30: 27–42.

Bergstrand, J. H. (1983) 'Measurement and Determinants of Intra-Industry International Trade' in P. K. M. Tharakan (ed.), *Intra-Industry Trade: Empirical and Methodological Issues* (Amsterdam: North Holland).

Davis, D. R. and D. E. Weinstein (2000a) 'Do Factor Endowments Matter for North–North Trade?', Mimeo, Columbia University.

Davis, D. R. and D. E. Weinstein (2000b) 'International Trade as an "Integrated Equilibrium"', *American Economic Review*, 90: 150–4.

Dixit, A. K. and G. M. Grossman (1982) 'Trade and Protection with Multistage Production', *Review of Economic Studies*, 43: 583–94.

Falvey, R. E. (1981) 'Commercial Policy and Intra-Industry Trade', *Journal of International Economics*, 11: 495–511.

Finger, J. M. (1975) 'Trade Overlap and Intra-Industry Trade', *Economic Inquiry*, 8: 581–9.

Finger, J. M. and M. E. Kreinen (1979) 'A Measure of "Export Similarity" and its Possible Uses', *Economic Journal*, 89: 905–12.

Fontagné, L. and M. Freudenberg (1997) *Intra-Industry Trade: Methodological Issues Reconsidered*, Centre d'Études Prospectives et d'Informations Internationales (Paris: CEPII).

Glick, R. and A. K. Rose (1998) 'Contagion and Trade: Why Are Currency Crises Regional?', NBER Working Paper Series No. 6806.

Gray, H. P. (1979) 'Intra-Industry Trade: The Effects of Different Levels of Data Aggregation' in H. Giersch (ed.), *On the Economics of Intra-Industry Trade* (Tübingen: J. C. B. Mohr).

Greenaway, D. and C. Milner (1981) 'Trade Imbalance Effects in the Measurement of Intra-Industry Trade', *Weltwirtschaftliches Archiv*, 117: 756–62.

Greenaway, D. and J. Torstensson (1997) 'Back to the Future: Taking Stock of Intra-Industry Trade', *Weltwirtschaftliches Archiv*, 133: 249–69.

Greenaway, D., P. J. Lloyd and C. Milner (2001) 'Intra-Industry Foreign Direct Investment and Trade Flows: New Measures of Global Competition' in L. K. Cheng and H. Kierzkowski (eds), *Global Production and Trade in East Asia* (Norwell, Mass.: Kluwer).

Grubel, H. G. and P. J. Lloyd (1971) 'The Empirical Measurement of Intra-Industry Trade', *Economic Record*, 47: 494–517.

Grubel, H. G. and P. J. Lloyd (1975) *Intra-Industry Trade: The Theory and Measurement of International Trade in Differentiated Products* (London: Macmillan).

Helpman, E. (1981) 'International Trade in the Presence of Product Differentiation, Economies of Scale and Monopolistic Competition: A Chamberlinian–
Heckscher–Ohlin Approach', *Journal of International Economics*, 11: 305–40.

Jones, R. (1956) 'Factor Proportions and the Heckscher–Ohlin Theorem', *Review of
Economic Studies*, 24: 1–10.

Kol, J. (1988) 'The Measurement of Intra-Industry Trade', Ph.D. thesis (Rotterdam:
Erasmus University).

Kol, J. and L. B. M. Mennes (1986) 'Intra-Industry Specialization and some Observations on Concepts and Measurement', *Journal of International, Economics*, 21:
1173–81.

Krugman, P. R. (1979) 'Increasing Returns, Monopolistic Competition and International Trade', *Journal of International Economics*, 9: 469–79.

Lancaster, K. (1980) 'Intra-Industry Trade under Perfect Monopolistic Competition', *Journal of International Economics*, 10: 151–75.

Lee, H-H and Y-Y Lee (1993) 'Intra-Industry Trade in Manufactures: The Case of
Korea', *Weltwirtschaftliches Archiv*, 129: 159–71.

Lipsey, R. E. (1976) 'Review of Grubel, H, G. and Lloyd, P. J., "Intra-Industry
Trade"', *Journal of International Economics*, 6: 312–14.

Lloyd, P. J. (1989) 'Reflections on Intra-Industry Trade and Factor Proportions', in
P. K. M. Tharakan and J. Kol (eds), *Intra-Industry Trade: Theory, Evidence and
Extensions* (London: Macmillan).

Lloyd, P. J. (1994) 'Aggregation by Industry in High-dimensional Models', *Review
of International Economics*, 2: 97–111.

Loertscher, R. and F. Wolter (1980) 'Determinants of Intra-Industry Trade among
Countries and across Industries', *Weltwirtschaftliches Archiv*, 116: 280–93.

Rayment, P. B. W. (1976) 'The Homogeneity of Manufacturing Industries with
Respect to Factor Intensity: the Case at the UK', *Oxford Bulletin of Economics and
Statistics*, 38: 203–9.

Rayment, P. B. W. (1983) 'Intra-"Industry" Specialization and the Foreign Trade of
Industrial Countries', in S. F. Frowen (ed.), *Controlling Industrial Economies,
Essays in Honour of C. T. Saunders* (London: Macmillan), pp. 1–28.

Trefler, D. and S. C. Zhu (2000) 'Beyond the Algebra of Explanation: HOV for the
Technology Age', *American Economic Review*, 90: 145–9.

Vanek, J. (1968) 'The Factor Proportions Theory: The N-Factor Case', *Kyklos*, 21:
749–56.

Verdoorn, P. J. (1960) 'The Intra-Bloc Trade of Benelux', in E. A. G. Robinson (ed.),
The Economic Consequence of the Size of Nations (London: Macmillan).

Watson, I. (1997) *Applying Case-Based Reasoning: Techniques for Enterprise Systems*
(San Francisco: Morgan Kaufman).

Part II
Models of Intra-Industry Trade

3
Horizontal Intra-Industry Trade and the Growth of International Trade

Nicolas Schmitt and Zhihao Yu

Introduction

The main question investigated in this chapter is whether a model of intra-industry trade with horizontal differentiation is able to explain the significant gap between the growth rates of trade and of output. We argue that it does, provided that the standard model of intra-industry trade (that is, the Dixit–Stiglitz–Krugman model) includes non-traded products.

It is well known that the post-Second World War period is characterized by a significantly higher growth rate in world manufactured trade than in world output. Roughly, world manufactured trade has grown on average by about 3 per cent per year faster than GDP since 1950 (Harris, 1993; Rose, 1991). Recent years have not changed this picture. The World Trade Organization reported recently that developing countries' merchandise exports expanded by 8.5 per cent in 1999, twice as fast as the global average, and more than seven times the growth rate of world commodity output (WTO, 2000). At the same time, the share of intra-industry trade has increased over the post-Second World War period and it represents today a significant proportion of overall trade.[1]

There is no well-accepted model explaining this gap in the growth rates (see, for example, Krugman, 1995). Rose (1991) investigates empirically the role of lower barriers to trade (tariff and transport cost), the relative decline in the price of traded goods with respect to non-traded goods,[2] and the role of the growth of international reserves and real income. Although lower tariffs do contribute towards explaining the growth of international trade, he finds no satisfying economic explanation that can capture most of the growth in trade. Ishii and Yi (1997) and Hummels *et al.* (2001) develop models of vertical specialization in production. The gap is then explained by the fact that countries specialize increasingly in intermediate inputs generating extensive trade since products cross borders repeatedly as intermediate inputs and then as components within more finished products. This is an interesting and important avenue of research, since a large, but apparently declining (see Ishii and Yi, 1997), share of international trade is in intermediate inputs. However, from their own account, vertical specialization explains, at best, 21 per cent of total exports in 1990 for ten OECD countries (representing 60 per cent of world trade).[3]

In this chapter, we want to argue that there is another, much simpler, channel through which the gap between growth in trade and in output can be explained: non-traded horizontally differentiated products are beginning to be traded as barriers to trade decrease.

This switch from non-traded to traded goods is consistent with Bernard and Jensen (1998), who investigate the US export boom between 1987 and 1992 at the firm level. Decomposing exports into a growth effect (that is, exports rise proportionally with the increase in the firms' overall shipment) and into an export intensity effect (indicating a relative increase in export with respect to firms' overall shipment), the authors find that 63 per cent of the change in US exports between 1987 and 1992 results from the change in the intensity effect alone. A further decomposition of this effect is particularly interesting since it is split equally between firms that were exporting in both 1987 and 1992, but are now simply exporting a larger fraction of their overall production, and the effect caused by firms that were *not* exporting in 1987 but were exporting in 1992. This last finding is important, because it indicates that a significant number of firms with non-traded goods in 1987 were trading these products in 1992.[4] It is this effect of non-traded products becoming traded that we wish to capture.[5]

Ishii and Yi (1997) argue that there is no intra-industry model explaining how trade could grow at a faster rate than production. Specifically, they argue that models such as Krugman (1980) are able to explain levels but not *changes*. However, none of the standard models of intra-industry trade used in the literature include non-traded goods. We show that the traditional Dixit–Stiglitz–Krugman model of intra-industry trade can indeed take into account non-traded goods and help to explain these gaps in growth rates.

Specifically, we find that in a model with both traded and non-traded goods, the effect of trade liberalization on the change in the share of export in total output almost doubles compared to the standard model, as some non-traded goods become traded when the cost of trade decreases. Furthermore, we also find that the change in the share of export is sensitive to higher degrees of scale economies.

As far as we know, Venables (1994) is the only existing paper that includes non-traded products in a standard model of intra-industry trade. However, his approach is different from ours, since non-traded goods emerge in his model from an asymmetry on the demand side (namely, preferences bias in favour of domestic products, as with the Armington hypothesis) whereas non-traded goods in our model emerge from an asymmetry on the supply side (namely different fixed cost of exporting among firms). His concern is also different from ours as he wants to assess how the presence of non-traded goods affects the gains from economic integration.

The chapter is organized as follows. In the next section, the basic model is developed. In the third section there is a brief review of well-known results without non-traded goods, and we discuss the implications of the standard model concerning the link between decreases in barriers to trade and the change in export shares. In the fourth section we introduce non-traded goods and contrast the results with the outcome with traded goods only. In the fifth section we argue that, in our model, changes in technology also help explaining higher rates of change in trade and in the share of trade with respect to output, while the sixth section concludes.

The model

Consider the standard model of intra-industry trade with horizontal differentiation among final goods *à la* Krugman (see, for example, Krugman, 1980). There are two identical countries, Home (d) and Foreign (f). Labor is the only factor of production, with $L = L_d = L_f$, and each worker supplies one unit of labour. Production of any differentiated goods requires a fixed cost α and a constant unit cost β. To export, a firm incurs two additional costs: a fixed cost, $\gamma_i \geq 0$, and an international barrier to trade such that, if $\tau = 1 + t > 1$ units are shipped abroad, only one unit arrives, where t represents the per-unit barrier to trade. Below we call it transport cost, although t also includes tariff and non-tariff barriers. While transport cost is identical for all firms, the fixed cost of exporting has subscript i and is thus firm-specific.

In terms of resources, if firm i supplies x_{id} units of its good to the domestic market and x_{if} units to the foreign market, the total labour requirement is:

$$l_i = \alpha + \beta x_{id} + \gamma_i + \beta \tau x_{if} \qquad (3.1)$$

so that firm i's profit is

$$\pi_i = p_{id} x_{id} + p_{if} x_{if} - (\alpha + \beta x_{id} + \gamma_i + \beta \tau x_{if}) w \qquad (3.2)$$

where w is the wage rate.

On the demand side, consumers in each country have identical preferences, and the utility of each of these consumers is represented by:

$$U = \sum_i c_{id}^\theta + \sum_j c_{jd}^\theta + \sum_l c_{lf}^\theta, \theta \in (0, 1) \qquad (3.3)$$

where c_{id} is the consumption of traded good i, c_{jd} is the consumption of non-traded good j, and c_{lf} is the consumption of imported good l. Consumer's income is the sum of individual labour income and the share of the profits from all domestic firms. It is apparent that a consumer sees traded and non-traded goods as well as domestic and foreign goods as being equally desirable. Indeed, the elasticity of substitution among these products is $\sigma = \frac{1}{1-\theta}$.

The model is closed, with the usual conditions that total consumption equals total production, that labour is fully employed, and that no firm has an incentive to enter or to exit the industry.

We first establish the equilibrium without non-traded goods. Although these results are well known, they constitute our benchmark as far as the sensitivity of the model to trade liberalization is concerned, since the equilibrium provides predictions concerning both the trade and the production response to trade liberalization.

Standard results without non-traded goods

In the standard model, firms do not face a fixed export cost. Hence, in this section, we impose $\gamma_i = 0$. Since the model boils down to the standard non-address model of intra-industry trade as developed by Krugman (1980), we do not dwell on the derivation of the equilibrium.

Maximizing Equation (3.2) with respect to x_{id} and to x_{if}, firm i's pricing rules follow standard Lerner conditions, such that:

$$p_{id} = w\beta(1 - \frac{1}{\varepsilon})^{-1} \quad \text{and} \quad p_{if} = w\beta\tau(1 - \frac{1}{\varepsilon})^{-1} \qquad (3.4)$$

where ε is the price elasticity of demand. Maximizing Equation (3.3), it is easy to establish that $\varepsilon = 1/1 - \theta$ whether the product is domestic or foreign, at least when the number of products is large. Since all firms are identical in this symmetric two-country case, the no-entry/no-exit condition is the zero-profit condition. Setting Equation (3.2) equal to zero and using the equilibrium prices just derived, the total production of firm i, X, is:

$$X = x_{id} + \tau x_{if} = \frac{\alpha\theta}{\beta(1-\theta)} \tag{3.5}$$

Utility maximization (and the equilibrium prices) requires that, in equilibrium, $c_d^{\theta-1}/c_f^{\theta-1} = 1/\tau$, so that, given $x_f = Lc_f$ and $x_d = Lc_d$ (supply equal demand conditions),

$$x_f = \tau^{1/\theta-1}x_d \tag{3.6}$$

Using Equations (3.5) and (3.6), it is then easy to establish that:

$$x_d = \frac{\alpha\theta}{\beta(1-\theta)(1+\tau^{\theta/(\theta-1)})} \tag{3.7}$$

Finally, the full-employment condition requires that $L = n(\alpha + \beta X)$, so that, in each country, the equilibrium number of products is:

$$n = \frac{L(1-\theta)}{\alpha} \tag{3.8}$$

It is apparent that trade liberalization has no effect on the overall production of a firm, and no effect on the overall number of products in each market, since both Equation (3.5) and Equation (3.8) are independent of τ. Simply, as τ falls, x_f increases and x_d decreases by exactly the same magnitude.

This also tells us that the autarkic equilibrium in each country can be characterized easily, since, in that case, the production of each firm is still given by Equation (3.5), the number of products by Equation (3.8) and the equilibrium price by p_d, as given by Equation (3.4).

Although we do not have an explicit model of economic growth, we can investigate how exports respond to trade liberalization. Trade liberalization is understood as being a bilateral decrease in τ, and thus in t. The total volume of exports by one country, net of the units devoted to international transportation, is:

$$T = nx_f = n\tau^{1/(\theta-1)}x_d \tag{3.9}$$

Taking the derivative with respect to τ, we obtain:

$$\frac{dT}{T} = \left[\frac{1}{1-\theta} - \left(\frac{\theta}{1-\theta}\right)\frac{\tau^{\theta/(\theta-1)}}{1+\tau^{\theta/(\theta-1)}}\right]\left(-\frac{d\tau}{\tau}\right) \qquad (3.10)$$

As expected, a decrease in τ increases trade, since the expression in square brackets is necessarily positive. The first term is the substitution effect. A decrease in the relative price of the imported goods relative to the domestic goods increases the consumption of foreign relative to domestic goods. Since the same occurs in both countries, then, everything else being equal, the net increase in the firm's overall production would be directly proportional to the elasticity of substitution. However, in equilibrium, the firm's overall production is independent of τ (see Equation (3.5)). The second term represents the necessary correction affecting the level of trade, making sure that firm's production remains constant.

In order to have a better idea of the implications of the standard model concerning the rate of change of the export share, we proceed as follows. First, observe that since total production is not affected by τ in the standard model, then, necessarily, the rate of change of exports is the same as the rate of change of the export share $\left(\text{that is,} \frac{dT}{T} = \frac{d(T/P)}{T/P}\right)$. Second, since $\tau = 1 + t$, then $\frac{d\tau}{\tau} = \frac{t}{1+t}\frac{dt}{t}$. Hence, Equation (3.10) can be rewritten as:

$$\frac{dt}{t} = \left[\frac{1}{1-\theta} - \left(\frac{\theta}{1-\theta}\right)\frac{\tau^{\theta/\theta-1}}{1+\tau^{\theta/\theta-1}}\right]^{-1}\left(\frac{\tau}{\tau-1}\right)\frac{d(T/P)}{T/P} \qquad (3.11)$$

The above relationship provides the rate of decrease in the barrier to trade t which, given the elasticity of substitution among goods and the initial level of the barrier to trade, is necessary to sustain a rate of increase of, say, 3 per cent in the share of exports with respect to output. Table 3.1 provides these rates assuming $\theta = 0.5$, and thus with an elasticity of substitution equal to 2, as used in many CGE models (see, for example, Mercenier and Schmitt, 1996).

Table 3.1 has two features. First, the higher the initial level of trade barriers, the lower the required rate of trade liberalization sustaining a 3 per cent increase in the share of exports. This results simply from the fact that, when the initial level of trade barriers is high, the effect of trade liberalization on the change in exports is necessarily large, since export volumes are low. Second, Table 3.1 shows that an increase in the share of exports of 3 per cent requires a high rate of trade liberalization. Rates are 'high' for the following reason: if one accepts that trade costs

Table 3.1   Trade liberalization in the standard model for $\frac{d(T/P)}{T/P} = 3$ per cent

t	100%	90%	80%	70%	60%	50%	40%	30%	20%	10%
$-(dt/t)$	3.6%	3.83%	4.11%	4.47%	4.95%	5.63%	6.63%	8.31%	11.7%	21.7%

(including tariffs and non-tariff barriers) have decreased by roughly 25 per cent over a period of thirty-five years, as it is sometimes suggested (see Ishii and Yi, 1997), then the average rate of trade liberalization is less than 1 per cent per year.[6] Table 3.1 shows that the standard model requires the rate of trade liberalization to be at least 3.6 per cent per year. However, an unrealistic initial barrier to trade of 100 per cent (that is, for every two units shipped abroad, only one arrives) is necessary to obtain this lower bound. In the next section, we develop a version of the model that generates significantly lower rates of trade liberalization.

Intra-industry trade with non-traded goods

The presence of non-traded products requires the introduction of an asymmetry between trading and non-trading firms. This asymmetry is introduced by imposing a fixed cost of exporting incurred by the firms engaged in trade. Of course, a fixed cost alone is not enough to generate two types of firms since either this cost is low enough and every firm chooses to engage in trade, or it is too high and none of them chooses to trade. We therefore assume that this fixed cost of exporting, γ_i, is firm-specific and is distributed according to the density function $\phi(\cdot)$ with support $[0, \gamma_{n_a}]$, where n_a is the autarkic number of goods produced in this market. We assume this distribution is the same in both countries and use $\Phi(\cdot)$ to denote the cumulated density function. To make sure that some firms trade and others do not, we assume that γ_i is distributed in such a way that firms with a high cost of exporting do not find it profitable to engage in international trade. It follows that, in equilibrium, an exporter's profit is necessarily non-negative.[7]

As with the standard model, firms segment the two markets (take separate decisions for each of them). Each trading firm maximizes Equation (3.2) with respect to x_d and x_f, while a non-trading firm maximizes:

$$\pi = p_d x_d - (\alpha + \beta x_d)w \tag{3.12}$$

with respect to x_d. Following the same methodology as in the previous section, any good produced for the domestic market is sold at price $p_d = \beta w/\theta$ and, given that $\pi = 0$, each of the non-trading firms produces:

$$x_d = \frac{\alpha\theta}{\beta(1-\theta)} \tag{3.13}$$

for the domestic market.

The above analysis implies that, in autarky and thus when all the firms are non-trading, the total number of goods produced in each country is determined by $L = n_a(\alpha + \beta x_d)$. Hence, this autarkic number of goods, n_a, is given by Equation (3.8).

Consumers do not differentiate between a domestic product sold by a trading firm and one sold by a non-trading firm. Since they are all sold at the same price, the total demand, and thus the total domestic production, of each trading firm is also given by Equation (3.13). It is now easy to derive the firm's behaviour on the export market. Firms maximize Equation (3.2) with respect to x_f. As in the previous section, $p_f = \beta w \tau/\theta = p_d \tau$ and, given the equilibrium prices, consumer's utility maximization requires $c_d^{\theta-1}/c_f^{\theta-1} = 1/\tau$. It follows that $x_f = \tau^{1/\theta-1}x_d$ (identical to Equation (3.6)), since all consumers buying both types of goods consume $x_k = Lc_k(k = d, f)$ units. Hence, unlike with the standard formulation of the model, a change in τ does not affect the production and the consumption of domestic products but only the level of trade (and the consumption of foreign products). This implies that an exporting firm necessarily produces a larger volume of output than a firm concentrating on its home market only, and thus that total firm production depends on the level of the barrier to trade. Indeed,

$$\begin{aligned} X &= x_d + \tau x_f \\ &= \frac{\alpha\theta}{\beta(1-\theta)}(1 + \tau^{\theta/\theta-1}) \end{aligned}$$

We are now able to find the level of fixed export cost that just ensures zero profit on the export market. We denote this fixed cost by $\tilde{\gamma}$, and it is obtained by solving $p_{if}x_{if} - (\tilde{\gamma} + \beta\tau x_{if})w = 0$. Using the relevant price and Equation (3.6), we get:

$$\tilde{\gamma} = \alpha\tau^{\theta/(\theta-1)} \tag{3.14}$$

This is an important relationship for several reasons. First, it is easy to show that $\gamma_i \leq \tilde{\gamma}$ corresponds to the condition that the average cost of an exporting firm is lower or equal to the average cost of the non-trading firm. Thus, in the present model, an exporting firm exploits economies of scale at least as well as a non-trading firm.[8] Second, and more importantly, this relationship indicates that any change in transport cost or in the fixed cost of production affects $\tilde{\gamma}$, and thus the number of traded goods $n_a\Phi(\tilde{\gamma})$. The fact that the number of traded goods increases with lower barriers to trade is, of course, not surprising. Simply, since the direct cost of exporting is decreasing, some non-trading firms find it profitable to export their product. It is more surprising that the number of traded goods increases with the fixed cost. The easiest way to understand this is to realize that an increase in α increases the cost of producing a good (whether or not it is traded) relative to the cost of exporting. Producing a non-traded good then becomes relatively more expensive relative to producing a trading good, thereby increasing the share of traded goods in this market. Below, we investigate these two effects separately.

Trade liberalization with non-traded goods

We first compute the rate of change of exports generated by trade liberalization. As before, we define the total volume of exports of the home country net of the units devoted to transportation. Recall, however, that the distribution of γ is defined with respect to the autarkic number of firms n_a so that the volume of exports is $T = n_a\Phi(\tilde{\gamma})x_f$, where $n_a\Phi(\tilde{\gamma})$ represents the number of trading firms given the overall distribution of γ. Changes in the export volume as a result of a decrease in transport costs can be captured by:

$$\frac{dT}{T} = \left[\frac{\tau}{x_f}\frac{dx_f}{d\tau} + \frac{\phi(\tilde{\gamma})}{\Phi(\tilde{\gamma})/\tilde{\gamma}}\frac{\tau}{\tilde{\gamma}}\frac{d\tilde{\gamma}}{d\tau}\right]\frac{d\tau}{\tau} \qquad (3.15)$$

There are two effects that contribute towards increasing the volume of exports. The first term is the change in export volume by the existing exporters, and the second is the change in the number of exporters as a result of trade liberalization. A decrease in τ increases profits from export and thereby, at the margin, the number of exporters.

Using Equations (3.6) and (3.14),

$$\frac{dT}{T} = \left[\frac{1}{1-\theta} + \frac{\theta}{1-\theta}\left(\frac{\phi(\tilde{\gamma})}{\Phi(\tilde{\gamma})/\tilde{\gamma}}\right)\right]\left(-\frac{d\tau}{\tau}\right) \qquad (3.16)$$

Comparing Equations (3.16) and (3.10), the change in exports following trade liberalization is unambiguously greater than without non-traded goods. The interpretation of the two terms in the square brackets of Equation (3.16) is straightforward. The first term is the same as in

Equation (3.10) and it represents the substitution effect. In this version of the model, there is no corrective effect like that in Equation (3.10), since total firm production is no longer constant. The second term represents the impact of the new exporters on trade volume, since some non-traded goods become traded as a result of trade liberalization. This effect has the same sign as the first one, making the volume of trade more sensitive to trade liberalization than in the standard version of the model.[9]

Share of trade with non-traded goods

We now want to determine how, in the presence of non-traded goods, trade liberalization affects the gap between trade and output, or, equivalently, how trade liberalization affects the share of trade in total output, in order to compare it with the rate implied by the standard model. To do so, we need first to determine the relationship between production and trade liberalization.

In this model, trade liberalization has two opposite forces on production. Since some firms become exporting firms without changing their domestic production, overall production must increase. However, this added production requires resources that can only come from non-trading firms exiting the market, since resources are fully employed. This, in itself, must decrease production. The net change in production results from these two opposite forces.

To compute the net change in production, we take the following steps. First, observe that the production embodied in exports is $P_x = \tau T = n_a \Phi(\tilde{\gamma}) \tau x_f$. This implies that a decrease in τ leads to the following increase in production:

$$dP_x = n_a \tau x_f d\Phi + n_a \Phi(\tilde{\gamma}) d(\tau x_f)$$

The first term represents the change in production caused by the change in the number of exporters, while the second term represents the change in production of the existing exporters. In terms of resources, this represents:

$$\beta dP_x + \tilde{\gamma} n_a d\Phi$$

that is, the variable cost associated with the added production and the additional fixed resources from the new exporters. Since these resources come from non-traded firms exiting the market, the number of non-traded firms leaving the market is equal to:

$$dn_{nt} = \frac{\beta dP_x + \tilde{\gamma} n_a d\Phi}{\alpha + \beta x_d}$$

The net change in production following trade liberalization must then be equal to:

$$dP = dP_x - x_d dn_{nt}$$
$$= \frac{1}{\alpha + \beta x_d} [\alpha n_a \Phi d(\tau x_f) + \alpha n_a \tau x_f d\Phi - x_d \tilde{\gamma} n_a d\Phi]$$

Using the relationship between x_d and x_f as well as Equation (3.14), the last two terms cancel out and we are left with:

$$\frac{dP}{d\tau} = \frac{\alpha n_a \Phi d(\tau x_f)}{\alpha + \beta x_d}$$
$$= -\theta n_a \Phi(\tilde{\gamma}) x_f \qquad (3.17)$$
$$= -\theta T$$

Hence, a decrease in τ increases overall production unambiguously.

We can now determine the relationship between trade liberalization and the change in the share of exports. To do so, we assume that γ_i is uniformly distributed and, therefore, that:

$$\frac{\phi(\tilde{\gamma})}{\Phi(\tilde{\gamma})/\tilde{\gamma}} = 1$$

Using Equations (3.16) and (3.17), trade liberalization as a function of the change of the export share can be found to be equal to:

$$\frac{dt}{t} = \left[\frac{\tau}{T} \frac{dT}{d\tau} - \frac{\tau}{P} \frac{dP}{d\tau} \right]^{-1} \left(\frac{\tau}{\tau - 1} \right) \frac{d(T/P)}{T/P}$$
$$= \left[b \frac{\theta + 1}{\theta - 1} + \theta \frac{\tau T}{P} \right]^{-1} \left(\frac{\tau}{\tau - 1} \right) \frac{d(T/P)}{T/P} \qquad (3.18)$$

The first term in square brackets represents the change in trade without the resource constraint, while the second term represents the change in production. Not surprisingly, this last term is proportional to the share of trade in total production. Of course, these two terms have opposite signs. Assuming, as in the previous Section, that $\theta = 0.5$ and $\frac{d(T/P)}{T/P} = 3$ per cent, Table 3.2 indicates the rates of trade liberalization implied by the model with non-traded goods.

Table 3.2   Trade liberalization and non-traded goods for $\frac{d(T/P)}{T/P} = 3$ per cent

T	100%	90%	80%	70%	60%	50%	40%	30%	20%	10%
$-(dt/t)$	2.1%	2.2%	2.3%	2.5%	2.7%	3.1%	3.6%	4.4%	6.1%	11%

Comparing Tables 3.1 and 3.2, the implied rates of trade liberalization sustaining an increase in the share of exports of 3 per cent are much lower (almost by half) in the present version of the model than in the standard model, and are thus more realistic despite the increase in production that trade liberalization generates. However, the implied rate of trade liberalization is still relatively high. We now go on to discuss the second feature of the model with non-traded goods that may also contribute to boost trade relative to production.

Economies of scale and non-traded goods

As we noticed with Equation (3.14), an increase in the fixed cost of production α increases the number of traded goods (that is, $d\bar{y}/d\alpha > 0$). In other words, a change in technology making the fixed cost of production larger relative to the unit cost of production and to the cost of exporting may be an added effect contributing to an increase in the volume of trade.

This is quite different from the standard model since, as can be seen from Equation (3.9), an increase in the fixed costs of production does not change the total volume of trade. Simply, an increase in α raises output and exports of an individual firm, but it also lowers the total number of products/firms, and these two effects have exactly the same magnitude.

In the presence of non-traded goods, a general increase of α (that is, by all the firms in both countries) raises output and exports of each trading firm, and increases the number of exporting firms as the relative cost of exporting falls. The intuition is as follows. An increase in α implies that more resources cannot be devoted to the direct production of goods. This leads to a decrease in the number of available variants and, because of the utility function, each consumer reacts by increasing the volume of consumption of each 'surviving' variant. This implies that the demand for foreign products increases, and thus that the firms that are indifferent between trading and not trading now make a profit (recall that prices are independent of α). Hence, more firms want to become exporters with higher α, establishing a link between the degree of scale economies and the share of trading firms in the total number of firms.

By implication, the total volume of exports necessarily goes up with α, just like as it does with trade liberalization.

Schmitt and Yu (2001) derive precisely the effects of a change in α on trade and on production. In particular, we show that an increase in α raises the volume of trade and decreases production, at least with uniform distribution of γ_i. Hence, an increase in α increases both the volume of trade and the share of trade in total output.

Although it is more difficult to compute a back-of-the-envelope rate of change in exports caused by a change in fixed cost than it is with trade liberalization, changes in technologies aimed first at exploiting economies of scale and more recently at economies of scope are often captured by increases in fixed costs relative to variable costs. To the extent that these changes have occurred over the post-Second World War period, and they have been significant, this model predicts that they have also contributed to the increase in international trade. It is interesting to note that, while we are not aware of any empirical evidence linking increases in scale economies and the growth rate of trade, Harrigan (1994) finds that the volume of trade is higher in sectors with larger scale economies. This is a direct implication of our model.

Conclusion

In a recent article, Krugman (1995) argues that the causes of the growth in world trade are surprisingly disputed. While some favour trade liberalization and falling transportation costs, others argue that income growth and countries' income convergence are the key. A third group underlines the role of technological changes, and in particular the forces leading to outsourcing.[10] This chapter not only underlines the role of trade liberalization and lower transportation costs in an environment where firms are heterogeneous, but also points out the role of technological changes – particularly those leading to higher degrees of economies of scale.

Specifically, we have argued that the simultaneous presence of non-traded horizontally differentiated goods and heterogeneity among firms in their ability to export is helpful in making trade and export shares more sensitive to trade liberalization and to changes in technology than in the standard model of intra-industry trade. This proves helpful if one wants to use intra-industry trade models to explain the wide and persistent gap between growth of trade and of output during the post-war period. Although our analysis has been cast in the standard framework of consumer final products, it must be clear that the conclusions would not be altered had we considered traded and non-traded intermediate products *à la* Ethier (1982).

We could imagine additional features of the model boosting further the sensitivity of trade to decreases in barriers to trade. One feature would be to consider multiproduct firms where, for each firm, some goods are traded and others are not. Another would be to have more than a single export market differentiated by fixed cost of exporting, or by the cost of transportation (for example, because some markets are more distant from the home market than others). Trade liberalization then induces products to become traded simultaneously with respect to more than one market, inducing thereby an even greater proportion of non-traded firms to exit the market in order to provide enough resources for these newly traded goods. In each of the above cases, however, the basic model remains the same and so is the message: the standard model of intra-industry trade in horizontally differentiated products can be amended to capture most, if not all, of the observed increase in the share of exports.

Notes

1 Concerning the EU, Fontagné, Freudenberg and Péridy (1997) find that the share of intra-industry trade increased from about 55 per cent in the early 1980s to 65 per cent in 1994. Brülhart and Elliott (1996) report that the number of European industries (at five digit level) where significant intra-industry occurs increased from 365 in 1961 to 2203 in 1992.

2 The argument is that the price of traded and non-traded goods is determined by the productivity in each sector, and that productivity in the traded good sectors increases faster with real income (Balassa, 1964).

3 This share may have increased to 30 per cent in 1995.

4 Note that it is quite possible that firms trading in both years increase their share of exports relative to shipment by selling in markets in which they were initially not engaged. Hence, products of these firms may simply become traded with respect to specific markets (for example, markets further away from the home market). See Hummels (1999) for evidence that transportation costs associated with increased distance have declined.

5 See also Roberts *et al.* (1995) for an empirical analysis of the importance of heterogeneity among firms and of export booms mainly explained by non-exporters re-tooling to sell in foreign markets; and Bernard *et al.* (2000) for a detailed analysis of plant-level heterogeneity in exporting.

6 This is obtained by solving $(1 + dt/t)^{35} = 0.75$.

7 Montagna (1998) generates differences in profits by introducing heterogeneous marginal costs of production. See also Jean (2000). Empirically, profitability differences among firms are found in Mueller (1990).

8 This contrasts with the standard model in which firms exploit economies of scale equally well in both autarky and free trade.

9 Note that Venables (1994) also finds that the volume of trade is more sensitive to trade liberalization with non-traded goods than with traded goods only.
10 See Baier and Bergstrand (2001) for a recent empirical attempt to disentangle some of these forces.

References

Baier, S. and J. Bergstrand (2001) 'The Growth of World Trade: Tariffs, Transport Costs and Income Similarity, *Journal of International Economics*: 53 (1), 1–27.

Balassa, B. (1964) 'The Purchasing-Power Parity Doctrine', *Journal of Political Economy*: 72 584–96.

Bernard, A. B., J. Eaton, J. B. Jensen and S. Kortum (2000) 'Plants and Productivity in International Trade', Unpublished manuscript, Boston University, Mass.

Bernard, A. B. and J. B. Jensen (1998) 'Understanding the U.S. Export Boom', NBER Working Papers No. 6438, March.

Brülhart, M. and R. J. R. Elliott (1996) 'Adjustment to the European Single Market: Inferences from Intra-Industry Trade Patterns', CREDIT Research Paper 96/15, September.

Ethier, W. J. (1982) 'National and International Returns to Scale in the Modern Theory of International Trade', *American Economic Review*, 72: 389–405.

Fontagné, L., M. Freudenberg and Péridy, N. (1997) 'Trade Patterns Inside the Single Market', Document de travail no. 97–07, CEPII.

Harrigan, J. (1994) 'Scale Economies and the Volume of Trade', *The Review of Economics and Statistics*, 76: 321–8.

Harris, R. G. (1993) 'Globalization, Trade and Income', *Canadian Journal of Economics*, 26: 755–75.

Hummels, D. (1999) 'Have International Transportation Costs Declined?', Unpublished manuscript, University of Chicago, July.

Hummels, D., J. Ishii and K. M. Yi (2001) 'The Nature and Growth of Vertical Specialization in World Trade', Journal of International Economics 54(1), 75–96.

Ishii, J. and K. M. Yi (1997) 'The Growth of World Trade', Research Paper 9718, Federal Reserve Bank of New York, May.

Jean, S. (2000) 'International Trade and Firms' Heterogeneity under Monopolistic Competition', CEPII Working Paper No. 00–13.

Krugman, P. R. (1980) 'Scale Economies, Product Differentiation, and Pattern of Trade', *American Economic Review*, 70: 950–9.

Krugman, P. R. (1995) 'Growing World Trade: Causes and Consequences', *Brookings Papers on Economic Activity*, 1: 327–77.

Mercenier, J. and N. Schmitt (1996) 'On Sunk Costs and Trade Liberalization in Applied General Equilibrium', *International Economic Review*, 37: 553–71.

Montagna, C. (1998) 'Efficiency Gaps, Love of Variety and International Trade', University of Dundee, Economics Discussion Paper No. 90.

Mueller, D. C. (1990) *The Dynamics of Company Profits: An International Comparison*, Cambridge: Cambridge University Press.

Roberts, M., T. Sullivan and J. Tybout (1995) 'What Makes Export Boom? Evidence from Plant-Level Panel Data', Unpublished manuscript, December.

Rose, A. K. (1991) 'Why Has Trade Grown Faster than Income?', *Canadian Journal of Economics*, 24: 417–27.

Schmitt, N. and Z. Yu (2001) 'Economies of Scale and the Volume of Intra-Industry Trade', Economics Letters 74(1), 127–32.

Venables, A. J. (1994) 'Integration and the Export Behaviour of Firms: Trade Costs, Trade Volumes and Welfare', *Weltwirtschaftliches Archiv*, 130 (1), 118–32.

WTO (2000) 'World Developments and World Trade in 1999', World Trade Organization Press Release 175, 6 April.

4
Intra-Industry Trade in Homogeneous Products

Daniel M. Bernhofen

Introduction

There seems to be a general consensus among trade economists that the phenomenon of intra-industry trade is linked directly to imperfect competition and economies of scale. Among the different theoretical explanations of intra-industry trade, the various models based on product differentiation in the presence of scale economies have obtained the highest level of popularity. This is possibly the case because the notion that intra-industry trade is linked to product differentiation had been postulated a decade before models of the new trade theory established the link formally in the late 1970s.

This chapter focuses on the literature of intra-industry trade in *homogeneous* products. Since we already know from casual observations that most economic transactions – at both national and international levels – take place in goods and services that are anything but homogeneous, a first reaction would be to classify these theories as having little or no empirical content. Unfortunately, this 'first reaction' has become a commonly held view by many trade economists.

One of the aims of this chapter is to convince the reader that the models of intra-industry trade in homogeneous products can play a very useful role in helping us to obtain a more complete understanding of the phenomenon of intra-industry trade. In this respect, it is important to remind ourselves of the purpose of the homogeneity assumption in all economic models: analytical tractability. Instead, the theoretical literature on intra-industry trade in homogeneous products should be viewed as a research agenda that focuses on economic environments where *taste for variety* (that is, horizontal product differentiation) or *product quality* (that is, vertical product differentiation) are not the driving forces behind intra-industry trade.

For the purpose of this chapter, I shall divide the literature into a 'comparative advantage' branch and a 'strategic' branch. The second section provides a short assessment of the debate about whether the phenomenon of intra-industry is compatible with competitive trade theory. I argue that the latest theoretical literature on this subject has inarguably refuted the popular view that the existence of intra-industry trade cannot be explained by models of comparative advantage. The third section focuses on the empirical and policy aspects of the strategic intra-industry trade model. I show that this model is quite useful in deriving industry hypotheses about intra-industry trade, and that recent empirical work using disaggregated industry data has confirmed the predictions of this model. I also demonstrate that a simple theoretical extension of the strategic intra-industry trade model provides some new insights on the interrelationship between the degree of product homogeneity and firms' incentives to engage in international collusion.

Intra-industry trade and comparative advantage

Background and overview

From its first vague formulation at the beginning of the nineteenth century up to very recently, the principal theoretical explanation for the existence of international trade was based on the concept of comparative advantage. Among the different sources of comparative advantage, the Heckscher–Ohlin explanation – with its emphasis on international differences in factor endowments coupled with factor intensity differences among goods – has played the dominant role in explaining international specialization and trade. Hence, it came as a shock to trade theorists when it was discovered that the trade liberalization patterns during the 1960s and 1970s, especially among the countries of the European Economic Community (EEC), were apparently at odds with the factor endowment predictions of the Heckscher–Ohlin model of international trade. Specifically, empiricists found that the majority of trade took place in *similar* goods among countries with *similar* rather than *different* factor endowments. In fact, Grubel and Lloyd's (1975) seminal demonstration of the importance of intra-industry trade created serious doubts on the empirical relevance of the Heckscher–Ohlin model and provided the impetus for the development of the new trade theory.

Since the new trade theory models were able to explain convincingly the existence of intra-industry trade, and economies of scale is the central element in these theories, it soon became conventional wisdom that economies of scale are a necessary condition for the existence of such trade. Helpman's (1981) seminal integration of the monopolistic competition trade model into a Heckscher–Ohlin framework, which has been extended and made popular by Helpman and Krugman (1985), has led to the widely-held belief that neoclassical and new trade theory are complementary in nature: *intra-industry* trade is best explained by product differentiation and scale economies, while *inter-industry trade* results from comparative advantage.

However, during the 1980s and 1990s a new literature emerged that has challenged the view that scale economies are necessary to explain intra-industry trade. In particular, Falvey (1981), Bhagwati (1982), Chipman (1988, 1991), Dinopoulos (1988), Davis (1995) and Bhagwati and Davis (1999) have demonstrated that intra-industry is quite compatible with neoclassical models based on constant returns to scale.[1] In what follows, I shall attempt to highlight the key issues raised by this literature, and make suggestions regarding in which direction future research might yield some fruitful results.

The notion of an industry: two views from two literatures

Intra-industry trade generally is defined as two-way trade in *similar* products. But what makes two goods *similar* or *dissimilar*? This question lies at the heart of the controversy on the compatibility/incompatibility of intra-industry trade with neoclassical trade theory, and implies the need for properly understanding how intra-industry trade has been defined in the literature. In particular, there is an important distinction between the industrial organization view of an industry and the view inherent in the Heckscher–Ohlin model of international trade, with the former being adopted in the intra-industry trade models of the new trade theory.[2]

The core intra-industry trade models of the new trade literature are *one-sector* industrial organization models, where the concept of an industry – or market – is assumed to be well defined.[3] Although the single-sector nature of these models precludes any discussion about the boundary of the industry, it is assumed implicitly that the goods in the industry are confined by their substitutability in consumption.[4] In this literature, intra-industry trade is defined as two-way trade of goods that are *similar* in consumption.

In contrast, the Heckscher–Ohlin model emphasizes the *boundaries* between two industries. Specifically, an industry is characterized by its relative factor intensity – that is, goods produced with the same factor intensity compromise an industry, while goods produced under a different factor intensity does not belong to that industry. Consequently, in a Heckscher–Ohlin framework, international trade is always inter-industry trade and intra-industry trade has been precluded by definition.

Helpman and Krugman's (1985) seminal contribution was to provide a nexus between new and neoclassical trade theory based on the analytical tool of an integrated equilibrium. A feature of the integrated equilibrium framework is that it singles out factor endowment differences as a single source of comparative advantage while neutralizing the other sources of comparative advantage, such as technology and taste. It is crucial to recognize that in an integrated equilibrium framework the primary emphasis is on the boundaries between two industries, since this analytical tool serves to explain the effects of factor endowment distributions on inter-industry specialization. An industry is treated like a black box. Helpman and Krugman's ingenious idea was to add some structure to that black box. Specifically, they postulate a two-industry model in which the first industry consists of differentiated varieties produced under increased returns to scale while the second industry consists of a single homogeneous good produced under constant returns to scale. Using the factor-intensity distinction of what constitutes an industry, the Helpman and Krugman monograph established the canon that inter-industry trade results from comparative advantage while intra-industry trade is results from economies of scale.

Intra-industry trade and constant returns to scale: a reconciliation

The question that now arises is whether scale economies are necessary for intra-industry trade. This issue has been addressed by a variety of models that can be distinguished by focusing on either the consumption or the production definitions of intra-industry trade.

An early explanation of intra-industry trade based on the consumption definition originated in Bhagwati (1982) and was formalized by Dinopoulos (1988). Bhagwati (1982) proposed a biological model of trade in which the type of product produced in a country is based on the interaction between 'country environment' (for example, relative factor endowments, sociological structures such as family size and so on) and country-specific genetic factors (for example, level of development, R&D capacities). Intra-industry trade, then, is the result of a dynamic process in which advertising producers, in their search for new markets, generate a diffusion of tastes and hence intra-industry trade of those varieties that an economy did not produce in a state of autarky. Hence, the biological model of intra-industry trade can be viewed as a dynamic explanation for the conjecture proposed by Linder (1961), in which intra-industry trade is the result of country-specific differences in demand.

Alternatively, Chipman (1988, 1991), and Davis (1995) and Bhagwati and Davis (1999) have demonstrated that intra-industry trade can also be generated in a multi-country Heckscher–Ohlin–Samuelson model. In particular, these papers have shown that intra-industry trade, defined as trade in goods produced under the same relative factor intensities, can be generated in a factor endowment model under a variety of assumptions and functional forms. Because of its intuitive appeal, we elaborate here only on the paper by Davis (1995).

Davis (1995) provides a pointed critique on the canon generated by Helpman and Krugman (1985), that increasing returns at the firm level is the main cause of intra-industry trade. His critique is more convincing than the earlier papers by Chipman because his analysis – like Helpman and Krugman's – is conducted in the integrated equilibrium framework. Specifically, Davis shows that intra-industry trade can be simply the result of Hicks-neutral technological differences in the production of two competitive goods. Assuming that these two goods are produced under the same factor intensity – which is as much justified as the assumption that differentiated varieties are produced under the same factor intensity in Krugman's monopolistic competition model – he demonstrates that the Ricardian model of international trade can be viewed as a model of intra-industry trade. Hence, from a theoretical viewpoint, technological differences can account for both inter-industry and intra-industry specialization.

What have we learned and where should we go from here?

Since the emergence of the new trade literature, trade economists have tended to categorize models as either increasing or constant returns to scale with respect to the phenomenon of intra-industry trade. However, based on the recent theoretical work in intra-industry trade, it should be clear that intra-industry trade is quite compatible with models based on constant returns to scale. Since most intra-industry trade is probably a result of economic specialization, it might be more appropriate to categorize intra-industry trade models according to the different forms of specialization that they emphasize.[5] For example, the Krugman model (1979, 1980) focuses on consumers' generic taste for variety as a source of intra-industry specialization. The paper by Davis (1995) suggests that small differences in technologies might be an alternative source of intra-industry specialization, while Bhagwati (1982) stresses initial differences in tastes.

The trade literature has provided us with several alternative explanations for the occurrence of intra-industry trade. However, the primary emphasis of the majority of studies has been on the question of the existence of such trade, and there has been little emphasis on the factors that determine the extent to which such trade will occur. Specifically, the theoretical models need to be investigated with respect to their empirical content and modified in such a manner that they yield propositions that are capable of being tested. Ultimately, further progress in our understanding of the phenomenon of intra-industry trade will depend on empirical work in this area.

Davis and Weinstein (1999, 2000) have recently completed a descriptive empirical study of the factor content of trade that addresses the issue of intra-industry trade. The authors argue that the use of a common (usually US) technology matrix in calculating the factor content of trade in a Heckscher–Ohlin–Vanek framework leads to a measurement error which precludes the factor content in intra-industry trade. Using technology matrices that are country-specific, Davis and Weinstein (1999) report that roughly 40 per cent of net factor trade is carried through intra-industry exchange. Although their analysis is creative, the conceptual foundation of their study is not quite clear. We already know from the empirical intra-industry trade literature that there is a large amount of trade overlap in many industries, and this is also true at fairly disaggregated levels. Hence, it is not too surprising to discover that intra-industry trade measured in factor content is also quite large. On a more profound level, the primary motivation for the empirical interest in the 'factor content of trade' versus 'actually observed trade' lies in the fact that the Heckscher–Ohlin–Vanek theorem yields a testable hypothesis on the relationship between relative factor endowments and net factor content of trade in higher dimensions. However, the theoretical foundation of the *factor content of intra-industry trade* is not quite clear and needs to be addressed in the future.

Strategic intra-industry trade

Background and overview

The core model of intra-industry trade in the presence of strategic interaction goes back to James Brander (1981). However, through the generalization and reformulation of the model by Brander and Krugman (1983), the model's original focus – which has been primarily on intra-industry trade – has been redirected to the phenomenon of 'reciprocal dumping'. Consequently, the model has had a much greater influence on the dumping literature than on the intra-industry trade literature. In fact, this model has been viewed as a more exotic explanation of intra-industry trade (Helpman and Krugman, 1989, p. 134) than the monopolistic competition model.

The relatively low degree of popularity of the Brander model as an explanation of intra-industry trade can perhaps be understood by realizing that international trade has been seen generally as the result of international economic specialization. In the neoclassical trade models, specialization occurs along the lines of comparative advantage. In the monopolistic competition trade model, specialization occurs (somewhat) arbitrarily with respect to different product varieties. In contrast, international trade does not lead to any specialization at all in the Brander model. From a national welfare point of view, trade in identical products seems pointless and even wasteful, if transportation costs are high enough.

The central feature of the Brander model is its emphasis on market power; intra-industry trade is the result of firms' incentives to penetrate into each other's market in a reciprocal manner. Unlike in the monopolistic competition trade model, where the 'the main concern is usually to get the issue of market structure out of the way as simply as possible' (Krugman, 1989, p. 1181), the imperfectly competitive market structure is at the heart of Brander's argument.

In the following sections we shall survey recent empirical research, which has demonstrated that the Brander model is quite useful in deriving industry hypotheses about intra-industry trade. In particular, the model yields robust predictions on the effects of industry characteristics on the intensity of bilateral intra-industry trade, as measured by the Grubel–Lloyd index. Also, the model is able to generate some hypotheses on the effects of market size and product homogeneity on the volume of bilateral trade.

With regard to policy implications, the strategic trade literature has focused primarily on the incentives of (national) welfare maximizing governments to intervene in the international market place with 'strategic trade policies'.[6] I will show how a simple extension of the Brander model has some lessons for international anti-trust policy by analyzing the incentives of private firms to actually engage in (or restrict) international competition (see page 000).

Explaining the intensity of intra-industry trade

An empirical investigation of a straightforward generalization of the original Brander model is given in Bernhofen (1999). The model is based on Cournot–Nash competition among a fixed number of domestic and foreign firms, and allows for country-specific differences in cost structures and market size. The paper relates the intensity of bilateral intra-industry trade, as measured by the Grubel–Lloyd index, to industry variables such as market size, production costs and industry concentration. Using a symmetry assumption, the paper shows that the intensity of intra-industry decreases the more dissimilar the two countries are in their industry characteristics. Specifically,

$$GL = 1 - \frac{|i - i^*|}{i + i^*} \tag{4.1}$$

where $i(i^*)$ pertains to the respective industry variable of the domestic (foreign) economy.

In contrast to the large number of empirical studies on the Grubel–Lloyd index that use relatively aggregated industry data for many countries and industries, the paper by Bernhofen (1999) is in the spirit of the new empirical industrial organization literature; it aims to explain bilateral intra-industry trade between the USA and Germany in the context of a single industry: homogeneous petrochemicals. A key argument is that the characteristics of the petrochemical industry and the product-specific data set are compatible with the underlying assumptions of the model. The estimates indicate that while country-specific differences in market size and costs are both significant economically and have the predicted sign, the market concentration variable is, for the most part, insignificant. The latter result might be because a simple count of the number of producers is a rather poor measure for the degree of market concentration.

Using slightly different approaches, Tang (1999) and Bernhofen and Hafeez (2001) show that the relationship in Equation (4.1) between the Grubel–Lloyd index and country-specific differences in various industry characteristics also holds under the assumption of Bertrand–Nash competition. Both papers provide supportive evidence for the predictions of the basic model beyond the bilateral trade patterns of a single country pair.

The paper by Tang (1999) is one of the few empirical intra-industry trade studies in a service sector – specifically, the international telephone industry. Tang employs an interesting panel data set to explain bilateral telephone traffic between the USA and 146 foreign destinations during 1990–7. She finds that the decreasing share of two-way telephone traffic between the USA and the foreign destinations is well explained by the larger country-specific differentials in cost, teledensity, market concentration and other control variables.

Motivated by the fact that the industry determinants of intra-industry trade in the Brander model are invariant to whether firms compete in homogeneous or differentiated products, Bernhofen and Hafeez (2001) investigate the predictions of the model using internationally comparable data for twenty-two ISIC manufacturing industries in twelve OECD countries during 1970–85. Using dummy variables to control for idiosyncratic industry and country-pair effects, the study also finds supportive evidence for the hypothesis that the intensity of bilateral intra-industry is lower, the larger the country-specific differences in production costs and market size.

Market size and the laws of gravity

The papers reviewed above focused on the predictions of the strategic trade model with respect to the Grubel–Lloyd (GL) measure of intra-industry. Since the GL index is a measure of the degree of asymmetry in trade flows, it provides no information on the direction of trade. With regard to explaining the directions of international trade, the gravity equation – which relates bilateral trade flows to income levels and distances between trading partners – has yielded the most successful results in the empirical trade literature.

While it has been noted that 'specialization... generates the force of gravity' (Grossman, 1998, p. 28), Feenstra *et al.* (2001) argue that the strategic trade model is also consistent with a gravity-type equation, although with pronounced differences with regard to the income sensitivity of net exports. While in the monopolistic competition free-entry model a country's net exports are more sensitive to home income than to foreign income, the opposite is true in a homogeneous good strategic trade model with restricted entry. Because of the lack of good measures of entry barriers, Feenstra *et al.* (2001) develop alternative hypotheses relating entry barriers to product differentiation, and use the measure of product differentiation developed by Rauch (1999).

Having found a statistically significant difference between the elasticity of exports with respect to home income versus the elasticity of exports with respect to foreign income, Feenstra *et al.* (2001) conclude that there must be a correlation between entry barriers and product differentiation. Estimating a gravity equation separately for exports according to their product type, the authors find that, for exports of differentiated goods, the domestic income effect is higher than the foreign income effect, and that the opposite is true for homogeneous goods. The authors claim that this finding provides evidence for the hypothesis that barriers to entry are strongest in homogeneous good industries.

The analysis by Feenstra *et al.* (2001) is interesting, since it is one of the few papers that tests empirically alternative predictions of alternative trade models under increasing returns to scale. However, the analysis is based on the implicit assumption that trade in homogeneous products is generated by strategic interaction and that – in contrast to Krugman's monopolistic competition model – intra-industry trade in the Brander model is *not* a consequence of product differentiation.

In my judgement, the Brander model has played a relatively minor role in the intra-industry trade literature precisely because of its alleged emphasis on product homogeneity, whereas the bulk of international trade takes place in goods that are, in fact, differentiated. Although it is true that product differentiation is not sufficient for the *existence* of strategic intra-industry trade, the subsequent discussion will demonstrate that if one relaxes the assumption of perfect product homogeneity in the Brander model, the model has a surprising prediction: the higher the degree of product differentiation (that is, the lower the degree of product homogeneity in the industry), the higher the volume of intra-industry trade.

Product homogeneity and the volume of intra-industry trade

To convey the relationship between product homogeneity and the volume of intra-industry trade in the most transparent way, consider a stripped-down reciprocal markets model with two identical countries, zero marginal production and transportation costs, and specific functional forms for demand. Under the assumption of perfect product homogeneity, the inverse demand function in each country is given by $p = 1 - (z + z^*)$, where p denotes the price of the homogeneous good and z (z^*) denotes the supply by the home (foreign) industry.

We relax now the perfect homogeneity assumption by introducing a parameter θ into the inverse demand function of the home economy: $p = 1 - (z + \theta z^*)$, $(0 \leq \theta \leq 1)$. The parameter θ can be thought of as measuring the intensity of strategic interaction between the home and the foreign industry. A lower value of θ reduces the intensity of competition, since consumers perceive the products to be less substitutable for each other. To preserve the symmetry of the model, we specify the same inverse demand function for the foreign economy: $p^* = 1 - (z^* + \theta z)$. Calculating the Cournot–Nash equilibrium prices and quantities, we obtain:

$$p = p^* = z = z^* = \frac{1}{2 + \theta} \tag{4.2}$$

From Equation (4.2), we can see immediately that the lower the value of θ (that is, the lower the degree of product homogeneity), the larger is the volume of trade. It should be noted that this holds whether the volume of intra-industry trade is measured in quantities (that is, $VT = z + z^*$) or in values ($VT = pz + p^*z^*$). It can also be shown that this relationship is robust with respect to the mode of oligopolistic competition (that is, assuming Bertrand rather than Cournot competition) and the assumption of restricted versus free market entry.[7]

Hence, while it is true that product differentiation is not central to the *existence* of strategic intra-industry, introducing production differentiation into the basic Brander model implies that there will be *more* intra-industry trade the less substitutable the products are in the industry. Since this prediction is robust with respect to a variety of model specifications, it would seem fruitful to test this hypothesis empirically in the future.

Product homogeneity and the profitability of international trade: some policy implications

The primary focus of the trade policy literature in the context of imperfectly competitive markets has been on the objectives of national governments to intervene in the international market place. However, there has been very little emphasis on investigating the incentives of private firms to actually engage in (or to restrict) international competition, together with its potential implications for international anti-trust policy. Anderson *et al.* (1989) is one of the few papers that addresses the question of whether trade liberalization is profitable in oligopolistic industries. Specifically, Anderson *et al.* (1989) find that some oligopolistic firms will always lose from trade liberalization in a homogeneous product industry. In what follows, we shall address this issue in an intra-industry trade model that, as in the previous section, relaxes the assumption of perfect product homogeneity.

We consider a two-country model, similar to Bernhofen (2001), where the domestic and the foreign economies are identical with respect to all industry characteristics. Because of the assumed symmetry, it is sufficient to describe and analyze the domestic economy.

Goods and consumers

We consider a representative consumer who has a taste for a predetermined set of n domestic and n^* foreign goods. The quasi-concave utility function of this consumer is assumed to take the following form:

$$U(y, z_1, \ldots, z_{n+n^*}) = y + \sum_{i=1}^{n+n^*} v(z_i) - \theta \sum_{i<j,\ i\neq j} z_i z_j, \quad v(z_i) = z_i - z_i^2/2,$$

$$0 \leq \theta \leq 1 \qquad (4.3)$$

where y denotes the quantity of a composite numeraire good, produced under constant returns to scale, and $z_i (i = 1, \ldots, n+n^*)$ pertains to the quantity of the ith sectoral good. Utility maximization then yields the following product demand system:[8]

$$p_i = 1 - z_i - \theta \sum_{j\neq i} z_j, \quad (i = 1, \ldots n+n^*) \qquad (4.4)$$

The parameter $\theta(0 \leq \theta \leq 1)$ is a measure of the degree of substitutability between each pair of goods. In the extreme case of $\theta = 0$, there is no substitutability between each pair of goods. Consequently, there are no cross-price effects of demand, that is, $p_i = 1 - z_i (i = 1, \ldots n + n^*)$. Since a higher value of θ is associated with a higher cross-price elasticity, the substitutability of firms' products is increasing in θ. If $\theta = 1$, the goods are perfect substitutes for each other. Although we assume that firms and the consumer know about the value of θ, it is our presumption that θ is an unknown industry characteristic for an anti-trust authority.

Firms

Each product is produced by a different firm but with identical costs, $C(z_i) = K + cz_i (i = 1, \ldots n + n^*)$, where K is a fixed cost and c is a constant marginal cost, both measured in terms of the numeraire. Since the representative consumer in the domestic economy has a taste for domestic and foreign goods, all firms have the opportunity to sell to the foreign and to the domestic consumer. However, the question arises whether firms will infact engage in international trade. In general, firms' incentives to engage in international competition will depend on the relative strength of two forces. On the one hand, trade leads to an enlargement of the market. In the context of our model, the market expansion effect of international trade enables firms to sell their product to the foreign market in addition to the domestic consumer, leading to an increase in profits. But on the other hand, international trade increases the number of competitors in the market. This intensified competition has a negative effect on firms' profitability. If the competitive effect of international trade is stronger than the market expansion effect, firms would be better off if there were no trade.

Equilibrium analysis

For the remainder of the model, we assume that the home and the foreign industry consist of the same number of firms; that is, $n_0 = n = n^*$ (where $n_0 > 1$). We compare two regimes: (i) a free trade regime; and (ii) a collusive regime. In the free trade regime, all the firms in the domestic and the foreign industry are engaged in international competition. The profit function of a representative firm is given by:[9]

$$\pi^f = 2(z_i(1 - z_i - \theta \sum_{\substack{j=1, \\ j\neq i}}^{2n_0} z_j) - cz_i) - F \qquad (i = 1, \ldots 2n_0). \qquad (4.5)$$

Alternatively, the firms in the domestic and foreign industry could form a collusive agreement which would specify that the domestic industry serves only the domestic consumer while the foreign industry serves solely the foreign consumer. Formally, this would be identical to a situation where the two economies would operate under autarky. Under this regime, firms' profits are given by:[10]

$$\pi^c = (z_i(1 - z_i - \theta \sum_{\substack{j=1, \\ j\neq i}}^{n_0} z_j) - cz_i) - F \qquad (i = 1, \ldots n_0). \qquad (4.6)$$

In general, the collusive agreement will be profitable for all participants, if and only if $\pi^c > \pi^f$, which will depend on: (i) the homogeneity parameter θ; and (ii) the degree of market concentration n_0.[11]

In order to focus clearly on the issue of international collusion, we assume implicitly that the firms in the domestic industry act noncooperatively on the home market, even if they decide to form a collusive agreement with the firms of the foreign industry.

Equations (4.4) to (4.6) can be used to solve for the Cournot–Nash equilibrium prices and quantities of a representative firm:

$$p(\theta, \ n_0) = \frac{1 + c(1 + (n_0 - 1)\theta)}{2 + (n_0 - 1)\theta} \qquad (4.7)$$

$$z(\theta,\ n_0) = \frac{1-c}{2+(n_0-1)\theta} \tag{4.8}$$

Using Equation (4.7), it can be shown that, for a given industry concentration parameter n_0, the price reduction resulting from foreign competition, $\Delta p(\theta, n_0) = p(\theta, n_0) - p(\theta,\ 2n_0)$, is larger, the higher the value of θ, that is, $\partial\Delta p(\theta,n_0)/\partial\theta > 0$. Hence, international trade has a larger effect on the reduction of domestic market power, the higher the degree of product substitutability in the industry. Hence, from an anti-trust point of view, the disciplining force of international trade should be the highest in industries characterized by a relatively low degree of product differentiation. However, the question of how the parameter θ affects the industries' incentives to diminish the welfare gains from trade by colluding internationally needs to be considered.

The home and the foreign industry will be interested in engaging in international trade as long as $\Delta\pi^{f-c}(\theta,n_0) = \pi^f - \pi^c = 2z(\theta,\ 2n_0)$ $(p(\theta,\ 2n_0) - c) - z(\theta,\ n_0)(p(\theta,\ n_0) - c) > 0$. Using Equations (4.7) and (4.8), it is straightforward to show that $\partial\Delta\pi^{f-c}(\theta,n_0)/\partial\theta < 0$ and $\Delta\pi^{f-c}(\theta,\ n_0) > 0$ if and only if $\theta < \frac{2}{n_0\sqrt{2}+1}$. The latter expressions imply an anti-trust dilemma in an international context.

Proposition 1

In industries in which unrestricted international trade has the largest disciplining effect, domestic and foreign competitors also have the highest incentive to restrict such trade through international collusion.

In the above discussion, we focused on variations of the product substitutability parameter θ, keeping the level of industry concentration n_0 unchanged. However, in general, anti-trust authorities have a good knowledge about the degree of concentration in an industry, but little or no information about the parameter θ. Consequently, for the rest of our analysis, we assume that the anti-trust authority has complete knowledge about the level of industry concentration, but is uncertain about the degree of product substitutability. An industry j is characterized by a vector $(n_j,\ \theta_j)$, where the parameter θ_j is unknown to the anti-trust authority. To keep the analysis as simple as possible, we assume that each value of θ_j is equally likely to occur. Formally, θ_j has a uniform distribution on the interval $[0, 1]$. From our discussion above, we know that the home and the foreign industry will have an incentive to collude internationally as long as $\Delta\pi^{f-c}(\theta_j,\ n_j) < 0$. From the point of view of the anti-trust office, the probability of picking an industry which has an incentive to engage in international collusion is then a function of the known concentration parameter n_j:

$$P(n_j) = P\{\theta_j | \Delta \pi^{f-c}(\theta_j, n_j) < 0; \ \theta_j \in [0, 1]\} \tag{4.9}$$

Since $\Delta \pi^{f-c}(\theta_j, n_j) < 0$ if and only if $\theta_j > \frac{2}{n_j \sqrt{2}+1}$, it follows that $\partial P(n_j)/\partial n_j > 0$.

Proposition 2

The likelihood that the anti-trust authority picks an industry that has an incentive to actually engage in international collusion increases, the less concentrated the domestic industry.

In general, domestic anti-trust offices pay special attention to domestic industries that are heavily concentrated. Proposition 2 has the interesting implication that the incentive for international collusion is stronger in industries with a relatively low degree of domestic industry concentration. The intuition is as follows: the larger the number of domestic competitors, the lower is the profit gain to an individual firm from the extra supply to the foreign market. On the other hand, the increased foreign competition will have a rather strong negative effect on domestic profitability. Hence, since the import competition effect is stronger than the market expansion effect of international trade, the domestic and foreign industries are both better off if they stay out of each other's national markets. The model suggests that a global cartel office should pay particular attention to industries that face strong competition in their national markets.

Concluding remarks

This chapter has focused on theoretical models of intra-industry trade in which product differentiation is not a sufficient condition for the existence of such trade. In my judgement, the key lessons we have learned from recent theoretical and empirical work in these research areas are as follows.

(i) It is important to recognize that there exist different (sometimes implicit) definitions of intra-industry trade in the literature. If intra-industry trade is defined as trade in goods that are produced under the same relative factor intensities, as it is done in a Heckscher–Ohlin framework, then intra-industry trade can result from small country-specific cost-differences in production. Hence, the existence of intra-industry trade is quite compatible with conventional comparative advantage explanations of international trade.

(ii)   Although we now have a fair number of models that suggest different theoretical causes for the existence of intra-industry trade, empirical studies that put these various theories under serious empirical scrutiny are in short supply. In the empirical comparative advantage literature, the research efforts have been directed primarily towards factor content studies of trade. However, because of their focus on factor endowments, these studies have used fairly aggregated data and hence, the theoretical linkages to the phenomenon of trade 'within an industry' are not well established.

(iii) Recent empirical work in the strategic trade literature has demonstrated that the seminal Brander (1981) model of intra-industry trade does not only yield robust hypotheses on the industry-determinants of intra-industry trade, but that the model's empirical predictions hold up in industries, such as petrochemicals and telephone services, which are compatible with the underlying assumptions of the model.

(iv)   Finally, I showed that relaxing the product homogeneity assumption in the standard strategic intra-industry trade model provides some new insights. Although intra-industry trade results from strategic interaction, relaxing the intensity of strategic interaction in the form of lowering the degree of product substitutability makes firms more eager to trade, and thus leads to more two-way trade. This characteristic feature of the model also has implications for anti-trust policy. Although a higher degree of product differentiation decreases firms' incentives to refrain from forming a collusive agreement not to sell into each other's national market, it also reduces the disciplining effect of foreign trade on domestic market power. Furthermore, it has been shown that – for a given degree of product substitutability – the incentives of international collusion are stronger in industries with a relatively low degree of market concentration.

Notes

1 From a chronological point of view, Falvey (1981) was one of the first to provide a model of intra-industry trade in a comparative advantage framework. However, since the Falvey model is based on vertical product differentiation, it will not be discussed it here.

2 See also the discussion in Bhagwati and Davis (1999).

3 See, for example, Krugman (1979, 1980) and Brander (1981).
4 Historically, the 'industrial organization idea' of an industry (or market) goes back to Robinson (1933) who suggested the following criteria: begin with a good, then look at the good's substitutes, and then at the substitutes for these substitutes, and so on, until one finds a significant gap in the chain of substitutes, which then constitutes the boundary.
5 As will be shown in the next section, strategic intra-industry trade does not necessarily lead to specialization.
6 See Brander (1995) for an excellent survey of this literature.
7 See Bernhofen (2001) for the explicit derivations.
8 All prices are relative prices with respect to the numeraire good.
9 The superscript f pertains to free trade.
10 The superscript c pertains to collusion.
11 Since I restrict myself to a static model, I abstract from the issue of enforceability of a collusive agreement, which would require a dynamic framework. Hence, I assume implicitly that no firm will deviate from collusion as long as the agreement is profitable for the industry.

References

Anderson, S., M. Donsimoni and J. Gabszewicz (1989) 'Is International Trade Profitable to Oligopolistic Industries?', *International Economic Review*, 30: 725–33.

Bernhofen, D. M. (1999) 'Intra-Industry Trade and Strategic Interaction: Theory and Evidence', *Journal of International Economics*, 47: 225–44.

Bernhofen, D. M. (2001) 'Product Differentiation, Competition and International Trade', *Canadian Journal of Economics*, 34: 1010–23.

Bernhofen, D. M. and Z. Hafeez (2001) 'Oligopolistic Competition and Intra-Industry Trade: Evidence from the OECD', *Australian Economic Papers*, 40: 77–90.

Bhagwati, J. N. (1982) 'Shifting Comparative Advantage, Protectionist Demands, and Policy Responses' in J. N. Bhagwati (ed.), *Import Competition and Responses* (Chicago: University of Chicago Press) 153–195.

Bhagwati, J. N. and D. R. Davis (1999) 'Intra-Industry Trade: Issues and Theory', in J. Melvin, J. Moore and R. Riezman (eds), *Trade, Theory and Econometrics: Essays in Honor of John S. Chipman* (New York: Routledge).

Brander, J. (1981) 'Intra-Industry Trade in Identical Commodities, *Journal of International Economics*, 11: 1–14.

Brander, J. (1995) 'Strategic Trade Policy', in G. Grossman and K. Rogoff (eds), *Handbook of International Economics*, Vol. 3 (Amsterdam: North-Holland), pp. 1395–455.

Brander, J. and P. R. Krugman (1983) 'A "Reciprocal Dumping" Model of International Trade', *Journal of International Economics*, 15: 313–21.

Chipman, J. S. (1988) 'Intra-Industry Trade in the Heckscher–Ohlin–Lerner–Samuelson Model', Mimeo, University of Minnesota.

Chipman, J. S. (1991) 'Intra-Industry Trade in a Loglinear Model', Mimeo, University of Minnesota.

Davis, D. R. (1995) 'Intra-Industry Trade: A Heckscher–Ohlin–Ricardo Approach', *Journal of International Economics*, 39: 201–26.

Davis, D. R. and D. E. Weinstein (1999) 'Trade in a Non-integrated Work: Insights from a Factor Content Study', Mimeo, Columbia University.

Davis, D. R. and D. E. Weinstein (2000) 'International Trade as an "Integrated Equilibrium": New Perspectives', *American Economic Review*, 90: 150–4.

Dinopoulos, D. (1988) 'A Formalization of the "Biological" Model of Trade in Similar Products', *Journal of International Economics*, 25: 95–110.

Falvey, R. E. (1981) 'Commercial Policy and Intra-industry Trade', *Journal of International Economics*, 11: 495–511.

Feenstra, R. C., J. R. Markusen and A. K. Rose (2001) 'Using the Gravity Equation to Differentiate among Alternative Theories of Trade', *Canadian Journal of Economics*, 34: 430–47.

Grossman, G. (1998) 'Comment', in J. A. Frenkel (ed.), *The Regionalization of the World Economy* (University of Chicago Press), pp. 29–31.

Grubel, H. G. and P. J. Lloyd (1975) *Intra-Industry Trade: The Theory and Measurement of International Trade in Differentiated Products* (London: Macmillan).

Helpman, E. (1981) 'International Trade in the Presence of Product Differentiation, Economies of Scale and Monopolistic Competition: A Chamberlin–Heckscher–Ohlin Approach', *Journal of International Economics*, 11: 305–40.

Helpman, E. and P. R. Krugman (1985) *Market Structure and Foreign Trade* (Cambridge, Mass.: MIT).

Helpman, E. and P. R. Krugman (1989) *Trade Policy and Market Structure* (Cambridge, Mass.: MIT).

Krugman, P. R. (1979) 'Increasing Returns, Monopolistic Competition, and International Trade', *Journal of International Economics*, 9: 469–79.

Krugman, P. R. (1980) 'Scale Economies, Product Differentiation, and the Pattern of Trade', *American Economic Review*, 70: 950–9.

Krugman, P. R. (1989) 'Industrial Organization and International Trade', in R. Schmalensee and R. D. Willig (eds), *Handbook of Industrial Organization*, Vol. 2. (Amsterdam: North-Holland), pp. 1179–223.

Linder, S. (1961) *An Essay on Trade and Transformation* (New York: John Wiley).

Rauch, J. E. (1999) 'Networks versus Markets in International Trade', *Journal of International Economics*, 48: 7–35.

Robinson, J. (1933) *The Economics of Imperfect Competition* (London: Macmillan).

Tang, L. (1999) 'Intra-Industry Trade in Services: A Case Study of the International Telephone Industry', Mimeo, Drexel University, Philadelphia, PA.

5
Fragmentation and Intra-Industry Trade

Ronald W. Jones, Henryk Kierzkowski and Gregory Leonard

Introduction

Hindsight is often invoked in order to point out where an original idea or exposition has really missed the mark. On re-reading the Grubel and Lloyd (1975) volume after twenty-five years we are, by contrast, struck by the extent to which they were prescient about developments in international trade theory that would follow their original work. Not only has their empirical measure of the extent of intra-industry trade been adopted by many researchers, but also their prose captures a number of ideas which, in subsequent hands, have provided the focal points of more detailed theoretical structures.

Some of these insights are spelt out as early as in their introductory chapter. For example, on pp. 5, 6 (Grubel and Lloyd, 1975) they stress the importance of modifying traditional trade theory by introducing increasing returns in production and imperfect competition. It was only a matter of a few years before the key original contributions of Krugman (1980), Lancaster (1980) and Helpman (1981) set out the ingredients of what is today a standard model of trade in differentiated products. In this model, simplifications are obtained by assuming that a wide variety of differentiated final consumer goods is capable of being produced in a number of countries. Each variety shares the identical technology with all others, and the Chamberlinian structure of the nature of market demand for differentiated products leads to production taking place at levels at which increasing returns are still obtainable. The mixture of demand for differentiated products and increasing returns yields a solution to the question of how many of these commodities will be produced, and the answer depends sensitively on whether the market is confined to one country or whether international trade in these products is allowed. In the latter case, all trade in these items exemplifies intra-industry trade. Of course, in some general equilibrium treatments, such as Helpman (1981), another sector, producing a homogeneous product under competitive conditions, is added, so that trade of both the intra-industry variety and more standard inter-industry type can take place simultaneously.

Not all intra-industry trade in final commodities is captured by models that insist on the same production function for each variety and the appearance of each in consumer taste patterns in the same manner. Instead, commodities can differ from each other in the quality dimension. Higher-income individuals demand higher-quality commodities. These commodities, in turn, may be produced by more capital-intensive techniques, which serves to open the door once again to a Heckscher–Ohlin type of explanation of trade patterns, in this case of intra-industry trade. In Grubel and Lloyd (1975, ch. 6), the authors discuss this variant of intra-industry trade. A more formal modelling approach was undertaken by Falvey and Kierzkowski (1987), who also questioned the assumption that trade in differentiated products needs to be undertaken in imperfectly competitive markets. More recently, Jones *et al.* (1999) considered the possibility that labour-abundant countries may indeed export commodities found in the labour-intensive sectors of the economy, but within such sectors these countries may export varieties that are produced by more capital-intensive techniques than the varieties that are consumed at home. The reason for this is that the more capital-abundant importing countries have higher wealth and income levels, and thus demand higher-quality goods than those that would be consumed in the labour-abundant exporting countries. This leads to the mixture of inter-industry selection of exports from labour-intensive sectors coupled with intra-industry exports of higher-quality, capital-intensive varieties. In the context of North–South trade, Grossman and Helpman (1991) introduced the concept of quality ladders, whereby investment in research and development is aimed at improving the quality of goods produced and exported by Northern firms.

Demand specifications in these various models of intra-industry trade typically followed one of two alternative forms. The first pursues the suggestions in Lancaster (1979) that individuals each have a most-preferred variety among the array available. This was the modelling form used by Helpman (1981) in his work on horizontally differentiated consumer goods. Others, such as Krugman (1980), have adapted the Dixit–Stiglitz (1977) 'love-of-variety' formulation, wherein consumers prefer a wider selection of final commodities to a more restricted one costing the same amount. Ethier (1982) has also used the Dixit–Stiglitz formulation to argue that a variety of intermediate inputs may be preferred to a narrower selection at the same cost. This kind of idea is suggested by Grubel and Lloyd (1975, p. 7): 'At higher levels of output it is possible to introduce machines which are more efficient *because they are special-purpose* or more automated' (emphasis added).

In addition to intra-industry trade in horizontally differentiated final goods, or vertically differentiated (by quality) goods, Grubel and Lloyd (1975 p. 101), also consider that countries may exchange final goods for intermediate inputs used in the same industrial classification or, indeed, exchange intermediate goods with each other, both within the same industry. In this chapter we focus on the phenomenon of *international fragmentation*, which often leads to the exchange of parts of a previously vertically integrated production process for other parts of the process which have been outsourced to other countries. If these various fragments are classified in the same industrial category (for example, automobiles and parts), they contribute yet another kind of example of intra-industry trade. Since some fragments may find a use in other industries, not all examples of international fragmentation represent intra-industry trade, any more than does all intra-industry trade reflect the fragmentation phenomenon. Furthermore, it does not follow that for a country that previously relied totally on imports of a final consumption item, the ability to produce some (labour-intensive, say) fragment of the item will result in a diminution of trade volume. The reason is that the fragment that is acquired is now not only produced for the local market but also exported to a variety of other countries. Outsourcing of this kind can greatly increase the volume of trade.

The next section of this chapter develops the basic ideas of the fragmentation scenario. As in much of the literature subsequent to the appearance of the Grubel and Lloyd volume, there is an important role to be found in the assumption of increasing returns to scale, albeit not in the manner utilized by earlier contributions. Following this exposition of the fragmentation model, the third section of the chapter turns to some examples of sectors in which the kind of fragmentation discussed in the second section seems to bulk large in the extent of intra-industry trade. We then provide a final section for concluding remarks.

Fragmentation of production and intra-industry trade

Although most of the formal modelling of intra-industry trade has adopted the Chamberlinian assumption that firm equilibrium takes place in the region in which costs are diminishing, standard competitive trade models can also illustrate the phenomenon. Indeed, much of the recent work addressing this issue has defended variations of the Heckscher–Ohlin model as supporting such trade. (As examples, see Chipman, 1992 or Davis, 1995). However, the two-commodity version of the Heckscher–Ohlin model would be too limited to illustrate the simultaneous existence of intra-industry trade and inter-industry trade. One of the basic characteristics of international trade is that a country needs to produce for the international market no more commodities than it has immobile factors. As a consequence, competitive Heckscher–Ohlin models with several countries and a large number of commodities can easily be constructed – for example, as found in the articles by Jones (1974) and Krueger (1977), appearing about the same time as the Grubel and Lloyd volume. A country could easily be exporting a differentiated commodity found in the same industrial category as many of its imports, as well as trading in a homogenous commodity.

The fragmentation scenario, as developed in Jones and Kierzkowski (1990), and in a following series of papers (Jones and Kierzkowski, 2001a, 2001b and 2001c)[1] makes use of the concept of increasing returns, as does the earlier literature on intra-industry trade, but in a different manner. Also, basic elements both of Ricardian trade theory and Heckscher–Ohlin theory are integral elements of the fragmentation process. A basic distinction is made between *production blocks* and *service links*. At low levels of production, a commodity might be produced in a manner suggested by the typical constant-returns-to-scale production function, in a single place and time, in a single production block. However, the advantages of possible increasing returns stemming from the kind of division of labour stressed by Adam Smith, suggests that production might be separated into two or more production blocks, perhaps in different locales, or even different countries. However, these blocks must be co-ordinated by certain service links, involving transportation, communication, and the elements of timing and matching of supplies. Services of this type may involve costs that are fixed primarily over a range of outputs (for example, the costs of obtaining information about supply networks abroad) and thus introduce increasing returns. Thus, as volumes of production expand, an increasingly fragmented production structure would replace an initial vertically-integrated structure, with a trade-off between lower marginal costs from being able to outsource production blocks to different locales and higher fixed costs because of greater reliance on service links. To the extent that fragmentation spills over national borders, the greater costs of co-ordinating production blocks in different countries (and perhaps different firms) can be more than offset by the advantages of such dispersal when production blocks differ in the composition of factor requirements, and countries differ in relative factor prices.

International fragmentation of vertical production chains results in intra-industry trade if the manner in which production categories are defined puts these various fragments into the same industrial category. Two significant characteristics of the last decades of the twentieth century have stimulated the process of international fragmentation greatly. The first is the greater degree of deregulation of the controls over production, both within countries and between them in terms of international freeing-up of controls on international trade and investment. The second is the nature and extent of technical progress affecting the costs of service links. The great strides taken in the development of information technology have caused the costs of communication to plummet. Such cost reductions are relatively even more severe in the international realm, as national borders and distance cease to impose any significant barriers. Additionally, transport costs have continued their traditional decline, and information about the costs of doing business abroad has vastly improved, with greater numbers of potential suppliers reducing the degree of uncertainty in obtaining supplies. These reductions in the costs of service links have fostered a great increase in the degree of international fragmentation of production. One consequence of this is that countries can now compete with each other in supplying fragments that are much more focused than is the integrated production chain. This allows a greater scope for Ricardian differences in comparative advantage to affect the location of productive activity. Some less developed countries might be able to compete successfully in world markets in some part of a production process, whereas they are not efficient enough to compete in other parts. Fragmentation allows them to participate in an internationally connected network.

The situation of other countries may be rather different: they may find that an initial position of comparative advantage in an *integrated* activity is based on being fairly good at each of the component fragments, whereas their rivals may have superiority in one or more fragments but have costs dragged down by inefficiency in others. Once improvements in technology and lowered costs of service links permit fragmentation, such countries may find they are no longer competitive in any part of the process. Fragmentation works in many ways like technological progress, lowering the costs of obtaining the final good, and in turn may stimulate technical progress as fragments of one industry might be used in other industries as well once certain modifications allow 'one size to fit all'. In the latter case, fragmentation can stimulate inter-industry trade as well as intra-industry trade.

The application of the Dixit–Stiglitz function that was stressed by Ethier (1982) focused on trade in intermediate goods, some of which might be used in the production of a given final good and appear as intra-industry trade. A feature of this approach is that increasing returns are generated by using a wider variety of intermediate inputs. In the Jones and Kierzkowski scenario, the number of internationally traded inputs (or fragments) can also be increased endogenously, with the increasing returns reflected in relatively fixed costs of service links helping to promote fragmentation of previously integrated production processes. In either case, growth can serve to promote intra-industry trade because of the multiplication of inputs or fragments belonging to the same industrial classification that can be traded internationally.

Fragmentation and intra-industry trade: some examples

Collecting data for the question at hand is not an easy process. In an ideal world, analysis of available data would enable general studies of the overall development and importance of fragmentation in the world economy. Perhaps this statistical picture concerning the extent of trade resulting from fragmentation is now beginning to emerge as countries introduce a new SITC system. Under the so-called SITC Revision 2, many components and parts are classified as separate product groups. In a pioneering work, Alexander Yeats (2001) began to analyze this new data source. It is estimated that, in the early 1990s, when the world trade in manufactures amounted to US$2.7 trillion, US$800 billion of the total represented exchange of parts and components.

With this new data in mind, traditional sources remain important. Fortunately, many countries have created programmes that reduce or eliminate duties on goods that are exported for processing and then re-imported. These programmes require imports to be categorized as part of a production-sharing arrangement and thus enable more analysis. This is especially fortunate since general evidence is difficult to assemble. For example, in the USA the customs service keeps the importer of goods confidential. Thus, it is not possible to link imports of particular intermediate inputs to a particular firm, or sometimes even a particular industry. This section discusses such production-sharing arrangements in the USA and Europe, paying particular attention to the contribution of fragmentation to intra-industry trade, and then summarizes other academic research that is attempting to quantify the development of the fragmenting of the production processes internationally.

Data collected under the US Production Sharing Provision of Harmonized Tariff Schedule (HTS PSP) Chapter 98 provide information on the imports of goods that are either assembled or processed abroad from US-made components or materials. These goods receive a duty exemption on the value of the US-made components they contain. These shipments make up a significant fraction of total imports. In 1997, the USA imported goods valued at US$79.2 billion under the HTS PSP, subchapter 9802, representing almost 10 per cent of total US merchandise imports.

The introduction of the Canada – US Free Trade agreement and NAFTA, however, has reduced the incentives of importers of goods from Mexico and Canada to utilize the production-sharing provisions of Chapter 98. The low duties on many imports from Mexico and Canada mean that the HTS PSP substantially under-report the degree of fragmentation occurring between the USA and Mexico and Canada. The US International Trade Commission estimates that imports resulting from production sharing with US firms make up at least 20 per cent of total imports. The especially low levels of duty on trade between the USA and Canada imply that the HTS PSP data reveal almost no information about the scope and type of fragmentation taking place across the US–Canada border. With this under-reporting in mind, data collected through the HTS PSP by the US International Trade Commission can provide a good picture of the degree of fragmentation in several industries.

The colour television industry[2]

The industry producing colour television sets provides a good example of firms fragmenting the production process to take advantage of differences in the costs of inputs. An oversimplified representation of the production of colour televisions breaks the process down into two general steps: production of colour picture tubes (cathode-ray tubes), and assembly of the television set. Production of colour picture tubes requires substantial capital investment. These plants are located primarily in the USA. There has been some recent activity to move this to Mexico, but this is a slow process, as replacing existing colour picture tube plants would cost from tens of millions to hundreds of millions of dollars. In 1999, the North American industry consisted of twenty-two companies assembling colour televisions and eight producing picture tubes. The location of production is largely dictated by the capital–labour mix in each production fragment and the costs of labour in each location. Since the labour costs to assemble a television set are almost constant across sets of different screen sizes, labour costs represent a larger share of total costs for smaller sets. Additionally, larger sets cost substantially more to transport from the point of assembly to the final market.

Television set manufacturer RCA opened its first Mexican plant in Mexico City in the 1960s, and since then both US and Asian colour television producers have increased their presence in Mexico for the more labour-intensive operations in the production of television sets destined for the US market. This trend continued strongly so that, by the close of the 1980s, the assembly of smaller sets bound for the US market took place in Mexico. At the time of the ratification of NAFTA, every US producer of colour televisions had located at least some assembly operations in Mexico.

More recently, two major US producers moved their remaining assembly operations to Mexico, so that every major US manufacturer now conducts the assembly of colour televisions smaller than 20 inches in diagonal measurement in plants just across the US–Mexico border. These facilities thus take advantage of the maquiladora programme. Both Zenith and Thompson Consumer Electronics, the latest firms to relocate assembly in Mexico, still continue manufacturing colour picture tubes in the USA. In addition, most assembly of larger-screen television sets as well as the design and R&D remain in the USA.

Table 5.1 shows the dominant pattern of trade in colour television receivers and parts with Mexico. Reflecting the high capital requirements in their production, the USA is the dominant exporter of cathode-ray picture tubes, exporting to Mexico more than six times the value imported from Mexico. US exports of cathode ray tubes were five times larger in 1999 than in 1994. In the realm of finished television sets, Mexico is the largest exporter, sending more than ten times the value of television sets to the USA than are sent in the opposite direction. With the liberalizing of trade between the USA and Mexico, this striking pattern of trade has only intensified. In 1992, the value of US shipments of cathode-ray tubes to Mexico was more than three times the value of cathode-ray tube imports from Mexico. By 1999, this had increased to more than six times. The development of trade in assembled television sets shows a similar trend. In 1992, the USA imported from Mexico almost eight times the value of television sets as it exported to Mexico. By 1999, US imports of television sets from Mexico were almost thirteen times greater than exports.

Both the recent developments in the industry and the direction of trade in picture tubes and assembled television sets suggest that much

Table 5.1 US imports of televisions and parts from Mexico and exports to Mexico, 1992–9 (US$000s)

	1992	1993	1994	1995	1996	1997	1998	1999
Imports								
Cathode ray tubes	101 560	117 980	184 810	217 583	216 794	296 299	272 949	283 056
Televisions	1 228 530	1 534 666	2 217 895	2 484 920	2 733 807	2 864 539	3 844 568	4 217 992
Total	**101 560**	**117 980**	**2 402 705**	**2 702 503**	**2 950 601**	**3 160 838**	**4 117 517**	**4 501 048**
Exports								
Cathode ray tubes	308 623	439 614	687 561	892 389	1 018 267	1 351 603	1 829 077	1 882 288
Televisions	158 708	139 082	167 007	54 019	93 641	174 943	249 108	326 772
Total	**467 331**	**578 696**	**854 568**	**946 408**	**1 111 908**	**1 526 546**	**2 078 185**	**2 209 060**

Source: All data from US International Trade Commission.

Table 5.2   Grubel-Lloyd measure of intra-industry trade in televisions, USA –
Mexico, 1992–9

Intra-industry trade	1992	1993	1994	1995	1996	1997	1998	1999
Cathode ray tubes	50	42	42	39	35	36	26	26
Televisions	23	17	14	4	6	11	12	14
Total	52	52	52	51	54	65	67	65

Source: As Table 5.1.

of the trade within the television industry is the result of fragmentation.
Table 5.2 presents measures of fragmentation for the television industry
as a whole as well as separately for the final sets and intermediate inputs.
While the industry as a whole appears to have a sizeable amount of intra-
industry trade (a Grubel–Lloyd measure of 65 in 1999), there is only a
small fraction of intra-industry trade in final television sets (14). Cathode
ray tubes also show a similar lack of two-way trade (26 in 1999). Additionally, the overall Grubel-Lloyd measure of intra-industry trade has increased from 52 to 65 from 1994 to 1999 yet over the same period intra-
industry trade declined in parts and has remained relatively stable at
around 14 in final television sets. Thus, while on the whole the television
industry appears to exhibit substantial intra-industry trade, interpreting
the industry in the framework of traditional intra-industry trade would be
misleading. In fact, trade between the USA and Mexico appears to con-
form much more closely to a classical Heckscher–Ohlin framework, with
its emphasis on the importance of factor proportions and factor prices.

The automobile industry

Accounting for 40 per cent of North American cross-border trade, the
automotive industry is the most internationally integrated in North
America. The integration process stems from the Automotive Products
Trade Act in 1965, the same year that the Mexican Border Industrialization Program began. While part of the growth in trade has come from
rationalization, a process whereby all cars of the same or similar models
are produced in one location for a large geographic region, specialization in types of production process by region has been motivated by the
differences in the costs of production inputs, namely labour costs. This
is especially true for Mexico, where the Mexican automobile industry
has focused traditionally on the more labour-intensive production processes. Mexico now dominates the production of engine castings and
wire harnesses, both labour-intensive products.

Table 5.3 Grubel-Lloyd measure of intra-industry trade in automobiles, USA – Mexico, 1992–9

Intra-industry trade	1992	1993	1994	1995	1996	1997	1998	1999
Parts	67	71	68	76	81	73	80	85
Autos	17	11	27	11	21	29	31	29
Total	91	86	87	61	56	67	64	61

Source: As Table 5.1.

Table 5.3 shows the degree of intra-industry trade between the USA and Mexico in automobiles. As in the case of televisions, the overall measure of intra-industry trade conceals the actual nature of trade in the industry. While the industry as a whole exhibits a substantial level of intra-industry trade (61 in 1999), intra-industry trade in final goods is relatively low (29). The increasing trend of intra-industry trade in parts from 67 in 1992 to 85 in 1999, however, contrasts with the declining trend of intra-industry trade in the industry as a whole, from 91 in 1992 to 61 in 1999.

The apparel industry

The apparel industry provides another good example of the fragmenting of the production process to take advantage of differences in the costs of inputs across locations. As with the colour television industry, data collected on HTS PSP imports allows detailed quantification of the magnitude and direction of production-sharing in the apparel industry. In fact, until the beginning of 1999, importers of apparel from Mexico had a significant incentive to declare items eligible under the production-sharing provisions, since apparel constructed from 'fabric wholly formed and cut in the United States' could enter completely free of duty. The removal of duties on most apparel imports from Mexico effective from 1 January 1999 eliminated this incentive to report production-sharing arrangements and hence renders current data collected under HTS PSP less representative of the industry as a whole.

Mexico and the countries benefiting from the Caribbean Basin Economic Recovery Act (CBERA) are the two largest suppliers of apparel to the USA under the HTS PSP. In 1998, Mexico and the CBERA countries accounted for 94 per cent of the fabric cut in the USA, sent abroad for processing and returned to the USA under the HTS PSP. HTS PSP apparel imports accounted for 84 per cent and 79 per cent of total apparel imports from Mexico and CBERA countries, respectively. In March 1999, almost a third of all Mexican maquiladoras, a total of 934, were manufacturing operations exporting apparel to the USA. These apparel imports consist primarily of garments assembled in Mexican industrial parks and free-trade zones in the CBERA countries from US fabric. US apparel firms continue to rely more heavily on these facilities for the labour-intensive operations to take advantage of lower labour costs. The reader may ask whether labour costs are not even lower in Asian economies such as China? Yes, but the costs of service links to the USA are higher: Asian facilities would be more difficult to manage, and shipments would incur higher transportation costs and longer lead times. Although Asia is still the principal supplier of apparel to the USA, it accounted for less than 1 per cent of the total US content in HTS PSP trade in 1997. This result arises not only because Asia enters into production-sharing arrangements less than do Mexico and CBERA countries, but also because when garments produced in Asia do incorporate US content, it is usually in the form of speciality items such as zips and buttons.

Trousers were the largest apparel item imported under the HTS PSP in 1997, with imports valued at US$4 billion. Along with shirts and blouses, trousers are the most labour-intensive garments, but their production requires only simple operations, and more standardized runs. These three categories of apparel show the greatest growth in HTS PSP imports. Imports of trousers alone increased by 95 per cent between 1994 and 1997. That the labour-intensive types of apparel show the greatest growth in production-sharing, suggests that apparel producers are locating their production fragments increasingly according to their relative capital and labour intensities.

Production sharing with Canada

While much of the previous discussion focused on Mexico, Canada is the other top production-sharing partner with the USA. After the UK, Canada was the the second-largest destination for US foreign direct investment in 1998, at US$104 billion. US companies owned about 75 per cent of the foreign-owned Canadian manufacturing companies, and 40 per cent of all Canadian manufacturing companies were foreign-owned in 1998. Much of the production-sharing trade with Canada does not claim preferential treatment because of small or zero duties on most trade. However, the high degree of integration in the automobile, aircraft and other industries is suggestive of the substantial contribution of fragmentation to trade between the USA and Canada. Trade in aircraft made up 3 per cent of total US–Canada trade in 1998. Bombadier Aerospace Group maintains ten manufacturing facilities in Canada and seven in the USA. Similarly, Boeing operated three facilities in Canada. Table 5.4 shows the

Table 5.4 Grubel-Lloyd measure of intra-industry trade in aircraft, USA–Canada, 1992–9

Intra-industry trade	1992	1993	1994	1995	1996	1997	1998	1999
Parts	97	92	96	97	93	93	97	95
Engines	92	99	93	95	95	90	98	92
Final goods	96	63	42	71	59	45	39	51
Total	71	62	74	65	71	79	83	81

Source: As Table 5.1.

level of intra-industry trade for the intermediate and final stages of production in the aircraft industry, inclusive of gas turbine engines. Interestingly, in the case of aircraft, the intra-industry trade measures for the total industry hide the true nature of the intra-industry trade. While the industry as a whole had a measure of 81 in 1999 for intra-industry trade, intra-industry trade in final goods was only 51. Parts and engines, on the other hand, showed substantial intra-industry trade, with measures of 95 and 92; respectively. This reflects the scattering of production fragments across the USA and Canada.

Semiconductors provide another good example of US–Canadian production-sharing. In 1998, total trade amounted to US$4.9 billion. While Canada does not have a large semiconductor industry, IBM fabricates semiconductors in the USA for final assembly in Bromont, Quebec. Table 5.5 shows that, indeed, intra-industry trade in semiconductors is high. The industry as a whole as well as semiconductors excluding parts had an intra-industry trade measure of 82 in 1999. This contrasts with the measure of intra-industry trade in parts, at 36. Thus, for semiconductors, while the total industry measure of intra-industry trade represents two-way trade in final goods accurately, the measure hides the lack of significant intra-industry trade in parts.

Table 5.5 Grubel-Lloyd measure of intra-industry trade in semiconductors, USA–Canada, 1992–9

Intra-industry trade	1992	1993	1994	1995	1996	1997	1998	1999
Parts	65	48	44	44	49	61	41	36
Semiconductors	95	96	87	84	89	90	92	82
Total	95	95	87	83	88	90	92	82

Source: As Table 5.1.

Other studies important for fragmentation

In the latter part of the 1990s, a number of studies attempted to quantify the development of fragmentation. This body of research establishes several important empirical facts relevant to a complete understanding of both the current importance and the changing role of fragmentation in intra-industry trade. Using various approaches and data sources, these studies develop a strong case that: (i) production processes are becoming increasingly fragmented across national borders; (ii) the degree of fragmentation varies across both countries and industries, often according to classical trade theory predictions using capital- and labour-intensities; and (iii) the level of fragmentation decreases with the distance between partner countries. In order to develop a general context for the industries examined, the remainder of this section looks at a number of empirical studies that have presented evidence relating to these three empirical characteristics of fragmentation.

In a comprehensive study, Feenstra *et al.* (2000) document each of these three empirical facts by analyzing US International Trade Commission USITC HTS PSP data for five industries: apparel; leather and footwear; machinery; electrical machinery; and transport equipment for the period 1981–93. By linking the data categorized under the HTS to the corresponding SIC categories, they are able make comparisons with US production data. They note several significant facts. First, in both apparel and leather and footwear, the share of total industry shipments accounted for by HTS PSP shipments has increased dramatically from 1 per cent to 6 per cent, and 1 per cent to 8.5 per cent, respectively. Second, the share of US components in HTS PSP trade differs across industries as well as source countries. Apparel has the highest share of US components, nearly twice the size of the share of foreign components. This feature of the HTS PSP trade may result from the differential treatment of apparel imports from Mexico where, unlike other HTS PSP trade, the US value-added is also not dutiable. Third, in transportation equipment, the share of US components decreased with the distance of the partner country. While US value-added accounted for over half of the value of transportation equipment imports from Mexico, and between 25 per cent and 33 per cent from Canada, imports from Germany, Japan and Korea contained less than 5 per cent US value.

Focusing on the trend of rising fragmentation of production processes, Chen and Sharma (2000) investigate the role of fragmentation and trade in intermediates for Canada. They find that the share of imported intermediates in total intermediate inputs used in production rose from 25 per cent in 1971 to 34 per cent in 1990. Office and computing machinery, radio, TV and communication equipment, and motor vehicles all had imported intermediate ratios above 70 per cent. Furthermore, by analyzing data on Canadian exports to the USA, Chen and Sharma are able to quantify the imported content in Canadian exports to the USA. This form of fragmentation – exports made from imported intermediate inputs – increased dramatically between 1981 and 1990. Of twenty-three industries examined, the share of export content attributable to imported inputs more than doubled. In 1990, imported inputs made up more than half the value in the three industries mentioned above, and in electrical apparatus and rubber and plastic products.

In two recent papers, both Görg (2000) and Celi (2000) analyze European production-sharing data to document both that fragmentation is generally increasing, and that the degree of fragmentation varies substantially across industries and countries. Görg presents evidence that US firms increasingly are locating intermediate fragments of the production process in Europe. By looking at the percentage of US imports accounted for by inward processing trade (IPT) from Europe, Görg argues that the EU increased the level of intermediate production for the USA over the period 1988–94. The inward processing trade designation applies to goods imported into the EU for processing and subsequent re-export. Between 1988 and 1994 the fraction of US imports accounted for by IPT trade with EU countries increased from 17.7 per cent to 19.8 per cent. The fraction of US imports from Ireland designated under the IPT programme increased from 23.7 per cent to 44.1 per cent.

Across industries, the fraction of imports accounted for by EU IPT varies greatly. In 1994, industrial machinery had the highest fraction of imports designated IPT – 34.6 per cent, and transportation equipment, leather, and electronics also had high ratios, at 24.8 per cent, 21.7 per cent and 21.0 per cent, respectively. In contrast, cork and wood, food, drink, and tobacco, and non-metallic minerals had the smallest ratios at 2.4 per cent, 4.4 per cent, and 6.7 per cent, respectively.

Celi (2000) analyzes European trade flows under the IPT's counterpart designation, outward processing trade (OPT). The outward processing trade designation is assigned to a good that is exported outside the EU for processing or assembly, and then re-imported by the original exporter. Over the period 1989–97, OPT trade flows increased in fourteen of the fifteen EU member countries. Over the 1989 levels, 1997 OPT flows represented a larger fraction of total trade in twelve of the fifteen countries. The shares of OPT in total trade vary across both countries and industries.

With more than 44 per cent of total EU OPT, Germany has both the greatest absolute amount of OPT flows as well as the largest OPT share of total trade, at 4.9 per cent. France and Italy generate 15 per cent and 10 per cent of EU OPT flows, respectively. In contrast, Spain, Portugal, Greece and Ireland each account for less than 1 per cent of total EU OPT trade. The OPT flows differ not only across the countries shipping the goods out for processing, but also by the countries processing the goods. In 1997, Central and Eastern European countries performed 46 per cent of all processing on OPT manufactured goods. Asia and North America followed, with 25 per cent and 22 per cent, respectively, of OPT flows.

Across sectors, the OPT flows showed substantial variation as well. In 1997, electrical machinery, and textiles and apparel, accounted for, respectively, 38 per cent and 37 per cent of all OPT flows. Transport flows accounted for 9 per cent of OPT. Interestingly, 82 per cent of all textile and apparel OPT flows were processed in Central and Eastern Europe. North America played a similarly dominant role in the processing of transport OPT flows by processing 88 per cent of EU transport OPT flows. Asia processed the most electrical machinery flows, with 52 per cent of the total. These differences in the location of processing in different industries appear to reflect the differences in capital intensities required for the industry production, and the differences in factor supplies across different regions.

Campa and Goldberg (1997) present broad evidence of two empirical characteristics of fragmentation: (i) manufacturing industries are becoming more reliant on imported inputs; and (ii) this reliance varies across industries and countries. In the USA over the period 1974–95, the average imported input share rose from 4.8 per cent to 8.2 per cent. Of the twenty industries examined, only one – petroleum and coal products – experienced a reduction in the share of imported inputs. The import shares for electronic equipment, apparel and other textiles, and transportation equipment increased, respectively, from 4.5 per cent to 11.6 per cent, 1.3 per cent to 3.2 per cent, and 6.4 per cent to 15.7 per cent.

Campa and Goldberg also find that the average imported input share for Canadian manufacturers increased from 15.9 per cent to 20.2 per cent over the period 1974–93. Only three industries showed decreased dependence on imported inputs. The import shares for textile industries and transportation equipment increased from 14.9 per cent to 20.2 per cent, and 29.1 per cent to 49.7 per cent, respectively. The import shares for the UK show a similar trend. The average import share increased over the period 1974–93 from 13.4 per cent to 21.7 per cent. Import shares for

Japan, however, show a markedly different picture of the evolving utilization of imported inputs: the average imported input share declined from 8.2 per cent in 1974 to 4.1 per cent in 1993. Against this trend, both textile products and transportation equipment show small increases in their shares of imported inputs. The share of imported inputs increased from 1.8 per cent to 2.8 per cent in transportation equipment, and from 4.5 per cent to 4.8 per cent in textile products.

Taken as a body of literature, these empirical studies demonstrate several important characteristics of the fragmenting of the production process across international borders. First, in most industries and in manufacturing more generally, fragmentation is increasing. Second, the degree of production-sharing varies substantially across both industries and partner countries, with relatively labour-abundant countries tending to specialize in the production of labour-intensive goods. Third, the level of fragmentation between any two countries decreases with the distance between the countries, suggesting perhaps that the linkages connecting production blocks are less effective and more costly when two countries are geographically far from each other.

Concluding remarks

Research since the 1970s, both empirical and theoretical in nature, has confirmed that the concept of intra-industry trade, as developed by P. J. Lloyd and Herb Grubel, is here to stay. The concept, however, may be richer than at first envisaged. Many final commodities do indeed appear in a number of differentiated varieties, and elements of monopolistic competition and increasing returns, suggested in the Grubel and Lloyd treatise, lend themselves to useful modelling techniques whereby countries exchange these varieties with each other. Furthermore, the varieties that do enter trade may differ from each other in a quality sense, with higher-quality varieties produced in more advanced countries. What we have attempted to suggest in this chapter is that yet a third type of intra-industry trade is gaining increasing importance. This trade is encouraged by technological improvements that lower the costs of the service links that bind the various fragments of a production process. These fragments may be located initially in a vertically connected form in one location, but with service links becoming less costly and formal regulatory barriers disappearing, increasingly it is possible that various fragments are outsourced among a number of countries.

We have surveyed some of the data available on the nature of trade, mainly among the NAFTA countries, to illustrate not only the process of international fragmentation, but also the different consequences in various industries on the nature of intra-industry trade. In some industries – for example, the television industry in the United States and Mexico – intra-industry trade remains at a high level for the industry as a whole, but much less so separately in fragments such as cathode ray tubes or final assembled sets. For other industries, such as the automobile sector, the aggregate measure of intra-industry trade has been falling, but the measure in parts alone has experienced a rapid increase. Thus, once again, a richer set of trade patterns is possible, but in all the importance of intra-industry trade, however 'industry' is defined, remains as a valued concept.

Notes

1   Other sources include Arndt (1997) and Venables (1999).
2   Much of the following discussion of industries draws heavily on the series of US International Trade Commission reports titled 'Production Sharing: Use of U.S. Components and Materials in Foreign Assembly Operations', December 1997, December 1998 and December 1999.

References

Arndt, S (1997) 'Globalization and the Gains from Trade', in K. Jaeger and K. Koch (eds), *Trade, Growth, and Economic Policy in Open Economies* (New York: Springer-Verlag).

Campa, J. and L. Goldberg (1997) 'The Evolving External Orientation of Manufacturing Industries: Evidence from Four Countries', NBER Working Paper No. 5919.

Celi, G. (2000) 'The Impact of International Trade on Labour Markets. The Case of OPT between the European Union and Central Eastern European Countries', Mimeo, University of Sussex.

Chen, S. and P. Sharma (2000) 'Canada's Trade and International Fragmentation of Production', Mimeo Trade and Economic Analysis Division, Department of Foreign Affairs and International Trade, Canada.

Chipman, J. S. (1992) 'Intra-Industry Trade, Factor Proportions and Aggregation', in W. Neuefeind and R. Riezman (eds), *Economic Theory and International Trade: Essays in Memoriam J. Trout Rader* (New York: Springer-Verlag).

Davis, D. R. (1995) 'Intra-Industry Trade: A Heckscher–Ohlin–Ricardo Approach', *Journal of International Economics*, 39: 201–26.

Dixit, A. and J. Stiglitz (1997) 'Monopolistic Competition and Optimum Product Diversity', *American Economic Review*, 67: 297–308.

Ethier, W. J. (1982) 'National and International Returns to Scale in the Modern Theory of International Trade', *American Economic Review*, 72: 389–405.

Falvey, R. E. and H. Kierzkowski (1987) 'Product Quality, Intra-Industry Trade and (Im)perfect Competition', in Henryk Kierzkowski (ed.), *Protection and Competition in International Trade* (Oxford: Basil Blackwell).

Feenstra, R. C., G. Hanson, and D. Swenson (2000) 'Offshore Assembly from the United States: Production Characteristics from the 9802 Program,' in R. Feenstra (ed.), *The Impact of International Trade on Wages* (Chicago: University of Chicago Press).

Görg, H. (2000) 'Fragmentation and Trade: US Inward Processing Trade in the EU', Mimeo, University of Ulster at Jordainstown.

Grossman, G. and E. Helpman (1991) 'Quality Ladders in the Theory of Growth', *Review of Economic Studies*, 58: 43–61.

Grubel, H. G. and P. J. Lloyd (1975): *Intra-industry Trade: The Theory and Measurement of International Trade in Differentiated Products* (London: Macmillan).

Helpman, E. (1981) 'International Trade in the Presence of Product Differentiation, Economies of Scale, and Imperfect Competition: A Chamberlin–Heckscher–Ohlin Approach', *Journal of International Economics*, 11: 151–75.

Jones, R. W. (1974) 'The Small Country in a Many Commodity World', *Australian Economic Papers*, 13: 225–36.

Jones, R. W. and H. Kierzkowski (1990) 'The Role of Services in Production and International Trade: A Theoretical Framework', in Jones and Krueger (eds), *The Political Economy of International Trade* (Oxford: Basil Blackwell), pp. 31–48.

Jones, R. W. and H. Kierzkowski (2001a) 'Globalization and the Consequences of International Fragmentation', in G. Calvo, R. Dornbusch and M. Obstfeld (eds), *Money, Capital Mobility and Trade: Essays in Honor of Robert A. Mundell* (Cambridge, Mass.: MIT Press).

Jones, R. W. and H. Kierzkowski (2001b) 'A Framework for Fragmentation', in S. Arndt and H. Kierzkowski (eds), *Fragmentation: New Production Patterns in the World Economy* (Oxford University Press).

Jones, R. W. and H. Kierzkowski (2001c) 'Horizontal Aspects of Vertical Fragmentation', in Cheng, L. and H. Kierzkowski (eds), *Global Production and Trade in East Asia*, (Boston: Kluwer).

Jones, R. W., H. Beladi and S. Marjit (1999) 'The Three Faces of Factor Intensities', *Journal of International Economics*, 48: 413–20.

Krueger, A. O. (1977) 'Growth, Distortions, and Patterns of Trade Among Many Countries', *Princeton Studies in International Finance*, No. 40 (Princeton University Press, Princeton).

Krugman, P. R. (1980) 'Scale Economies, Product Differentiation, and the Pattern of Trade', *American Economic Review*, 70: 950–9.

Lancaster, K. (1979) *Variety, Equity and Efficiency* (New York Columbia University Press).

Lancaster, K. (1980) 'Intra-Industry Trade under Perfect Monopolistic Competition', *Journal of International Economics*, 10: 151–75.

US International Trade Commission (1997) 'Production Sharing: Use of U.S. Components and Materials in Foreign Assembly Operations, 1993–1996' (Washington, DC).

US International Trade Commission (1998) 'Production Sharing: Use of U.S. Components and Materials in Foreign Assembly Operations, 1994–1997' (Washington, DC).

US International Trade Commission (1999) 'Production Sharing: Use of U.S. Components and Materials in Foreign Assembly Operations, 1995–1998' (Washington, DC).

Venables, A. (1999) 'Fragmentation and Multinational Production', *European Economic Review*, April.

Yeats, A. J. (2001) 'How Big Is Global Production and Trade in East Asia', in L. Cheng and H. Kierzkowski (eds), *Globalization of Production and Trade in East Asia* (Boston: Kluwer).

6

The Geography of Intra-Industry Trade

Mary Amiti and Anthony J. Venables

Introduction

One of the most robust empirical finds in the literature on intra-industry trade (IIT) is that measures of intra-industry trade relative to inter-industry trade, such as the Grubel–Lloyd index, decline with distance. The objective of this chapter is to investigate why relative intra-industry trade (RIIT) declines in this way. There are two quite distinct ways in which this decline could arise. The first is that there are differences in the nature of the trading process that make IIT attenuate more rapidly with distance than do other forms of trade. For example, products in which IIT is important may also be products where shipping costs are particularly high, so RIIT measures decline with distance. Alternatively, industry may locate in such a way that neighbouring countries produce a similar mix of products, in which case IIT will be higher on short- rather than long-distance trades. Then, even if the trading process is the same for all products, the data may show a systematic relationship between RIIT and distance.

We start, in the second section of the chapter, by reviewing the literature in order to identify the empirical regularities that need to be explained. We then turn to theoretical analysis of these issues, for which we need a model that has some geographical structure – a number of countries at different distances from each other. We develop such a model, and show how it yields a natural benchmark case, in which IIT occurs but RIIT measures are independent of distance. We then use the model to explore a variety of deviations from this benchmark, and show how they create patterns of RIIT that are correlated with distance. The deviations include letting transport costs and demand elasticities vary across industries, and letting factor endowments vary systematically with geography. Spatial models create their own forces for industrial location, and we show how these alone create a relationship between RIIT and distance. Overall, our conclusions are that the negative relationship between RIIT and distance is explained more plausibly as a corollary of industrial location than as a consequence of trading technologies.

Empirical findings

Numerous studies have examined the determinants of RIIT, generally regressing some measure of intra-industry trade on various explanatory variables, usually in a cross-section analysis for one year. Intra-industry trade measures can be defined at the level of separate industries and for bilateral trade flows, thus $RIIT_i(j, k)$ denotes such a measure for the bilateral trade between countries j and k in industry i.[1] Some of the studies we review below aggregate over countries, and some over industries. (In the latter case we replace subscript i by A). The most consistent and clear finding across these studies is that RIIT is related inversely to distance.

Country studies

Balassa (1986a) shows that $RIIT_A$ was related inversely to distance in a study of thirty-eight countries in 1971. He constructs a measure of $RIIT_A$ for each country by aggregating across industries and across partner countries. This measure is regressed on distance, measures of trade costs and country characteristics. The distance variable is a weighted average of the inverse of distance between a single country and all its partner countries, with GNP used as weights. There are two trade cost variables. One is a trade orientation variable to reflect openness, which is defined as the percentage deviation of actual from hypothetical values of per capita trade. The hypothetical values are derived from regression analysis, with exports per capita regressed on per capita income, population, availability of mineral resources and distance from foreign markets. Positive deviations indicate low barriers, so the hypothesized sign is positive, which was confirmed by the empirical analysis. The second trade cost variable is a border dummy to proxy for economic integration – this was found to be insignificant. The country characteristics included are the level of development (proxied by GNP per head) and the size of domestic markets (GNP), and both were positively (and significantly) related to $RIIT_A$.

The significance of distance is also robust in pooled cross-section and time series analysis. In a study of Australia and fourteen of its trading partners, Matthews (1998) estimates a static and dynamic model. She separates the sample into traditional trading partners (mainly European) and Asia Pacific countries (which are much closer geographically), and finds a negative coefficient on distance in all the estimations. A trade orientation variable is included, as in the Balassa study, and this has the expected positive and significant coefficient in the group of traditional trading partners but the reverse sign for the Asia Pacific countries. All the country characteristics had the expected signs, including differences in per capita income between countries, used to proxy for taste and cultural similarity (negative and significant).

This finding on the distance variable is also robust to the inclusion of relative factor endowment differences. Hummels and Levinsohn (1995)[2] regress an $RIIT_A$ index on distance, while controlling for relative factor endowment differences, measured by differences in land-to-labour ratios and capital-to-land ratios, and country size differences, measured by the minimum and maximum GDP of the two countries. The expected signs on the relative factor endowments variables are negative, and positive on minGDP and negative on maxGDP. They estimate separate cross-section regressions for each year, from 1962 to 1983, for bilateral country pairs of OECD countries, and they find a consistently negative and significant coefficient on distance. They find that the land-to-labour variable is negative and significant only in the early years (1963 to 1978), whereas the capital-to-labour ratio is insignificant for most years, and positive and significant in the final few years (1980 to 1983); the minGDP variable has the expected positive and significant sign for most years, but maxGDP has the wrong sign, with a positive and significant coefficient for most years.

Interestingly, the signs on the factor endowments and country size variables are sensitive to whether distance is included. Without controlling for distance in the cross-section regressions, the land-to-labour variable is negative and significant in all the years, whereas the capital-to-labour variable changes its sign, with a negative significant coefficient in the early years, insignificant in the middle years and positive in the final years; minGDP is positive and significant for fewer years, and maxGDP now has the correct sign but is insignificant for all years. When the twenty-two years of data are pooled into a single panel (in which case they drop the land-to-labour ratio because there was little variation over time), the capital per worker variable becomes insignificant, whereas if income per worker is included to proxy for factor differences the coefficient is negative and significant. The coefficient on minGDP is positive and significant (as expected), while maxGDP is insignificant. With fixed effects, the sign on capital per worker is positive and significant (and on income per worker is positive and significant). Hummels and Levinsohn conclude that, instead of factor differences explaining much of RIIT, it appears to be specific to country pairs, with distance being the most important variable empirically.

Industry studies

In cross section studies using industrial disaggrated data, Loertscher and Wolter (1980), Balassa (1986b) and Balassa and Bauwens (1987) find that distance is related negatively to $RIIT_i$ after controlling for other barriers to trade, country characteristics and industry characteristics. Loertscher and Wolter construct a measure of $RIIT_i$ for each 3-digit industry in their sample for each OECD country pair (except Australia and New Zealand). The trade barrier variables include dummies for customs unions, common borders and similar language, which were all positive and significant, and a cultural group dummy, which was insignificant. The country characteristics included were the average level of development (which was insignificant), the difference in levels of development (negative and significant), the average market size (positive and significant), and the difference in market size (negative and significant). The industry characteristics included were measures of product differentiation (which was insignificant), scale economies (which had an unexpected negative sign), and the comprehensiveness of the definition of an industry, proxied by the number of 4-digit industries in a 3-digit category (positive and significant).

The results in Balassa (1986b) and Balassa and Bauwens (1987) are similar, though their samples differ and they include some additional industry and country characteristics in their regressions. Balassa (1986) regresses an industry $RIIT_i$ index between the USA and other countries. The country characteristics include income and size inequality, which were both negative and significant. Additional industry characteristics included (not in Loertscher and Wolter) that were significant in the non-linear least squares estimation are marketing (positive), standard deviation of profit rates (positive), and the concentration ratio (negative). Balassa and Bauwens (1987) extend this study to include an observation for all country pairs for each industry in the sample. They find that distance and average country size contribute the most explanatory power to the regression. One of the most significant industry characteristics to be related positively to RIIT is product differentiation.

Trade costs

Measuring trade costs has turned out to be one of the most difficult industry characteristics to calculate because it includes so many different dimensions. As a proxy for industry-specific transaction costs, a number of studies use the mean distance travelled within the USA, as calculated by Weiss (1972), defined as the ratio of the ton-miles shipped and the tonnage shipped. For example, Pagoulatos and Sorensen (1975), and Toh (1982), hypothesize that $RIIT_i$ is higher for goods that have smaller transport costs, drawing on a theory by Gray (1971). They hypothesize that the mean distance travelled should have a positive effect on $RIIT_i$, arguing that the further the good is shipped, the less important transport costs are relative to other factors. Both studies indicate a positive coefficient (but insignificant in Toh). Loertscher and Wolter also hypothesize that $RIIT_i$ is related positively to the mean distance travelled, which is meant to be an inverse proxy of transaction costs. Strangely, although their results indicate a negative coefficient, they do not comment on it.[3]

Balassa (1986b) criticizes the use of the mean distance as a measure of transport costs, arguing that transport costs should not be equated to distance, and that it is inappropriate to use a measure of inland transportation within a country to proxy international transport costs that usually take place on a sea route. He uses an alternative measure of transport costs, based on a model developed by Lipsey and Weiss (1974), where transport costs are a function of product unit value and stowage. However, this measure is statistically insignificant.

It is difficult to glean which types of industry are subject to higher trade costs from these studies on the determinants of $RIIT_i$. More recently, Davis (1998) and Rauch (1999) assess whether differentiated goods industries are subject to higher trade costs than are homogenous goods industries. Rauch (1999) divides commodities into three groups: (i) those traded on organized exchanges; (ii) those not traded on organized exchanges but possessing a 'reference price'; and (iii) all other commodities, which can be interpreted as representing homogenous goods, near-homogenous goods and differentiated goods, respectively. Transport costs are measured by taking the ratio of customs, insurance and freight as a proportion of total customs value of imports between the USA and Japan (as data was not available for all countries). This variable is interpreted as a measure of 'transportability'. He finds that these costs are lowest on differentiated goods. In order to assess whether search and networks are more important for differentiated goods, he estimates a gravity model separately for each of the three commodity groups, and finds that proximity and common language/colonial ties are more important for differentiated goods (but only weakly so, since differences in coefficients between three equations were small in magnitude).

Davis divides trade costs into conventional and non-conventional types. In the conventional trade costs group, he draws on Rauch's transportability measure and supplements this with tariffs, strengthening the result that conventional trade costs are lower for differentiated product industries compared to homogenous goods. He examines correlations between these conventional measures and indicators of scale economies (meant to proxy differentiated goods industries) such as the Grubel–Lloyd index and R&D expenditure, and finds there is a negative correlation. As with Rauch, he concludes that conventional trade costs are lower for differentiated goods. But to assess which type of industry has the highest total trade costs, the non-conventional trade costs must also be included. Studies by McCallum (1995), Helliwell (1996), and Engel and Rogers (1996) provide evidence that non-conventional trade costs, such as non-tariff barriers, do matter for international trade. But work by Harrigan (1993) and Wei (1996) cast doubt on the importance of non-tariff barriers. Yet Rauch provides evidence that non-conventional trade costs, such as search, are higher for differentiated goods. Hence, which type of industry is subject to higher total trade cost remains an open question. However, Davis (1998) argues that there is little evidence to suggest that total trade costs are higher for the differentiated goods.

A reference case

There are two broad reasons why RIIT measures might be decreasing functions of distance. One is that relative costs of trade for high IIT products change in a way that causes trade in these products to decline sharply with distance. The other is that production patterns have a geographical structure, a corollary of which is that there is more inter-industry trade (relative to intra-) between distant countries. A model to illuminate these effects must contain the following ingredients. First, a geographical structure, so there are many countries at different distances from each other. Second, a basis for net trade, arising from differences in preferences, technologies, endowments or geographical characteristics. And third, a basis for intra-industry trade, arising from product differentiation or strategic behaviour. To capture these effects at (we think) minimum complexity we make the following set of assumptions.

We suppose that there are many countries, and that they are located at equal distances around the circumference of a circle (the 'racetrack' economy of Fujita *et al.*, 1999). Though unrealistic, this geographical space has the advantages of being one-dimensional and permitting countries to be symmetrical. In the final section of the chapter we move from a circle to a line, where geography is fundamentally different, because the existence of ends to the line creates a natural pattern of periphery and centre.

Each country is endowed with quantities of two factors, which we shall refer to as labour and capital. These factors are geographically immobile, and cross-country variation in factor endowments will be the main (and until we reach the sixth section of this chapter, the only) basis for inter-industry trade.

There are three industries, labelled 1, 2 and 3. Industry 1 is labour-intensive, industry 3 is capital-intensive, and industry 2 lies between these two. Intra-industry trade is generated by letting each industry produce differentiated products, and this is modelled in the usual CES way, with elasticities of substitution σ_1, σ_2, σ_3 between pairs of varieties in the three industries. We assume initially that the numbers of varieties produced in each country are fixed exogenously, production is constant returns, and market structures are perfectly competitive. As $\sigma_i \to \infty$, the model tends towards a model of trade with homogenous products; at finite values of σ_i it is an 'Armington' model, in which product differentiation supports intra-industry trade. In the sixth section of the chapter we let the number of varieties be determined endogenously by free entry and exit of increasing returns to scale firms (each producing a single variety), so generating a Helpman and Krugman (1985) structure.

Transport costs are iceberg, and depend on distance shipped round the circumference of the circle. The iceberg cost factor for shipping goods from industry i a distance d is $\exp[\tau_i d]$. The circumference of the circle is 1, and as a measure of transport costs we define t_i as the cost of shipping a good one unit distance, $t_i \equiv \exp[\tau_i]$, $i = 1$, 2, 3.

This structure generates patterns of both inter- and intra-industry trade. Our starting point is to construct a reference case in which there is no systematic relationship between RIIT and distance. We assume that all industries have the same values of σ_i and t_i, but differing factor intensities, as outlined above. If all locations have the same endowments, then all would have the same structure of production, so there would be intra-industry trade, but not inter-industry. We therefore need to have variations in endowments that are – in some sense – uncorrelated with each country's location. The simplest way to do this is by supposing that there are two types of country – labour-abundant and capital-abundant – and they alternate around the circle; this ensures there is no geographical grouping of countries by endowments.[4]

The geographical pattern of a country's imports and exports of goods 1 and 3 is illustrated in Figure 6.1. There are sixteen economies, and the

94

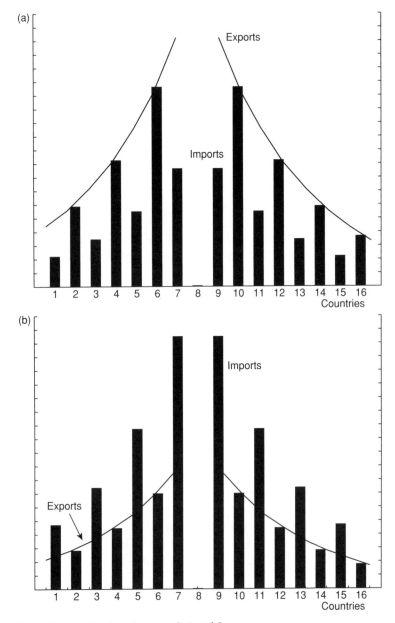

Figure 6.1   Country 8 trade in goods 1 and 3

trade of country 8 is illustrated. This country is labour-abundant and its trade in the labour-intensive good (good 1) is illustrated on Figure 6.1(a). The solid line is country 8 exports of good 1 to different countries (arranged on the horizontal axis), and these exports fall off quite steadily with distance. The bars are imports of good 1 from different countries, and these reflect each country's comparative advantage. Thus all trade in good 1 with even-numbered countries (which have the same endowments as country 8) is intra-industry trade, while trade with odd-numbered countries has both intra- and inter-industry components. For good 3 (Figure 6.1(b)) country 8 exports are lower; it is a net importer from odd-numbered countries and trade is balanced (RIIT only) with even numbered countries. Good 2 is not illustrated, but is virtually all intra-industry trade.

The point of this example is that, for all industries and in aggregate, RIIT is independent of distance. This is summarized in Table 6.1. $RIIT_i$ refers to the Grubel–Lloyd index for industry i, computed on a bilateral basis with partner countries. For industries 1 and 3 this takes values 1 and 0.64, with even- and odd-numbered partners, respectively. The aggregate Grubel–Lloyd index ($RIIT_A$), combining all industries, is higher as industry 2 is averaged in, and takes values 1 and 0.76 with even- and odd-numbered partners. A further point worth noting is that although there are cross-industry differences in $RIIT_i$, these result only from the factor intensities of the industries, and reveal nothing about market structure, product differentiation or returns to scale.

Transport costs and demand elasticities

We can now see how parameters that have a direct effect on trade volumes shape the relationship between distance and RIIT. Trade volumes

Table 6.1 Benchmark case: $\sigma_1 = \sigma_2 = \sigma_3$, $t_1 = t_2 = t_3$

	Production	*Industry, $RIIT_i$*	*Aggregate, $RIIT_A$*
Industries 1 and 3	Comparative advantage because of factor endowments: uncorrelated with distance	$RIIT_i = \{1, \ 0.64\}$ uncorrelated with distance	$RIIT_A = \{1, \ 0.76\}$ uncorrelated with distance
Industry 2	Same for all countries	$RIIT_i = \{1, \ 0.999\}$ uncorrelated with distance	

will decline relatively little with distance in the case where transport costs are low, or if the elasticity of demand for the product is small (so transport costs imply a small reduction in demand for imports). The key parameter is the product $\tau_i(\sigma_i - 1)$, and industries for which this is low will have higher trade volumes, *and* trade volumes falling off less sharply with distance.[5] Can cross-industry variation in this parameter generate RIIT varying with distance?

To answer this question, we illustrate the case in which industry 2 has a greater amount of product differentiation (that is, lower elasticity of substitution) and/or lower transport costs than industries 1 and 3, so $\sigma_2 < \sigma_1 = \sigma_3$, and/or $t_2 < t_1 = t_3$. The effects of this on measured RIIT are given in Table 6.2. First, notice that, for all sectors, the industry-level Grubel–Lloyd indices, $RIIT_i$, are once again unrelated to distance.[6] However, at the aggregate level, $RIIT_A$ is now increasing with distance. The reason is that industry 2 has more intra-industry trade than other sectors (because of its middle factor intensity), and the share of this industry in overall trade now increases with distance.[7]

This example fails to produce the results found in the empirical literature – industry $RIIT_i$ measures are still independent of distance, and the aggregate measure $RIIT_A$ goes in the opposite direction. Clearly, the aggregate measure would be decreasing with distance if the industry with the high level of $RIIT_i$ was also the industry with high elasticity of substitution or high transport costs, (so, in terms of our example, $\tau_2(\sigma_2 - 1) > \tau_1(\sigma_1 - 1) = \tau_3(\sigma_3 - 1)$). Empirically, what do we know about this relationship? It seems likely that elasticities of substitution between varieties are very much lower in industries with high levels of $RIIT_i$. A low σ_i means that product differentiation is important in the industry, thus supporting intra-industry trade, as compared to 'traditional' comparative advantage industries where each industry's product is close to homogeneous. Cross-industry variation in transport costs is less clear-cut, and we saw in the second section of this chapter that there is little significant evidence on the cross-industry relationship between $RIIT_i$ and transport costs. This suggests that the parameter configuration used in Table 6.2 is the appropriate one.

It is also possible that there are cross-industry differences, not just in levels of transport costs, but also in the functional form of the relationship between distance and transport costs. For example, some products might experience a very rapid increase in transport costs for the first 1000 km, then little change thereafter, or vice versa. This would certainly change the story, but we know of no evidence nor a priori basis for

Table 6.2 Transport costs and demand elasticities: $\sigma_2 < \sigma_1 = \sigma_3$, $t_2 < t_1 = t_3$

	Production	Industry, $RIIT_i$	Aggregate, $RIIT_A$
Industries 1 and 3	Comparative advantage because of factor endowments: uncorrelated with distance	$RIIT_i = \{1, 0.64\}$ uncorrelated with distance	$RIIT_A = \{1, \ 0.73 - 0.81\}$ increasing with distance
Industry 2	Same for all countries	$RIIT_i = \{1, \ 0.999\}$ uncorrelated with distance	

thinking that there is a systematic relationship between the shape of this function and level of $RIIT_i$.

The example of this section suggests that, in the absence of a systematic spatial structure to the comparative advantage of economies, it is more likely that $RIIT_A$ would be increasing with distance, rather than decreasing. At the industry level, $RIIT_i$ is uncorrelated with distance. We now turn to looking at systematic spatial structure in production.

Factor endowments

The argument of the fourth section suggests that it is unlikely that the observed decline in $RIIT_A$ with distance can be explained by differences in transport costs or demand elasticities. We must therefore look to systematic spatial differences in the location of industry. For example, suppose that industries are as described in the benchmark case above, but factor endowments vary systematically across space, with capital-abundant economies tending to be bunched together, and labour-abundant countries bunched together. In this case it is very easy to see that $RIIT_A$ will tend to diminish with distance. Neighbouring countries will have similar endowments, and therefore little inter-industry trade. Remote economies will have more inter-industry trade, and lower *relative* intra-industry trade.

An example of this is given in Figures 6.2 and 6.3. We suppose that country 8 is the most labour-abundant location, and the location opposite (country 16) is the most capital-abundant, with endowments of labour and capital taking the form of a sine wave form around the circle. The associated pattern of production is illustrated in Figure 6.2, which

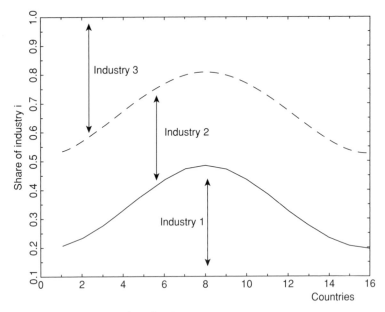

Figure 6.2 The location of production

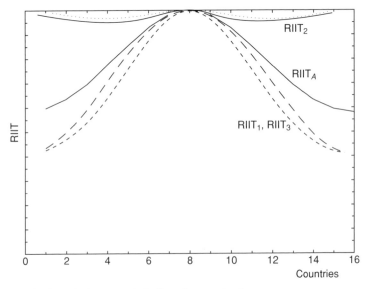

Figure 6.3 Intra-industry trade indices for country 8

gives the share of the three industries in countries' output. Industry 1 is concentrated in the most labour-abundant countries, industry 3 in the most capital-abundant, and industry 2 is more evenly spread. Figure 6.3 gives RIIT measures – for each industry and in aggregate – for country 8, with each of its partners (arrayed on the horizontal axis). We see that in industries 1 and 3, and in aggregate, RIIT declines with distance.

What do we learn from this? First, as before, $RIIT_i$ levels vary across industries, although the industries are identical, except in factor intensities. This means that cross-industry differences in $RIIT_i$ cannot necessarily be taken to reveal anything about transport costs, product differentiation or market structure in the industries. Second, the model generates the observed inverse correlation between distance and RIIT, although there is nothing 'causal' in this relationship. It is simply that if endowments vary systematically with location, then so does both production and RIIT. Their correlation results from their being jointly determined by a third factor – endowments – which should be observable to the econometrician. However, the model is non-linear, and it is worth asking how simple linear estimation would perform confronted with data generated by this model. Suppose that we take the endowment and distance data used in the model, and the (deterministic) trade flows and RIIT values it generates, and investigate the linear least squares relationships between these variables. A linear function of the absolute value of cross-country differences in capital/labour ratios (as used by Hummels and Levinsohn, 1995) explains 95 per cent of the variation in bilateral RIIT, while distance explains 42 per cent. In a linear regression with both distance and differences in capital/labour ratios (which have correlation coefficient of 0.63), both have negative coefficients.[8]

The same point can be made more sharply by changing the geography of this world. Suppose that the racetrack economy is replaced by a 'beach economy' (linear, with ends and a centre), and that the capital endowment declines linearly and labour endowment increases linearly with distance from one end. In this case, distance and the difference between capital/labour ratios are nearly collinear,[9] and the linear regression of RIIT on capital/labour ratios and distance gives the former the wrong sign, and attributes all explanatory power to the latter. It therefore appears as if distance is driving the behaviour of RIIT, although in fact it is being determined by factor endowments.

The conclusion of this section is that, if there is spatial bunching of endowments, then distance may appear to be a significant determinant of RIIT, even if it plays no causal role in determining these flows. In principle, the use of endowment information can control for this, but in practice – and given the non-linearity of the theoretical relationships – there must be doubts as to whether it does so successfully.

Geography, industrial location and intra-industry trade

Up to this point in our study we have ignored imperfect competition, letting Armington product differentiation drive intra-industry trade flows. We now switch to monopolistic competition, identifying varieties with monopolistically competitive firms that choose location in response to profit opportunities. From now on we also replace the 'racetrack economy' with the 'beach economy' that we used at the end of the previous section. In the racetrack economy, all locations have a fundamental symmetry, whereas the beach economy has a geographical structure, containing a central region and two peripheries. The combination of monopolistic competition and this geographical structure means that different countries will, in general, have different industrial structures even if they have identical factor endowments – an assumption that we shall make from now on. The question we pose is, therefore: if industrial location is determined by the geography of this linear economy, what pattern of RIIT will emerge?

Figure 6.4 illustrates the location of production in this economy, when there are just two industries, both monopolistically competitive, and differing only in transport costs (the figure is constructed with 32 countries rather than 16, purely in order to generate smoother figures). Industry 1 has higher transport costs, with $t_1 = 1.2$, and industry 2 has $t_2 = 1.1$. The higher transport cost industry is drawn into the central location, because of a 'home market effect', while the lower transport cost industry is located predominantly in the periphery.

This spatial clustering of industry generates a complex pattern of RIIT which we (partially) illustrate in Figure 6.5. The curves labelled $RIIT_A(j, k)$ indicate the values of the Grubel–Lloyd intra-industry trade index for selected countries $j(j = 4, 10, 16)$ with all other countries, k, arrayed on the horizontal axis. For a location very close to the centre, such as, $j = 16$, the $RIIT_A$ index decreases with distance; clearly, more distant locations have more different industrial structures, and this gives rise to declining $RIIT_A$. For location 10, $RIIT_A(10, k)$ decreases with distance locally, but then increases over some range. The reason is that location 10 is on one side of the centre, and has a similar industrial structure to locations on the other side of the centre. A similar pattern emerges for country 4, with $RIIT_A$ declining with distance locally, but then increasing for its trade with the other periphery. Although

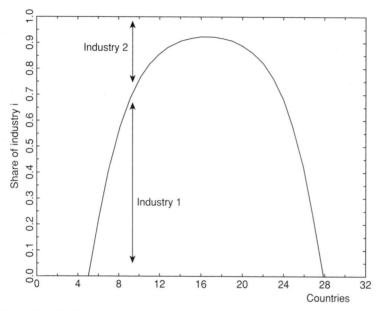

Figure 6.4 The location of production

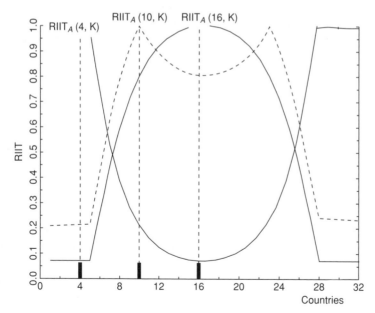

Figure 6.5 Intra-industry trade of countries 4, 10 and 16

Figure 6.5 indicates the non-monotonicity of the relationship between $RIIT_A$ and distance, a simple linear regression of the data generated by this model, over all pairs of locations, produces a negative relationship.

The pattern of industrial location illustrated in Figure 6.4 captures a simple 'home market' effect, but the geography of industrial location rapidly becomes more complex than this. Figures 6.6 and 6.7 are analogous to Figures 6.5 and 6.6, but for a case in which there are three industries, differing only in transport costs and with $t_1 > t_2 > t_3$. The location of production (Figure 6.6) can be understood as follows. As usual in models of this type, the 'home market effect' is strongest for industries with intermediate levels of transport costs. This is because high-transport-cost industries have to be near consumers, so tend to be distributed relatively uniformly, and low-transport-cost industries will locate where labour is cheapest, tending to go to the periphery (see also Venables, 1999, and Fujita *et al.*, 1999). In this example, industry 2 is the 'intermediate'-transport-cost industry, and consequently clusters in central regions. Locations 3 and 30 have no industry 2, although this industry reappears in the extreme periphery to meet local demand. Industry 1 has the highest transport costs, and is active in all locations; there is a

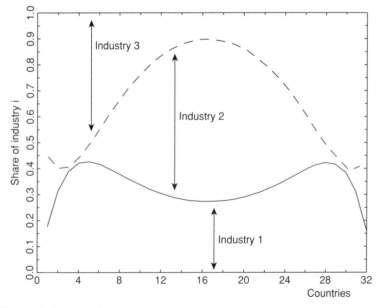

Figure 6.6   The location of production

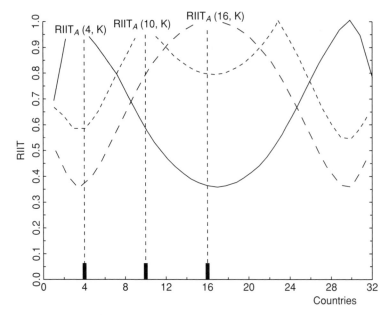

Figure 6.7 Intra-industry trade of countries 4, 10 and 16

home market effect pulling the industry into the centre, although high wages (caused by factor market competition from industry 2) reduce the level at which it operates in the very centre. Industry 3 has the lowest transport costs, so is the most 'footloose'. It consequently locates predominantly in the low wage periphery, from which it can supply central locations.

The corresponding pattern of $RIIT_A$ is illustrated, for selected countries, on Figure 6.7. The central country, country 16, has $RIIT_A$ with most of its partners being a decreasing function of their distance, essentially because more distant countries are more different from 16 – except for the non-monotonicity in the extreme periphery. For countries 4 and 10, the pattern is more complex, as $RIIT_A$ indices first fall then rise to a second distinct maximum. The reason is simply that a country on one side of the periphery has an industrial structure unlike that at the centre, but similar to other countries on the far side of the centre. These are countries with which most trade will be with intra-, rather than inter-industry.

In both these cases, the relationship between RIIT and distance is essentially a corollary of the pattern of industrial location that is generated by the geography of the economy. However, simple linear regression indicates that in this case, once again, RIIT declines with distance. One can imagine adding controls to capture geographical effects (such as a bilateral comparison between measures of how central or peripheral countries are). However, these are likely to be imperfect, so the econometrician might again expect to observe a negative relationship between RIIT and distance. The general point is that if the location of production is determined by geography, there is a likelihood that neighbouring locations will have similar production structures. As a consequence RIIT measures are likely to decrease with distance.

Concluding comments

The spatial pattern of trade is determined by many forces, depending on differences in production structure and preferences, as well as demand elasticities, transport costs, and other trade frictions such as tariffs and information barriers. Our investigation has abstracted from some of these forces in order to try to assess the reasons why intra-industry trade should decline more rapidly with distance than does inter-industry trade. It seems implausible that differences in trade technologies (transport costs combined with import demand elasticities) can account for the decline, and more likely that it is caused by spatial clustering of production, making inter-industry trade levels relatively low between countries in close proximity. The spatial clustering of production could result from the spatial distribution of endowments, or simply that geography influences the location of production. In either case, it might be difficult for econometricians to control for these considerations, which would account for the empirical finding that measures of intra-industry trade decline with distance.

Appendix

Parameter values used in simulation:
Table 6.1, Figure 6.1: $\sigma_1 = \sigma_2 = \sigma_3 = 10$, $t_1 = t_2 = t_3 = 1.25$.
Table 6.2, $\sigma_1 = \sigma_3 = 10$, $\sigma_2 = 5$, $t_1 = t_3 = 1.25$, $t_2 = 1.2$.
Figures 6.2 and 6.3: $\sigma_1 = \sigma_2 = \sigma_3 = 10$, $t_1 = t_2 = t_3 = 1.5$.
Pages 000–000:
Two-industry case: $\sigma_1 = \sigma_2 = 10$, $t_1 = 1.2$, $t_2 = 1.1$.
Three-industry case: $\sigma_1 = \sigma_2 = \sigma_3 = 10$, $t_1 = 1.2$, $t_2 = 1.15$, $t_3 = 1.05$.

Notes

1   The Grubel–Lloyd index is $\mathrm{RIIT}_i(j,\ k) \equiv 2\min(X_i(j,\ k),\ X_i(k,\ j))/[X_i(j,\ k)+ X_i(k,\ j)]$ where $X_i(j,\ k)$ denotes exports from country j to country k in products

of industry i. At the aggregate level, $RIIT_A(j, k) \equiv 2\sum_i \min(X_i(j, k), X_i(k, j))/ \sum_i [X_i(j, k) + X_i(k, j)]$.

2 Hummels and Levinsohn build on Helpman (1987), which was the first study to attempt to link empirical analysis of RIIT determinants to theory with hypotheses developed from the Helpman and Krugman (1985) model. However, since transport costs do not appear in the theory, Helpman did not include distance in the empirical analysis. Hummels and Levinsohn modify Helpman (1987) in terms of econometric techniques, the units of measurement, which are bilateral country observations rather than aggregate measures for each country, and the measure of differences in relative factor endowments. Instead of using income per capita, which Helpman finds to be negative and significant, they use actual relative capital to labour endowments and relative labour to land endowments and they add distance.

3 Caves (1981) also conducts an industry study. He hypothesizes that the inverse of the average distance moved by domestic shipments should have a positive effect on RIIT, which is confirmed by his analysis. His hypothesis seems to contradict the others but he claims that 'Pagoulatos and Sorensen (1975) and Loertscher and Wolter (1980) both confirm this result statistically.' The evidence on this is confusing.

4 An alternative would be to take random distributions of endowments and compute average values of endogenous variables taken over many random draws.

5 If all products have the same price and the same demand functions, then the value of demands are proportional to $\exp[\tau_i d(1 - \sigma_i)]$. This function is lower, and falling more steeply with d, the larger is $\tau_i(\sigma_i - 1)$.

6 And since the only parameters that are changed are σ_2 and t_2 the actual values of $RIIT_1$ and $RIIT_3$ are unchanged.

7 Similar results hold if we let the number of product varieties in industry 2 be determined endogenously by entry and exit of increasing returns to scale firms.

8 There is no error structure in this exercise. We simply find the linear function that best fits (minimizes the sum of squared deviations from) a non-linear relationship. Significance levels are not meaningful or reported.

9 Not perfectly collinear, as the ratio of capital to labour is strictly convex in distance.

References

Balassa, B. (1986a) 'Intra-Industry Specialization: A Cross-Country Analysis', *European Economic Review*, 30: 27–42.

Balassa, B. (1986b) 'The Determinants of Intra-Industry Specialization in United States Trade', *Oxford Economic Papers*, 38: 220–33.

Balassa, B. and L. Bauwens (1987) 'Intra-Industry Specialization in a Multi-Country and Multi-Industry Framework', *The Economic Journal*, 97: 923–39.

Caves, R. E. (1981) 'Intra-Industry Trade and Market Structure in the Industrial Countries', *Oxford Economic Papers*, 33(2) 203–53.

Davis, D. R. (1998) 'The Home Market Effect, Trade and Industrial Structure', *American Economic Review*, 88(5): 1268–76.

Engel, C. and J. H. Rogers (1996) 'How Wide is the Border?', *American Economic Review*, 88(5): 1112–25.

Fujita, M., P. R. Krugman and A. J. Venables (1999) *The Spatial Economy: Cities, Regions and International Trade* (Cambridge Mass.: MIT Press).

Gray, H. P. (1971) 'Two-Way International Trade in Manufactures: A Theoretical Underpinning', *Weltwirtschaftliches Archiv*, 109: 19–39.

Grubel, H. G. and P. J. Lloyd (1975) *Intra-Industry Trade* (London: Macmillan).

Harrigan, J. (1993) 'OECD Imports and Trade Barriers in 1983', *Journal of International Economics*, 35(1–2): 91–111.

Helliwell, J. (1996) 'Do National Borders Matter for Quebec's Trade?', *Canadian Journal of Economics*, 29(3): 507–22.

Helpman, E. (1987) 'Imperfect Competition and International Trade: Evidence from Fourteen Industrial Countries', *Journal of the Japanese and International Economies*, 1: 62–81.

Helpman, E. and P. R. Krugman (1985) *Market Structure and Foreign Trade* (Cambridge, Mass.: MIT Press).

Hummels, D. and J. Levinshohn (1995) 'Monopolistic Competition and International Trade: Reconsidering the Evidence', *Quarterly Journal of Economics*, 110(3): 799–836.

Lipsey, R. E. and M. Y. Weiss (1974) *The Structure of Ocean Transport Charges* (New York: NBER).

Loertscher, R. and F. Wolter (1980) 'Determinants of Intra-Industry Trade: Among Countries and Across Industries', *Weltwirtschaftliches Archiv*, 116: 280–93.

Matthews, K. (1998) 'Intra-Industry Trade: An Australian Panel Study', *Journal of Economic Studies*, 98: 84–97.

McCallum, J. (1995) 'National Borders Matter: Canada–US Regional Trade Patterns', *American Economic Review*, 85(3): 615–23.

Pagoulatos, E. and R. Sorensen (1975) 'Two-Way International Trade: An Econometric Analysis', *Weltwirtschaftliches Archiv*, 111(3): 454–65.

Rauch, J. E. (1999) 'Networks versus Markets in International Trade', *Journal of International Economics*, 48(1): 7–36.

Toh, K. (1982) 'A Cross-Section Analysis of Intra-Industry Trade in US Manufacturing Industries', *Weltwirtschaftliches Archiv*, 118: 281–300.

Venables, A. J. (1999) 'Geography and Specialization: Industrial Belts on a Circular Plain', in R. Baldwin, D. Cohen, A. Sapir and A. J. Venables (eds), *Market Integration, Regionalism and the Global Economy* New York: Cambridge University Press.

Wei, S.-J. (1996) 'Intra-National versus International Trade: How Stubborn are Nations in Global Integration', NBER Working Paper 5531.

Weiss, L. W. (1972) 'The Geographic Size of Markets in Manufacturing', *The Review of Economics and Statistics*, 54: 245–57.

Part III

Empirical Studies and Policy Issues of Intra-Industry Trade

7
Marginal Intra-Industry Trade: Towards a Measure of Non-Disruptive Trade Expansion

Marius Brülhart

Introduction

When Verdoorn (1960) found that the formation of a customs union among the Benelux countries had stimulated large, two-way trade flows of similar products, and Drèze (1961) discovered the same phenomenon in the fledgling six-nation EEC, economists took note for one main reason: adjustment costs. Instead of inter-sectoral specialization according to countries' comparative advantage, the national economies seemed to preserve their broad industrial structures and to specialize predominantly at the intra-sectoral level. A 'smooth adjustment hypothesis' (SAH) soon became firmly rooted in economic thinking, according to which intra-industry trade (IIT) expansion generally entails lower adjustment costs than does inter-industry trade.

In time, the early conjectures on the shape of emerging trade patterns were confirmed by a number of high-profile studies such as those of Grubel and Lloyd (1975), Greenaway and Milner (1986), Greenaway and Hine (1991), and OECD (1994). These empirical studies have, without exception, uncovered a secular increase in the share of intra-industry flows in trade among developing as well as developed economies, and many scholars have cited this fact as a powerful force for attenuating trade-induced economic frictions within and between countries since the 1950s.

The choice of IIT measure used in empirical work, however, has until recently been guided not so much by its relevance for factor-market adjustment but rather by its significance for the theory of international trade. Since trade theory consists to the most part of static models, the static Grubel–Lloyd index of IIT has been by far the most widely employed measure. High static IIT is difficult to reconcile with the predictions of neoclassical trade theory, and its discovery has therefore driven the development of the 'new trade theory', which can accommodate the existence of IIT. For that reason, measures of static IIT can be a useful gauge of the determinants of trade flows.

However, Hamilton and Kniest (1991) have pointed out in a seminal contribution that, in the context of adjustment, dynamic measures of IIT may be more informative than static measures. They proposed an index of 'marginal IIT' (MIIT) to be used in studies of the SAH. A number of authors have since proposed different measures of MIIT, and some empirical tests of the SAH have been carried out. This contribution provides a survey of that growing literature.

The survey is organized as follows. The second section provides some theoretical background to the SAH. In the third section there is a brief review the properties of the most widely used measure of IIT – the Grubel–Lloyd index. The fourth section presents some alternative measures which capture changes in IIT but not MIIT in the strict sense. An overview of MIIT measures is given in the fifth section while the sixth section is dedicated to a special class of MIIT measures, namely those that combine information on the symmetry of trade changes with information on a country's sectoral trade performance. In the seventh section I conclude with some generalizations and suggestions for future research.

The smooth adjustment hypothesis

Adjustment costs arise from temporary inefficiencies when markets fail to clear instantaneously in the wake of a change of demand or supply conditions. More specifically, the adjustment costs that are normally studied in the context of trade expansion are those welfare losses that arise in labour markets from temporary unemployment resulting from factor–price rigidity or from costs incurred through job search, relocation and retraining.

Trade *per se* cannot be called a cause for adjustment costs. The size and pattern of trade flows are not exogenous. Rather, they are shaped by underlying factor endowments, demand patterns, technologies, income levels and policy regimes of the trading countries. The concept of 'trade-induced' changes therefore alludes implicitly to ulterior causes that are manifested in the structure of trade flows. This conception is easiest to grasp in a setting of trade liberalization. There, any change that can be tracked to the change in the trade-policy regime is defined as 'trade-induced'.

The models of the new trade theory are consistent with the smooth adjustment hypothesis. Krugman (1981, p. 970), in a general equilibrium model considering only price adjustments (changes in relative wages), found 'a one-for-one relationship between similarity of factor endowments and intra-industry trade', which he interpreted as 'a vindication... that intra-industry trade poses fewer adjustment problems than inter-industry trade'. This result stems effectively from the fact that all the influential models explaining IIT through scale economies and monopolistic competition assume the products of an industry to be perfectly homogenous in terms of quantitative and qualitative factor requirements. Intra-industry adjustment costs are thus eliminated simply by assumption.

Unfortunately, the industry concept that underlies the empirical measurement of IIT does not contain only goods with perfectly identical production requirements. For the analysis of empirically-observed IIT, there are three conceivable reasons why IIT might entail smaller labour-market adjustment costs than does inter-industry trade:

(i) The mobility of labour across firms and occupations might be greater within industries than between industries;
(ii) Relative wages might be more flexible within industries than between industries; or
(iii) Other production factors might be more mobile within than between industries.

The first hypothesis has much intuitive appeal. If one defines IIT as the exchange of goods with similar production requirements, then it is implied that labour requirements are more similar within industries than between industries. If the skills acquired by the workers and managers of a contracting firm can be applied without much retraining in an expanding firm of the same industry, then labour mobility may well be higher within industries than between them. If specialization occurs inside firms, then workers can simply be transferred from one department to another. Where industries are spatially concentrated, labour is likely to be more mobile within than between industries. The problem is that one cannot assume *a priori* that the statistical product categories underlying empirical calculations of IIT in fact correspond to this definition of industries.

The second hypothesis relates to the intra-industry, specific-factors model where asymmetric trade shocks across producers in one industry, combined with short-term immobility of workers, will result in temporary unemployment if wages are not flexible across producers. The main impediments to wage flexibility are minimum-wage legislation and contractual wage agreements at the industry level. Since such constraints generally apply at the level of the entire economy or of individual industries, they might in fact be expected to allow greater wage flexibility between industries than within them. If wage inflexibility through industry-wide centralized bargaining is the dominant cause of adjustment problems, then adjustment would be greater when trade shocks are intra-industry than when trade alters the relative competitiveness among industries.

The third hypothesis, like the first, is plausible if we assume that 'industries' are delineated according to supply-side substitutability of goods. In the specific-factors model it is normally assumed that all production factors except labour are non-transferable among products. If we relax this assumption and allow for increasing mobility of the complementary factor(s), then smaller wage adjustments will be needed to restore labour-market equilibrium. Hence, the third hypothesis offsets to some extent the caveat provided by the second hypothesis.

In sum, while the SAH has not yet been embedded rigorously in a fully specified theoretical model, existing trade theory does supply some arguments in its favour.[1] Ultimately, however, the homogeneity and adaptability of industries defined in trade statistics can only be determined through empirical investigation.

This section has been concerned with the effect on an asymmetric demand shock between or within industries on labour-market adjustment. The main focus of this survey, however, is on how to measure the relevant degree of (a)symmetry of trade-induced shocks in empirical work.

Static IIT: the Grubel–Lloyd index

By far the most widely used measure of IIT stems from Grubel and Lloyd (1975), who suggested the following formula:

$$GL_i = 1 - \frac{|X_i - M_i|}{(X_i + M_i)} \tag{7.1}$$

where X_i and M_i refer to a country's exports and imports of goods contained in industry i in one particular year. This measure takes values between zero and one, and increases in IIT.

Furthermore, Grubel and Lloyd (1975) have represented the summary IIT index calculated over several industries as a trade-weighted (rather than simple arithmetic) average of the industry indices:

$$GL = \sum_{i=1}^{n} w_i GL_i = \sum_{i=1}^{n} \left(\frac{X_i + M_i}{\sum_{i=1}^{n}(X_i + M_i)} \right) GL_i = 1 - \frac{\sum_{i=1}^{n} |X_i - M_i|}{\sum_{i=1}^{n}(X_i + M_i)} \qquad (7.2)$$

Equivalent to this definition is the following formula:

$$GL = \frac{\sum_{i=1}^{n} 2 \, (\min X_i, M_i)}{\sum_{i=1}^{n}(X_i + M_i)} \qquad (7.3)$$

The *GL* index can be calculated for a country's world-wide trade, or for a subset of trade partners, as well as for total merchandise trade or for a subset of industries. The statistical properties and limitations of the *GL* index have been scrutinized carefully in the literature. An authoritative survey can be found in Greenaway and Milner (1986). I will therefore give only a brief summary of the four main measurement issues.

Categorical aggregation

As seen above, the definition of an 'industry' central to the SAH and probably the most contentious issue in applied IIT research. Grubel and Lloyd (1975, p. 86), have defined IIT as 'trade in differentiated products which are close substitutes'. Over time, it has become accepted generally that the relevant criterion is substitutability in production (rather than in consumption), since this is the aspect of industries that (a) distinguishes IIT from comparative-advantage based trade; and (b) lies at the heart of the link between IIT and factor-market adjustment. While statistical product classifications inevitably are imperfect in this respect, they are nevertheless guided largely by the correct criterion – that is, an effort to group together goods with similar input requirements.[2] This still leaves open the question about the most appropriate level of statistical aggregation for the calculation of IIT indices. While the majority of empirical studies use data at the 3-digit level, this choice is in the main motivated by expediency rather than any *a priori* reason for favouring that level of aggregation.

Adjustment for overall trade imbalance

The upper bound of a country's mean *GL* index is related negatively to the share of the overall trade surplus or deficit in total trade. Hence, imbalance in the trade account will tend to bias the *GL* index downwards. Adjustment methods have therefore been suggested, with the one brought forward by Aquino (1978) having been used most widely. The Aquino index is defined as follows:

$$GL_i^A = 1 - \frac{\left| \hat{X}_i - \hat{M}_i \right|}{(\hat{X}_i + \hat{M}_i)} \tag{7.4}$$

where $\hat{M}_i = M_i^*(\{\sum X_i + M_i\}/2 \sum M_i) =$ 'expected imports', and $\hat{X}_i = X_i^*(\{\sum X_i + M_i\}/2 \sum X_i) =$ 'expected exports'.

The rationale for such adjustment measures has been questioned, on the grounds that visible trade imbalances, both bilateral and multilateral, may well be compatible with balance of payments equilibrium (Greenaway and Milner, 1986; Kol and Mennes, 1989; Vona, 1991). Given the difficulty in estimating equilibrium trade imbalances, the professional consensus has been to work with unadjusted *GL* indices.

Scale invariance

The *GL* index for an individual industry is not related to the absolute size of imports and exports in that sector, nor indeed to the size of the industry in terms of domestic production or consumption. What matters for studies of trade-induced adjustment is not only the structure of trade flows, which is captured by the *GL* index, but also the degree of openness of individual sectors. In regression analysis it is therefore advisable to interact the *GL* index with a measure of sectoral trade openness or simple trade volumes.

Static nature

The GL index refers to the pattern of trade in one year. In the context of structural adjustment, however, it is the structure of *changes* in trade patterns that is important. This insight, attributable to Hamilton and Kniest (1991), has motivated the development of measures of *marginal* IIT (MIIT) and thus provides the key issue for this survey.[3]

Quasi-dynamic measures: changes in IIT

Some measures have been developed that are neither static nor measures of MIIT in the strict sense. These 'quasi-dynamic' measures take account of trade flows in two different years, but, as I shall argue below, they may not present the most appropriate gauge of trade patterns in the adjustment context.

First-differenced GL indices

Prior to the introduction of the MIIT concept, the evaluation of IIT changes over time was confined to the comparison of *GL* indices for different time periods, where

$$\Delta GL = GL_t - GL_{t-n} = \left(1 - \frac{|M-X|}{(M+X)}\right)_t - \left(1 - \frac{|M-X|}{(M+X)}\right)_{t-n} \qquad (7.5)$$

Δ is the first-difference operator, t is the end year, and n is the number of years separating the base and end years.[4]

The nature and limitations of this approach to measuring IIT are best illustrated in a simple diagram. Figure 7.1(a) plots one country's imports and exports of one particular industry (i).[5] All points along any ray from the origin share the same *GL* index, since they represent equal sectoral import–export proportions. The *GL* index equals 1 along the 45° line, and zero along either of the axes.

Assume that P represents the sectoral trade balance in the base year $(t-n)$. In this initial year, home-country imports in industry i exceed exports by a ratio of 3:1. The industry thus exhibits a *GL* index of 0.5.[6] Assume further that the *GL* index is higher in the end year (t). In Figure

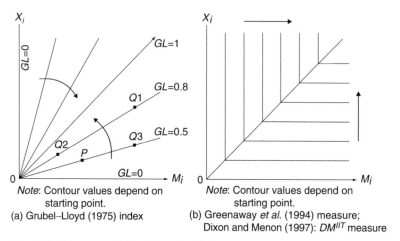

Note: Contour values depend on starting point.

(a) Grubel–Lloyd (1975) index

Note: Contour values depend on starting point.

(b) Greenaway *et al.* (1994) measure; Dixon and Menon (1997): DM^{IIT} measure

Figure 7.1 Measures of IIT and quasi-MIIT

7.1(a), both points Q1 and Q2 fit this scenario, since they both correspond to a sectoral *GL* index of 0.8. Both a move from *P* to Q1 and a move
from *P* to Q2 would thus show up as an increase in the *GL* index from 0.5
to 0.8. However, the pattern of trade change is quite different between
the two scenarios. Consider, first, a shift from *P* to Q1· Q1 lies at a 45°
angle to the north-east of *P*. Exports and imports of *i* have thus increased
at the same absolute rate, and both countries (assuming there are only
two) have captured an equal share of the increased volume of trade in
this sector. If this pattern appears for other industries as well, then the
adjustment process is *intra*-industry, since all countries share equally in
the growth (or decline) of all these sectors. Now consider a move from *P*
to Q2. In this scenario, the amount of home country exports has declined, while imports have increased. If this pattern also appears in other
industries – with the home country not necessarily always on the 'los-
ing' side – the adjustment process is *inter*-industry. A rise in the *GL* index
can thus hide both a process of *intra*- and *inter*-industry trade change.
Thus, the juxtaposition of corresponding *GL* indices for different
periods conveys some information on the structure of trade in each of
these time periods, but it does not allow conclusions on the structure of
the *change* in trade flows.[7]

   This, however, is not to say that intertemporal analysis of corresponding *GL* indices is useless or misleading in itself. If the aim of the analysis
is 'comparative static', meaning that what is sought is a comparison of
the structure of trade at different points (years) in time, then the comparison of *GL* indices may well be adequate. It is only when the aim of
the analysis is 'dynamic' in nature, meaning that the structure of the
change in trading patterns is to be scrutinized, that the comparison of
GL indices is inadequate. Since simple logic suggests that the costs of
adjustment depend on the latter rather than on the former, an alternative measurement method is warranted.

The Greenaway–Hine–Milner–Elliott measure

Greenaway *et al.* (1994) have suggested the following measure:

$$\text{GHME} = [(X + M) - |X - M|]_t - [(X + M) - |X - M|]_{t-n} \qquad (7.6)$$

or:

$$\text{GHME} = \Delta[(X + M) - |X - M|] \qquad (7.7)$$

The *GHME* measure differs fundamentally from the *GL* index in that it
reports IIT in absolute values rather than as a ratio. This feature can be

desirable because it facilitates the scaling of IIT relative to gross trade levels, production or sales in a particular industry, which in turn is useful for the econometric analysis of the forces that determine structural adjustment. The drawback in this is that the unscaled *GHME* measure says nothing about the proportion of (marginal) intra-relative to inter-industry trade and it lacks the presentational appeal of a simple bounded index. Hence, its *raison d'être* rests upon the fact that 'it can be related to corresponding levels of gross trade or real output' (Greenaway *et al.*, 1994, p. 424).[8]

The *GHME* measure belongs to the 'quasi-dynamic' class, since it corresponds to the difference in the amounts of IIT in two periods, and it therefore shares limitations of the *GL* index for the assessment of the structure of *change* in trading patterns. Hamilton and Kniest's (1991) insight on the *GL* index thus also applies to the *GHME* measure. Assume, for example, that over the period of investigation a particular sector experiences a shift from a trade deficit to balanced trade while exports remain unchanged. The *GHME* measure will show a positive value of twice the increase in exports, even though this is an obvious case of *inter*-industry adjustment, because the increase in exports is not matched by any corresponding increase in imports. This can be seen in Figure 7.1(b), which gives a mapping of iso-*GHME* contours: the inter-industry trade change represented by a change from *P* to *Q*2 in Figure 7.1(a) would yield a positive value of the *GHME* measure.

The Dixon–Menon measures

Dixon and Menon (1997) have developed two alternative 'quasi-dynamic' measures. The first measure captures base-year weighted percentage growth of IIT:

$$\text{DM}^{\text{IIT}} = GL_{t-n}\left(\frac{\Delta[(X+M) - |X-M|]}{[(X+M) - |X-M|]_{t-n}}\ 100\right) \qquad (7.8)$$

and the second measure captures the base-year weighted percentage growth of net trade:

$$\text{DM}^{\text{NT}} = (1 - GL_{t-n})\left(\frac{\Delta|X-M|}{|X-M|_{t-n}}\ 100\right) \qquad (7.9)$$

These measures can take values from -100 to infinity. An appealing feature is that these two measures add up to the percentage growth in total trade of the relevant industry. However, the Dixon–Menon measures belong to the 'quasi-dynamic' class, because they cannot consistently separate MIIT from marginal inter-industry trade. For illustration, suppose again that over the period of investigation a particular sector experiences a shift from a trade deficit to balanced trade while exports remain unchanged. $DM^{IIT}(DM^{NT})$ will yield a positive (negative) value, even though this is an obvious case of *inter*-industry adjustment. A mapping of iso-DM^{IIT} contours looks identical to the one derived from the *GHME* measure (Figure 7.1(b)): the inter-industry trade change represented by a change from *P* to *Q2* in Figure 7.1(a) would yield a positive value of the DM^{IIT}.[9]

To summarize, the 'quasi-dynamic' measures are representations of the change in the share or the amount of matched trade between two years, using different scaling yardsticks. They can thus be useful for an analysis of the evolution of IIT over time. However, these measures do not relate consistently to the degree of 'matchedness' in trade changes – that is, they do not capture MIIT in the strict sense.

Marginal IIT: matched trade changes

Measures of MIIT quantify the degree of intra-sectoral symmetry of trade *changes*. Hence, they are computed from first differences in exports and imports, ΔX and ΔM – that is, they can be unrelated to the level of trade or of IIT in either the base or end period. In a nutshell, MIIT is about the importance of IIT in trade changes, and not about the change in IIT.

The Hamilton–Kniest index

The first measure of MIIT was proposed by Hamilton and Kniest (1991):

$$HK = \begin{cases} \dfrac{\Delta X}{\Delta M} & \text{for } \Delta M > \Delta X \geq 0 \\[2mm] \dfrac{\Delta M}{\Delta X} & \text{for } \Delta X > \Delta M \geq 0 \\[2mm] 1 & \text{for } \Delta X = \Delta M > 0 \\[2mm] \text{undefined} & \text{for } \Delta M < 0 \text{ or } \Delta X < 0 \end{cases} \qquad (7.10)$$

This measure is related strictly to the structure of the *change* in trading patterns – information on levels of exports or imports is not required. Hence, the *HK* index can be mapped on to a plane that is defined by ΔX and ΔM (Figure 7.2(a)). The possibility of such a mapping is what distinguishes MIIT measures from IIT and quasi-MIIT.

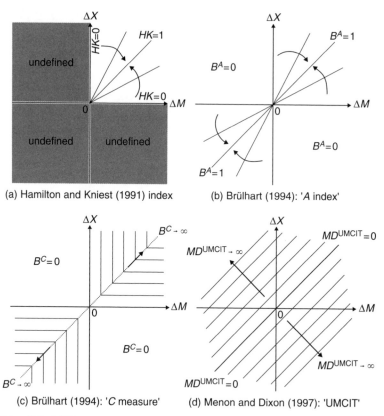

(a) Hamilton and Kniest (1991) index   (b) Brülhart (1994): '*A* index'

(c) Brülhart (1994): '*C* measure'   (d) Menon and Dixon (1997): 'UMCIT'

Figure 7.2   MIIT measures

This index, however, has some important limitations. Greenaway *et al.* (1994) have highlighted that the *HK* index is undefined when either *X* or *M* has decreased which can lead to a non-random omission of a significant number of statistical observations and therefore to potentially misleading results. Furthermore, Hamilton and Kniest (1991) have interpreted any situation where their index is undefined as representing 'an increase in exports and a decrease in imports (or vice versa), which indicates inter-industry trade'. Yet, the *HK* index is also undefined where both imports and exports have decreased (the bottom left quadrant of Figure 7.2(a)), a situation in which the matched decreases should be recorded as MIIT.

A Grubel–Lloyd style measure of MIIT

The following index is derived in Brülhart (1994):

$$B^A = 1 - \frac{|\Delta X - \Delta M|}{|\Delta X| + |\Delta M|} \qquad (7.11)$$

This index, like the *GL* coefficient, varies between 0 and 1, where 0 indicates marginal trade in the particular industry to be completely of the *inter*-industry type, and 1 represents marginal trade to be entirely of the *intra*-industry type. The main appeal of the B^A index lies in the fact that it reveals the structure of the *change* in import and export flows, similar to the HK index. Yet, unlike the latter measure, the B^A coefficient is defined in all cases and shares many familiar statistical properties of the GL index. This can be seen in the mapping given in Figure 7.2(b).

Oliveras and Terra (1997) have shown that the statistical properties of the B^A index differ from those of the *GL* index in two particular respects. First, this index does not fall systematically as the level of statistical disaggregation is increased. Second, there is no functional relationship between the B^A index for a certain period and the B^A indices of constituent subperiods.

Note that B^A can be summed, like the *GL* index, across industries of the same level of statistical disaggregation by applying the following formula for a weighted average:

$$B^A_{tot} = \sum_{i=1}^{k} w_i B^A_i$$

where

$$w_i = \frac{|\Delta X|_i + |\Delta M|_i}{\sum\limits_{i=1}^{k} (|\Delta X|_i + |\Delta M|_i)} \qquad (7.12)$$

and where B^A_{tot} is the weighted average of MIIT over all industries of the economy or over all the sub-industries of an industry, denoted by $i \ldots k$.

Extensions to the MIIT index

Several authors have put forward amended versions of the B^A index, tailored to particular underlying assumptions on the nature of the adjustment problem.

Lloyd (1998) has argued that it may be useful in certain contexts to incorporate local sales of foreign affiliates ('international production') in an analysis of trade flows. He suggested that the B^A index could be computed for $\hat{X}_i = \sum_{j=1,2} X_i^j$ and $\hat{M}_i = \sum_{j=1,2} M_i^j$, where i again denotes the industry, and j stands for the 'mode of supply'. If a particular flow is a cross-border import or export in the traditional sense, then $j = 1$; and when we look at local sales of foreign affiliates then $j = 2$. This index could be useful for a study of the adjustment implications of globalization in a broader sense, since it can be decomposed into the separate contributions to MIIT of changes in international goods trade and of changes in the pattern of international production.[10]

Another variant of the MIIT index was developed by Thom and McDowell (1999) to take account of the increasing fragmentation of international production:

$$\text{TM}_i = 1 - \frac{|\Delta X_i - \Delta M_i|}{\sum_{l=1}^{L} |\Delta X_l| + \sum_{l=1}^{L} |\Delta M_l|} \qquad (7.13)$$

where l denotes sub-industries of i. The TM index is bounded between zero and one, but it differs from B_{tot}^A aggregated over sub-industries j or i (Equation (7.12)).

The rationale underlying the *TM* index is that offsetting net trade changes across subsectors should be counted as MIIT if those subsectors are linked vertically. This is best illustrated with a simple example. Assume that country A increases its exports and reduces its imports of finished watches *vis-à-vis* country B, and that A simultaneously reduces its exports and increases its imports of watch components. Furthermore, suppose that the two trade changes are of equal size. If we apply the B^A index to the industries 'finished watches' and 'components' separately, we diagnose zero MIIT. On the other hand, if we define finished watches plus components as an industry, then the B^A index is undefined, since we observe zero aggregate trade change. The *TM* index, however, will return a value of 1 (that is, perfect MIIT), since the two net changes at sub-industry level offset each other perfectly. In an application to data on trade between the EU and some Eastern European countries, Thom and McDowell (1999) have found their index to return significantly higher values on average than B^A.

The validity of the *TM* index hinges on the appropriate definition of industries and sub-industries. If one had a classification with sub-industries defined according to the stages of production of the industry's final product, then the *TM* index provides an elegant measure of the international fragmentation process of production. In the face of the un-tidy existing statistical classification schemes, however, it is difficult to state *a priori* which might be the appropriate level of aggregation, and whether one should prefer the *TM* or B^A indices.

Annicchiarico and Quintieri (2000) have suggested a third extension of the MIIT index. They propose that the index should take a negative sign when the matched trade change is negative, so that the index would range from -1 to 1:

$$AQ = \begin{cases} -B^A & \text{if } \Delta M < 0 \text{ and } \Delta X < 0, \\ B^A & \text{otherwise} \end{cases} \qquad (7.14)$$

This touches on an important point. Underlying the B^A index is the implicit assumption that the quantity of production factors displaced by a one unit increase in imports (decrease in imports) is identical to the quantity of production factors required for a one-unit increase in exports (decrease in imports). One corollary is that a matched increase in imports and exports has a zero net effect on factor demand at the industry level, and similarly for a matched decrease in imports and exports.[11] Unless we are in the context of multiple regression, where one can control for trade-independent changes in sectoral demand and productivity, we may assume plausibly that matched expansion of trade will be associated with growing sectors, while matched contraction of trade would be indicative of sectors that are in general decline. Hence, unless we can control for non-trade determinants of structural change, it appears plausible that the adjustment implications of matched trade expansion differ from those entailed by matched trade contraction, and the transformed index suggested by Annicchiarico and Quintieri (2000) may well be informative in descriptive studies.

Unscaled MIIT measures

There are undeniable advantages in a simple bounded index for presentation and interpretation. Yet, as pointed out by Greenaway *et al.* (1994), it can be useful in certain applications to have gross measures of MIIT, or to scale MIIT to production variables. For this reason, the following measure has been suggested by Brülhart (1994):

$$B^C = (|\Delta X| + |\Delta M|) - |\Delta X - \Delta M| \qquad (7.15)$$

which is strictly non-negative and can be scaled even at the disaggregated industry level, like the *GHME* measure:

$$B_V^C = \frac{B^C}{V} \qquad (7.16)$$

where V is any relevant scaling variable. Figure 7.2(c) presents a mapping of iso-B^C contours in the trade-change space.

Menon and Dixon (1997) have proposed a similar measure. Instead of capturing absolute values of sectorally matched trade changes, like B^C, theirs is a 'measure of unmatched changes in trade':

$$\text{MD}^{UMCIT} = |\Delta X - \Delta M| \qquad (7.17)$$

MD^{UMCIT} and B^C are closely related, as B^C shows the absolute magnitude of MIIT and MD^{UMCIT} shows the absolute magnitude of marginal *inter*-industry trade. The relative properties of MD^{UMCIT} and B^C are easily grasped through a comparison of their respective mappings in Figures 7.2(d) and 7.2(c).

Absolute values of MIIT, such as B^C and MD^{UMCIT}, are difficult to interpret in isolation, since they give no indication of the proportion between intra- and inter-industry trade, which, after all, is central to the definition of the very concept of IIT and MIIT. Therefore, it might be appropriate for studies investigating MIIT and adjustment to use a two-stage approach, where MIIT is expressed both in relation to marginal *inter*-industry trade and in relation to other scaling variables.

Marginal IIT and sectoral performance

As noted above, a latent assumption underlying the basic MIIT index is that the adjustment costs of a net improvement in a sectoral trade balance are identical to those of a net deterioration in that sectoral trade balance. In other words, an additional million dollars of net exports will create a number of jobs equal to the number of jobs that would have been destroyed by an additional million dollars of net imports in that industry, and the adjustment costs of a job lost and of a job created are equal. In a labour market with unemployment and on-the-job learning, the assumed symmetry of adjustment costs between job creation and job destruction is clearly unrealistic. MIIT indices have therefore been developed to take account of the asymmetry between net import growth and net export growth.

For those reasons, the following index was put forward in Brülhart (1994):

$$B^B = \frac{\Delta X - \Delta M}{|\Delta X| + |\Delta M|} \qquad (7.18)$$

where

$$|B^B| = 1 - B^A \qquad (7.19)$$

This coefficient can take values ranging between -1 and 1. It is two-dimensional, containing information about both the proportion of MIIT and country-specific sectoral performance. First, the closer B^B is to zero, the higher is MIIT. B^B is equal to zero where marginal trade in the particular industry is entirely of the *intra*-industry type, whereas at both -1 and 1 it represents marginal trade to be entirely of the *inter*-industry type. Second, sectoral performance is defined as the change in exports and imports in relation to each other, with exports representing good domestic performance, and imports reflecting weak domestic performance, in a particular sector. Thus defined, B^B is related directly to sectoral performance. When $B^B > 0$, ΔX was $> \Delta M$. The opposite holds for $B^B < 0$. A mapping of B^B into the trade-change plane is given in Figure 7.3(a).

Unlike the B^A index, B^B cannot be aggregated meaningfully across industries, except where the Bs of all sub-industries have the same sign. Since high marginal inter-industry trade is expressed by values close to either -1 or 1, the weighted average of two sub-industries might yield a value close to zero (high MIIT) even where high marginal *inter*-industry trade prevails in both of them. Therefore, B^B cannot be used for summary statistics resulting from calculations at a disaggregated level.

A related measure has been proposed by Azhar and Elliott (2001):

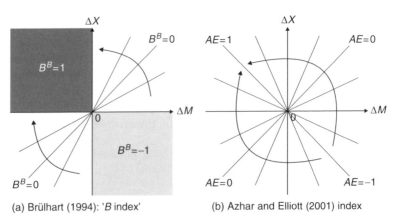

(a) Brülhart (1994): '*B* index' (b) Azhar and Elliott (2001) index

Figure 7.3 Measures of MIIT and sectoral performance

$$AE = \frac{\Delta X - \Delta M}{2(\max [|\Delta X|, |\Delta M|])} \qquad (7.20)$$

This index also ranges from -1 to 1, and it is negative (positive) if the sectoral trade balance has deteriorated (improved) over the relevant time interval. The difference lies in the data range where ΔX and ΔM have opposite signs (that is, where there is no MIIT). The B^B index returns a value of -1 or 1 for all configurations within that data range. The AE index, however, differentiates between the relative sizes of opposing net trade changes. This means that the AE index provides further detail in a data range where B^B always returns one of its polar values. This additional information conveyed by the AE index does not come at a cost, since the information contained in $B^B \in (-1, 1)$, which is the same data range as that for which $B^A \in (0, 1]$, is fully contained in $AE \in (-0.5, 0.5)$. Hence, the information conveyed by B^B is a subset of that given by the AE index. The apparent advantage of the AE index also presents its main difficulty: it is not clear how one should interpret different configurations of pure marginal inter-industry trade – that is, what to infer from different index values in the ranges $(-1, -0.5)$ and $(0.5, 1)$. There is no ready interpretation for index values in these intervals.

Some conjectures: which measure is best?

The SAH has undeniable intuitive appeal and is firmly established in the canon of international economics.[12] As this survey of measurement issues shows, however, the seemingly straightforward hypothesis is mired in ambiguity once one tries to define it rigorously. I have argued that a measure of MIIT – that is, one that reflects the degree of intra-sectoral (a)symmetry in trade *changes*, should be preferred to static or 'quasi-dynamic' measures of IIT when one seeks information on the likely implications of trade changes for factor-market adjustment.

Unfortunately, the ambiguity does not stop here. There are now a number of different measures that capture different aspects of the structure of trade changes. The problem is, of course, that no one-dimensional measure can ever fully describe the three-dimensional distribution of adjustment costs over the trade-change plane. Take, for example, the hypothetical mapping of trade-induced adjustment costs given in Figure 7.4. That particular map of iso-adjustment contours assumes that adjustment costs rise monotonically as one moves away from the origin of the Cartesian space, i.e. as the combined size of trade

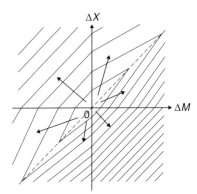

Figure 7.4 Hypothetical map of adjustment costs and trade changes

changes increase; but that this rise does not occur at the same rate depending on the direction in which one departs from the origin. The debate about which MIIT measure to use boils down to the question about which is the most important direction of skewness in this distribution, departing from one that is symmetric around the origin.

Figure 7.4 is based on the following linear model of adjustment costs (*AC*) in a certain industry (*i* subscripts implied):

$$AC = \alpha|\Delta X - \Delta M| + \beta(\Delta X - \Delta M) + \gamma(|\Delta X| + |\Delta M|) \qquad (7.21a)$$

with

$$\alpha > 0, \qquad (7.21b)$$
$$\beta < 0, \qquad (7.21c)$$
$$|\alpha| > |\beta|, \qquad (7.21d)$$
$$\gamma > 0. \qquad (7.21e)$$

The model (Equation (7.21a)) is fairly general, its main restriction being that of linearity – which could easily be relaxed by adding non-linear terms. The four restrictions that are then imposed on this model to generate the mapping of Figure 7.4 are rooted in assumptions that have been made, mainly implicitly, in the MIIT literature. Restriction (7.21b) reflects the assumption that adjustment costs increase in the absolute amount of unmatched trade change, (7.21c) that export expansion (contraction) causes lower (higher) adjustment costs than import expansion (contraction), (7.21d) that for given volumes of trade changes adjustment costs are minimized where changes in imports and exports are of equal size, and (7.21e) that a adjustment costs increase in the absolute amount of total trade change.

Estimation of a model such as Equation (7.21a) might shed some light on the debate about the most appropriate measure of low-adjustment-cost trade change. One could assess the validity of the SAH assumptions by testing restrictions (Equations, (7.21b–7.21e)). In particular, the relevance of MIIT would be confirmed if the estimated α were significant, since this would indicate that the degree of 'matchedness' of trade changes within sectors matters for adjustment costs, as the variable $|\Delta X - \Delta M|$ is the Menon–Dixon (1997) measure of marginal inter-industry trade (MD^{UMCIT}). The relevance of the Grubel–Lloyd-style MIIT index (B^A) would be confirmed if α were large relative to γ. Similarly, a significant estimated β would indicate that sectoral trade performance matters for adjustment costs, and that indices such as B^B of Brülhart (1994) or the Azhar–Elliott (2001) index are important.

There is some empirical evidence to support the claim that MIIT is relevant to labour-market adjustment costs, derived from a specification that is similar that in Equation (7.21a) (Brülhart, 2000).[13] However, this question still deserves to be explored further. Two major challenges need to be addressed. First, explicit estimation of factor-market adjustment *costs*, rather than measures of structural change that are merely assumed to relate to the adjustment costs, has only recently begun to be applied to this context (Haynes *et al.*, 2000; and Wright *et al.*, 2001). Second, there still does not exist a formal theoretical model that can generate marginal intra- and inter-industry trade, and thus serve as a base for the specification of empirical models. The choice of control variables in such exercises therefore still lacks a coherent theoretical base.

Notes

1 Lovely and Nelson (2000) have explored changes in IIT in an Ethier (1982) trade model. In that model, trade liberalization can yield both changes in countries' relative specialization and changes in the size of industries at world level. In the conventional understanding of the SAH, the latter effect is subsumed into the *ceteris paribus* assumption, but the Lovely–Nelson (2000) analysis highlights the importance of controlling for world-wide structural change – be it induced by trade liberalization, technology or taste changes – in empirical analyses of the relationship between (M)IIT and factor-market adjustment.

2 In the list of five similarity criteria used by the experts in charge of the third revision of the SITC code, for example, the first principle was 'the nature of the merchandise and the materials used in its production', while 'the uses of

the product' only ranked third (United Nations, 1986, p. viii). Evidence in favour of reasonable homogeneity of statistical sectors in terms of factor requirements has been found by Elliott *et al.* (2000). Some researchers, including Aquino (1978), Balassa (1985), Balassa and Bauwens (1987) and Christodoulou (1992), have rearranged trade data into groups that would seem more appropriate in the IIT context.

3 A note on terminology. I refer to the *GL* index as a 'static' measure, and to MIIT as a 'dynamic' concept. The *GL* index is calculated on the basis of cross-border flows of goods and is thus not a static measure in the strictest sense. Yet, 'static' IIT in the sense of the *GL* index contrasts with 'dynamic' measures of MIIT, since the latter relate to the change in these flows between two different years.

4 Industry subscripts are implied. This will also be the case for all subsequent equations, unless stated otherwise.

5 This graphical representation originated in Shelburne (1993) and has been developed as the 'trade box' by Azhar *et al.* (1998).

6 If the (constant) slope of a ray is defined as $S = M_i/X_i$, then the *GL* index on any point along a particular ray is given by: $GL = 1 - (|1 - S|/\{1 + S\})$.

7 These considerations are supported by empirical evidence in Little (1996, p. 16), who observed that 'regions with rising IIT tended to experience a relatively large shift in the composition of their exports, imports, or both. By contrast, regions with declines in IIT faced somewhat less structural change. These results suggest the need to re-examine the conventional wisdom that increasing IIT automatically smoothes adjustment to trade liberalisation'.

8 Greenaway *et al.* (1994) also pointed out the importance of using deflated trade values for the calculation of ΔM and ΔX. This is true for all measures which use first differences of trade flows, hence it applies to all the MIIT measures discussed below.

9 Note also that the first measure is undefined if base-year IIT is zero, and the second measure is undefined where base-year net trade is zero.

10 Greenaway *et al.* (1998) have applied this definition of 'extended trade' to compute *GL* indices for the USA and five of its major trading partners. They found that two-way, foreign-owned production is significantly larger than arm's-length IIT.

11 Another implication is that the magnitude of adjustment costs is unaffected by whether net trade changes are positive or negative. This assumption is relaxed in the fifth section.

12 For a list of references to the SAH in the recent literature, see Brülhart (1999).

13 The exercise of Brülhart (2000), which is conducted on Irish data and where adjustment costs are proxied by plant-level job turnover rates, includes among the independent variables the MIIT index (B^A) and a measure of trade intensity ($(X + M)/$output). It does not consider measures of sectoral trade performance.

References

Annicchiarico, B. and B. Quintieri (2000) 'Aggregated Measures of Intra-Industry Trade: A Critical Comparison', Mimeo, University of Rome Tor Vergata.

Aquino, A. (1978) 'Intra-Industry Trade and Intra-Industry Specialisation as Concurrent Sources of International Trade in Manufactures', *Weltwirtschaftliches Archiv*, 114: 275–95.

Azhar, A. K. and R. J. R. Elliott (2001) 'A Note on the Measurement of Trade-Induced Adjustment', Mimeo, University of Manchester.

Azhar, A. K., R. J. R. Elliott and C. Milner (1998) 'Static and Dynamic Measurement of IIT and Adjustment: A Geometric Reappraisal', *Weltwirtschaftliches Archiv*, 134: 404–22.

Balassa, B. (1985) 'Intra-Industry Specialisation', *European Economic Review*, 30: 27–42.

Balassa, B. and L. Bauwens, (1987) 'Intra-Industry Specialisation in a Multi-Country and Multi-Industry Framework', *Economic Journal*, 97: 923–39.

Brülhart, M. (1994) 'Marginal Intra-Industry Trade: Measurement and Relevance for the Pattern of Industrial Adjustment', *Weltwirtschaftliches Archiv*, 130: 600–13.

Brülhart, M. (1999) 'Marginal Intra-Industry Trade and Trade-Induced Adjustment: A Survey', in M. Brülhart and R. C. Hine *Intra-Industry Trade and Adjustment: The European Experience* London: Macmillan.

Brülhart, M. (2000) 'Dynamics of Intraindustry Trade and Labor-Market Adjustment', *Review of International Economics*, 8: 420–35.

Brülhart, M. and R. Elliott, (1998) 'Adjustment to the European Single Market: Inferences from Intra-Industry Trade Patterns', *Journal of Economic Studies*, 25: 225–47.

Brülhart, M. and R. C. Hine, (eds) (1998) *Intra-Industry Trade and Adjustment: The European Experience*. (London: Macmillan).

Christodoulou, M. (1992) 'Intra-Industry Trade in Agrofood Sectors: The Case of the EEC Meat Market', *Applied Economics*, 24: 875–84.

Dixon, P. B. and J. Menon, (1997) 'Measures of Intra-Industry Trade as Indicators of Factor Market Disruption', *Economic Record*, 73: 233–7.

Drèze, J. (1961) 'Les Exportations intra-C.E.E. en 1958 et la Position Belge', *Recherches Économiques de Louvain*, 27: 717–38.

Elliott, R. J. R., D. Greenaway, and R. C. Hine, (2000) 'Tests for Factor Homogeneity and Industry Classification', *Weltwirtschaftliches Archiv*, 136: 355–71.

Ethier, W. (1982) 'National and International Returns to Scale in the Modern Theory of International Trade', *American Economic Review*, 72: 388–405.

Greenaway, D. and R. C. Hine, (1991) 'Intra-Industry Specialization, Trade Expansion and Adjustment in the European Economic Space', *Journal of Common Market Studies*, 24: 603–22.

Greenaway, D. and C. Milner, (1986) *The Economics of Intra-Industry Trade*. (Oxford, Basil Blackwell).

Greenaway, D., P. J. Lloyd, and C. Milner (1998) 'Intra-Industry FDI and Trade Flows: New Measures of Globalisation of Production', *GLM Research Paper*, No. 98/5, Centre for Research on Globalisation and Labour Markets, University of Nottingham.

Greenaway, D., R. C. Hine, C. Milner and R. Elliott (1994) 'Adjustment and the Measurement of Marginal Intra-Industry Trade', *Weltwirtschaftliches Archiv*, 130: 418–27.

Grubel, H. and P. J. Lloyd, (1975) *Intra-Industry Trade* (London: Macmillan).

Hamilton, C. and P. Kniest, (1991) 'Trade Liberalisation, Structural Adjustment and Intra-Industry Trade: A Note', *Weltwirtschaftliches Archiv*, 12: 356–67.

Haynes, M., R. Upward, and P. Wright, (2000) 'Smooth and Sticky Adjustment: A Comparative Analysis of the US and UK', *Review of International Economics*, 8: 517–32.

Kol, J. and L. B. M. Mennes, (1989) 'Corrections for Trade Imbalance: A Survey'. *Weltwirtschaftliches Archiv*, 125: 703–17.

Krugman, P. (1981) 'Intraindustry Specialization and the Gains from Trade', *Journal of Political Economy*, 89: 959–73.

Little, J. S. (1996) 'U.S. Regional Trade with Canada during the Transition to Free Trade', *New England Economic Review*, January: 3–22.

Lloyd, P. J. (1998) 'Globalisation, International Factor Movements and Market Adjustments', *CREDIT Research Paper*, No. 98/7, University of Nottingham.

Lovely, M. and D. Nelson, (2000) 'On the Economic Relationship between Marginal Intra-Industry Trade and Labour Adjustment in a Division of Labour Model', *Review of International Economics*, 8: 436–47.

Menon, J. and P. B. Dixon, (1997) 'Intra-Industry versus Inter-Industry Trade: Relevance for Adjustment Costs', *Weltwirtschaftliches Archiv*, 133: 164–9.

OECD (1994) *The OECD Jobs Study, Part I: Labour Market Trends and Underlying Forces of Change* (Paris: OECD).

Oliveras, J. and I. Terra, (1997) 'Marginal Intra-Industry Trade Index: The Period and Aggregation Choice', *Weltwirtschaftliches Archiv*, 133: 170–9.

Shelburne, R. L. (1993) 'Changing Trade Patterns and the Intra-Industry Trade Index: A Note', *Weltwirtschaftliches Archiv*, 129: 829–33.

Thom, R. and M. McDowell, (1999) 'Measuring Marginal Intra-Industry Trade'. *Weltwirtschaftliches Archiv*, 135: 48–61.

United Nations (1986) Standard International Trade Classification, Revision 3, Series M, No. 34/Rev. 3, New York.

Verdoorn, P. J. (1960) 'The Intra-Block Trade of Benelux', in Robinson, E. A. G. (ed.), *Economic Consequences of the Size of Nations*. (London: Macmillan).

Vona, S. (1991) 'On the Measurement of Intra-Industry Trade', *Weltwirtschaftliches Archiv*, 127: 678–700.

Wright, P., M. Haynes, and R. Upward, (2001) 'Estimating the Wage Costs of Inter- and Intra-Sectoral Adjustment', *CEPR Discussion Paper*, No. 2710.

8
Long-term Trends in Intra-Industry Trade

Lionel Fontagné and Michael Freudenberg

Introduction

This chapter examines European trade patterns over the period 1980–99, using data on values and unit values of bilateral trade flows at a very detailed level. Reviewing the related concerns for economic policy permits the identification of a key issue: quality matters. A new method of measurement highlights the fact that the development of intra-industry trade is associated with a specialization of countries along quality lines. This result sheds light on the often neglected potential adjustment costs of intra-industry trade in vertically differentiated products.

The first section of the chapter highlights the major theoretical foundations and implications of the inter- versus intra-industry nature of trade for economic policy, using the European framework as a benchmark. It argues that determinants and consequences of IIT depend clearly on the nature of product differentiation. In fact, inter-industry trade (implying a displacement of resources between industries), intra-industry trade in vertically differentiated products (associated with a specialization along quality ranges), and intra-industry trade in similar products (associated with a specialization in varieties) have different determinants and consequences.

In the second section different methods to measure intra-industry trade are discussed briefly. It argues in favour of an approach which, by using information on unit values at a very detailed level of trade nomenclatures (some 10 000 product items), allows bilateral trade to be separated into three trade types: one-way trade, two-way trade in horizontally differentiated goods, and two-way trade in vertically differentiated goods.

Using this approach, the third section offers empirical evidence of the nature of European trade, both within the EU and with non-EU members. One of the main findings is that the observed increase in intra-industry trade between 1980 and 1999 in Europe is almost entirely a result of two-way trade in *vertical* differentiation. This phenomenon of simultaneous exports and imports of products with similar main technical characteristics, but under different prices (unit values), suggests that countries increasingly are specializing along ranges of qualities within products. Thus gains to trade are created not only though a larger choice of varieties, but also because of a broader choice among different qualities.

Determinants of shares of trade types in bilateral trade are addressed econometrically in the fourth section. Traditional explanations of IIT are shown to be relevant here, augmented by ones of the Falvey type. This exercise also sheds light on the potential effects of the next step of integration in Europe, namely the monetary union. The fifth section focuses on policy implications: which segment of the market different member states are positioned is an important issue, as this has consequences in terms of adjustment costs, income distribution, or catching-up. The last section of the chapter draws conclusions.

European integration and the political economy of trade patterns

The first wave of European integration, following the creation of the Common Market in the late 1950s, shed serious doubts on the validity of traditional theories of international trade associating integration and specialization through *inter*-industry trade (see Table 8.1). According to these theories, increased specialization along lines of comparative advantage provides gains to trade. In turn, it also implies the abandon of comparatively disadvantaged industries, the displacement of factors towards a limited number of export-orientated industries, and the impoverishment of certain categories of agents along the Stolper–Samuelson mechanism. Thus fears were expressed at its creation that the Common Market might drive the most advanced countries to specialize in high-value-added industries, with the others countries specializing in the remaining sectors. However, even though European integration was accompanied, as expected, by a strong increase in the volume of intra-European trade, it did not translate into an increased specialization of the member states. Indeed, empirical studies since the 1960s have shown that an important part of intra-European trade was of an *intra*-industry nature (that is, simultaneous exports and imports within industries), a phenomenon that has continued to increase since then.

Table 8.1 Trade patterns and economic policy concerns

	Theory	*Political economy*
1950s	Traditional trade theory: Integration = specialization = *inter*-industry trade	The Common Market might lead to excessive specialization of member countries
1960s		Rise in intra-European trade, but no increased specialization: existence of *intra*-industry trade
1970s/1980s	'New international economics' based on imperfect competition (internal scale economies and gains in variety)	
Mid-1980s	Synthesis by Helpman and Krugman: • Between different countries: inter-industry trade • Between similar countries: intra-industry trade in similar; that is, horizontally differentiated goods	European Commission White Paper for a Single European Market, with an optimistic scenario: Integration = intra-industry trade = gains in variety and limited adjustment costs
Still 1980s	• Products can differ by quality (because of, for example, capital intensity, R&D, qualifications of labour force) • Differences between countries favour not only inter-industry trade, but also IIT in vertically differentiated goods • Specialization along quality spectrum matters	Instead of favouring a catch-up of less developed member states, European integration might lead to a potential income divergence among countries.
1990s	Inter-industry trade is not only based on macroeconomic differences between countries. The 'new economic geography' suggests that asymmetry between countries might be increased through external scale economies and agglomeration effects	One market and one money might be incompatible: successful liberalization according to Single Market criteria might impede a successful monetary union.

'New trade theory' models developed towards the end of the 1970s and in the early 1980s challenged the traditional theories and provided a simple explanation for the observed intra-industry trade patterns in Europe. They emphasized the gains to trade associated with intra-industry trade in horizontally differentiated products based on imperfect competition, consumer preferences and other features of industrial organization. Such trade patterns are based on the similarity of nations; they lead to increased efficiency through the achievement of scale economies, and to welfare gains thanks to a larger choice of varieties for consumers. Accordingly, consumers' demand for varieties of (horizontally) differentiated goods produced under increasing returns is satisfied by the specialization of producers. But since firms in each country follow this pattern, there is no increased specialization of countries. If the diversity in production declines (firm exits), the variety offered to consumers on a larger market increases, thus bringing new gains to trade and reinforcing the competition. Krugman (1980) provides a stylized framework associating the costs of inter-industry trade and the gains of IIT: similar-enough countries or differentiated-enough products authorize the traditional Stolper–Samuelson effect to be compensated for by gains in variety for the scarce factor. Then Helpman and Krugman (1985) provided a synthesis that quickly became the key reference in the literature: it associates similarity between countries with intra-industry trade, and comparative advantage with inter-industry trade.

A key issue associated with this synthesis between the traditional view (incomplete specialization of nations) and the new perspective (complete specialization of firms) is the potential (social) cost of displacing resources between alternative uses: gains are not *net* gains, since factors being industry-specific in the short run must be displaced. Invested capital and qualifications become obsolete because of incomplete portability of factors and assets across industries. In this case, moving from one industry to another as a result of inter-industry adjustment is costly: workers have to be retrained, since their human capital is depreciated.[1] In the case of IIT, in contrast, human capital is portable across firms even if some firms exit the market: adjustment costs in that case are supposed to be much smaller than for *inter*-industry trade that has distribution effects for factor rewards. These costs are limited to specific assets of firms that have dropped out of the market, in the case of exits.

During the early 1980s, the European Commission made the *diagnosis of 'Non Europe'*. Despite decades of European integration, differences in prices, non-tariff barriers, exclusive public procurement procedures, public monopolies and underachieved economies of scale remained

(European Commission, 1988). In response, the 1985 White Paper entitled *Completion of the Internal Market* (European Commission, 1985) suggested the cancelling of border formalities and remaining non-tariff barriers, the opening public markets, and, more generally, the implementation of the principles of free movement of goods and factors within the integrated area. The European Commission, comforted by past experiences and the new view of imperfect competition in international trade, hoped that the rather optimistic scenario of a relatively painless integration in Europe would work again in the case of the Single Market, even if some studies (such as the European Commission, 1990) expected that not all sectors or member states would be affected in the same way.[2]

However, the new (synthetic) view of international trade popularized in the mid-1980s missed an important issue: products are not only differentiated horizontally but also vertically. Accordingly, determinants and consequences of intra-industry trade in horizontally differentiated products are different from those in vertical differentiation. In the former case, products sold at the same price are perfect substitutes, while in the second a common ranking of consumer preferences can be associated with differences in quality, based on factor endowments (Falvey, 1981; Falvey and Kierzkowski, 1987), on fixed costs in R&D (Gabszewicz et al., 1981) or on the qualification of the labour force (Gabszewicz and Turrini, 1997). Hence associating inter-industry trade with painful adjustments and intra-industry trade with less costly adjustments might be challenged by the development of IIT in vertically differentiated products. As far as the specificity of qualifications is concerned, specializing in top-quality varieties will be associated with adjustment costs if the qualification of labour employed intensively to produce in low-quality varieties is specific. Indeed, the portability of qualifications might be limited, even within sectors, across the quality range of products. More generally, the adjustment costs associated with IIT in vertical differentiation (exchange of qualities) might be sizeable, as it may not be equivalent to specialize in high- or low-quality products in the same industry. Specializing along the quality spectrum, as a result of R&D expenses, endowments in human capital, or simply advertising, might be associated with a costly displacement of resources.

Incidentally, *inter*-industry trade is not based exclusively on comparative advantages: external economies and agglomeration effects, spillover effects, or more generally the country size (and differences in size) do matter. Inter-industry trade is no longer associated with perfect competition and constant returns to scale.

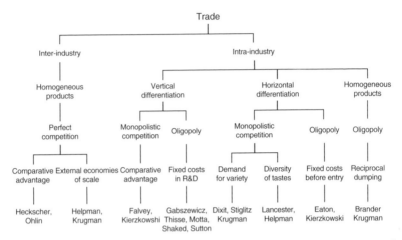

Figure 8.1   Market structure, differentiation of products and the determinants of trade

Finally, intra-industry trade can be determined by market structures only, independently from any diversification of products. The latter explanation, to be referred to as the reciprocal dumping model of IIT (Brander and Krugman, 1983), increasingly is receiving empirical support (Feenstra *et al.*, 1998; Fung and Lau, 1998).

In total, a wide spectrum of determinants of trade patterns is to be considered, going far beyond the popular perception of the new international trade theory (see Figure 8.1).

Measuring trade types

This chapter does not rely on the traditional Grubel–Lloyd (GL) indicator. It uses a complementary method that allows the whole of a given flow to be classified in one and the same *trade type*. This strategy contrasts with the assimilation of IIT to balanced trade. In addition, differences in unit values have to be interpreted; we shall assume that these represent differences in quality.

Early studies on intra-industry trade overestimated strongly the extent of intra-industry trade, as an insufficient country and/or product disaggregation led to the well-known sectoral[3] or geographic[4] aggregation biases. While these biases may arise with any indicator of IIT, the widely used Grubel–Lloyd indicator (based on the degree of overlap in trade) may set an additional problem of interpretation for studies focusing on changes rather on levels. This is why a different method will be suggested here.

The GL index relies on the decomposition of total trade in trade overlap (representing intra-industry trade) and the imbalance (inter-industry trade). Accordingly, the (net) flows related to inter-industry trade remain explained by traditional theory, whereas the trade overlap is explained by the 'new international trade theory'. This helps to reconcile what are, a priori, two incompatible paradigms (after Helpman and Krugman, 1985), but raises a problem when used in dynamics: how must an increase in the GL index be interpreted? A long-run study of trade patterns should consider this measurement issue carefully.

There has been growing concern about the consequences of increasing IIT over time: according to the static view referred to here, a move towards IIT would mean painless adjustments, at least as far as the distinction between horizontal and vertical differentiation is ignored. Hamilton and Kniest (1991), however, noticed that this was not necessarily the case. What matters is the intra-industry nature of marginal trade (Greenaway *et al.*, 1994). Accordingly, an inter-industry adjustment can lead to an increasing Grubel–Lloyd index. In total, increasing values of the GL index would hardly be interpreted systematically as carrying painless adjustments.

This difficulty with the traditional GL simply results from a definition of IIT based on the trade overlap.[5] Azhar *et al.* (1998), and Lovely and Nelson (1999), tackle this issue in partial and general equilibrium, respectively. Intra-industry trade may induce inter-industry adjustment and carry changes in factor prices; however, measures of marginal intra-industry trade are poor predictors of such adjustment. The intuition is very simple: when opening the economy, the number of varieties falls in each country. Marginal trade is of an intra-industry nature, but since the number of varieties shrinks in each country at the same pace, resources leave the manufacturing sector and the adjustment is of an inter-industry nature.

The second issue is associated with the interpretation of differences in unit values. How to interpret such differences remains to a large extent an open question. The idea of defining a product as a 'bundle of attributes' has found its empirical counterpart in so-called 'hedonic prices'. These implicit prices of attributes are derived through econometric estimates which relate observed prices of goods to specific amounts of characteristics associated with them: a product with a higher amount of a specific attribute (quality) usually sells at a higher price. However, several factors can undermine the positive link between quality and price. While high-priced goods need to have a minimum (objective or subjective) quality to be sold on the market (non-price competitiveness), low-priced goods are not necessarily of low quality, because of lower production costs (price-competitiveness) or firms' strategies (mark-up). Prices of goods are also influenced by factors such as market structure, firm strategies, income distribution, consumer tastes and behaviour, and consumers' perception of quality. In addition, prices of imported goods are influenced by factors such as exchange rate movements and trade restrictions. A final difficulty arises because unit values are imperfect proxies for prices.

Notwithstanding such unresolved issues, unit values are used increasingly in the literature as a proxy for quality, noticeably because there is no alternative to systematic empirical analysis covering all industries and all products. Elaborating along this interpretation, goods differing by quality can be sold at different prices; they can be considered as the outputs of distinctive production functions. Factors that play a key role in vertical product differentiation and have a positive influence on the quality of goods include: more capital (Falvey, 1981; Falvey and Kierzkowski, 1987); more R&D (Gabszewicz *et al.*, 1981); a highly qualified labour force (Gabszewicz and Turrini, 1997); and a specific work organization of firms.

Departing from Grubel/Lloyd-related methodologies, but also from indicators of marginal IIT, our analysis of intra-EC trade is based on a methodology initiated by Abd-El-Rahman (1986) and refined by Fontagné and Freudenberg (1997), that has four characteristics. First, it considers, depending on the degree in overlap, both exports and imports as being as being part of either two-way trade or one-way trade. This allows a breaking of the link between the two notions of IIT and trade balance at stake. Second, the method minimizes the bias of geographic aggregation by considering only bilateral flows. Third, it minimizes the bias arising from sectoral aggregation by using far more disaggregated classifications. Finally, the method distinguishes between vertical and horizontal differentiation by incorporating price (unit value) differences.

The analysis of trade patterns is conducted on a strict bilateral basis and at the most detailed level for which statistics are available: data published by Eurostat in the classification of the 8-digit Combined Nomenclature (CN) (and, until 1987, the 6-digit Nimexe) concerns some 10 000 product items.

Trade at the elementary level will be either inter-industry or intra-industry; when the value of the minority flow (for example, imports) represents at least 10 per cent of the majority flow (exports, in that case), both the flows are considered to be part of 'two-way trade'. Otherwise, both flows would be considered as part of 'one-way trade'.

Since products may differ in quality, even at the most detailed level of disaggregation, it is assumed that differences in prices (unit values) at the 8-digit level reflect quality differences. Products whose unit values are close are considered to be differentiated horizontally. The criterion is necessarily arbitrary: if the export and import unit values differ by more than 15 per cent, products are considered to be differentiated vertically.

This method allows elementary trade flows to be broken down into different categories according to the similarity in unit values and to the overlap in trade:

- One-way trade (no or insignificant overlap between exports and imports);
- Two-way trade in similar, horizontally differentiated, products (significant overlap and limited differences unit value);
- Two-way trade in vertically differentiated products (overlap and large differences in unit value).

This approach permits the totality of trade to be broken down according to these criteria, each elementary trade flow being associated with a unique trade type. Notice that each trade type can be presented both in value or, alternatively, in share of total trade.

This method is therefore complementary to the one developed by Greenaway, Hine and Milner (1994, 1995), but addresses directly the shares of trade types, whereas Greenaway, Hine and Milner consider a mix of trade shares and trade types notwithstanding their use of the Grubel and Lloyd reference.

Empirical evidence of EU trade patterns

Using such methodology authorizes drawing an original picture of the long-term trends in IIT within the EU, and *vis-à-vis* third countries. IIT is particularly important for Europe, especially in intra-EU trade; it expands continuously, but quite exclusively, because of a development of two-way trade in vertically differentiated products.

Table 8.2 shows the relative importance of the three trade types among the fifteen EU members in 1999.[6] Half of the trade between the EU members and the world (that is, both intra- and extra-EU partners) is one-way – that is, it takes the form of either exports or imports with no significant flows in the other direction. The trade type second in importance, with about a third of total trade, is two-way trade in vertically differentiated goods which can be interpreted as an exchange of different qualities. Finally, two-way trade in horizontal differentiation has a relatively small share, with less than 15 per cent. In total, two-way trade in vertically differentiated goods is about twice as important as two-way trade in horizontal differentiation.

A more detailed examination, in cross-section, yields two major results. First, the share of two-way trade in total trade is much more important in intra-EU trade than in trade with non-members, and this is true for each individual member country. Thus, while two-way trade represents about 60 per cent of intra-EU trade, it accounts for about 30 per cent of trade with extra-EU partners. Second, there are striking differences among member states concerning the relative importance of the three trade types. For example in *intra*-EU trade, two-way trade is most pronounced for France, Germany, Belgium-Luxembourg, and the UK. In contrast, trade is mainly one-way for small periphery countries, especially for Greece, Finland and Portugal.

Of course, a threshold other than 15 per cent for unit value differences would have given a different relative importance of vertical versus horizontal differentiation. Nevertheless, the increase over time of the share of IIT in vertically differentiated products reveals a process of specialization that operates at a very detailed level, by quality ranges, inside products.

Since there are no data for a sufficiently long time period for all EU-15 members, an analysis of the dynamics of trade patterns must focus on trade patterns among EU-12 countries. Figure 8.2 indicates the evolution of the share of the three trade types in intra-EU-12 trade from 1980 to 1999, and, for comparison's sake, the Grubel–Lloyd indicator. The considered time period was characterized by an increase in intra-industry trade: the Grubel–Lloyd indicator was around 33 per cent in the beginning of the 1980s, and fairly regularly gained about five points until the late 1990s.[7]

One-way trade, with a share of some 45 per cent, the most important trade type at the beginning of the 1980s, experienced a decline from the mid-1980s onwards. In that sense, one-way trade and the Grubel–Lloyd indicator are the opposite sides of the same coin. However, and in contrast to what is often assumed implicitly, including *ex ante* studies on the impact of the Single Market, the rise in intra-industry trade in intra-EU-12 trade concerns vertically differentiated products and not those that are horizontally differentiated. In fact, two-way trade in

Table 8.2 Share of trade types in EU-15 trade, 1999 (%)

	Intra-EU			Extra-EU			World		
	Horizontal two-way trade	Vertical two-way trade	One-way trade	Horizontal two-way trade	Vertical two-way trade	One-way trade	Horizontal two-way trade	Vertical two-way trade	One-way trade
France	23.1	47.2	29.7	10.3	29.1	60.6	18.5	40.7	40.8
Germany	18.8	49.9	31.3	5.7	33.2	61.1	13.1	42.6	44.3
Belgium-Luxembourg	24.8	41.2	34.0	10.9	17.9	71.2	20.9	34.7	44.3
United Kingdom	13.6	52.3	34.1	4.8	31.0	64.2	9.8	43.0	47.2
Austria	15.0	42.2	42.8	8.3	25.1	66.5	12.8	36.6	50.7
Netherlands	16.2	43.1	40.6	3.0	16.0	80.9	11.9	34.2	53.9
Spain	20.8	35.2	44.0	2.1	11.6	86.4	15.3	28.2	56.6
Italy	14.8	39.8	45.4	2.8	20.1	77.1	9.8	31.6	58.6
Sweden	7.2	38.1	54.6	4.2	23.4	72.4	6.1	32.5	61.5
Denmark	9.1	35.4	55.5	4.7	16.8	78.6	7.7	29.4	62.9
Ireland	5.6	35.1	59.3	5.9	23.3	70.8	5.7	30.7	63.6
Portugal	11.5	27.3	61.1	1.1	3.8	95.1	9.4	22.5	68.1
Finland	5.5	25.6	68.8	2.3	12.5	85.3	4.2	20.3	75.5
Greece	2.9	11.4	85.7	1.1	6.1	92.8	2.2	9.4	88.4
EU-15	17.2	43.8	39.0	5.7	25.5	68.8	12.9	36.8	50.3

Note: Countries are ranked by the relative importance of one-way trade with the world.
Source: Eurostat comext trade data base, authors' calculations.

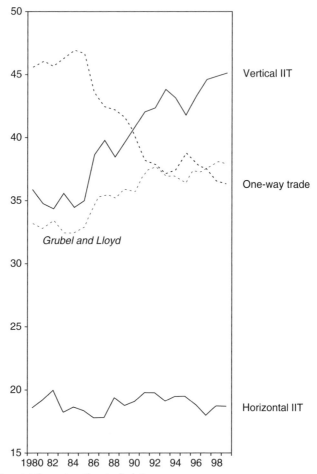

Source: Eurostat Comext, authors' calculations.

Figure 8.2   Trade types in intra-EU-12 trade, 1980–99 (%)

similar products remains rather stable and represents less than 20 per cent of all intra-EU trade, whereas two-way trade in vertically differentiated products increased from less than 35 per cent in 1980–5 to about 45 per cent in 1999. However, this phenomenon, the pre-eminent feature of intra-European trade, has until recently received little attention in the theoretical literature when compared to intra-industry trade in horizontal differentiation.

The evolution of trade patterns by country is an important concern in view of the potential divergence across countries caused by increasing specialization. Between 1980 and 1999, the share of one-way trade in total intra-EU trade has fallen for virtually all countries (see Figure 8.3). Thus, contrasting with often-expressed fears, this evidence does not support a possible scenario of concentration of industries in a limited number of countries. At least at this level of aggregation, it appears that theoretically possible agglomeration effects, detrimental to European cohesion, are not observed empirically.

While the relative importance of trade types differed substantially in the early 1980s between European 'core' and 'periphery' countries, the observed dynamics of trade patterns is quasi-general: European integration has been accompanied by an increase in intra-industry trade, with the exception of Greece (stability) and Ireland (slight decline). For most countries, the corresponding rise in IIT is related almost exclusively to the vertical product differentiation.

The rise in IIT is most pronounced for Spain and Portugal, who seem to have integrated successfully in intra-EU trade, away from a residual specialization on activities abandoned by more advanced countries, thereby contrasting strongly with Greece's situation. For Portugal, and even more so for Spain, foreign direct investment may have accelerated the convergence towards the trade structure observed in more advanced countries. At the same time, structural funds engaged by the EU may have smoothed the transition period for these countries.

Trade patterns have a clear bilateral dimension according to the new trade theory: similarities in GDP, in GDP per capita, and the average size of the market increase the share of IIT in bilateral trade. Accordingly, in 1999, the share of two-way trade (see Figure 8.4) is most important in bilateral trade between Germany, France, the UK, and Belgium-Luxembourg. In contrast, some bilateral trade relations (of little importance when measured in the value of the transaction) are almost exclusively one-way; this is the case, for example, in trade between Ireland and Greece, or Ireland and Portugal. In short, trade between peripheral countries is characterized by one-way trade, and trade among core countries by two-way trade. And when peripheral countries engage in two-way trade, it is primarily in vertical differentiation with the core.

Determinants of trade types

The latter remarks lead us to address the determinants of the three trade types: to what extent inter-industry trade and IIT in vertically

144

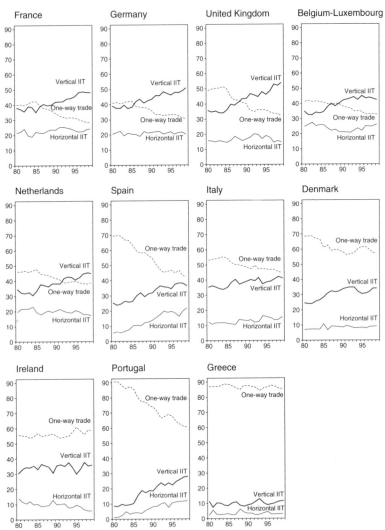

Note: Countries art ranked in decreasing order by the relative importance of one-way trade

Source: Eurostat-Comext, authors' calculations.

Figure 8.3 Evolution of trade types in intra-EU-12 trade by country, 1980–99 (%)

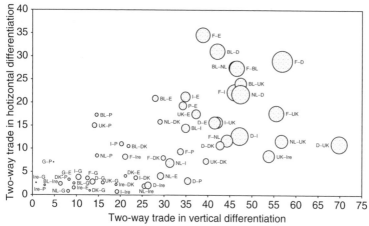

Notes: The area of the bubbles represents the relative inportance of total bilateral trade in totalintra-EU trade.
source: Eurostat by the Comext, authors' calculations.

Figure 8.4   Trade types in bilateral intra-EU-12 trade, 1999

differentiated products share common determinants, as opposed to IIT in horizontally differentiated products, is a key issue. We consider here a panel of bilateral trade flows between EU-12 members for fourteen industries, from 1980 to 1994. Fixed effects on periods and industries are introduced. The latter control for the unobserved characteristics of industries. The dependent variable is the share of each trade type in total industry, by country/partner/industry/year. Results in Table 8.3 confirm the arguments developed here. The average economic size of the trading partners has a positive influence on the share of two-way trade of both types. A larger, integrated market is associated with more varieties and/ or qualities to be traded. The difference in economic size hinders IIT in varieties, a classical outcome under monopolistic competition. Two-way trade seems to be a 'superior' trade type, since its share increases with income per capita. Importantly, the difference in per capita income (a proxy for the intensity of bilateral comparative advantages) promotes one-way trade *and* two-way trade in vertically differentiated products. Conversely, the share of IIT decreases for less similar countries. Finally, the exchange rate volatility reduces intra-industry trade, a result that needs to be discussed in more detail.

Table 8.3   Determinants of the share of trade types in bilateral trade between EU-12 member countries, panel of 14 industries and 11 countries, 1980–94

	Two-way trade in horizontal differentiation	*Two-way trade in vertical differentiation*	*One-way trade*
Average economic size	1.697	0.884	−0.228
	(58.847)	(43.903)	(−50.938)
Difference in economic size	−1.109	0.178	0.515
	(−13.666)	(3.139)	(40.983)
Per capita income	3.515	3.119	−0.364
	(40.684)	(51.682)	(−27.217)
Difference in per capita income	−0.253	0.057	0.089
	(−12.784)	(4.138)	(28.876)
Exchange rate volatility	−5.704	−2.718	0.941
	(−13.945)	(−9.514)	(14.848)
Intercept	9.481	2.586	1.521
	(4.843)	(1.891)	(5.014)
Number of observations	22836	22836	22836
Adjusted R^2	0.465	0.432	0.444
F-statistic	602.4	527.9	553.8
Probability	0.0001	0.0001	0.0001

Notes: t-statistics in parentheses. Fixed time and group (industries) effects not reported
Definition of variables:
Trade types in percentages of trade values (industry, declaring country, partner, time).
Average economic size: average GDP of the two trading partners.
Difference in economic size: normalized difference in GDPs.

$$GDPD_{kk'} = 1 + \frac{[w \ln w + (1 - w) \ln (1 - w)]}{\ln 2}$$

where $w \equiv \dfrac{GDP_k}{GDP_k + GDP_{k'}}$

Income per capita: average per capita income of the two trading partners.
Intensity of comparative advantage: differences in per capita income.

Exchange rate volatility: $EXVAR2_{kk't} = 100\dfrac{\max (e_{kk'}^{t}, \ e_{kk'}^{t-1})}{\min (e_{kk'}^{t}, \ e_{kk'}^{t-1})}$.

The deep integration of European economies has not implied, so far, increased inter-industry specialization. However, the possibility that reduced transaction costs lead to agglomeration economies should not be excluded. Accordingly, inter-industry trade would increase, in the same manner as in the USA, where states and regions exhibit a high degree of industrial specialization (Krugman, 1993). This is important with respect to Monetary Union in Europe: if the single market pushes towards intra-industry trade, 'one market' is complementary to 'one money', as structural asymmetries between member states are reduced. In contrast, if it pushes towards an inter-industry specialization, asymmetries between countries may increase, and sectoral shocks may have different macroeconomic consequences for individual member states; in this case, the coexistence of the single market and a single currency might lead to tensions in Europe.

As far as a macroeconomic perspective is used, structural asymmetries among EU countries are large enough to authorize identifying core and peripheral countries (Bayoumi and Eichengreen, 1993). The corresponding debate about a 'two-speed Europe' has then shifted to the examination of arguments related to the endogeneity of asymmetries. Boone (1997) identifies that structural asymmetries are not so structural: they decrease rapidly over time. Frankel and Rose (1998) argue that fostering integration in Europe will lead to more symmetrical shocks, along the increasing diversification of economies and the rise in IIT.

This replicates the informal argument lagging behind the Euro-optimism of the Commission, as illustrated by the so-called 'Mechanism 13' of the Emerson Report (Emerson *et al.*, 1990): the general idea was that the combination of Single Market effects and Monetary Union effects would lead to a reduction of asymmetries between individual member countries. Comparative advantages having lost their significance as determinants of trade patterns, sector-specific shocks would thus affect a large number of member countries in similar ways. It deserves further comment stressing that, as Kenen (1969) highlighted in a seminal contribution, diversified economies, that is countries having a large share of *intra*-industry trade in their total trade will experience more symmetric shocks. Results in Table 8.3 confirm, in contradiction to what is generally assumed on the basis of the reduction in transaction costs only, that the European Monetary Union is likely to foster intra-industry trade in Europe, thus leading to more symmetric shocks between member states.[8] The Monetary Union could create the conditions of its success endogenously, since inter-industry trade and the corresponding specialization are expected to shrinking, to the benefit of both types of IIT.

Why quality matters

The question regarding in which market segments (in terms of price–quality) different member states are positioned matters, as this has consequences in terms of adjustment costs, income distribution, or catching-up. In addition to the problem of imperfect portability of qualifications referred to above, specialization in high-quality goods allows the extraction of important rents: demand for high-quality goods is characterized generally by high income elasticity and low price elasticity.

Advanced countries are expected to specialize in high quality, and less advanced countries in low quality goods. However, while advanced countries need constantly to improve the technological content or the quality of goods, there is also a possibility that less advanced countries will engage in a catch-up or leapfrogging process through technology spillovers,[9] or in terms of quality upgrading (Herguera and Lutz, 1997).

In order to characterize the corresponding specialization of EU countries, let us continue to assume that differences in unit values reflect quality differences.[10] As exports and imports are analyzed separately, flows for the same product with a given trade partner can exist in different European price–quality ranges (Freudenberg and Müller, 1992): up-market products (with unit values exceeding the intra-EU average by at least 15 per cent), down-market products (more than 15 per cent below the norm), as well as medium-market products (the remainder).[11]

While the structure of imports by price–quality range is quite close among EU countries (suggesting harmonized consumption patterns in Europe), some striking differences across countries can be detected with respect to the structure of exports (see Table 8.4). Up-market goods represent more than half of total exports for Ireland, Germany, Sweden, Denmark and the UK. If the results for most of these countries seem compatible with their image of exporters of expensive but high-quality goods, the presence of foreign affiliates of multinational firms certainly plays a major role in Ireland's situation (Ruane and Görg, 1997). Possible transfer pricing between headquarters and affiliates in this country with a favourable fiscal system cannot be excluded a priori. At the other extreme are the Southern countries that joined the European Community in the 1980s: Greece, Spain and Portugal export in the main down-market and medium-market goods.

As an indictor of revealed comparative advantage, we use the 'contribution to the trade balance' (Lafay, 1987), which tries to eliminate business cycle variations by comparing an industry's trade balance to the overall trade balance.[12] Ireland, Germany, Sweden, Denmark and France specialize strongly in up-market goods, whereas countries such as Spain, Greece, Portugal and Italy specialize in down-market goods (see Table 8.4). Italy's presence in the latter group may come as a surprise, but analysis at a more detailed level points up that Italy specializes strongly in up-market goods in some of its key industries such as textiles, wearing apparel, and wood and paper products.

These results suggest a qualitative division of labour among the countries, and often, a structural surplus in one price–quality range coexists with a deficit in another within the same industry. Also, for example,

Table 8.4 EU-15 members trade by price-quality range, 1999

	Imports (% of total)			Exports (% of total)			Contribution to the trade balance (%)		
	Low	Medium	High	Low	Medium	High	Low	Medium	High
Ireland	20.2	27.3	52.5	16.7	12.1	71.2	-17.2	-73.4	90.6
Germany	23.9	36.9	39.2	14.1	32.1	53.8	-48.6	-23.9	72.5
Sweden	21.2	31.8	47.0	15.3	29.4	55.3	-29.3	-11.5	40.8
Denmark	23.4	32.6	44.0	18.7	29.6	51.7	-23.3	-15.2	38.6
France	24.0	38.4	37.6	19.9	35.0	45.1	-20.5	-16.9	37.4
Netherlands	25.3	36.8	37.9	17.4	38.5	44.1	-39.5	8.5	31.1
UK	23.3	29.7	47.0	17.3	32.4	50.3	-29.6	13.1	16.4
Austria	19.0	33.8	47.3	20.5	30.3	49.2	7.4	-17.1	9.7
Belgium-Luxembourg	20.7	42.3	37.0	19.1	42.2	38.7	-7.9	-0.5	8.3
Italy	21.4	38.5	40.0	28.7	30.6	40.7	36.5	-39.7	3.3
Finland	21.6	31.6	46.8	14.6	38.3	47.1	-34.3	33.0	1.2
Spain	28.1	40.0	31.9	33.2	40.5	26.3	24.9	2.3	-27.2
Portugal	25.3	37.6	37.0	27.1	42.5	30.4	8.4	22.6	-30.9
Greece	33.9	29.1	36.9	40.8	36.1	23.2	26.7	27.2	-53.9

Note: Countries are ranked by the decreasing importance of the contribution to the trade balance for up-market goods (see note 12).
Source: Eurostat-Comext and CEPII-CHELEM, authors' calculations.

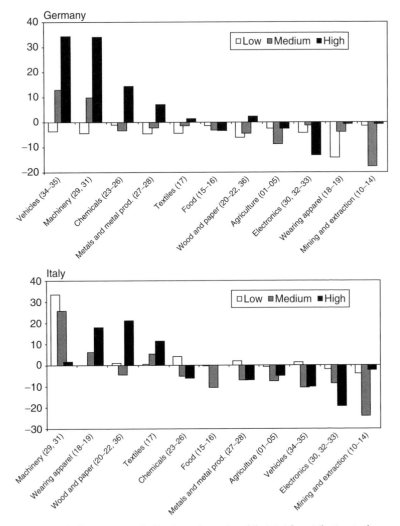

Notes: In ‰ Industries are ranked in decreasing order of their total contribution to the bilateral trade balance. (See note 12.)
Source: Eurostat-Comext and CEPII-CHELEM, authors' calculations.

Figure 8.5 Germany's and Italy's strengths and weaknesses by price–quality range in bilateral trade, 1999

the major European exporters of machinery – Germany and Italy – seem to have found a division of labour: Italy specializes in down-market and medium-market goods, and Germany in up-market goods within the same industry (see Figure 8.5).

Turning to trade with third countries, analysis reveals that the EU as a whole clearly specializes in up-market goods. Figure 8.6 shows the contribution of the different industries to EU-15's trade balance. Europe's major strengths are machinery, vehicles and chemicals, and its major weaknesses are in mining and extraction, electronics, agriculture and wearing apparel. But, more interestingly, Europe has a structural surplus in up-market goods, not only in its key industries, but also in industries that are disadvantaged globally, such as wearing apparel. In total, the EU is often advantaged for one price–quality segment (often up-market goods) and disadvantaged for other segments within that same product group, suggesting a 'reversal of comparative advantages by price ranges'.[13]

To conclude this section, an analysis of bilateral trade between EU-15 and China points out interesting trade patterns (see Figure 8.7). EU's trade with China, which is almost exclusively of a one-way nature,

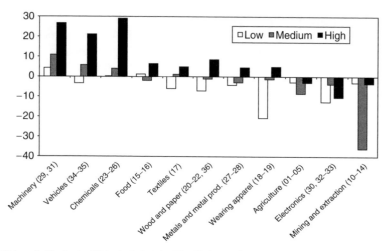

Notes: In % of extra-EU trade. Industries (classified according to the Nace Rev 1) are ranked in decreasing order of their total contribution to the trade balance.
Source: Eurostat-Comext and CEPII-CHELEM, authors' calculations.

Figure 8.6 Contribution to EU-15's trade balance, by industry and price–quality range, 1999

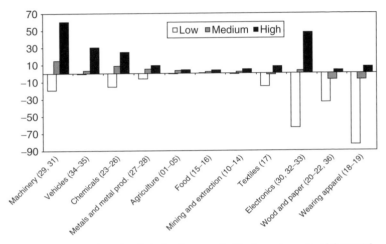

Notes: In % of total bilateral trade. Industries are ranked in decreasing order of their total contribution to the bilateral trade balance. (See note 12.)
Source: Eurostat-Comext and CEPII-CHELEM, authors' calculations.

Figure 8.7 EU-15's strengths and weaknesses by price–quality range in bilateral trade with China and Hong Kong, 1999

shows a substantially different pattern once price–quality ranges are taken into account. The EU is advantaged in up-market goods in a range of industries, and disadvantaged in down-market goods (especially in wearing apparel, wood and paper, and electronics).

Conclusion

The analysis presented here shows that European integration has proceeded in a manner that is both original and quite unexpected. The first years of the functioning of the Single Market have neither 'validated' the optimistic scenario of the European Commission, where integration should translate into IIT in horizontal differentiation (gains in variety, limited adjustment costs), nor the more pessimistic scenario of inter-industrial specialization caused by agglomeration economies. In the latter case, integration would have translated into stronger asymmetries among member states.

Accordingly, the *ex post* appraisal of the completion of the internal market draws a balanced picture (CEPII, 1997; Fontagné *et al.*, 1998). As expected from *ex ante* studies, one-way trade has declined strongly in Europe: this evidence does not support a possible scenario of concentration of industries in a limited number of countries. However, contrasting with the conclusions of *ex ante* studies, the share of intra-industry trade of varieties has remained remarkably stable over time, whereas the share of intra-industry trade of qualities has increased rapidly, and is now the most important trade type in intra-European trade. The corresponding rise in IIT is most pronounced for Spain and Portugal, who seem to have integrated successfully in intra-EU trade, away from a residual specialization in activities abandoned by more advanced countries. In total, gains to trade are not only the result of a larger choice of varieties, but also because there is a larger choice among different qualities. A new form of specialization, more difficult to assess empirically but with important consequences, is emerging. There is increased specialization, but within industries: the quality of goods and the positioning on the quality ladder are now playing a crucial role. R&D efforts, technological progress or the qualification of the labour force are determinants of this qualitative division of labour.

Indeed, it is not neutral for countries to specialize in up-market or down-market goods. Quality matters, and there seems to be a 'qualitatively division of labour' in Europe. There is evidence that countries globally are specialized differently along the quality spectrum, roughly corresponding to a dividing line between the 'North' (up-market goods) and the 'South' (medium- and down-market goods) of Europe. At the industry level, a structural surplus in one quality segment often coexists with a deficit in another within a same industry.

The future enlargement of the EU raises similar issues: IIT increasingly is becoming important in trade with Central (less so with Eastern) European countries, but which remain disadvantaged globally in up-market goods in their trade with EU countries, and advantaged in down-market and medium-market goods (Freudenberg and Lemoine, 1999). However, some Central European countries have revealed comparative advantages in up-market goods in some of their leading industries. At this stage, the evidence does not support the scenario of the integration into the EU of a first wave of countries based on a 'residual' specialization in down-market products.

Notes

1 Labour economists have addressed this issue extensively (Neal, 1995, is a good example).
2 For a certain number of so-called 'sensitive' sectors with important NTBs in the 'pre-completion' situation, conversion costs, implying factor mobility, possibly

sunk costs and cohesion costs could not be excluded. In addition, the sectoral adjustment occurring in the less developed member states was not clear. One possible scenario was an increased specialization along comparative advantages giving rise in inter-industry trade, whereas a convergence in production and demand structures might increase intra-industry trade. Trade would thereby contribute to reducing the asymmetries in production and trade structures among member states.

3   The sectoral bias stems from an insufficient disaggregation in the trade classifications: the lesser the detail of the classification used, that is, the more products that are lumped together into a single industry, the more trade becomes of an intra-industry nature. A specific problem arises when an exchange of intermediate goods (for example, motors) for final goods (for example, cars) belonging to the same industry is considered as 'intra-industry' trade. Simultaneous exports and imports within an industry, but at different production stages, should not be considered as intra-industry trade, but as a fragmentation of the production processes.

4   Similarly, geographic bias arises from an insufficient disaggregation of partner countries, and in the extreme case, only a country's trade relations with 'the rest of the world' are examined. However, the sign of the trade balance for a particular product may change from one partner to another, corresponding to the accumulation of various inter-industry flows for the same item of the product classification. Such 'multilateral' intra-industry trade is a pure artefact and is perfectly compatible with traditional theories (see, for example, Deardorff, 1979; and Lassudrie-Duchêne and Mucchielli, 1979) for the concept of the 'chain of comparative advantages').

5   Brülhart (1994) and Greenaway Hine, Milner and Elliott (1994) explore the same issue.

6   Concerning extra-EU partners, EU trade statistics are available for some 250 partners, some of which were aggregated, leading in total to some fifty non-EU partners. The calculations being done bilaterally for these partners, the share of two-way trade with the aggregates, and thus with the 'world', is overestimated.

7   The level of the Grubel and Lloyd indicator may seem low when compared to other studies, but this is, of course, because of the strong disaggregation of trade flows.

8   Fontagné and Freudenberg (1999) reach the same conclusion using a different methodology.

9   See Soete (1985); Brezis *et al.* (1993); Coe and Helpman (1995); or Coe *et al.* (1996).

10   It is important to mention that, despite their common use of unit values, trade types and price–quality ranges are two distinct and strictly independent notions. For example, two-way trade in *similar* products can be done in *different* European price segments. Similarly, two-way trade in *vertically differentiated* products can be done in the *same* market segment.

11   Clearly, this approach differs from Aiginger (1997) and Erkel-Rousse and Le Gallo (1998) who use relative unit values to discriminate between price and quality competition. In our approach, we are not interested if a country has higher relative unit values (compared to another country, or exports com-

pared to imports), but whether a country exports (imports) more of the high (medium, low) quality product.

12 It examines whether an industry performs relatively better or worse than the manufacturing total, no matter whether the manufacturing total itself is in deficit or surplus. This 'contribution' is defined as the difference between the actual and the theoretical balance:

$$\underbrace{\left(X_j - M_j\right)}_{\text{observed industry trade balance}} \quad - \quad \underbrace{\left(X - M\right)\frac{\left(X_j + M_j\right)}{\left(X + M\right)}}_{\text{theoretical industry trade balance}}$$

The indicator is additive, and individual industries can be grouped together by summing up their respective values.

13 A more detailed examination of the contribution of industries by price–quality ranges separately for the three trade types clearly shows the importance of one-way trade to yield the overall result (Freudenberg, 1998).

References

Abd-El-Rahman, K. S. (1986) 'Réexamen de la définition et de la mesure des échanges croisés de produits similaires entre les nations', *Revue économique*, 1: 89–115.

Aiginger, K. (1997) 'The Use of Unit Values to Discriminate between Price and Quality Competition', *Cambridge Journal of Economics*, 21: 571–92.

Azhar, A. R. Elliott and C. Milner (1998) 'Static and Dynamic Measurement of Intra-Industry Trade and Adjustment: A Geometric Reappraisal', *Weltwirtschaftliches Archiv*, 134(3): 404–22.

Bayoumi, T. and B. Eichengreen (1993) 'Shocking Aspects of European Monetary Unification', in F. Torres and F. Giavazzi (eds), *Adjustment and Growth in the European Monetary Union* (Cambridge University Press), pp. 193–230.

Bergstrand, J. H. (1990) 'The Heckscher–Ohlin–Samuelson Model, the Linder Hypothesis and the Determinants of Bilateral Intra-industry Trade,' *The Economic Journal*, 3: 1216–29.

Boone, L. (1997) 'Symmetry and Asymmetry of Supply and Demand Shocks in the European Union: A Dynamic Analysis', CEPII Working Paper No. 97–03. (http://www.cepii.fr/anglaisgraph/workpap/pdf/1997/wp97_03.pdf)

Brander, J. A. and P. Krugman (1983) 'A Reciprocal Dumping Model of International Trade,' *Journal of International Economics*, 15(3–4): 313–21.

Brezis, E. S., P. R. Krugman and D. Tsiddon (1993) 'Leapfrogging in International Competition: A Theory of Cycles in National Technological Leadership', *American Economic Review*, 83(5): 1211–19.

Brülhart, M. (1994) 'Marginal Intra-industry Trade: Measurement and Relevance for the Pattern of Industrial Adjustment', *Weltwirtschaftliches Archiv*, 130(3): 600–13.

Brülhart, M. and J. R. Elliott (1998) 'Adjustment to the European Single Market: Inferences from Intra-industry Trade Patterns', *Journal of Economic Studies*, 25(3): 225–47.

Brülhart, M. and R. C. Hine (eds) (1998) *Intra-industry Trade and Adjustment: The European Experience* (London: Macmillan).

CEPII (1997) 'Trade Patterns inside the Single Market', *The Single Market Review*, Subseries IV, Vol. 2 (Kogan Page).

Coe, D. and E. Helpman (1995) 'International R&D spillovers', *European Economic Review*, 39(5): 859–87.

Coe, D. and E. Helpman and A. Hoffmaister (1996) 'North–South R&D Spillovers', NBER Working Paper No. 5048.

Deardorff, A. (1979) 'Weak Links in the Chain of Comparative Advantage', *Journal of International Economics*, 9(2): 197–209.

Emerson, M., D. Gros, A. Italianer, J. Pisani-Ferry and H. Reichenbach (1990) *One Market, One Money* (Oxford University Press).

Erkel-Rousse, H. and F. Le Gallo (1998) 'Quality and Price Competition in International Trade: An Empirical Study Based on the Trade Between Twelve OECD Countries', Paper presented at the European Economic Association Congress, Berlin, September.

European Commission (1985) White Paper on Completing the Internal Market, Brussels.

European Commission (1988) ' "The Economics of 1992", An Assessment of the Potential Effects of Completing the Internal Market of the European Community', *European Economy*, 35.

European Commission (1990) 'L'impact sectoriel du marché intérieur sur l'industrie: les enjeux pour les États membres', *Économie Européenne*, special issue.

Evenett, S. J. and W. Keller (1997) 'On Theories Explaining the Success of the Gravity Equation', SSRI Working Papers No. 9722, University of Wisconsin.

Falvey, R. E. (1981) 'Commercial Policy, and Intra-industry Trade', *Journal of International Economics*, 11(4): 495–511.

Falvey, R. E. and H. Kierzkowski (1987) 'Product Quality, Intra-industry Trade and (Im)perfect Competition', in H. Kierzkowski (ed.), *Protection and Competition in International Trade* (Oxford: Basil Blackwell), pp. 143–61.

Feenstra, R. C., J. A. Markusen and A. K. Rose (1998) 'Understanding the Home Market Effect and the Gravity Equation: The Role of Differentiating Goods', NBER Working Paper No. 6804.

Fontagné, L. and M. Freudenberg (1997) 'Intra-industry Trade: Methodological Issues Reconsidered', CEPII Working Paper No. 97–01 (http://www.cepii.fr/anglaisgraph/workpap/pdf/1997/wp97_01.pdf).

Fontagné, L. and M. Freudenberg (1999) 'Endogenous Symmetry of Shocks in a Monetary Union', *Open Economies Review*, 10(3): 263–87.

Fontagné, L., M. Freudenberg and N. Péridy (1997) 'Trade Patterns inside the Single Market', CEPII Working Paper No. 97–07 (http://www.cepii.fr/anglaisgraph/workpap/pdf/1997/wp97_07.pdf)

Fontagné, L., M. Freudenberg and N. Péridy (1998) 'Intra-industry Trade and the Single Market: Quality Matters', CEPR Discussion Paper No. 1959.

Frankel, J. A. and A. K. Rose (1998) 'The Endogeneity of the Optimum Currency Area Criteria', *Economic Journal*, 108(449): 1009–25.

Freudenberg, M. (1998) 'Échanges intra-branche et nature des relations internationales des pays de la Communauté européenne' Ph.D. thesis, University of Paris i (Panthéon-Sorbonne), May.

Freudenberg, M. and F. Lemoine (1999) 'Central and Eastern European Countries in the International Division of Labour in Europe', CEPII Working Paper No. 99–05 (http://www.cepii.fr/anglaisgraph/workpap/pdf/1999/wp99_05a.pdf)

Freudenberg, M. and F. Müller (1992) 'France et Allemagne: quelles spécialisations commerciales?', *Économie prospective internationale*, 52: 7–36.

Fung, K. C. and L. F. Lau (1998) 'A Price-Based Empirical Test of the Reciprocal Dumping Model', Mimeo, University of California.

Gabszewicz J. and A. Turrini (1997) 'Workers' Skills, Product Quality and Industry Equilibrium', CORE Discussion Paper No. 9755.

Gabszewicz, J., A. Shaked, J. Sutton and J. F. Thisse (1981) 'International Trade in Differentiated Products', *International Economic Review*, 22(3): 527–34.

Greenaway, D. and J. Torstensson (1997) 'Back to the Future: Taking Stock on Intra-industry Trade', *Weltwirtschaftliches Archiv*, 133(2): 249–69.

Greenaway, D., R. Hine and C. Milner (1994) 'Country-Specific Factors and the Pattern of Horizontal and Vertical Intra-industry Trade in the UK', *Weltwirtschaftliches Archiv*, 130(1): 77–100.

Greenaway, D., R. Hine and C. Milner (1995) 'Vertical and Horizontal Intra-industry Trade: A Cross Industry Analysis for the United Kingdom,' *The Economic Journal*, 105(433): 1505–18.

Greenaway, D., R. Hine, C. Milner and R. Elliott (1994) 'Adjustment and the Measurement of Marginal Intra-industry Trade', *Weltwirtschaftliches Archiv*, 130: 414–27.

Grubel, H. G. and P. J. Lloyd (1975) *Intra-industry Trade, the Theory and Measurement of International Trade in Differentiated Products* (London: MacMillan).

Hamilton C., P. Kniest (1991), Trade Liberalisation, Structural Adjustment and Intra-industry Trade: A Note, *Weltwirtschaftliches Archiv* 127(2): 356–67

Helpman, E. (1987) 'Imperfect Competition and International Trade: Evidence from Fourteen Industrial Countries', *Journal of the Japanese and International Economies*, 1(1): 62–81.

Helpman, E. and P. Krugman (1985) *Market Structure and Foreign Trade* (Cambridge, Mass.: MIT Press).

Herguera, I. and S. Lutz (1997) 'Trade Policy and Leapfrogging', Universidad Carlos III de Madrid Working Paper No. 97–04, Economics Series 01.

Hummels, D. and J. Levinsohn (1995) 'Monopolistic Competition and International Trade: Reconsidering the Evidence', *The Quarterly Journal of Economics*, 110(3): 799–836.

Kenen, P. J. (1969) 'The Theory of Optimum Currency Areas: An Eclectic View', in R. Mundell and A. K. Swoboda (eds), *Monetary Problems of the International Economy* (University of Chicago Press), pp. 41–60.

Krugman, P. R. (1980) 'Scale Economies, Product Differentiation, and the Pattern of Trade', *American Economic Review*, 70(5): 950–9.

Krugman, P. R. (1981) 'Intraindustry Specialization and the Gains from Trade', *Journal of Political Economy*, 89(5): 959–74.

Krugman, P. R. (1993) 'Lessons of Massachusetts for EMU', in F. Torres and F. Giovezzi (eds), *Adjustment and Growth in the European Monetary Union* (CEPR Cambridge University Press).

Lafay, G. (1987) 'La mesure des avantages comparatifs révélés', *Économie prospective internationale*, 41. Reprinted as 'The Measurement of Revealed Comparative

Advantages', in M. G. Dagenais and P.-A. Muet (eds), *International Trade Modelling* (1994) (London: Chapman & Hall).

Lassudrie-Duchêne, B. and J. L. Mucchielli (1979) 'Les échanges intra-branche et al hiérarchisation des avantages comparés dans le commerce international', *Revue Économique*, 30(3): 442–86.

Lovely, M. E. and D. R. Nelson (1999) 'On the Economic Relationship between Marginal Intra-Industry Trade and Labour Adjustment in a Division of Labour Model', Mimeo, Syracuse University.

Markusen, J. R. (1995) 'The Boundaries of Multinational Enterprises and the Theory of International Trade', *Journal of Economic Perspectives*, 9(2): 169–89.

Markusen, J. R. and A. J. Venables (1995) 'Multinational Firms and the New Trade Theory', NBER Working Paper No. 5036.

Markusen, J. R. and R. M. Wigle (1990) 'Explaining the Volume of North–South Trade', *Economic Journal*, 100(403): 1206–15.

Neal, D. (1995) 'Industry-Specific Human Capital: Evidence from Displaced Workers', *Journal of Labor Economics*, 13(4): 653–77.

Ruane, F. and H. Görg (1997) 'The Impact of Foreign Direct Investment on Sectoral Adjustment in the Irish Economy', *National Institute Economic Review*, 160: 76–86.

Soete, L. (1985) 'International Diffusion of Technology, Industrial Development and Technological Leapfrogging', *World Development*, 13(3) (March): 409–22.

9
Intra-Industry Trade in Services

Hyun-Hoon Lee and P. J. Lloyd

Hitherto, all empirical studies and analyses of intra-industry trade have been confined to trade in goods. The only discussion of intra-industry trade in a service industry, to our knowledge, are those of the transportation services by Kierzkowski (1989) and the international telephone industry by Tang (1999). Yet, for the purpose of analysis of trade flows and their effects on the allocation of resources and the welfare of national residents, there is no reason to separate trade in goods from trade in services. In principle, intra-industry trade should cover both goods and services. In practice, the two trade flows have been separated because the Standard International Trade Classification (SITC) applies only to goods and there has been no readily comparable classification of trade in services.

This chapter seeks to remedy this gap in the study of intra-industry trade by using data compiled recently under an OECD classification of trade in services. We also carry out an empirical analysis of inter-country differences in intra-industry trade in services, and examine the effect that inclusion of trade in services has on the observed levels of intra-industry trade in goods and services combined. The last section comments on some areas for future research in intra-industry trade in services.

The nature of trade in services and intra-industry trade in services

Trade in services received little attention from international trade economists until the conclusion of the General Agreement on Trade in Services (GATS) in the Uruguay Round. GATS made national government measures affecting trade in services subject to multilateral discipline for the first time. Since then there has been more interest in trade in services, chiefly in the measurement of the market access and national treatment that are subject to the discipline of the GATS (see, especially, Hoekman and Braga, 1996; and Findlay and Warren, 2000).

The definition of service trade has always been troublesome. Two definitions are currently in use. The oldest, and the one that is used to provide statistics of service trade, is that from the IMF *Balance of Payments Manual* (IMF, 1993), the fifth edition known as 'BMP5'. The balance of payments statement summarizes transactions that take place between an economy and the rest of the world, for the most part between residents and non-residents. Trade in services records current account transactions that are neither goods transactions nor income payments.

The second definition is that given in the GATS. GATS Article I defined a service as any service that is supplied across national borders by one of four modes. These are the cross-border supply of the service (known as Mode 1 or 'cross-border'); supply to a service consumer who moves to the country of the service supplier (Mode 2 or 'consumption abroad'); supply by a service supplier who moves to the country of the consumer (Mode 3 or 'commercial presence'); and supply through the temporary movement of natural persons (Mode 4 or 'presence of natural persons'). The IMF definition corresponds roughly to Modes 1 and 2 only. In Mode 1, the services are supplied in the same manner as the cross-border supply of goods, and in Mode 2 there is a cross-border sale of services such as those provided to foreign tourists or for international transport.

The supply by the GATS mode of commercial presence defines as international trade supplies that traditionally have been regarded as domestic production in the host country. Hence, many services that were regarded as non-tradeable commodities are now defined as traded; for example, electricity or gas generation and distribution when supplied by a foreign-controlled corporation. The last three modes of supply all involve some movement by the service supplier or the service consumer, with the service being supplied in the location of the consumer. This interaction between the service provider and consumer makes the international supply of such services quite distinct from the international supply of goods.[1]

Both definitions will give rise to intra-industry trade in services. The partitioning of the service sector into service industries is unlikely to differ between the two definitions. Industries are defined by the nature of the service and most use Mode 1 and Mode 3, at least for the delivery of some services within the industry. However, the introduction of new technologies of supply is changing industry boundaries. E-commerce is revolutionizing the supply of services, such as financial services, rapidly.

There is a substantial difference between the magnitude of international trade in services according to the two definitions because of the importance of Mode 3: 'Although services comprise about a fifth of world-wide trade in balance of payments terms, it is estimated that as much again in sales is generated by subsidiaries of firms established in markets abroad, their so-called foreign affiliates' (Commission of the European Union, 1999, p. 8).

It is not clear which of the two definitions should be preferred in principle. Most international trade economists now think in terms of GATS modes. However, this reflects the importance of the agreement for negotiations and for actual market entry rather than the logic of the GATS definition. GATS modes combine quite unlike transactions. Snape (1998) suggested that, in the event of a new multilateral agreement on foreign direct investment, the provisions of GATS relating to delivery by Mode 3 ('commercial presence') and 4 ('presence of natural persons') be removed from the GATS. It is doubtful that supplies by Mode 3 should be classified as international trade. Statistics compiled according to the *Balance of Payments Manual* do not record these transactions. They record the changes in the asset position of the foreign investing and host countries, and that part of the income generated which accrues to foreign factor owners, rather than the outputs of the foreign investors once these come on stream.

In practice, we are compelled to use the balance of payments definition. No statistics of service trade by GATS modes are available. The draft Manual on Statistics of International Trade in Services being prepared jointly by the Commission of the EU, the IMF, OECD, UN and WTO outlines how they might be collected (see Commission of the European Union *et al.*, 1999). In particular, it will be very difficult to collect statistics of services supplied by Mode 4, as no statistics are compiled currently of these transactions, and they lie outside the BMP5 coverage. The international agencies are also considering the collection of statistics by all countries on foreign affiliates sales, which have become known in these circles as Foreign Affiliates Trade Statistics (FATS).

If FATS were available, we could examine intra-industry affiliate 'trade' and relate it to intra-industry goods trade. Greenaway *et al.*, (1999) have done this for the USA, using Bureau of Economic Analysis statistics of US affiliate production abroad and foreign affiliate production in the USA, but these statistics are not available for most OECD countries.

The use of statistics compiled on the basis of the balance of payments definitions has two advantages. First, the services traded are comparable more directly with goods traded as they are supplied by the cross-border Mode 1 and by Mode 2. Second, when we wish to make a correction of the statistics of intra-industry trade for the aggregate trade imbalance, the BMP5 service trade statistics all relate to items that are (or should be) recorded in the current account of the balance of payments accounts.

We do not have a model or models of intra-industry trade in services. The widely different nature of services in terms of modes of delivery and technologies means that there cannot be a single theory of international trade in services. Existing models of intra-industry trade that incorporate FDI might be applicable to services supplied by GATS Mode 3, but these services are excluded from the balance of payments statistics of services. Other existing models of horizontally and vertically differentiated products are not applicable to services supplied by Modes 2, 3 and 4, because the service products are differentiated by location of the supplier and/or consumer.

However, the reason for intra-industry or two-way supply of these services is obvious. In the case of services supplied by Mode 2 (consumption abroad), the nature of the service gives rise automatically to two-way trade. Thus, foreign travel can be supplied to domestic residents only by their travelling to other countries, and vice versa. Therefore, there will always be two-way trade in foreign tourism services. Telecommunications services provided to final consumers is two-way because communications between natural persons living in different countries is two-way. Intra-industry trade is inherent in such services. One can expect a high level of intra-industry trade in the services supplied by these industries.

An important category of services is service inputs into the production and delivery of goods: transportation, insurance, financial services, telecommunications and other business services. These services must be two-way because goods trade is two-way. At first sight, it appears that the model of goods-in-process developed by Dixit and Grossman (1982) might be extended to include service inputs. Unlike goods-in-process, however, these services cannot be fragmented and delivered by the cheapest global supplier as they are either associated with the international movement of goods themselves (transport), or must be provided in the country of exportation or importation. The latter services are closer to the model of 'middle products' of Sanyal and Jones (1982).

And, unlike foreign travel, it is possible that these services in one direction could be supplied by service providers from a third country, such as shipping companies registered in a third country, though service suppliers resident in the country of supply have a natural advantage in some instances.

In the case of telecommunications and international passenger air transport, there is the added complexity of a network of suppliers. International telecommunications operators require a domestic carrier to terminate the service, and international passenger transport operators require rights of access to foreign airspace and landing slots. Networks introduce an element of natural monopoly. A second implication is that there is a high degree of government regulation affecting the nature of the international sale of these services and levels of intra-industry trade. In the telecommunications industry there is a system where bilateral agreements fix the settlement rates for sale of services, and in the airline industry there is a system of bilateral inter-government air service agreements that specify access to domestic facilities and the various air transport freedom rights.

Measurement of intra-industry trade in services

The data are obtained from computer disks of the 1998 edition of *Services Statistics on International Transactions, 1987–1996*. A more detailed discussion on the data is provided in the Appendix on page 000.

Table 9.1 shows the share of the total amount of services trade in total goods and services trade for twenty individual OECD countries over the period 1992–6. For the entire period, Austria shows the largest share of services trade (33.3 per cent) and Norway the second largest (26.5 per cent). The smallest shares are for Canada and Ireland, with 14.5 per cent and 15.5 per cent, respectively. The simple average of the share of services trade in total trade remained stable at above 20 per cent. None the less, the total amount of services trade for all of the included countries increased by 26.1 per cent from US$65.8 billion in 1992 to US$82.9 billion in 1996.

Now we provide a description of intra-industry trade patterns among twenty countries of the OECD. Unadjusted Grubel–Lloyd (GL) indices for the service sector were calculated for twenty individual countries. The GL index is the trade share-weighted mean of the proportions of intra-industry trade in each of the service industries.

The indices are calculated using 1-digit categories. At this level, the nine categories correspond to industries commonly identified by

Table 9.1   Share of services trade, 1992–6 (percentages)

Country	1992	1993	1994	1995	1996	Average (1992–6)
Australia	21.5	21.6	21.9	21.9	22.3	21.8
Austria	31.6	34.4	32.8	33.1	34.5	33.3
Belgium-Luxemburg	19.5	20.9	21.6	17.9	18.0	19.6
Canada	15.5	15.2	14.3	13.6	14.0	14.5
Finland	20.1	19.0	18.3	19.6	17.9	19.0
France	25.8	27.5	25.9	20.8	20.7	24.2
Germany	15.2	16.8	16.1	16.3	16.8	16.2
Ireland	16.4	15.2	15.4	14.9	15.8	15.5
Italy	23.7	24.1	22.5	21.5	23.3	23.0
Japan	19.4	19.4	19.2	19.0	19.9	19.4
Netherlands	21.5	22.9	22.6	20.8	21.1	21.8
Norway	27.9	28.4	27.2	25.2	23.6	26.5
New Zealand	24.8	24.0	24.4	24.7	25.0	24.6
Portugal	17.5	23.0	20.4	20.0	19.3	20.0
Spain	24.4	25.7	23.8	22.6	23.0	23.9
Sweden	24.1	20.8	18.8	17.7	18.5	20.0
Switzerland	18.3	19.2	18.7	18.5	19.2	18.8
Turkey	24.8	23.7	25.6	25.1	20.0	23.9
UK	20.4	20.6	20.3	20.3	20.4	20.4
USA	19.2	19.1	18.6	17.9	19.1	18.6
Average	**21.6**	**22.1**	**22.4**	**20.6**	**20.6**	**21.2**

Notes: Share represents the percentage of the total amount of services trade in terms of total trade of goods and services. Royalties and licence fees (8) and Government services (11) are excluded from the services sector. 'Average' represents the unweighted averages.
Source: See Appendix, page 176.

analysts and economists: Transportation, Travel, Communications services, etc. All these industries provide multiple services; in fact, a very large number of services these days. There is substitution in demand and/or supply among services within these industries. For example, although the insurance industry makes a distinction between general and life insurance and reinsurance, and some suppliers specialize in only one of these categories, many individual insurance companies can and do provide a wide variety of insurance services across these categories. This is also true of other 1-digit industries. Transportation is the industry with perhaps the clearest division. The intersection of suppliers in the two subcategories Sea transport and Air transport is relatively small, but a few suppliers supply both and there is substitutability between air and sea transport for an increasing range of goods transported that have high unit values.

Table 9.2 summarizes the results. As shown in the table, the shares of intra-industry trade in services trade for most countries are high. The country average GL indices over the entire period range from 0.49 (Turkey) to 0.88 (Belgium-Luxembourg). The average GL index for all countries and all periods is 0.73. It is interesting to note that for most countries the shares of IIT remained very stable.

A more disaggregated classification of service industries might be considered in order to minimize the 'categorical aggregation' problem arising from intra-category product heterogeneity. For eight countries, Table 9.3 reports the results for the three 1-digit industries for which disaggregation of trade flows to a 2-digit level is possible. These are

Table 9.2 Intra-industry trade in services by country, 1992–6, 1-digit industries

Country	1992	1993	1994	1995	1996	Average (1992–6)	MIIT (1992–6)
Australia	0.85	0.84	0.81	0.80	0.82	0.82	0.67
Austria	0.76	0.82	0.83	0.89	0.92	0.84	0.74
Belgium-Luxemburg	0.88	0.89	0.89	0.87	0.87	0.88	0.77
Canada	0.81	0.80	0.85	0.87	0.88	0.84	0.70
Finland	0.77	0.79	0.88	0.87	0.87	0.84	0.68
France	0.88	0.88	0.88	0.87	0.87	0.87	0.78
Germany	0.74	0.73	0.71	0.73	0.75	0.73	0.68
Ireland	0.74	0.72	0.74	0.69	0.68	0.71	0.58
Italy	0.84	0.81	0.75	0.72	0.76	0.78	0.56
Japan	0.65	0.66	0.66	0.64	0.66	0.65	0.50
Netherlands	0.88	0.88	0.87	0.83	0.82	0.86	0.49
Norway	0.75	0.74	0.76	0.74	0.73	0.74	0.52
New Zealand	0.82	0.83	0.83	0.77	0.77	0.80	0.59
Portugal	0.55	0.74	0.68	0.74	0.75	0.69	0.75
Spain	0.61	0.63	0.61	0.59	0.61	0.61	0.45
Sweden	0.62	0.76	0.76	0.81	0.77	0.74	0.69
Switzerland	0.75	0.75	0.77	0.79	0.82	0.78	0.62
Turkey	0.50	0.48	0.46	0.47	0.53	0.49	0.34
UK	0.82	0.84	0.82	0.84	0.78	0.82	0.68
USA	0.79	0.79	0.80	0.79	0.79	0.79	0.79
Average	**0.72**	**0.73**	**0.73**	**0.73**	**0.74**	**0.73**	**0.63**

Notes: Calculated from nine 1-digit service industries. Royalties and licence fees (8), and Government services (11) are excluded (see Appendix on page 000 for details). Intra-industry trade indices are the weighted average of unadjusted Grubel–Lloyd indices over all industries. 'Average' represents the unweighted averages of intra-industry trade indices for individual years. 'MIIT' is the weighted average of the Brülhart A indices over all industries.
Source: See Appendix, page 177.

Table 9.3   Intra-industry trade in services by country, 1992–6, comparison between 1-digit and 2-digit industries

Country	Digit	1992	1993	1994	1995	1996	Average (1992–6)
Belgium-Luxemburg	1-digit	0.93	0.95	0.92	0.90	0.91	0.92
	2-digit	0.93	0.93	0.91	0.87	0.88	0.91
Canada	1-digit	0.85	0.81	0.84	0.87	0.91	0.86
	2-digit	0.85	0.80	0.83	0.86	0.88	0.84
Finland	1-digit	0.87	0.79	0.89	0.91	0.93	0.88
	2-digit	0.84	0.76	0.85	0.88	0.91	0.85
France	1-digit	0.95	0.94	0.95	0.95	0.94	0.95
	2-digit	0.93	0.91	0.90	0.92	0.91	0.91
Ireland	1-digit	0.68	0.66	0.65	0.56	0.56	0.62
	2-digit	0.68	0.66	0.65	0.56	0.56	0.56
Italy	1-digit	0.82	0.83	0.81	0.79	0.82	0.81
	2-digit	0.80	0.83	0.81	0.79	0.82	0.81
Norway	1-digit	0.76	0.74	0.78	0.76	0.75	0.76
	2-digit	0.72	0.69	0.73	0.70	0.71	0.71
Spain	1-digit	0.86	0.88	0.91	0.89	0.92	0.89
	2-digit	0.80	0.82	0.83	0.83	0.83	0.83
Average	**1-digit**	**0.84**	**0.83**	**0.84**	**0.83**	**0.84**	**0.84**
	2-digit	**0.82**	**0.80**	**0.81**	**0.80**	**0.81**	**0.81**

Notes: Calculated from three 1-digit sectors and eight 2-digit categories, respectively. The 1-digit sectors are (1), (9) and (10). The 2-digit categories are (1.1), (1.2), (1.3), (9.1), (9.2), (9.3), (10.1) and (10.2) (see Appendix on page 000 for details). Intra-industry trade indices are the weighted average of unadjusted Grubel–Lloyd indices over all industries. 'Average' represents the unweighted averages.
Source: See Appendix, page 177.

(1) Transportation, (9) other business services, and (10) personal, cultural and recreational services. Comparing the intra-industry trade in these industries at the 1-digit and 2-digit levels, we see that the share of intra-industry trade at the 2-digit level is lower than at the 1-digit level in most cases, though in a few cases it remains the same. (The GL index has the property that disaggregation must lower the index except in cases where the subcategories have trade balances that all have the same sign.) However, the decrease in the indices is remarkably small. This indicates that the trade imbalance generally have the same sign in a country with little offsetting of surpluses and deficits within 1-digit categories ('industries'). It should be noted that there are only three subcategories (Sea transport, Air transport, and Other transport) in the Transportation industry, three subcategories in the Other business services industry, and only two in the Personal, cultural and recreational services industry.

Now we consider the industry pattern of intra-industry trade. The shares of intra-industry trade by nine 1-digit individual industries were calculated and reported in Table 9.4. All these service industries have high levels of intra-industry trade, but with some differences. Transportation and Other business services have the largest shares, of 0.89 and 0.83, respectively, for the entire period, while Personal, cultural and recreational services has the smallest share, at 0.56.

As pointed out by Hamilton and Kniest (1991) and others, the traditional GL index is a static measure, in the sense that it describes intra-industry trade patterns at a single point in time. Brülhart (1994) proposed an index that is now commonly used by many researchers as a measure of changes in intra-industry trade or marginal intra-industry trade. Specifically, the weighted average of the Brülhart indices over all industries is calculated as follows:

$$A = \sum w_i A_i \qquad i = 1, \ldots, S \qquad (9.1)$$

where

$$A_i = \frac{|\Delta X_i| + \Delta |\Delta M_i| + |\Delta X_i - \Delta M_i|}{|\Delta X_i| + |\Delta M_i|}$$

$$w_i = \frac{|\Delta X_i| + |\Delta X_i|}{\sum_i (|\Delta X_i| + |\Delta M_i|)}$$

Table 9.4 Intra-industry trade in services by industry, 1992–6

		1992	1993	1994	1995	1997	Average (1992–6)	MIIT (1992–6)
1	Transportation	0.89	0.90	0.90	0.89	0.89	0.89	0.78
2	Travel	0.69	0.68	0.67	0.67	0.68	0.68	0.51
3	Communications services	0.79	0.74	0.74	0.78	0.76	0.76	0.64
4	Construction services	0.73	0.72	0.70	0.73	0.75	0.73	0.52
5	Insurance services	0.80	0.75	0.76	0.63	0.72	0.73	0.73
6	Financial services	0.77	0.79	0.83	0.74	0.77	0.78	0.80
7	Computer and information services	0.68	0.70	0.72	0.76	0.72	0.72	0.53
8	Other business services	0.83	0.84	0.84	0.84	0.83	0.83	0.78
9	Personal cultural and recreational services	0.55	0.53	0.57	0.58	0.55	0.56	0.32

Source: See Appendix, page 177.

These measures are calculated at the 1-digit level of the classification, and the estimated results are shown in the last column of Table 8.2. The average levels of marginal intra-industry trade are also high for most of the individual countries. The simple average is 0.63. This may imply that the recent expansion of trade in services has entailed relatively low adjustment costs for the OECD countries. It is also interesting to note that Turkey, the country with the lowest GL index, has the lowest value of MIIT in the table (0.34). Belgium-Luxembourg, with the highest GL index, has a value of MIIT of 0.77, the third highest value after the USA (0.79) and France (0.78). This pattern is in contrast to the findings of Hamilton and Kniest (1991) who argued that the observation of a high proportion of intra-industry trade does not justify a priori any prediction of the likely pattern of *change* in trade flows. Brülhart's indices of MIIT for each service industry were also calculated over all countries, and presented in the last column of Table 9.4. Again, they are large.

A cross-country analysis of trade in services

This section studies the determinants of intra-industry trade in services. There are many different models offering alternative explanations of intra-industry trade. Some explanations are country specific and others industry specific. Since Balassa and Bauwens (1987), most empirical studies on intra-industry trade have tended to combine 'country specific' and 'industry specific' determinants of 'bilateral' intra-industry trade of 'goods' in one equation.

The empirical study here is different from others in that, first, our focus is on intra-industry trade in 'services'. Second, we believe that empirical studies of intra-industry trade should relate to multilateral rather than bilateral trade. The effects of intra-industry trade on a country's welfare and resource allocation stem from a country's total trade with 'the rest of the world'. A majority of empirical studies of traditional endowments-based trade theory are done on the multilateral basis. Third, we consider only country-specific determinants of intra-industry trade.

The first hypothesis is that the extent of intra-industry trade in services will be related positively to the country's per capita income. This relationship is predicted by models of intra-industry trade in goods which carry over to intra-industry trade in services of the cross-border type. In the model of Helpman and Krugman (1985), the differentiated good is assumed to be capital intensive. In the model of Falvey (1981), the higher-quality varieties of the differentiated good are produced using relatively capital-intensive techniques. A higher-income country indicates a relatively capital abundant country, and hence it specializes in the production of both horizontally and vertically differentiated goods and 'services'. On the demand side, the extent of intra-industry trade may be correlated with the country's per capita income, through a more diversified pattern of demand. This variable is measured as the log of the per capita gross domestic product (PCGDP) in US dollars, deflated by the US GDP deflator (IMF, 1999).

The second hypothesis is that the larger a country, the higher the extent of intra-industry trade. Lancaster (1980) shows that the extent of intra-industry trade is higher in industries with scale economies. The larger a country, the greater the opportunities for domestic economies of scale and the higher the extent of intra-industry trade, although national scale is distinct from scale in a specific industry. On the demand side, a large home market indicates a more diverse demand and hence a greater potential for intra-industry trade. The size of a country is measured as the log of the gross domestic product (GDP) in billions of US dollars, deflated by the US GDP deflator (IMF, 1999).

Third, Falvey (1981) demonstrates that countries with lower trade barriers have higher levels of intra-industry trade. Following Balassa and Bauwens (1987), we define a proxy for trade orientation (TROR) as the residuals from a regression of the log of per capita services trade (PCT) on the log of per capita income (PCGDP) and the log of population (POP). Per capita trade here is the sum of trade in services (in millions of US dollars) divided by population (in thousands). Year dummies are included to control for year specific factors. The estimated results are as follows, with t-values in parentheses:

$$PCT = -7.040 + 0.896PCGDP - 0.308POP + YEAR \text{ Dummies; } R^2(Adj) = 0.811$$
$$(-12.22) \quad (15.84) \qquad (12.21) \qquad\qquad\qquad (9.2)$$

Finally, the GL index becomes smaller as the size of the trade imbalance increases. As will be shown in the fourth section of the chapter, the magnitude of the trade imbalance is substantial in our sample.

Following Lee and Lee (1993), and Stone and Lee (1995), a measure of trade imbalance is included in estimating the determinants of intra-industry trade. Trade imbalance (TIMB) is defined as $TIMB_j = |X_j - M_j|/(X_j + M_j)$, where X_j is country j's exports of services to the world, and M_j country j's imports.

Thus our basic equation (with predicted signs) is:

$$\overset{+}{\quad}\quad\overset{+}{\quad}\quad\overset{+}{\quad}\quad\overset{-}{\quad}$$
$$B = f(\text{PCGDP, GDP, TROR, TIMB}) \qquad (9.3)$$

where B is the unadjusted GL index. With regard to the specification of the above equation, two points are to be made. First, estimation of a linear function may have predicted values of B that lie outside the interval $[0, 1]$, while the index can take values only within this interval. Therefore, in addition to the linear regression specification, we estimate a non-linear regression of the logit probability function as follows:

$$B = 1/(1 + \exp(-\beta Z)) + \mu \qquad (9.4)$$

where Z is the vector of explanatory variables and μ is the disturbance term.

Second, because we have only twenty observations in a given year, we pool our data across years (1992–6) and include year dummies. Thus our fixed-effects model can pick up cross-country variation in the index of intra-industry trade. We may also include country dummies, as they may take care of all other country-specific factors of intra-industry trade, such as geography, language and culture. Country dummies are not included, however, because, as shown in Table 9.2, there is very little time series variation in the GL indices during the time period of interest. In addition, any time variation in the right-hand side variables for a given country will affect the share of intra-industry trade only with a substantial time lag, but the limited data prevent us from considering time lags.

Results of the estimation are presented in Table 9.5. Estimates made by ordinary least squares (OLS) are presented in the first two columns and those by non-linear least squares (NLS) are in the last two columns. The overall explanatory power (in terms of Adjusted R^2) of the model is relatively high and remains very stable, in all of the estimated equations (0.672–0.699). We begin by considering the estimates of OLS from pooling the data without year dummies. The effect on the extent of intra-industry trade is significantly positive for per capita gross domestic product (PCGDP) at the 1 per cent level, but is not significant for either gross domestic product (GDP) or the constructed measure of trade orientation (TROR). Trade imbalance (TIMB) is in fact the most significant variable affecting the variation of intra-industry trade among countries during the period 1992–96. This qualitative result does not change when year dummies are included in the OLS model. In fact, none of the year dummies has a significant coefficient at any statistically significant level.[2]

Table 9.5   Determinants of IIT in services

	Pooled OLS	Fixed-effects OLS	Pooled NLS	Fixed-effects NLS
CONSTANT	0.307**	0.289***	−0.486	−0.562
	(2.339)	(2.139)	(0.736)	(0.830)
PCGDP	0.054***	0.055***	0.214***	0.220***
	(3.835)	(3.863)	(3.014)	(3.031)
GDP	0.0004	−0.0002	−0.0005	−0.0009
	(0.076)	(0.096)	(0.018)	(0.032)
TROR	0.031	0.032	0.212*	0.218*
	(1.431)	(1.442)	(1.662)	(1.672)
TIMB	−0.513***	−0.508***	2.786***	−2.763***
	(7.846)	(7.617)	(7.899)	(7.675)
R^2 (Adjusted)	0.682	0.672	0.699	0.689

Notes: Dependent variable is unadjusted GL indices. PCGDP and GDP are in logarithms.
NLS model estimates a logistic function. Fixed-effects models include year dummies, whose
estimated coefficients are not shown for brevity. *t*-values are shown in parentheses. ***, **
and * denote 1, 5, and 10 per cent levels of significance, respectively, for a two-tailed test.

In the non-linear regression specification (the last two columns), the
estimated coefficient of trade orientation (TROR) becomes significant at
the 10 per cent level and has a predicted positive sign. PCGDP and TIMB
remain significant at the 1 per cent level, while GDP remains insignificant
at any plausible level. Again, none of the year dummies is significant.

Hence, intra-industry trade in services is explained relatively well by
the country's per capita income and trade orientation. This evidence
might be viewed as giving more support for product differentiation than
economies of scale, as a cause of intra-industry trade in services. In
addition, the trade imbalance factor is strongly significant in our regression. This implies that the unadjusted GL index is biased strongly downwards with the trade imbalance, and therefore including a measure of
trade imbalance is desirable to control for any possible bias.

Trade in goods and services and adjustment for the trade imbalance

There is one further issue that arises when we have calculated measures of
intra-industry trade in services. This is the effect of combining trade in
services with trade in goods. We noted in the introduction to the chapter
that there is no reason to separate trade in goods from trade in services.
Measures of intra-industry should relate to trade in goods and services combined.

The difficulty here is to choose a level of disaggregation in the SITC and in the OECD–Eurostat classification of trade in services that are comparable and can be combined. For reasons explained above, it is necessary to choose the 1-digit level of classification for services. At this level, we have considered nine 'service' industries. At the 1-digit level of the SITC there are ten categories, and at the 2-digit level over thirty categories in the goods sector. Ideally, one should choose levels that give categories in both the goods and the services sector which are meaningful aggregates of production. From this point of view, both classifications are somewhat arbitrary. In terms of the value of trade in categories, the 2-digit SITC categories correspond more closely to the 1-digit service classification categories.

Rather than carry out an arbitrary aggregation of trade in goods and in services, we examine the likely effects of aggregation. There are two reasons why this aggregation could increase the observed level of intra-industry trade compared to the calculations based on goods trade alone if there was an agreed matching of the classifications. The first reason is that the observed level of intra-industry trade in services might be higher on average than that in goods trade alone. The second reason relates to trade imbalances.

Grubel and Lloyd (1975, p. 22) argued that their measure of intra-industry trade for all goods traded in an economy had the undesirable feature that, when the aggregate goods trade was unbalanced, it could not attain a value of 1. It was therefore 'biased downwards'. Such biases will be particularly large when the measure is applied to bilateral rather than multilateral flows.

They recommended the adjusted measure:

$$C = \frac{\sum_i (X_i + M_i) - \sum_i |X_i - M_i|}{\sum_i (X_i + M_i) - |\sum_i X_i - \sum_i M_i|} \qquad i = 1, \ldots, S \qquad (9.5)$$

By simple manipulation,

$$C = B \bullet 1/(1 - k_g) \qquad (9.6)$$

where B is the unadjusted GL index:

$$B = \frac{\sum_i (X_i + M_i) - \sum_i |X_i - M_i|}{\sum_i (X_i + M_i)} \qquad i = 1, \ldots, S \qquad (9.7)$$

and

$$k_g = \frac{\left| \sum_i X_i - \sum_i M_i \right|}{\sum_i (X_i + M_i)} \tag{9.8}$$

is the balance of payments deficit/surplus as a percentage of total (goods) trade. Hence, $C > B$ unless there is a zero deficit/surplus ($k_g = 0$), in which case $C = B$.

The need for an adjustment to the average level of intra-industry trade has been hotly debated. Some form of adjustment in the presence of a trade imbalance has been generally accepted. A number of authors have, however, criticized the method of adjustment in Equation (9.5) and offered alternative adjustments.[3]

The present section explores a new approach to the adjustment for the aggregate trade imbalance. As noted above, one should, in principle, study intra-industry trade patterns in goods and services simultaneously. This would, of course, change the trade imbalances as a proportion of total trade, the factor k in Equation (9.7).

Consider the factor k for trade in goods and services combined in one country. This may be written as:

$$\begin{aligned}
k &= \frac{\left| (X_g + X_s) - (M_g + M_s) \right|}{(X_g + X_s) + (M_g + M_s)} = \frac{\left| (X_g - M_g) + (X_s - M_s) \right|}{(X_g + X_s) + (M_g + M_s)} \\
&\leq \frac{\left| (X_g - M_g) \right| + \left| (X_s - M_s) \right|}{(X_g + X_s) + (M_g + M_s)} \\
&= \frac{\left| X_g - M_g \right|}{X_g + M_g} \bullet \frac{(X_g + X_g)}{(X_g + X_s) + (M_g + M_s)} + \frac{\left| X_s - M_s \right|}{M_g + M_s} \bullet \frac{(X_s + X_s)}{(X_g + X_s) + (M_g + M_s)} \\
&= k_g \bullet w_g + k_s \bullet w_s \tag{9.9}
\end{aligned}$$

The subscripts g and s indicate the summations over all goods and all services, and W_g and W_s are the proportions of goods trade and services trade, respectively, in total goods and services trade. The inequality follows from the Triangle Inequality. These relations state that the trade imbalance factor k for goods and services trade combined is less than or equal to the weighted average trade imbalances for goods trade and services trade separately. It is equal to the weighted sum if the trade imbalance in goods has the same sign as the trade imbalance in services (that is, there is a surplus or a deficit on both the goods and the services accounts). It is strictly less than the weighted sum if the trade

Table 9.6   Trade imbalance factors , 1992–6 (averages)

Country	(a) Goods trade (%)	(b) Services trade (%)	(c) Goods and services trade (%)	(c)/(a)	(c)/(b)
Australia	1.92	3.17	1.42	0.74	0.45
Austria	9.62	14.34	1.96	0.20	0.13
Belgium-Luxemburg	2.72	2.90	2.76	1.02	0.95
Canada	5.24	13.93	2.58	0.49	0.18
Finland	14.48	12.44	9.35	0.65	0.75
France	1.80	9.86	3.63	2.02	0.37
Germany	5.86	25.00	1.18	0.20	0.05
Ireland	16.82	23.90	10.56	0.63	0.44
Italy	9.25	2.46	7.47	0.81	3.03
Japan	20.10	31.31	10.17	0.51	0.32
Netherlands	6.43	3.43	5.78	0.90	1.69
Norway	12.67	1.96	9.84	0.78	5.02
New Zealand	5.88	4.99	3.29	0.56	0.66
Portugal	17.90	14.52	11.53	0.64	0.79
Spain	10.90	29.87	2.23	0.20	0.07
Sweden	9.39	6.27	6.27	0.67	1.00
Switzerland	0.85	20.76	3.87	4.57	0.19
Turkey	20.04	47.22	6.10	0.30	0.13
UK	4.43	5.15	2.57	0.58	0.50
USA	12.48	16.11	7.17	0.57	0.45
Average	**9.44**	**14.48**	**5.49**	**0.58**	**0.38**

Notes: Trade imbalance is calculated as $100^* |X_j - M_j|/(X_j + M_j)$, where X_j is exports of country j to the world, and M_j is imports of country j for the relevant category of goods and/or services. 'Average' represents the unweighted average.

imbalance in goods has the opposite sign to the trade imbalance in services.

We can now see the effect of adding trade in services to trade in goods on the trade imbalance factor. The effect will depend on two factors: the sign of the trade imbalance on the services account compared to that on the goods account, and the magnitude of the trade imbalance in services, k_s. If a country has opposite signs for the two trade imbalances and/or a small relative trade imbalance on the services account, the trade imbalance for goods and services combined will be less than the trade imbalance on the goods account alone. In such cases, the magnitude of the adjustment that might be made for a trade imbalance, and therefore the importance of adjustment, is reduced.

The sizes of the trade imbalances for goods trade and for services trade alone, and for goods and services trade combined, are reported in Table 9.6 for our twenty OECD countries. Column (a) reports the trade imbalance for goods trade alone. This is the relevant factor in previous studies of intra-industry trade that have been confined to goods trade. This can be compared to the factor for goods and services combined in column (c). For seventeen of the twenty countries combining goods and services trade reduces the magnitude of the trade imbalance. For Belgium-Luxembourg, there is a small increase, and for France and Switzerland a large increase. In the latter two cases, there is no offsetting as both countries have surpluses on both the goods and services account, and the average is increased by the higher relative imbalance for services trade alone. Thus, in general, combining goods and services trade in intra-industry trade studies would reduce the magnitude of the imbalance substantially.[4] This, in turn, will tend to raise the level of intra-industry trade because of the negative empirical relationship between the level of intra-industry trade and the trade imbalance, as noted in the previous section.

Concluding remarks

Our initial investigation of intra-industry trade in services has shown that it is uniformly high in twenty OECD countries and nine service industries, and is stable over time. Given the high levels of intra-industry trade in service industries and the attention to liberalization in trade in services in the WTO under the Built-in Agenda, there is an urgent need for further work on this topic. Several directions of research need to be pursued.

There is a great need for the development of theoretical models of intra-industry trade that incorporate the key features of service industries. Such models should predict the determinants of intra-industry trade in services and be able to shed light on its welfare implication. There is also a need for studies of barriers to trade in services, including barriers to foreign investment in the case of services supplied by the commercial presence mode. These should take account of the multiple services traded internationally within industries and the associated patterns of national specialization and intra-industry trade. They could be used to predict the effects of liberalization of trade and FDI on international trade and investment, and production of services, and thereby on the gains from trade and the costs of adjustment to increased trade in services.

The industry categories used here are very broad and subject to an aggregation problem. Hence there is a need for the collection of more detailed statistics on international trade in services, including new statistics of services supplied according to the GATS modes. In particular, FATS in the case of supply by the mode of commercial presence need to be linked to trade in services supplied by other modes.

Appendix: joint OECD–Eurostat trade in services classification

The data are obtained from computer disks of the 1998 edition of *Services Statistics on International Transactions, 1987–1996*. This is the first edition of a joint publication on statistics of international trade in services by the Organization for Economic Co-operation and Development (OECD) and the Statistical Office of the European Community (Eurostat). There are four levels in this classification: 1-digit, 2-digit, 3-digit and 4-digit levels. At the 1-digit level, the items of the OECD–Eurostat classification are the same as those in the BMP5. At the 2-, 3- and 4-digit level, they are fully compatible with those in the BMP5.

Countries, however, do not fully provide data at all of the digit levels in the OECD–Eurostat classification. The following is the list of service industries whose data are available for most of OECD countries during 1992–6.

(1)   Transportation
      1.1   Sea transport
      1.2   Air transport
      1.3   Other transport
(2)   Travel
(3)   Communications services
(4)   Construction services
(5)   Insurance services
(6)   Financial services
(7)   Computer and information services
(8)   Royalties and licence fees
(9)   Other business services
      9.1   Merchanting and other trade-related services
      9.2   Operational leasing services
      9.3   Miscellaneous business, professional, and technical services
(10)   Personal, cultural, and recreational services
      10.1   Audiovisual and related services
      10.2   Other personal, cultural and recreational services
(11)   Government services, not included elsewhere

Royalties and licence fees (8) is not a service industry and these intellectual property payments occur in all industries. Hence they are excluded. Government services, n.i.e. (11) is also excluded because they are not driven by market forces.

Tables 9.2 and 9.4: At the 1-digit level, we examine trade for the nine 'industries'; that is, for items (1), (2), (3), (4), (5), (6), (7), (9) and (10). There is a further problem with missing values. When missing values for some industries appear for a certain country, intra-industry indices are calculated with the remaining industries. The countries with their omitted industry(ies) are: Australia (1); Ireland (5); Japan (7); Netherlands (5) (7) (10); New Zealand (3) (4); Portugal (7); Switzerland (4) (6) (7); Turkey (3) (7); UK (6).

Table 9.3: Six of the above 1-digit industries cannot be disaggregated as no data are provided by most of the reporting countries. Hence, at the 2-digit level, we are able to consider the effects of disaggregation only for the sub-items for which data are available; that is, for those in items (1) Transportation, (9) Other business services and (10) Personal, cultural and recreational services.

Notes

1   But the problems of definition are more fundamental. The GATS definition is not exhaustive. Many services can be supplied by more than one mode. And a single act of supply may involve more than one mode. Even the boundary between trade in goods and trade in services is unclear; for example, 'how long does the rental of a movie have to be before the transaction becomes one in a good rather than in a service?' (Snape, 1998, n.1). The newly emerged Information Technology (IT) industry is a major supplier of both goods and services (see US Department of Commerce, 2000, ch. vi). Some new technologies mean that services that were previously supplied by one mode can now be supplied by another; for example, broking firms in, say, the USA, are now offering their services to customers residing in other countries, whereas previously they had to compete in foreign markets with a commercial presence.

2   For brevity, they are not shown in the table.

3   This literature is surveyed by Kol (1988, ch. 4).

4   One should note that the combining of trade in goods and services, as defined here, still omits some items from the current account of the balance of payments statistics. Royalties and licence fees were omitted from the service industries, and the current account also includes factor service payments and receipts (employee compensation and investment income) and the value of current transfers.

References

Balassa, B. and L. Bauwens (1987) 'Intra-Industry Specialisation in a Multi-Country and Multi-Industry Framework', *Economic Journal*, 97: 923–39.

Brülhart, M. (1994) 'Marginal Intra-Industry Trade: Measurement and Relevance for the Pattern of Industrial Adjustment', *Weltwirtschaftliches Archiv*, 130: 600–13.

Commission of the European Union, International Monetary Fund, Organization for Economic Co-operation and Development, United Nations, World Trade Organization (1999), *Manual on Statistics of International Trade in Services*, Provisional Draft.

Dixit, A. K. and G. M. Grossman (1982) 'Trade and Protection with Multistage Production', *Review of Economic Studies*, 43: 583–94.

Falvey, R. (1981) 'Commercial Policy and Intra-Industry Trade', *Journal of International Economics*, 11: 495–511.

Findlay, C. and T. Warren (eds) (2000) *Impediments to Trade in Services: Measurement and Policy Implications* (Sydney: Routledge).

Greenaway, D., P. J. Lloyd and C. Milner (2001) 'Intra-Industry Foreign Direct Investment and Trade Flows: New Measures of Global Competition' in L. K. Cheng and H. Kierzkowski (eds), *Global Production and Trade in East Asia* (Norwell, Mass.: Kluwer).

Grubel, H. G. and P. J. Lloyd (1975) *Intra-Industry Trade: The Theory and Measurement of International Trade in Differentiated Products* (London: Macmillan).

Hamilton, C. and P. Kniest (1991) 'Trade Liberalization, Structural Adjustment and Intra-Industry Trade: A Note', *Weltwirtschaftliches Archiv*, 127: 356–67.

Helpman, E. and P. R. Krugman (1985) *Market Structure and Foreign Trade* (Brighton : Harvester Wheatsheaf).

Hoekman, B. and C. A. P. Braga (1996) 'Trade in Services, the GATS and Asia', *Asia-Pacific Economic Review*, 2: 5–20.

IMF (International Monetary Fund) (1993) *Balance of Payments Manual*, 5th edn (Washington, DC: International Monetary Fund).

IMF (International Monetary Fund) (1999) *International Financial Statistics Yearbook* (Washington, DC: International Monetary Fund).

Kierzkowski, H. (1989) 'Intra-Industry Trade in Transportation Services', in P. K. M. Tharakan and J. Kol (eds), *Intra-Industry Trade: Theory, Evidence and Extensions* (London: Macmillan), pp. 92–120.

Kol, J. (1988) 'The Measurement of Intra-Industry Trade', Ph. D. thesis, Erasmus University, Rotterdam.

Lancaster, K. J. (1980) 'Intra-Industry Trade under Perfect Monopolistic Competition', *Journal of International Economics*, 10: 151–75.

Lee, H.-H. and Y.-Y. Lee (1993) 'Intra-Industry Trade in Manufactures: The Case of Korea', *Weltwirtschaftliches Archiv*, 129: 159–71.

Organization for Economic Co-operation and Development and the Statistical Office of the European Commission (1998) *Services Statistics in International Transactions, 1987–1996* (Paris: OECD).

Sanyal, K. K. and R. W. Jones (1982) 'The Theory of Trade in Middle Products', *American Economic Review*, 72: 16–31.

Snape, R. H. (1998) 'Reaching Effective Agreements Covering Services' in A. O. Krueger (ed.), *The WTO as an International Organisation* (University of Chicago Press), pp. 279–93.

Stone, J. and H.-H. Lee (1995) 'Determinants of Intra-Industry Trade: A Longitudinal, Cross-Country Analysis', *Weltwirtschaftliches Archiv*, 131: 67–84.

Tang, L. (1999) 'Intra-Industry Trade in Services: A Case Study of the International Telephone Industry', Mimeo, Drexel University.

US Department of Commerce (2000) *Digital Economy 2000*, US Department of Commerce (website http://www.esa.doc.gov/de).

10
Intra-Industry Trade and the C–H–O Model: Evidence and Implications for Adjustments

David Greenaway and Chris Milner

Introduction

By the late 1980s many of the basic issues relating to modelling the determinants of intra-industry trade appeared to be resolved. There was a core theoretical foundation which offered a widely accepted explanation for intra-industry specialization and two-way trade in horizontally differentiated goods. In its single-sector form (Krugman, 1979) it offered a pure non-H–O explanation of such specialization and exchange between identical economies, based upon individuals' preference for variety and the existence of decreasing costs in production. The subsequent incorporation of both H–O and non-H–O sources of trade into a general equilibrium framework (Helpman, 1981; Helpman and Krugman, 1985) allowed for inter-industry specialization in homogenous goods and intra-industry specialisation in horizontally differentiated goods, and is often referred to as the Chamberlin–Heckscher–Ohlin (C–H–O) model. Thus a theoretical coherence was provided for the contrast between 'new' and 'old' (factor endowment) explanations of trade. Interest was also generated in the opportunities created by this 'new' type of model for affecting the pattern of comparative advantage through the strategic use of trade and industrial policies.

Alongside this theoretical development, a clear consensus or apparent consistency emerged from the large empirical literature (see Greenaway and Milner, 1984, 1987), the presumption being that horizontal IIT was the dominant form of IIT.

Empirical work, while often not closely linked to the testing of a specific model, consistently supported hypotheses about the determinants of IIT that were compatible with the C–H–O explanation. The share of intra-industry in total trade was predicted to expand with rising and increasing similarity of per capita incomes. Indeed, this process was likely to be most pronounced in the new industrializing economies of the world (especially in Asia). High levels of IIT had already been achieved in the industrialized economies, but the rapid growth of incomes and greater regional integration and trade liberalization offered opportunities for IIT in 'South–South' trade. Indeed, the attraction of this view of specialization and trade expansion was that it offered the prospect of relatively costless trade expansion. Specialization in and exchange of horizontally-differentiated products was not expected to impose high adjustment or dislocation costs on industrializing economies (see, for example, Krugman, 1981).

In this chapter it is argued that the above view of the nature and determinants of IIT was largely misplaced. There have recently been a number of studies (for example, Greenaway, Hine and Milner, 1994 and 1995; Hummels and Levinsohn, 1995; Gullstrand, 2001) that cast serious doubt upon the dominance of the horizontal IIT explanation of intra-industry trade and the robustness of the earlier empirical testing of the C–H–O model. Increasingly, evidence points to IIT in vertically differentiated goods as the dominant form of IIT. We therefore need to revisit alternative theoretical explanations, including comparative advantage or factor endowment explanations (for example, Falvey, 1981; Falvey and Kierzkowski, 1987; Flam and Helpman, 1987) of within-industry specialization and IIT. Here we focus on the relative importance of H–O and non-H–O factors in explaining the pattern of intra- and inter-industry trade. The thrust of this chapter is similar to that of Davis (1997), who demonstrates that factor endowment and technological factors can explain the volume of 'North–North' trade in a H–O setting. The presumed similarity of industrial countries is often cited as evidence of a need for non-H–O explanations for the volume of 'North–North' trade. We also need to investigate the implications of this for the likely pattern of IIT and adjustment in industrializing countries. The remainder of the chapter is organized as follows. In the second section the monopolistic competition model of IIT in horizontally differentiated goods is set out, and evidence from the first generation of empirical testing is reviewed. The robustness of the earlier evidence is challenged in the light of a number of recent developments in the third section. This challenge to the existing orthodoxy provides a rationale for reconsidering in the fourth section the theory and evidence relating to the alternative model of vertical intra-industry trade. Given the displacement of the horizontal IIT by the vertical IIT model, we consider the implications of this for policy and adjustment. The sixth section offers some conclusions.

C–H–O model and IIT: traditional view

Theory

The Chamberlin–Heckscher–Ohlin model (Helpman, 1981; Helpman and Krugman, 1985) provides an explanation of both inter- and intra-industry trade; H–O factors explain inter-industry specialization, while scale economies and horizontal product differentiation explains IIT. If countries have identical factor endowments, the model predicts that all trade will be IIT in similar, but horizontally differentiated, products (hereafter referred to as horizontal IIT), while there will be both IIT and inter-industry trade (that is, a net imbalance in non-differentiated, H–O goods) if factor proportions differ between countries.

Consider a two-country, two-factor capital (K) and labour (L) model with one homogenous goods sector (constant returns) and one differentiated goods sector (increasing returns). Consumers (with identical and homothetic preferences) are assumed to like variety, but products are produced by identical production functions and have equal prices, and therefore it is not differences in quality or technological characteristics of products that drive the demand for variety. Let us assume that the differentiated sector is relatively capital intensive and the home country relatively capital abundant. In which case, the model predicts that the foreign country will export homogenous goods, but both countries will export and import differentiated goods; with the home country being a net exporter of differentiated goods to offset its imports of the homogeneous goods at balanced trade. If $s(s^*)$ is the share of home (foreign) country in world income and spending (where $s + s^* = 1$), then home (foreign) country produces $n(n^*)$ varieties and $s^*(s)$ of the output of each is exported to the foreign (home) country. Because trade is balanced, the volume of gross trade (GT) equals twice the exports of the home country; that is

$$GT = 2s^*pX \qquad (10.1)$$

where X is the output of differentiated goods in the home country, and p is the price of differentiated goods.

Similarly, the gross volume of intra-industry trade (GIIT) between the two countries is twice the exports of differentiated products by the (net importing) foreign country; that is

$$GIIT = 2spX^*$$ (10.2)

in which the share of IIT in total trade is

$$\frac{GIIT}{GT} = \frac{2spX^*}{2s^*pX} = \frac{sX^*}{s^*X}$$ (10.3)

The model can be extended to more general circumstances, but the clear implication from Equation (10.3) is that the share of intra-industry trade depends (positively) on the similarity of relative factor endowments and on country size effects.

Evidence

A large number of tests of the country specific determinants of IIT was undertaken in the 1980s. Some researchers were explicitly testing a C–H–O model (for example, Helpman, 1987), but most were drawing implicitly upon this model to frame estimating equations. Invariably, however, the similarity of factor composition was proxied by the similarity of per capita income (GDP). Thus the hypothesis tested was that *the share of intra-industry between two countries (j and k) was expected to be larger the difference in per capita incomes between the countries*; that is

$$IIT_{jk} = \alpha_0 + \alpha_1 \left| \frac{GDP^j}{L_j} - \frac{GDP^j}{L_k} \right| + \alpha_i V_{jk} + \varepsilon_{jk}$$ (10.4)

where L is population, V_{jk} is a vector of other control variables (such as market size, trade policy), and IIT_{jk} is the Grubel and Lloyd index (Grubel and Lloyd, 1975)

Some of the econometric evidence relating to the sign and significance for the coefficient on α_1 is summarized in Table 10.1, which distinguishes between evidence for trade with all countries and trade between different groups of countries. For trade with all countries and for 'North–South' trade there is strong support for the factor similarity hypothesis of IIT. Indeed, it is from these types of study that the empirical literature is generally interpreted as supporting the negative relationship between per capita income differences and IIT. However, Table 10.1 indicates much less support for the hypothesis when dealing with trade within groupings of more similar countries, that is, 'North–North' and 'South–South' trade. Only in Helpman (1987) for 'North–North' intra-industry trade is a significant, negative sign identified for the years at the start of the period. After 1976, the negative sign becomes

Table 10.1   Summary of some econometric evidence on relationships between share of intra-industry trade in bilateral trade and per capita income differences

Study	Coverage	Years	Sign on relationship (α_1)
All trade			
Balassa and	OECD	1979	-*
Bauwens (1987)	Industrializing and		
	Developing countries	1988	-*
Greenaway, Hine	UK with 62 industrialized		
and Milner (1994)	and developing		
'North–North'			
Helpman (1987)	OECD countries	1970–6	-*
		1976–81	-
Balassa and	OECD countries	1979	-
Bauwens (1987)			
'North–South'			
Balassa and	OECD and developing	1979	-*
Bauwens (1987)	countries		
Nolle (1990)	Latin Amnerica with		-*
	OECD countries		
'South–South'			
Hellvin (1994)	Asian countries	1984	-
Nolle (1990)	Latin-American countries		-
Balassa and	Developing countries	1979	-
Bauwens (1987)			

Note: *denotes significance at minimum 5 per cent level.

insignificant. The above evidence was interpreted as giving support for a similarity in demand rather than in factor composition effect. Although small differences in per capita income may not generate large inter-country differences in the share of intra-industry trade, the positive influence of high income on demand for variety and demand similarity or taste overlap on encouraging two-way trade in horizontally differentiated goods was posited.

IIT and horizontal differentiation: revised view

Recent developments in empirical work cause one to question the interpretation in the previous section of evidence relating to the determinants of IIT and the robustness of the C–H–O model. There are a number of challenges that can be offered to the traditional view. First, does the similarity thesis hold if factor proportions or composition are measured directly rather than proxied by per capita income? Second, are there country-specific effects that are obscured by the use of cross-sectional analysis? Third, are we confident that intra-industry trade in horizontally differentiated goods is being measured properly? We look at each in turn.

Direct measurement of factor composition

Hummels and Levinsohn (1995) estimate the following equation for OECD countries for each of the years 1962–83:

$$IIT_{jk} = \alpha_0 + \alpha_1 \log \left| \frac{K^j}{L^j} - \frac{K^k}{L^k} \right| + \alpha \log \left| \frac{T^j}{L_j} - \frac{T^k}{L^k} \right|$$
$$+ \alpha_3 \min \left(\log GDP^j, \log GDP^k \right)$$
$$+ \alpha_4 \max \left((\log GDP^j, \log GDP^k) + \varepsilon_{jk} \right)$$

(10.5)

where L^j is working population of country j, T^j is the land endowment of country j, and K^j is the capital stock of country j.

Their results are summarized in Table 10.2. The relative capital intensity differential is significantly negative up to 1968, but loses significance and its negative sign until it becomes significantly positive at the end of the period. By contrast, differences in the land-to-labour ratio are significantly positive throughout the period. This latter finding may be because there is relatively little IIT in agricultural products, and (arable) land-abundant countries exchange homogenous products for differentiated manufactures and therefore have relatively low IIT overall. The finding for capital-to-labour ratios, however, is less supportive for the C–H–O explanation of IIT in manufactured products.

Country-specific effects and panel estimation

In cross-section analysis we seek to explain the variation in IIT between, say, Germany and Japan, and the USA and Canada, in terms of differences in their relative factor endowments. The first pair may be more similar in terms of factor endowments than the second, but this effect may be swamped consistently by other factors such as geographical proximity, trade policy measures and so on – that is, there may be country-pair specific effects. Panel estimation techniques offer the potential to capture cross-sectional and time-stationary special influences.

Hummels and Levinsohn (1995) provide panel estimates for the same countries and time period as in Table 10.2. We report results from their

Table 10.2   Summary of cross-sectional tests of the C–H–O model for US-OECD trade, 1962–83

Year	Capital/labour differential	Land/labour differential	Min GDP	Max GDP	R^2
1962	−**	−**	+**	−	0.357
1963	−**	−**	+**	−	0.390
1964	−*	−**	+**	−	0.392
1965	−*	−**	+**	−	0.382
1966	−*	−**	+**	−	0.416
1967	−*	−**	+**	−	0.426
1968	−*	−**	+**	−	0.442
1969	−	−**	+**	−	0.435
1970	−	−**	+**	−	0.442
1971	−	−**	+**	−	0.421
1972	−	−**	+**	−	0.393
1973	−	−**	+**	−	0.354
1974	−	−**	+**	−	0.395
1975	−	−**	+**	−	0.313
1976	+	−**	+**	−	0.277
1977	+	−**	+	−	0.260
1978	+	−**	+	−	0.225
1979	+	−**	+	−	0.203
1980	+	−**	+	−	0.197
1981	+*	−**	+	−	0.209
1982	+*	−**	+	−	0.216
1983	+**	−**	+	−	0.237

Notes: * = 5 per cent significance level; ** = 1 per cent significance level.
Source: Hummels and Levinsohn (1995), table IV.

fixed effects models in Table 10.3. This model, which sweeps out all the specific, country-pair effects, produces a positive and significant relationship between IIT and both per capita income and capital-to-labour differentials. Allowance for these apparently important fixed effects produces results contrary to those predicted by the C–H–O model, and robust to controls for the influence of factors such as distance and common borders that may be colinear with income or resource similarity.

The measurement of horizontal IIT

One reason for these unexpected findings is that the C–H–O model is being used to explain inter-country variation in the share in *total* IIT in all forms of differentiated products, when only IIT in horizontally differentiated products should be measured. Clearly, in practice, most

Table 10.3 Panel equation tests of C–H–O model for US–OECD trade, 1962–83

	Fixed effects estimates	
	(1)	(2)
Per-capita income differential	0.038	
	(3.609)	
Capital–labour differential		0.029
		(3.235)
Min. GDP	1.315	1.327
	(18.483)	(18.666)
Max. GDP	−0.005	−0.013
	(−0.079)	(−0.197)
R^2 (with country dummies)	0.524	0.523
	(0.965)	(0.966)

Note: t-ratios in brackets.
Source: Hummels and Levinsohn (1995), table v.

products are differentiated to varying degrees by price and quality. However, it is sensible to distinguish between those bilateral exchanges of products with similar prices and qualities and those with markedly dissimilar prices and qualities (that is, IIT in vertically differentiated products). Rigorous methods of capturing quality differences in trade have been used for a restricted range of products at a fine level of product disaggregation – for example, Aw and Roberts (1988). At the aggregate level, one must of necessity fall back on cruder but more comprehensive methods of decomposing total IIT in horizontal and vertical IIT. Extending the work of Abd-el-Rahman (1991), Greenaway, Hine and Milner (1994) proposed a methodology for this decomposition based on unit value differentials (at common levels of disaggregation – usually SITC digit 5) between exports and imports; with those two-way exchanges where unit values lie within the differential being classified as horizontal IIT and otherwise as vertical IIT. Despite its relative crudeness and arbitrariness, the methodology has been applied (with some sensitivity analysis) to a number of countries with some gains in our understanding of the determinants of IIT, and with a degree of consistency emerging from the results.

Table 10.4 reports evidence for the USA using this decomposition. The critical issue for present purposes is to emphasize how unimportant horizontal IIT is, and, in general, how relatively important is vertical IIT. In line with previous findings for the UK (Greenaway, Hine and Milner, 1994, 1995), vertical IIT accounts on average for about 70 per

Table 10.4   Shares[1] of horizontal and vertical[2] IIT in USA's bilateral trade in manufactures

Country	Horizontal IIT	Vertical IIT
Canada	0.15	0.20
Germany	0.03	0.22
Switzerland	0.03	0.18
UK	0.03	0.25
Norway	0.01	0.04
Luxembourg	0.02	0.04
Austria	0.00	0.08
Sweden	0.02	0.14
New Zealand	0.00	0.03
Australia	0.00	0.04
Spain	0.01	0.07
Finland	0.01	0.07
Ireland	0.01	0.13
Italy	0.02	0.19
Japan	0.03	0.09
France	0.03	0.27
Denmark	0.01	0.11
Belgium	0.02	0.11
Mexico	0.02	0.19
Netherlands	0.03	0.25

Notes: 1   Grubel–Lloyd index.
         2   Using $+/-$ 15 per cent unit value differential, though the study reports also results of a $+/-$ 25 per cent differential which are very similar to those shown above.
Source: Durkin and Krygier (1997).

cent of total IIT, and while this figure falls as the unit value differential is raised, it falls relatively slowly.

Note also that there is a consistent pattern of vertical IIT being the dominant form of IIT across the industrial countries in Table 10.4. This consistency is found also for the UK's trade with industrial countries and for its trade with developing and industrializing countries. As Table 10.5 shows, the share of vertical in total IIT rises to about 90 per cent in these countries. This pattern is also evident across low income (distant) developing countries and the industrializing economies of East Asia.

Given this dominance of vertical IIT, it is perhaps not surprising that recent panel econometric testing of the C–H–O model, using total IIT to proxy horizontal IIT, should reject the per capita income similarity explanation of IIT. If one controls for all the country-specific effects, then the finding that IIT is related positively to per capita income and

Table 10.5 Relative importance of vertical and horizontal IIT in UK's bilateral intra-industry trade, manufactured goods, 1988

	Share (%) in total IIT	
	Horizontal	*Vertical*
With EU countries	33	67
With OECD countries	33	67
With developing/industrializing countries	9	91
Including:		
Singapore	10	90
Korea, Rep.	9	91
China	7	93
Malaysia	6	94
Thailand	9	91
With all countries	32	68

Source: Information for groups of countries taken from Grubel and Lloyd indices in Greenaway, Milner and Elliott (1997), and for individial countries from SITC product coverage data in Greenaway, Hine and Milner (1994).

factor (capital-to-labour) composition differences is less of a puzzle if vertical, rather than horizontal, IIT is the dominant form of IIT. We need to revisit our theory of IIT.

Testing the vertically differentiated model of IIT

This section first reviews briefly the model of IIT in vertically differentiated products of Flam and Helpman (1987), the results of which are very similar to those in Falvey and Kierzkowski (1987), then considers the limited, available evidence on empirical testing of this type of model.

There are two countries, one factor (labour) and two goods in the Flam and Helpman model. The homogenous good is produced with Ricardian technology (with equal efficiency in both countries), and one qualitydifferentiable good where quality is a positive function of labour inputs. Demand for variety arises because of variation in income across consumers, who purchase a specific quality according to their preferences and income constraint; consumers with higher effective labour endowments (and by implication higher income) demand higher-quality varieties.

Let us assume that the home country had an absolute advantage in producing all qualities, but that a foreign country may have comparative advantage in low-quality varieties. Thus the unit labour requirement in the foreign country [$a^*(q)$] is always higher than in the home country [$a(q)$], that is, $2(q) = a^*(q)/a(q)$ as shown in Figure 10.1 as a positive function of q. In Figure 10.1 we also map out two different density functions g and g^* that could describe the distribution of demand for different qualities, given the distributions of income (effective labour endowments), preferences and prices in the two countries; the lower and upper bars on the quality (q) levels represent the qualities demanded by the lowest and highest income groups in each country. Given that the wage (w) per unit of labour is higher in the home country and assuming that it therefore specializes completely in differentiated goods, we are able to predict the pattern of trade at balanced trade. For the relative wage ($= w/w^*$) assumed in Figure 10.1, the foreign country exports the homogenous good and varieties with quality levels between q^* and q_d and the home country exports varieties between q_d and $\bar{q}^*$ (subject to the condition for intra-industry trade that $q < q_d < \bar{q}^*$)

The model does not predict an unambiguously positive relationship between the share of vertical IIT in total trade and relative wages, (that is, the proxy for inter-country per capita income difference given that labour is the only input). However, if we hold these constant (in particular, income distribution) then a rise in 2 (that is, more dissimilar per capita incomes across countries) will raise the share of IIT. To the extent that per capita income also proxies capital/labour ratios, this model can predict the opposite relationship between IIT and per capita income differentials across countries to that of the monopolistic competition

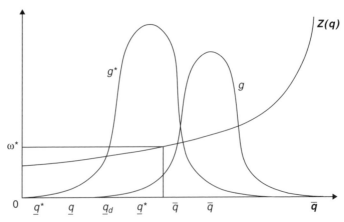

Figure 10.1   Trade in vertically differentiated varieties

model. This, as was argued in the previous section, may help us to understand the results of econometric testing of the monopolistic competition model.

But what of the evidence on the country determinants of the vertical IIT model? In one sense there is very little evidence on which to report, because it is only recently that efforts have been made to disentangle vertical and horizontal IIT. In another sense we could argue that, in fact, we have a lot of evidence because we now know that most IIT appears to be vertical IIT. In which case, the large cross-section evidence (referred to in the second section of this chapter) would appear to reject the vertical IIT model; since IIT is invariably found to be related negatively to per capita income differentials in cross-country/cross-section studies. However, if we accept the need to control for bilateral/country-specific effects and use a panel approach, then the results from this methodology (for example, Hummels and Levinsohn, 1995) are consistent with the vertical IIT model, IIT being related positively to GDP per head differentials.

Although the direct testing of the vertical IIT model using the decomposition of IIT outlined in the previous section is limited, what is available confirms the earlier contrasting pattern of results for cross-section and panel testing. Greenaway, Milner and Elliott (1999) in a cross section (country and industry in a single year) study of the separate determinants of horizontal and vertical IIT find that vertical IIT is related negatively to per capita income differentials across EU countries. By contrast, Durkin and Krygier (1997) testing the vertical IIT model for US trade with OECD countries (1989–92) find the supportive positive relationship when using a fixed effects panel model or when controlling in cross-section for distance (between the USA and the trading partner), and for the extent of income distribution overlap between countries. These results are summarised in Table 10.6, and are strongly supportive of the vertical IIT model. In another recent paper, Gullstrand (2001) tests a modified version of the Falvey–Kierkowski model for a sample of sixty countries. He disentangles income distribution both between and within countries and finds strong support for the importance of income distribution, so long as trade was in vertically differentiated products.

Implications for adjustment and policy

With the monopolistic competition model as the dominant paradigm, it became common during the 1980s to view H–O or comparative advantage as a driver of inter-industry trade between dissimilar economies and

Table 10.6 Summary of cross-section and panel testing of vertical IIT model for USA–OECD trade, 1989–92

Effects	Cross section/OLS		Panel/fixed	
	Vertical IIT		Vertical IIT	
	(± 15%)	(± 25%)	(± 15%)	(± 25%)
Per-capita income differential	+*	+*	+***	+***
GDP of trading partner	+***	+***	+	+
GDP of USA	−	−	−*	−*
Distance	−***	−***		
Income distribution overlap	+**	+**		
$\bar{R}^2$	0.56	0.55	0.87	0.86
N	80	80	80	80

Note: *** / ** / * denotes 1%, 5% and 10% level of significance, respectively.
Source: Durkin and Krygier (1997).

non-H–O factors as a driver of intra-industry trade between similar economies. Alongside this view of the world developed a number of related policy themes. Regional integration and trade liberalization, involving as it does trade between often relatively similar economies, would promote disproportionately intra-industry specialization and trade in differentiated manufactured goods. This would satisfy industrialization aims (technology transfer, greater external economies and so on), but would not involve adjustment problems associated with trade expansion arising out of factor composition differences. Indeed, in its extreme representation, the location of production of particular varieties is arbitrary and not dependent on country-specific factors. In these circumstances, trade and industry policy might be used strategically to fashion the location of production in the hope of deriving future scale advantages; that is, the use of policy as a determinant of comparative advantage.

In Table 10.7 we report on some estimates of the average levels of intra-industry trade among Asian countries in 1984. This evidence could be interpreted as being in line with the prevailing wisdom: the greater the scope for IIT in manufactured goods, the greater the importance of IIT in trade between the higher and more similar (per capita) income economies of Asia, and the greater scope for promoting IIT through narrower rather than broader definitions of regional trading groups. But the earlier sections of this chapter have challenged the prevailing wisdom, and a number of the above policy propositions need to be

Table 10.7 Average levels of bilateral intra-industry trade in Asia, 1984 (percentages)

	Manufactures	*Non-manufactures*
NICS–NICs	17.2	1.9
NICs–NECs	29.7	9.2
NECs–NECs	28.4	1.4
LDCs–LDCs	1.0	17.1
NICs–LDCs	4.0	3.4
NECs–LDCs	2.5	0.3

Notes: NICs = Singapore, Hong Kong, Korea.
         NECs = Malaysia, Thailand, Philippines, Indonesia.
         LDCs = India, Sri Lanka, Pakistan.
Source: Hellvin (1994).

reconsidered in the light of this. Of course, it would be helpful to confirm the earlier results about the importance of vertical IIT and the validity of the vertical IIT model, and as a minimum the chapter sets a research agenda for the analysis of intra-Asian trade flows. However, the earlier evidence is strongly supportive of the view that factor composition or H–O factors are central to explaining intra-industry trade, once we have controlled appropriately for overlapping incomes and factors such as distance, culture and transnational activity. In which case, regional groupings of geographically close and economically similar economies will not have a significant (positive) effect on increasing the share of IIT. If factor composition effects are important, then broader regional groupings may be more desirable. Indeed, there may be considerable scope for (vertical) IIT in Asia's trade outside the region (for example, with industrialized countries). This would argue in favour of non-discriminatory trade liberalization.

The restoration of H–O or factor composition explanations to both inter- and intra-industry trade also serves to strengthen the arguments in favour of non-interventionist trade policies for governments in Asia as in other regions. If the location of production of specific varieties or qualities is not arbitrary, and comparative advantage in homogenous product industries and differentiated product industries is fashioned by relative national endowments, then policy-makers have a reduced incentive to intervene for strategic reasons. Governments will, however, need to recognize that the expansion of vertical IIT (that is, exchange of different qualities) may involve factor market adjustments more similar to inter-industry specialization than intra-industry specialization associated with horizontal IIT. The story of smooth adjustment to intra-industry trade, as presented in, for example, Krugman (1981), is one based on the production and exchange of horizontally differentiated goods where there is low wage and skills dispersion within industries. The issue remains ultimately an empirical one, but there is already quite a lot of evidence of substantial intra-industry variation in skills and wages, certainly sufficient to undermine the smooth adjustment hypothesis.

Conclusions

The Chamberlin–Heckscher–Ohlin monopolistic competition model of inter-industry trade in homogenous products, and of intra-industry trade in horizontally differentiated (but similar quality) products has appeared for some years to provide a coherent explanation of international trade in broad terms. It neatly contains H–O or factor composition and non-H–O (scale economies and demand for variety) factors in a unified, general equilibrium framework. It also offers a rationale for the observed importance of intra-industry trade in 'North–North' trade – that is, trade between similar countries in terms of per capita incomes and factor endowments – and of inter-industry trade in 'South–North' trade. Although there was limited explicit testing of the C–H–O model, there was a large empirical literature that provided evidence implicitly about factor composition (proxied by per capita incomes) similarity hypothesis that derived from the model. The evidence for trade with all types of economies and for 'North–South' trade was consistent with the similarity hypothesis; a significant negative relationship in cross-section (country) regressions between the share of IIT in gross trade and the per capita income differential between countries. The evidence for more culturally and geographically similar countries in a 'North–North' or 'South–South' setting was much weaker, and for the later years in the study by Helpman (1987) a positive sign – that is, a dissimilarity relationship – is evident. Indeed, this puzzle is reaffirmed (for both capital–labour and per capita differentials) by the panel estimation approach to testing the C–H–O model used by Hummels and Levinsohn (1995), who argue that the negative sign may be found in cross-sections of countries where all the fixed effects on the bilateral exchange between a specific pair of countries (for example, distance, cultural links, commercial policies and so on) are not taken into account. These authors point also to other sources of factor composition differences (for example, land-to-labour), which may explain in part their puzzling results. But their results would appear much less puzzling if the world was described by a model of IIT in vertically differentiated goods such as in Flam and Helpman (1987). In this model, a positive relationship may well exist between vertical IIT and per capita income differences between countries, if one controls fully for income distribution overlap and for other country-specific effects. Recent developments in the measurement and testing of vertical IIT are consistent with the view that vertical, rather than horizontal, IIT is the dominant form of IIT in 'North–North' and 'North–South' trade, and that US vertical IIT is, controlling for other factors, related positively to the differential between US and other OECD (average) income levels.

If these recent findings are confirmed for a wider set of countries, then the puzzle is completely resolved. The implication for policy-makers is that they need readjust their thinking about the means of promoting and adjusting to intra-industry trade and specialization that is driven by factor composition and comparative advantage influences.

Notes

1 Bergstrand (1990) also demonstrated subsequently the importance of demand or taste factors in models of monopolistic competition with non-homothetic demand.
2 Of course, the corollary of the greater (short-run at least) adjustment costs of vertical IIT than those associated typically with horizontal IIT is that the long-run welfare gains of IIT expansion driven by comparative cost differences, as well as the demand for variety, may be correspondingly greater than those associated with horizontal IIT.

References

Abd-el-Rahman, K. (1991) 'Firms Competitiveness and National Comparative Advantages as Joint Determinants of Trade Composition', *Weltwirtschaftliches Archiv*, 127: 83–97.

Aw, B. W. and M. J. Roberts (1988) 'Pure and Quality Comparisons for US Footwear Imports: An Application of Multilateral Index Numbers', in R. Feenstra (ed.), *Empirical Methods for International Trade* (Cambridge, Mass.: MIT Press).

Balassa, B. and L. Bauwens (1987) 'Intra-Industry Specialisation in a Multi-country and Multi-industry Framework', *Economic Journal*, 97: 923–39.

Bergstrand, J. H. (1990) 'The Heckscher–Ohlin–Samuelson Model, the Linder Hypothesis and the Determinants of Bilateral Intra-Industry Trade', *Economic Journal*, 100: 1216–29.

Davis, D. R. (1997) 'Critical Evidence on Comparative Advantages? North–North Trade in a Multilateral World', *Journal of Political Economy*, 105: 1051–60.

Durkin, J. T. and M. Krygier (1995) 'Empirical Analysis of Intra-Industry Trade: A Vertically Differentiated Approach', Revised version of a paper presented at the Empirical Issues in International Trade Conference, Perdue University, November.

Falvey, R. (1981) 'Commercial Policy and Intra-Industry Trade', *Journal of International Economics*, 11: 495–511.

Falvey, R. and H. Kierzkowski (1987) 'Product Quality, Intra-Industry Trade and (Im)perfect Competition', in H. Kierzkowski (ed.), *Protection and Competition in International Trade* (Oxford: Basil Blackwell).

Flam, H. and E. Helpman (1987) 'Vertical Product Differentiation and North–South Trade', *American Economic Review*, 76: 810–22.

Greenaway, D. and C. R. Milner (1984) *The Economics of Intra-Industry Trade* (Oxford: Basil Blackwell).

Greenaway, D. and C. R Milner (1987) 'Intra-Industry Trade: Current Perspectives and Unresolved Issues', *Weltwirtschaftliches Archiv*, 123: 39–57.

Greenaway, D., R. C. Hine and C. R Milner (1994) 'Country Specific Factors and the Pattern of Horizontal and Vertical Intra-Industry Trade in the UK', *Weltwirtschaftliches Archiv*, 130: 77–99.

Greenaway, D., R. C. Hine and C. R Milner (1995) 'Vertical and Horizontal Intra-Industry Trade: A Cross Industry Analysis for the UK', *Economic Journal*, 105: 1505–18.

Greenaway, D., C. R. Milner and R. Elliott (1999) 'UK Intra-Industry Trade with EU North and South', *Oxford Bulletin of Economics and Statistics*, 61: 365–84.

Grubel, H. G. and Lloyd, P. J. (1975) *Intra-Industry Trade: The Theory and Measurement of International Trade in Differentiated Products* (London: Macmillan).

Gullstrand, J. (2001) 'Demand Patterns and Vertical Intra-Industry Trade', Mimeo, Lund University.

Hellvin, L. (1994) 'Intra-Industry Trade in Asia', *International Economic Journal*, 8: 27–40.

Helpman, E. (1981) 'International Trade in the Presence of Product Differentiation, Economies of Scale and Monopolistic Competition', *Journal of International Economics*, 11: 305–40.

Helpman, E. (1987) 'Imperfect Competition and International Trade: Reconsidering the Evidence', *Journal of Japanese and International Economics*, 1: 62–81.

Helpman, E. and P. Krugman (1985) *Market Structure and Foreign Trade* (Cambridge, Mass.: MIT Press).

Hummels, D. and J. Levinsohn (1995) 'Monopolistic Competition and International Trade: Reconsidering the Evidence', *Quarterly Journal of Economics*, 110: 799–836.

Krugman, P. R. (1979) 'Increasing Reforms, Monopolistic Competition and International Trade', *Journal of International Economics*, 9: 469–79.

Krugman, P. R. (1981) 'Intra-Industry Specialisation and the Gains from Trade', *Journal of Political Economy*, 89: 959–73.

Nolle, D. E. (1990) 'The Determinants of Intra-Industry Trade for Developing Countries', *Rivista Internationale di Scienze Economiche et Commerciali*, 37: 409–23.

Part IV

Intra-Industry Trade, Affiliate Production and FDI

11
A Unified Approach to Intra-Industry Trade and Foreign Direct Investment

James R. Markusen and Keith E. Maskus

Introduction

The theory of international trade has long been relatively disjoint from the theory of foreign direct investment, the latter being viewed traditionally as part of the macroeconomic theory of capital flows. The foreign investment 'regime' (that is, restricted, liberal) could, of course, affect trade in this view, but only through changing the host country's capital stock. This conceptual approach to direct investment began to break down in the 1980s as researchers noted that direct investment seemed to relate more to firm-specific assets than to measures of aggregate capital. Firms in the developed countries penetrated each other's markets with intra-industry direct investment, and the directions of investment did not seem to bear any particular relationship to interest rates or other measures of returns to capital. Other studies refined the evidence by showing that direct investment was related closely to knowledge-based and other intangible assets, and not to physical capital intensity (Eaton and Tamura, 1994; Brainard, 1997; Ekholm, 1998; Carr, *et al.*, 2001; Markusen and Maskus, 2001). For recent surveys of empirical findings, see Markusen (1995, 1998) and Caves (1996).

We have now come to appreciate direct investment as quite different from portfolio capital flows, and our theoretical understanding of FDI has become related more closely to real trade theory than to international finance. It might be best to think of a firm's decision to build or acquire a foreign factory as a 'real'-side decision, with the decision of where and how to raise financial capital for the factory as a separate and distinct decision. Financial capital sometimes comes from the parent country, sometimes from the host country, and sometimes it is raised on world markets in a manner that makes it difficult to define its origin.

In this chapter, we shall concentrate on the 'real' side of direct investment; that is, decisions on the location of production and sales by firms. We shall try to integrate these choices with a trade model, permitting firms to serve foreign markets either by exports or by branch-plant production, or indeed to serve the home market by exports from the foreign branch plant. This permits a much-needed integration of trade and investment theories, and is particularly important in discussions of intra-industry trade and the 'new trade theory' (the industrial-organization approach to trade). These two literatures generally have ignored the role of multinational firms, even though most of the industries that are widely cited as examples of the new trade theory are dominated by multinational firms.

The next section of the chapter provides a few statistics on intra-industry trade and intra-industry affiliate sales (sales by the foreign affiliates of multinational firms). We use real affiliate sales rather than investment stocks or flows, because the latter are a conceptual mismatch when compared to trade flows.

Section three of the paper outlines a formal general equilibrium model with endogenous multinational firms, and notes how Grubel–Lloyd intra-industry trade (IIT) indices and intra-industry affiliate sales (IIAS) indices depend on country characteristics and the restrictiveness of the trade and investment regimes.

The results of section three provide hypotheses for econometric testing and estimation in section four. We relate IIAS and IIT indices to their theoretical determinants, including joint market size, differences in market size, differences in skill endowments, and the costs of engaging in investment and trade. The IIAS regressions fit the theory very well. The index grows higher as two countries become more similar in size and in relative endowments. The IIT regressions fit somewhat less well, but generally support the theory. A final set of regressions use the ratio of the IIAS to the IIT index as the dependent variable. The results suggest that 'balanced' (high index) affiliate activity, much more so than trade, is encouraged by higher incomes and country similarity in terms of size and labour-force composition.

IIT and IIAS indices

We shall use indices for trade and affiliate activity following the formula developed by Grubel and Lloyd (1975). The IIT index is defined as follows, for industry i and countries j and k; $exports_{ijk}$ are exports from j to k, and $imports_{ijk}$ are imports into j from k in industry i:

$$IIT_{ijk} = \left[1 - \frac{|\, exports_{ijk} - imports_{ijk}\,|}{exports_{ijk} + imports_{ijk}} \right] 100 \qquad (11.1)$$

The IIT index ranges from a low of zero, when trade in one-way only, to a value of 100 when trade is perfectly balanced. The IIAS index is similarly defined, where AS_{ijk} are industry i affiliate sales by affiliates in country k of country j parent firms:

$$IIAS_{ijk} = \left[1 - \frac{|\, AS_{ijk} - AS_{ikj}\,|}{AS_{ijk} + AS_{ikj}} \right] 100 \qquad (11.2)$$

Our data set covers the USA and ten countries or regions: Canada, France, Germany, the Netherlands, Switzerland, the UK, Australia, Japan, other Asia-Pacific, and Latin America. The industrial sectors are total manufacturing and seven broad subcategories: food and kindred products (FOOD), chemicals (CHEM), primary metals (PRIM), machinery (MACH), electrical machinery (ELEC), transport equipment (TRAN), and other manufacturing (OTHE). In the econometric estimation in the fourth section of this chapter we employ data for three years: 1988, 1991 and 1994. The affiliate sales data are from the United States Bureau of Economic Analysis. One unfortunate feature of these data is that all observations are bilateral with the USA. Thus, for example, Germany–UK activity is not available, and the USA is always one side of each observation.

Table 11.1 presents the IIAS and IIT indices for 1987 and 1997 (TMFG is total manufacturing). Because these are highly aggregated industrial sectors and the figures are averaged across all countries, the indices are quite high. For most sectors, intra-industry sales ratios exceeded intra-industry trade ratios in 1987, except for machinery and transport equipment. The sales and trade indices came closer together by 1997.

Because we are interested in the evolution of intra-industry activity, in Table 11.2 we present some comparative statistics. In columns (a) and (b) of Table 11.2, we show the change in the IIAS and IIT indices between 1987 and 1997. The IIT index for total manufacturing rose more than its counterpart IIAS index and substantial variation across industries is shown.

Columns (c) and (d) of Table 11.2 show the percentage change in the IIAS index minus the percentage change in the IIT index between 1987

Table 11.1   Grubel–Lloyd indices, 1987 and 1997

	(a) Affiliate sales 1987	(b) Total trade 1987	(c) Affiliate sales 1997	(d) Total trade 1997
TMFG	73.4	69.4	82.9	84.4
FOOD	71.3	66.6	73.5	86.1
CHEM	97.4	80.4	86.8	86.5
PRIM	82.3	39.8	71.5	68.5
MACH	32.6	93.9	52.3	93.2
ELEC	93.6	75.5	98.4	90.9
TRAN	17.2	66.9	52.6	86.9
OTHE	93.0	41.4	81.6	63.0

Source: Calculations for Affiliate Sales use data from US Department of Commerce, Bureau of Economic Analysis, *Foreign Direct Investment in the United States: Operations of US Affiliates of Foreign Companies* (Washington, DC: US Department of Commerce, various years) and *US Direct Investment Abroad: Operations of US Parent Companies and their Foreign Affiliates* Washington, DC: US Department of Commerce, various years). Calculations for Total Trade use data on computer diskettes from United Nations, *Commodity Trade Statistics* (COMTRADE) (Geneva: United Nations).

and 1997, and a similar statistic for the changes in the levels of total (two-way) affiliate sales and total trade. The statistics indicate that the IIAS index grew somewhat none slow than the IIT index over the period, except in machinery and transport equipment. However, the numbers in column (b) indicate that the level of affiliate activity grew faster than the level of trade for total manufacturing. Considering the results in columns (c) and (d) of Table 11.2, we can say that affiliate activity grew faster than trade over the period, but trade became somewhat more balanced than affiliate activity. It is thus important to keep in mind that the indices of intra-industry activity measure proportions and say nothing about volumes. Affiliate activity in the food, electrical machinery, and transport equipment industries grew much faster than trade, but affiliate activity became more balanced relative to trade in the machinery and transport equipment industries.

A general-equilibrium model of trade and affiliate activity

Consider the two-country, two-good, two-factor general-equilibrium model as an extension of the model in Markusen and Venables (1998, 2000). The principal features of the model are as follows. First, there are two homogeneous goods (X and Y), two countries, (h and f), and two

Table 11.2 Changes in Grubel–Lloyd indices for affiliate sales and total trade, 1987–97

	(a) Affiliate sales index	(b) Total trade index	(c) $\Delta IIAS/IIAS - \Delta IIT/IIT$	(d) $\Delta AS/AS - \Delta T/T$
TMFG	9.5	14.9	−5.4	16.7
FOOD	2.1	19.6	−17.4	69.8
CHEM	−10.7	6.1	−16.7	−60.4
PRIM	−10.7	28.6	−39.4	−6.3
MACH	19.7	−0.7	20.4	−24.5
ELEC	4.8	15.5	−10.7	52.3
TRAN	35.4	20.0	15.4	98.3
OTHE	−11.4	21.6	−33.0	−29.0

Source: Calculations were made from the figures in Table 11.1.

factors, (unskilled labour L and skilled labour S). Second, the Y sector is competitive, has constant returns to scale, and is L-intensive. Third, the X sector is imperfectly competitive, has increasing returns to scale, and is S-intensive overall. In this good, 'headquarters' and 'plant' may be separated geographically. Thus firms may have plants in one or both countries.

Fourth, there are six firm types, with free entry and exit into and out of firm types. We use the term *regime* to denote a set of firm types active in equilibrium.

Type m_h Horizontal multinationals that maintain plants in both countries, with headquarters located in country h.

Type m_f Horizontal multinationals that maintain plants in both countries, with headquarters located in country f.

Type n_h National firms that maintain a single plant and headquarters in country h. Type h firms may or may not export to country f.

Type n_f National firms that maintain a single plant and headquarters in country f. Type f firms may or may not export to country h.

Type v_h Vertical multinationals that maintain a single plant in country f and headquarters in country h. Type v_h firms may or may not export to country h.

Type v_f Vertical multinationals that maintain a single plant in country h and headquarters in country f. Type v_f firms may or may not export to country f.

Fifth, good X is homogeneous, firms engage in Cournot competition, and the h and f markets are segmented. Sixth, a firm's mark-up over marginal cost is decreasing in its market share. This creates a 'reciprocal dumping' motive for intra-industry trade and investment. Seventh, there are firm-level scale economies arising from the joint-input ('public good') nature of knowledge-based assets, as well as plant-level scale economies. Finally, the factor-intensity assumptions of the various activities, ranked from most skilled-labour-intensive to least skilled-labour-intensive, are

$$[\text{headquarters only}] \; > \; [\text{integrated } X] \; > \; [\text{plant only}] > \; [Y]$$

The firm-level scale economies create a motive for horizontal multinationals, which spread the fixed costs of knowledge capital across multiple plants. The different factor intensities between activities combined with the different factor endowments (and prices) across countries create a motive for vertical firms. We now describe circumstances under which one firm type is encouraged relative to another in equilibrium.

National firms

National firms wish to locate in the larger market (to save transport costs) and/or the skilled-labour-abundant country (for factor-price motives). The number of firms in the two countries will be relatively balanced, and hence the IIT index higher, if the countries are relatively similar, or if the smaller country is skilled-labour-abundant, and trade costs are low.

Horizontal firms

Horizontal multinationals will be more important when trade costs are high, the countries are relatively similar in size and in relative endowments, and total income is high (as then firms bear the fixed costs of branch plants instead of the variable costs of exports). The location of a firm's headquarters depends only on factor prices (but these are influenced by the location of production in general equilibrium). Intra-industry affiliate sales should be highest when the countries have very similar endowments (headquarters' locations are balanced) and when the countries are relatively similar in size and trade costs are high (type *m* firms are important).

Vertical firms

Vertical firms will be important when the countries have very different relative endowments, and trade costs are relatively low. We have included a small cost to fragmenting the headquarters and plant, so that, other things being equal, a type v firm has higher costs than a type n firm. The consequence of this is that there will never be type v firms operating in both countries. One type v firm from each country could be replaced by one type n in each country, and the same output could be generated with lower costs. Combining this notion with the previous result, we do not expect intra-industry affiliate sales when the countries have quite different relative factor endowments.

What do these general results imply about the relationship of the IIT and IIAS indices to each other and to country characteristics? Clearly, if countries are quite similar and trade costs moderate to high, then we would expect type m firms to substitute for trade. Similarly, if countries grow in total income, we expect horizontal firms to substitute for trade (because of plant-level scale economies).

Figures 11.1 to 11.6 illustrate contours for the levels of IIT and IIAS indices over the 'world' (two-country) Edgeworth box. On the horizontal axis is the total two-country endowment of unskilled labour and the vertical axis is the total two-country endowment of skilled labour. The origin for country h is at the south-west (SW) corner of the box, and the origin for country f is at the north-east (NE) corner of the box. For points along the SW–NE diagonal, the countries differ in relative size but not in relative endowments. The line of approximately equal incomes, in which countries differ in relative endowments but not in size, is steeper than the NW–SE diagonal, and runs from approximately column 9 to column 11 through the centre of the box.

We simulate the model repeatedly over a grid of endowment values, solving for the equilibrium regime and trade pattern for each point in the box. Then we compute IIT and IIAS indices for each solution. These are then plotted in Figures 11.1–11.6. Four different combinations of trade and investment restrictions are considered:

  (i) NL involves no liberalization and includes high trade costs (20 per cent) and a prohibition on FDI;
 (ii) TL involves trade liberalization, adopting low trade costs (1 per cent) and a prohibition on FDI;
(iii) IL involves investment liberalization, permitting FDI but maintaining high trade costs (20 per cent); and
 (iv) FL involves both trade and investment liberalization.

Figure 11.1 shows the intra-industry trade index under NL (trade costs 20 per cent, multinationals prohibited). Intra-industry trade occurs

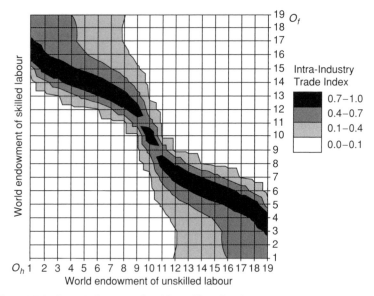

Figure 11.1 Intra-industry trade with no liberalization

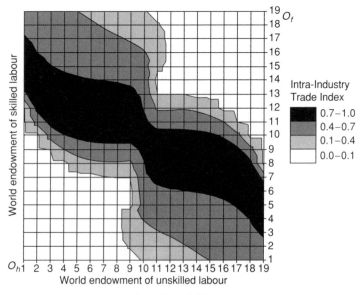

Figure 11.2 Intra-industry trade with trade liberalization

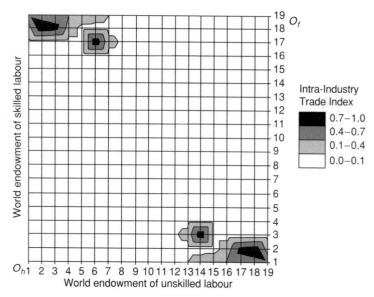

Figure 11.3   Intra-industry trade with investment liberalization

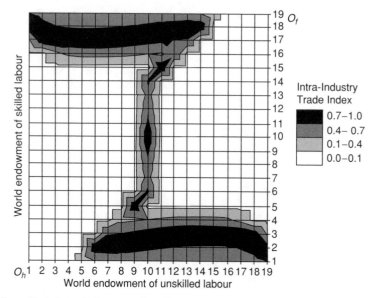

Figure 11.4   Intra-industry trade with investment and trade liberalization

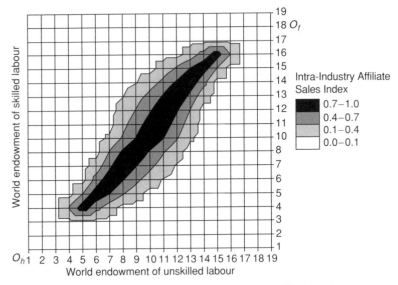

Figure 11.5 Intra-industry affiliate sales with investment liberalization

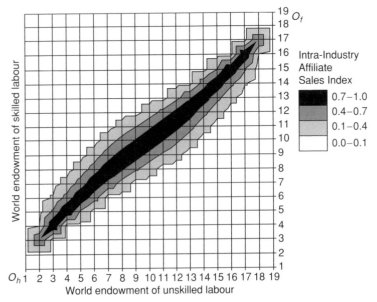

Figure 11.6 Intra-industry affiliate sales with investment liberalization, countries twice as big

when the countries are very similar, or when the smaller country is skilled-labour-abundant. Because good X has increasing returns to scale and is skilled-labour-intensive, size and skilled-labour-abundance are both sources of comparative advantage in that sector. These results will be used in the specification of the regression equations in the next section.

Figure 11.2 shows the IIT index under TL, with trade costs reduced to 1 per cent and multinationals still prohibited. The effect of trade liberalization is to increase the areas where intra-industry trade occurs, but the same general pattern holds: the IIT index is high when countries are similar or when the small country is skilled-labour-abundant.

Figure 11.3 plots the IIT index under the investment liberalization (IL) experiment, retaining high trade costs. Intra-industry trade almost entirely disappears. Near the centre of the box, type n firms are replaced by type m firms so that there is, in fact, no trade in good X. In the region where the small country is skilled-labour-abundant, type v firms headquartered in that country dominate. Thus, headquarters are located there and plants are located in the large, unskilled-labour-abundant country.

Figure 11.4 plots the IIT index under the full liberalization (FL) scenario. Because of plant-level scale economies, type m firms are not active near the centre of the box, and there is once again intra-industry competition between type n firms located in the two countries. The other regions where the index is high are where one country is very skilled-labour-abundant, and of similar size or smaller than the other country. Consider the N–NW region of Figure 11.4. In this region, the dominant firms are type n_h and type v_h. Thus all firms are headquartered in country h, but there are plants in both countries and intra-industry trade occurs while (as noted below), intra-industry affiliate activity does not.

Figure 11.5 shows the IIAS index under investment liberalization (IL) and trade costs at 20 per cent. Positive IIAS occurs where countries are similar in relative endowments, and not too different in size. As the countries become very different in size, type n firms headquartered in the large country come to dominate. Figure 11.6 shows the effect of doubling the world factor endowment. The region of intra-industry affiliate sales stretches to include countries that are more different in size, but not more different in relative endowments.

No intra-industry affiliate sales occur under the full liberalization (FL) scenario, so we have not shown the IIAS index under FL. There are regions in which type v firms are dominant under FL, but they are always headquartered in the skilled-labour-abundant country. Thus there are no intra-industry affiliate sales, even though the level of multinational activity is high. As noted earlier, it is important to remember that the IIAS index is a measure of the *balance* of activity, not its *level*.

What are the general conclusions from the theory? Trade liberalization can increase the IIT index for many country pairs (compare Figure 11.1 to Figure 11.2). However, investment liberalization can largely eliminate IIT if trade costs are high (compare Figure 11.1 to Figure 11.3) or reduce IIT if trade costs are low (compare Figure 11.2 to Figure 11.4). We expect IIT to be highest when, on the one hand, the countries are similar in size, or the small country is skilled-labour-abundant and, on the other hand, when trade costs are low and investment costs are high.

We expect the IIAS index to be higher when the countries are similar in size and in relative endowment, trade costs are high, and investment costs low. One final hypothesis not shown in a diagram relates to total world income. As the two-country total income rises, we expect a shift from intra-industry competition by type *n* firms to intra-industry affiliate sales competition by type *m* firms at points near the centre of the box. Thus there is a hypothesis that a growth in total world income should increase the ratio of the IIAS index to the IIT index.

Empirical results

The theory suggests hypotheses about how IIT and IIAS should be related to country characteristics. Thus, in our regression equations, the dependent variables are the IIT index, the IIAS index, and the ratio IIAS/IIT. The country characteristics identified by our theory include the following. First, SUMGDP is the sum of US and country *j* GDP. This is a measure of joint market size. Second, GDPDIFSQ is the squared difference between US and country *j* GDP. It captures similarity in size between partners and is squared in order to capture non-linearities in the indices as we move toward the north-east in the endowment box.

Third, SKDIFSQ is the squared difference between the share of the labour force that is skilled in the USA and the same share in country *j*. Differences in skill endowments play a strong role in the theory. Fourth, GDPDIF*SKDIF is an interaction term that is important in the IIT regressions. Next, INVCJ is an index of costs of investing in country *j*, and TCJ is an index of the costs of overcoming trade barriers in country *j*.

Data for the estimation form a panel of cross-country and cross-industry observations for the years 1988, 1991 and 1994. Again, the countries and regions involved are Canada, France, Germany, the Netherlands, Switzerland, the UK, Australia, Japan, other Asia-Pacific, and Latin America. We take real sales volume of non-bank manufacturing affiliates in each country to indicate production activity. The US Department of Commerce, Bureau of Economic Analysis (BEA) provides annual data on sales of foreign affiliates of American parent firms and on sales of US affiliates of foreign parent firms. Because the focus of our inquiry is on intra-industry sales, we use the sectoral breakdown indicated in Table 11.1. Clearly, it would be better to investigate data with far greater industry disaggregation, but when BEA data on both outward and inward sales activity are combined, the resulting number of sectors and partner countries or regions becomes severely limited.

The data are bilateral with the USA, which is either the parent country or the host country in every observation. Annual sales values abroad were converted into millions of 1990 US dollars using an exchange-rate-adjusted local wholesale price index, with exchange rates and price indices taken from the International Monetary Fund.

In our theory, intra-industry trade emanates from country character-istics. Thus the appropriate usage is bilateral trade by sector rather than intra-firm trade. For this purpose, figures on bilateral US exports *to* each trading partner, and US imports *from* each trading partner, were com-piled from the COMTRADE database, using the Standard International Trade Classification, version 2, and aggregated to our sectoral classifica-tion. Details of this aggregation are available on request. The export and import data were in current US dollars and we converted them into millions of 1990 US dollars.

Real gross domestic product (GDP) is measured in billions of 1990 US dollars for each country. For this purpose, annual real GDP figures in local currencies were converted into dollars using the market exchange rate. These data are also from the IFS. Skilled labour abundance is defined as the sum of occupational categories 0/1 (professional, tech-nical, and kindred workers) and 2 (administrative workers) in employ-ment in each country, divided by total employment. These figures were compiled from annual surveys reported in the *Yearbook of Labor Statistics* published by the International Labor Organization (various years). In cases where some annual figures were missing, the skilled–labour ratios were taken to equal the period averages for each country. The variable SKDIFFSQ is the squared difference between relative skill endowment of the parent country and the affiliate country.

The cost of investing in the affiliate country is a simple average of several indices of perceived impediments to investment, reported in the

World Competitiveness Report of the World Economic Forum (various years). The investment barriers include restrictions on the ability to acquire control in a domestic company, limitations on the ability to employ foreign skilled labour, restraints on negotiating joint ventures, strict controls on hiring and firing practices, market dominance by a small number of enterprises, an absence of fair administration of justice, difficulties in acquiring local bank credit, restrictions on access to local and foreign capital markets, and inadequate protection of intellectual property. The resulting indices are computed on a scale from zero to 100, with higher numbers indicating higher investment costs.

A trade cost index was taken from the same source and is defined as a measure of national protectionism, or efforts to prevent importation of competitive products. It also runs from zero to 100, with 100 being the highest trade costs. All of these indices are based on extensive surveys of multinational enterprises. It should be noted that both the investment-cost and trade-cost indices are ordinal and qualitative in nature. Thus regression coefficients represent the partial effects of a change in the average perceived costs of investing and trading.

The variables suggested above form the basic specifications we estimate. However, there is likely to be heterogeneity in effects across sectors and investment partners. Thus we add industry effects in a second specification, and industry effects and dummies for Japan and Canada in a third specification. Finally, because of the bilateral nature of the data, the USA is one of the partners in each observation. Thus, the US values of INVC and TC are constant for all observations and cannot provide independent information. Accordingly, impacts of the US trade and investment costs are subsumed into the constant term.

In the IIT and IIAS regressions, the dependent variable is limited in range from 0 to 100. Accordingly, ordinarily least squares (OLS) is an inappropriate estimation technique. For this reason we employ the standard logit approach for those equations. However, the equations involving the ratio IIAS/IIT are not so constrained in principle and we use OLS.

Table 11.3 shows the results for the regressions with intra-industry affiliate sales as the dependent variable. There were a number of industry–country pairs for which data were suppressed, leaving a sample size of 181. For the IIAS regressions, the hypothesized sign on SUMGDP is positive following Figure 11.6. The hypothesized signs on GDPDIFSQ and SKDIFSQ are negative from the results in Figures 11.5 and 11.6. INVCJ should have a negative sign if two-way affiliate sales are relatively balanced at low investment costs. TCJ should have a positive sign, as

Table 11.3 Intra-industry affiliate sales logit regressions

RHS variable	Basic (1)	Basic Ind. Dum. (2)	Basic Ind. Dum. J, C Dum. (3)	Basic INVC, TC (4)	Basic INVC, TC Ind. Dum. (5)	Basic INVC, TC Ind. Dum.J, C Dum. (6)
Constant	**48.9**	**86.3**	**86.1**	**125.4**	**112.8**	**120.2**
	(4.54)	(14.8)	(14.1)	(12.2)	(13.5)	(14.3)
SUMGDP	**0.007**	**0.004**	**0.005**	**0.006**	**0.005**	**0.007**
	(3.71)	(4.24)	(4.26)	(4.87)	(4.92)	(6.34)
GDPDIFSQ	$-8.3e-7$	$-6.2e-7$	$-8.6e-7$	$-9.6e-7$	$-8.1e-7$	$-16.7e-7$
	(-1.28)	(-1.90)	(-2.07)	(-2.25)	(-2.56)	(-4.28)
SKDIFSQ	-2574	-1009	-867	-178	-429	-172
	(-5.11)	(-3.46)	(-3.01)	(-0.50)	(-1.50)	(-0.61)
INVCJ				**-3.15**	**-1.05**	**-1.34**
				(-10.3)	(-3.53)	(-4.20)
TCJ				**0.64**	-0.07	0.08
				(1.81)	(0.82)	(0.25)
No. of observations	181	181	181	181	181	181
Adj. R^2	0.62	0.91	0.91	0.85	0.92	0.93

213

type *m* firms should substitute for type *n* firms as trade costs in the host country rise.

In Table 11.3 there are six regressions listed. The first is the basic model without investment costs, trade costs, or industry and country effects. The second adds industry dummies, and the third adds dummy variables for Japan and Canada. The final three regressions repeat this structure but include INVCJ and TCJ.

The results in Table 11.3 give good support to the theory, both in terms of correct signs and statistical significance, with coefficients that achieve at least 90 per cent confidence shown in bold type. It is evident that market size, as captured by SUMGDP, exerts a positive and significant impact on IIAS. Thus increases in size raise the ratio of two-way affiliate sales to total affiliate sales. In virtually all specifications, GDPDIFSQ has a significantly negative effect on IIAS, as anticipated. Thus the greater the dissimilarity in sizes, the smaller the share of intra-industry sales. In the regressions without cost variables, SKDIFSQ also has a significant and negative effect on IIAS, consistent with the theory. The signs and significance of the central variables SUMGDP, GDPDIFSQ, SKDIFSQ are robust to the inclusion or exclusion of the industry dummies, and Japan and Canada dummies. We should note that the coefficient on the Japan dummy is always negative and usually significant, while that on the Canada dummy is always positive and significant. Industry fixed effects typically are also significant.

When the trade and investment cost variables are added, the results on SUMGDP and GDPDIFSQ remain intact. SKDIFSQ retains its appropriate sign but loses its statistical significance. Skill differences in our data are correlated positively with investment costs, which are higher in the developing countries. This collinearity explains the reduction in magnitude and significance of SKDIFSQ. As for INVCJ and TCJ themselves, their coefficients generally have the right signs. Investment costs clearly reduce incentives to engage in intra-industry affiliate activity. Overall, these results are very positive for the theory.

The IIT regressions in Table 11.4 have 264 observations because there are no missing observations in the trade data, and we include total bilateral trade in addition to the sectoral flows. The results are less supportive of the theory. In principle, SUMGDP should have a negative sign, as type *m* firms replace type *n* firms when total two-country income grows, and this holds in four of the six regressions. GDPDIFSQ and SKDIFSQ should each have negative signs. However, GDPDIFSQ comes out positive in four specifications. Note that it takes on the correct sign when idiosyncrasies in the IIT flows with Japan and Canada are con-

Table 11.4 Intra-industry trade logit regressions

RHS variable	Basic (1)	Basic Ind. Dum. (2)	Basic Ind. Dum. J, C Dum. (3)	Basic INVC, TC (4)	Basic INVC, TC Ind. Dum. (5)	Basic INVC, TC Ind. Dum. J, C Dum. (6)
Constant	**89.2**	**91.8**	**91.5**	**83.4**	**86.9**	**91.2**
	(14.0)	(13.5)	(12.7)	(9.91)	(9.82)	(10.1)
SUMGDP	**−0.002**	−0.001	**0.002**	**−0.003**	**−0.002**	**0.002**
	(−2.09)	(−1.46)	(2.39)	(−2.86)	(−2.29)	(1.74)
GDPDIFSQ	**4.3e−7**	**4.0e−7**	**−7.7e−7**	3.8e−7	3.6e−7	**−7.4e−7**
	(2.00)	(1.87)	(−2.84)	(1.72)	(1.66)	(−2.65)
SKDIFSQ	−198	−225	−339	−98.4	−120	−274
	(−0.73)	(−0.84)	(−1.34)	(−0.36)	(−0.44)	(−1.05)
GDPDIFF*SKDIFF	**−0.01**	−0.01	−0.001	**−0.02**	**−0.02**	−0.006
	(−1.68)	(−0.84)	(−0.07)	(−2.77)	(−2.45)	(−0.67)
INVCJ				**0.84**	**0.84**	0.35
				(2.81)	(2.81)	(1.22)
TCJ				**−0.43**	**−0.44**	−0.25
				(−1.96)	(−1.96)	(−1.16)
No. of observations	264	264	264	264	264	264
Adj. R^2	0.87	0.88	0.90	0.87	0.88	0.90

trolled with country dummies. As is well known, Japan displayed mark-edly low IIT ratios in its trade with the USA during our estimation period. Controlling for this unusual case, we find that differences in GDP affect intra-industry trade negatively. Skill differences have consistently negative signs but do not achieve statistical significance in the explanation of IIT.

The interaction term GDPDIFF*SKDIFF should be negative. Figures 11.1, 11.2 and 11.4 suggest that IIT should be high when one country is small and skilled-labour abundant, implying that IIT should be large when GDPDIFF*SKDIFF is negative. The interaction term always has the right sign and achieves statistical significance in three cases. Note that this variable performs better when investment and trade costs are included.

The INVCJ variables should be positive and the TCJ variable negative, and these hypotheses are generally confirmed in the data. Without controlling for Japan and Canada, we find that an increase in host-country investment costs significantly expands intra-industry trade. Again, however, Japanese history suggests an anomaly: it is costly to invest in Japan but there is relatively little IIT between the USA and that country.

In Table 11.5, the ratio IIAS/IIT is the dependent variable and there are 181 observations. Again, these are OLS regressions because the dependent variable may range without limit. Joint market size, or SUMGDP, should be positive as type *m* firms displace type *n* firms. This result is robust and powerful in the econometric estimates. The diagrams discussed above suggest that the impacts of SKDIFSQ should be negative, as they are. Thus, intra-industry sales rise in comparison with intra-industry trade as countries grow richer and are more similar in size.

However, the theory does not suggest a very sharp hypothesis with respect to GDPDIFSQ. An increase in the size difference should lower the ratio when countries have similar endowments (the numerator falls, the denominator is constant) but raise the ratio when the countries have different relative endowments (the numerator is constant, the denominator falls). Yet in spite of some theoretical ambiguity, the signs are consistently negative, even if significance levels are low. Thus, the IIAS index seems to grow relative to the IIT index as countries become more similar in relative endowments.

A puzzle is why the trade and investment cost variables have the 'wrong' signs in Table 11.5 (although they always have very large standard errors), since they do well in the IIAS and IIT regressions and have opposite signs in those regressions. The results in Tables 11.3 and 11.4

Table 11.5 Ratio of intra-industry affiliate sales to intra-industry trade OLS regressions

RHS variable	Basic (1)	Basic Ind. Dum. (2)	Basic Ind. Dum. J, C Dum. (3)	Basic INVC, TC (4)	Basic INVC, TC Ind. Dum. (5)	Basic INVC, TC Ind. Dum. J, C Dum. (6)
Constant	**1.05** (7.34)	**1.11** (6.74)	**1.08** (5.97)	**1.01** (4.05)	**1.06** (4.18)	**0.97** (3.59)
SUMGDP	**6.5e−5** (3.38)	**6.1e−5** (3.43)	**5.3e−5** (2.32)	**6.6e−5** (3.35)	**6.2e−5** (3.40)	**4.7e−5** (2.00)
GDPDIFSQ	**−2.4e−8** (−3.63)	**−2.2e−8** (−3.72)	**−1.9e−8** (−2.23)	**−2.4e−8** (−3.65)	**−2.3e−8** (−3.75)	**−1.6e−8** (−1.89)
SKDIFSQ	−1.56 (−0.34)	−1.22 (−0.29)	−1.43 (−0.33)	−1.81 (−0.35)	−1.62 (−0.34)	−1.71 (−0.35)
INVCJ				0.007 (0.71)	0.009 (0.93)	0.013 (1.26)
TCJ				−0.006 (−0.72)	−0.007 (−0.90)	−0.01 (−1.26)
No. of observations	181	181	181	181	181	181
Adj. R^2	0.06	0.23	0.22	0.06	0.22	0.22

lead us to expect that the coefficients on INVCJ should be negative, and those on TCJ should be positive, in Table 11.5. Why they are not is unclear to us at this point.

Summary and conclusions

The purpose of this chapter is to present a unified model of intra-industry trade and intra-industry affiliate production and sales where the pattern of firm location, production and trade are determined simultaneously and endogenously. This model is then used to generate predictions about how IIT and IIAS indices should be related to country characteristics and to trade and investment costs. The principal conclusions of the chapter are as follows.

The IIAS regressions fit the theory very well. The index is higher as the two countries are richer and more similar in size and in relative endowments.

The IIT regressions fit less well. The sign on GDPDIFSQ is inconsistent, though it works as hypothesized when trade with Japan is controlled for. The interaction term between differences in country size and differences in relative endowments always has the correct sign (negative) and is generally statistically significant.

While the theory regarding the ratio IIAS/IIT does not always give sharp predictions, the positive sign on the SUMGDP coefficient is robust. The ratio regressions suggest that balanced direct investment, much more than trade, is encouraged by higher incomes and country similarity in terms of size and labour-force composition. Note that skill differences could also be considered a proxy for per capita income. This last result complements earlier findings in Carr *et al.* (2001), and Markusen and Maskus (2001), that the *level* of affiliate sales rises with country incomes, and with their similarity in size and relative endowments. Combining the findings of those papers with the current analysis, we conclude that increased incomes and increased similarity in size and relative endowments increases both the level of affiliate activity and the balance of affiliate activity between country pairs.

References

Brainard, S. L. (1997) 'An Empirical Assessment of the Proximity-Concentration Tradeoff between Multinational Sales and Trade', *American Economic Review*, 87: 520–44.

Carr, D., J. R. Markusen and K. E. Maskus (2001) 'Estimating the Knowledge-Capital Model of the Multinational Enterprise', *American Economic Review*, 91, 693–708.

Caves, R. E. (1996) *Multinational Enterprise and Economic Analysis*, 2nd edn (Cambridge: Cambridge University Press).

Eaton, J. and A. Tamura (1994) 'Bilateralism and Regionalism in Japanese and US Trade and Foreign Direct Investment Relationships', *Journal of Japanese and International Economies*, 8: 478–510.

Ekholm, K. (1998) 'Headquarter Services and Revealed Factor Abundance', *Review of International Economics*, 6: 545–53.

Grubel, H. G. and P. J. Lloyd (1975) *Intra-industry Trade* (London: Macmillan).

International Labour Organization (various years), *International Labour Statistics Yearbook* (Geneva: International Labour Organization).

Markusen, J. R. (1995) 'The Boundaries of Multinational Firms and the Theory of International Trade', *Journal of Economic Perspectives*, 9: 169–89.

Markusen, J. R. (1998) 'Multinational Firms, Location and Trade', *The World Economy*, 21: 733–56.

Markusen, J. R. and K. E. Maskus (2001) 'Multinational Firms: Reconciling Theory and Evidence', in M. Blomstrom and L. Goldberg (eds), *Topics in Empirical International Economics: A Festschrift in Honor of Robert E. Lipsey* (Chicago: University of Chicago Press). 71–95.

Markusen, J. R. and A. J. Venables (1998) 'Multinational Firms and the New Trade Theory', *Journal of International Economics*, 46: 183–203.

Markusen, J. R. and A. J. Venables, (2000) 'The Theory of Endowment, Intra-Industry and Multinational Trade', *Journal of International Economics*, 52: 209–234.

World Economic Forum (various years), *World Competitiveness Report* (Lausanne: IMD).

12
Factor Endowments and Intra-Industry Affiliate Production by Multinational Enterprises*

Karolina Ekholm

Introduction

The increased importance of foreign direct investment (FDI) and activities by multinational enterprises (MNEs) has created an interest among trade economists to explain the cross-country pattern of foreign activities by MNEs. Recent theories of FDI have provided a basis for empirical studies of this pattern. According to models of so-called horizontal FDI – that is, foreign direct investment in similar activities as the ones that are undertaken at home – FDI arises as a consequence of multiplant economies of scale and trade costs (for example, Horstmann and Markusen, 1992; Brainard, 1993; Markusen and Venables, 1998, 2000). The resulting country pattern of FDI is one where similarities with respect to incomes and relative factor endowments are conducive to FDI. According to models of vertical FDI – that is, investment in activities that are either upstream or downstream in relation to the activities conducted at home – FDI arises as consequence of the firms' desire to locate different stages of production at the locations with the lowest production costs (for example, Ethier, and Horn, 1990; Helpman, 1984, 1985). The resulting country pattern from these models is one where differences in relative factor endowments promote FDI. More recently, models of horizontal and vertical FDI have been synthesized in the so-called knowledge-capital model of FDI (see Markusen *et al.*, 1996; Markusen, 1998).

The empirical literature on the cross-country pattern of FDI and activities of MNEs has tended to favour the theory of horizontal FDI over the theory of vertical FDI. Brainard (1997) has shown, using US data, that similarities rather than differences in relative factor endowments explain volumes of affiliate sales. Similar findings are reported by Ekholm (1997, 1998) using Swedish data. Markusen and Maskus (1999) nest models of horizontal and vertical FDI within a more general model (the knowledge-capital model) and show that US data decisively reject the restrictions associated with the model of vertical FDI, whereas the restrictions associated with the model of horizontal FDI cannot be rejected. This has led researchers to conclude that, although production cost differentials may be important in explaining FDI in certain countries and certain sectors, market access is the predominant motive at the aggregate level.

It is evident that a substantial part of the FDI that takes place, much like trade, occurs within industries. However, there are very few studies that analyze the determinants of this intra-industry FDI empirically. In a number of early studies, the importance of intra-industry FDI was documented (that is, Dunning, 1981; Dunning and Norman, 1986). The amount of foreign penetration of MNEs through affiliate sales that are two-way-directed is studied in a recent paper by Greenaway *et al.* (1998) using US data.

In this chapter, we investigate the pattern of intra-industry affiliate production based on data from Sweden. We construct Grubel–Lloyd (GL) indices of intra-industry affiliate production as well as trade. This enables us to compare the country patterns for both measures. We then examine to what extent the variation in these indices can be explained by the degree of similarity in relative factor endowments between countries. In particular, we distinguish between the role played by relative endowments of physical and human capital on the basis that we would expect relative endowments of human capital to play a more important role.

The rest of the chapter is organized as follows: in the second section, we discuss the implications of different models of FDI for the pattern of intra-industry affiliate production. The third section 3 presents the data and methods used in the empirical analysis and the fourth section presents and discusses the empirical results. Finally, some concluding remarks are given in the fifth section.

Determinants of IIAP and IIT according to trade theory

According to the theory of horizontal FDI, a firm has an incentive to set up a foreign affiliate if the saving on trade costs associated with exporting the good exceeds any fixed costs involved in setting up the new plant. A precondition for such a situation to arise is that the firm faces multiplant economies to scale. One reason for such multiplant economies of scale to exist is that the firm has to incur fixed costs in order to invest in knowledge capital. The knowledge capital of the firm may also create incentives for the firm to internalize its production abroad (see Markusen, 1995).

Another way in which the firm's investment in knowledge capital may give rise to FDI is to generate scope for a separation between the firm's headquarters and its production plants. Because ideas are often more easily transferred than goods across national borders, a firm may choose to locate its headquarters where highly-skilled labour is relatively cheap, while production is located where product markets are large and/or where other factors of production are relatively cheap. In such a case, a particular form of vertical FDI arise where upstream headquarters activities take place in one country, while downstream production of final goods take place in another (Markusen *et al.*, 1996; Markusen, 1998).

Clearly, there are also other forms of vertical FDI: for example, investment in component production or assembly activities. However, the theory of this type of vertical FDI is not as well developed as the theory of horizontal FDI and vertical FDI stemming from a separation between headquarters and plants. In an early paper, Helpman (1985) analyzed FDI in intermediate input production in a monopolistic competition framework with zero trade costs, showing that this type of FDI increases with differences in relative factor endowments.[1]

An implication of the theory of horizontal FDI is that the amount of affiliate production that takes place is affected basically by the same set of factors as the amount of trade that takes place. The volume of horizontal FDI is affected by similarity in relative factor endowments and market size, much like the volume of intra-industry trade according to the two-sector monopolistic competition trade model developed by Dixit and Norman (1980), Lancaster (1980), Helpman (1981) and Krugman (1981). Since horizontal FDI is driven by the firms' desire to avoid trade costs, one might think that the only difference between the pattern of affiliate production and trade would be that high trade costs favour affiliate production over trade, whereas low trade costs favour trade over affiliate production. However, the introduction of trade costs in monopolistic competition trade models changes the relationship between market size and trade, so that the relative size of the market becomes an additional source of comparative advantage. This means that the volume of intra-industry trade tends to be high when there are small differences in relative factor endowments as well as market size, and when the smaller country is relatively abundant in factors used intensively in the monopolistic competition sector. The volume of intra-industry affiliate production, on the other hand, increases unambiguously with the degree of similarity in relative factor endowments (see Markusen and Venables, 2000).

Another possible difference between the patterns of trade and affiliate production is that we would expect to find affiliate production to be more important in industries in which knowledge capital is an important input. However, depending on the extent to which knowledge capital at the level of the firm is associated with product differentiation at the level of the industry, the industry pattern of intra-industry affiliate production and trade may be quite similar.

An implication of the theory of vertical FDI is that the volume of affiliate production motivated by a separation between headquarters and production plants increases with differences in relative factor endowments, just as we would expect that the volume of inter-industry trade increases with such differences.

In a multicountry setting, we can define intra-industry affiliate production as the proportion of the bilateral volume of affiliate production that is two-way-directed. Let us define the following Grubel–Lloyd index for intra-industry affiliate production (Grubel and Lloyd, 1975):

$$IIAP_{jkt} = 1 - \frac{\sum_{i=1}^{n} \left| A_{ijkt} - A_{ikjt} \right|}{\sum_{i=1}^{n} \left(A_{ijkt} + A_{ikjt} \right)}, \qquad 0 \leq IIAP_{jkt} \leq 1 \qquad (12.1)$$

A_{ijk} is affiliate production in industry i by country j's firms in country k; A_{ikj} is affiliate production in the same industry by country k's firms in country j; and n is the number of industries. Defined in this way, $IIAP_{jk}$ is a weighted average of the degree of intra-industry affiliate production within industries.

According to the theory of horizontal FDI, we would expect $IIAP_{jk}$ to be high when countries are similar with respect to relative factor endowments. In particular, we expect it to be high when countries have similar relative endowments of highly-skilled labour and other resources important for investment in knowledge capital, since differences in relative endowments of such factors may give rise to one-way FDI of the vertical type discussed above.

Let us also define a similar index for the share of intra-industry trade (IIT_{ijk}):

$$IIT_{jkt} = 1 - \frac{\sum\limits_{i=1}^{n} |X_{ijkt} - M_{ijkt}|}{\sum\limits_{i=1}^{n} (X_{ijkt} + M_{ijkt})}, \qquad 0 \le IIT_{jkt} \le 1 \qquad (12.2)$$

where $X_{ijk}(M_{ijk})$ is country j's exports to (imports from) country k in industry i. IIT_{jk} would be expected to be high when countries have similar relative factor endowments, provided that trade costs are negligible. However, for levels of trade costs sufficiently high for firms to take market size into account in their location decision, but still sufficiently low for them to concentrate production in one location, we expect IIT to be affected by the interaction between relative market size and relative factor endowments.[2] More specifically, we expect IIT to decrease with the product of the difference in market size and the difference in relative endowments of factors used intensively in increasing returns to scale (IRS) industries. Such a product would be positive when the larger country is relatively rich in factors used intensively in IRS industries. It would be negative when the smaller country is relatively rich in such factors. We expect IIT to be high when the smaller country is relative rich in factors used intensively in IRS industries, since the comparative advantage in IRS production stemming from relative factor endowments is then counteracted by a comparative disadvantage stemming from relative market size. Hence we expect a negative relationship between IIT and the product of the difference in market size and the difference in relative endowments of factors used intensively in IRS industries.

Relative market size does not play a similar role in determining $IIAP$, since horizontal FDI is the alternative to concentrating production in large markets in order to save on trade costs.

To summarize, we expect $IIAP$ to be related negatively to the degree of dissimilarity in relative factor endowments. For low trade costs, we also expect IIT to be related negatively to the degree of dissimilarity in relative factor endowments. For high trade costs, however, we expect IIT to be related negatively to the product of differences in market size and differences in relative endowments of factors used intensively in IRS industries.

Data and methods

In this chapter, we shall use Swedish data on affiliate activity as well as trade in order to study the relationship between $IIAP$ and relative factor endowments, on the one hand, and IIT and relative factor endowments and market size, on the other.

In general, data on the actual volume of output of foreign firms in a country are not available from national official sources. Data on affiliate sales for both outward and inward activities are only available for the USA (for studies that use US data to calculate measures of intra-industry affiliate sales, see Greenaway *et al.* (1998), and Chapter 11 by Markusen and Maskus in this volume). In this study, we shall use Swedish data on MNE employment instead. These data show the number of people employed in affiliates of foreign firms, so that outward affiliate production is measured by the number of employees in foreign affiliates of Swedish firms, and inward affiliate production by the number of employees in Swedish affiliates of foreign firms.

A drawback with using affiliate employment instead of affiliate production or sales is that this variable will tend to overestimate activity in labour-intensive sectors, and underestimate activity in capital-intensive sectors. However, the correlation between the employment data and the available data on affiliate production is 0.95.[3] Therefore, affiliate employment is likely to be a reasonable proxy for affiliate production.

The Swedish data on affiliate employment originate from two sources: the Research Institute of Industrial Economics (IUI) and Statistics Sweden. IUI has collected extensive data on the foreign operations of Swedish multinationals about every fourth year since the early 1970s.[4] Statistics Sweden has collected information about employment by Swedish affiliates of foreign firms since the early 1980s. We shall use data for four years: 1986, 1990, 1994 and 1998.

Our data cover the manufacturing sector only, and the level of industry aggregation corresponds roughly to the 2–3-digit level of ISIC (International Standard Industrial Classification).[5] In order to ensure comparability, the same level of aggregation is used for calculating both IIAP and IIT.[6] Affiliate employment is classified according to the primary activity of the affiliate.

Tables 12.1 and 12.2 present bilateral GL indices of IIAP and IIT, respectively, for Swedish trade with most of the other OECD countries. These tables reveal that there is a somewhat similar pattern for these indices in so far as both tend to be high for trade with other Northern EU countries, the USA, Canada and Japan, and tend to be low for the Southern EU countries, Australia and New Zealand. Tentatively, this suggests that relative factor endowments, economic size and geographical distance affect the country pattern of both variables.

We shall run regressions on the GL indices, trying to explain the country pattern with the degree of similarity with respect to relative factor endowments. We want to distinguish between labour, on

Table 12.1   Grubel-Lloyd indices of intra-industry affiliate production between Sweden and other OECD countries

	1986	1990	1994	1998
All countries	0.467	0.529	0.458	0.500
Northern EU				
Austria	0.006	0.006	0.005	0.008
Belgium	0.050	0.095	0.076	0.081
Denmark	0.392	0.292	0.504	0.328
Finland	0.517	0.232	0.291	0.337
France	0.216	0.112	0.218	0.223
Germany	0.104	0.103	0.178	0.175
Ireland	0	0	0.234	0.441
Italy	0.009	0.034	0.027	0.029
Luxembourg	0	0.250	0	0
Netherlands	0.367	0.180	0.277	0.244
Norway	0.300	0.365	0.342	0.193
Switzerland	0.240	0.111	0.101	0.055
UK	0.534	0.305	0.333	0.365
Southern EU				
Greece	n.a.	0	0	0
Portugal	0	0	0	0
Spain	0	0	0	0
North America				
Canada	0.087	0.111	0.201	0.086
USA	0.370	0.295	0.188	0.335
Other OECD				
Australia	0	0	0	0
Japan	0.012	0.009	0.022	0.214
New Zealand	0	0	0	n.a.
Turkey	0	0	0	0

Note: Affiilate production is measured in terms of employment in foreign affiliates in the manufacturing sector and the calculations are based on a level of industry disaggregation corresponding to the 2–3-digit level of ISIC.
Source: IUI database and Statistics Sweden (own calculations).

the one hand, and capital, on the other. However, in order to test whether IIAP is affected by similarity in relative endowments of factors relevant for the creation of knowledge capital, we want to distinguish between human capital and physical capital. In the two-factor case, relative capital endowments will be measured simply by GDP per capita (denoted GC).[7] In an alternative specification, however, we distinguish between physical and human capital. We use two alternative measures

Table 12.2   Grubel-Lloyd indices of intra-industry trade between Sweden and other OECD countries

	1986	1990	1994	1998
All countries	0.614	0.809	0.797	0.778
Northern EU				
Austria	0.530	0.659	0.638	0.636
Belgium	0.455	0.543	0.589	0.604
Denmark	0.532	0.795	0.751	0.710
Finland	0.575	0.837	0.819	0.716
France	0.553	0.676	0.693	0.676
Germany	0.543	0.541	0.624	0.636
Ireland	0.637	0.620	0.517	0.426
Italy	0.384	0.539	0.541	0.566
Luxembourg	n.a.	n.a.	n.a.	n.a.
Netherlands	0.564	0.537	0.580	0.584
Norway	0.416	0.657	0.542	0.567
Switzerland	0.666	0.573	0.560	0.471
UK	0.534	0.666	0.683	0.725
Southern EU				
Greece	0.079	0.127	0.124	0.105
Portugal	0.173	0.265	0.265	0.307
Spain	0.378	0.343	0.461	0.416
North America				
Canada	0.336	0.408	0.334	0.333
USA	0.434	0.718	0.647	0.586
Other OECD				
Australia	0.083	0.078	0.076	0.110
Japan	0.241	0.442	0.605	0.638
New Zealand	0.065	0.043	0.058	0.132
Turkey	0.033	0.099	0.116	0.124

Note: Calculations are based on a level of industry disaggregation corresponding to the 2–3-digit level of ISIC.
Source: Statistics Sweden (own calculations).

of relative physical capital endowments: capital stock per worker reported in Penn World Tables Mark 5.6 (denoted *KW*) and commercial energy use per capita (*EC*).[8] As a proxy variable for relative human capital endowments we use gross enrolment ratios in secondary education (denoted *HK*).[9]

The variables measuring degree of dissimilarity take the following form:

$$Xdis_{jkt} = \left| 1 - \frac{X_{jt}}{X_{kt}} \right| \qquad (12.3)$$

where X is a measure of relative factor endowments, taken to be either GDP per capita (GC), capital per worker (KW), commercial energy consumption per capita (EC) or gross enrolment ratios in secondary education (HK).

Since the GL index is bounded between 0 and 1 we specify the estimated equation as a logistic function. More specifically, we estimate functions of the following form:

$$y_{jkt} = \frac{1}{1 + e^{-x'\beta}} \qquad (12.4)$$

where y_{jkt} is either the $IIAP_{jkt}$ or IIT_{jkt}, x is a vector of explanatory variables, and β is a vector of regression coefficients.

In the analysis, we want to utilize the panel nature of our data, exploring whether any effects of the degree of similarity with respect to relative factor endowments are detectable in the time series dimension as well as the cross-section dimension. Hummels and Levinsohn (1995) claim that the results from cross-section analyses in this area are sensitive to taking the time series dimension into account. However, it should be noted that we have very few observations over time, which makes it somewhat difficult to apply panel data techniques in this context.

An additional reason for focusing on the time dimension of $IIAP_{jk}$ and IIT_{jk} is that it may reveal differences in how these indices have responded to changes in trade costs. Based on the theory of horizontal FDI, we would expect that a decrease in transportation and other trade costs would have a depressing effect on the amount of horizontal FDI. At the same time, a reduction of trade costs might increase the scope for vertical FDI. The end result would be a decreased relative importance of intra-industry affiliate production. For trade, on the other hand, we would not expect a similar effect. In order to examine whether $IIAP_{jk}$ and IIT_{jk} in fact exhibit different patterns over time, the vector of explanatory variables includes time dummies.

Results

Table 12.3 presents results from non-linear estimations of Equation (12.4) with GL indices for IIT and IIAP as dependent variables. In these

Table 12.3   Non-linear estimations of logistic functions

Independent variables	Dependent variable: IIT			Dependent variable: IIAP		
	(1)	*(2)*	*(3)*	*(1)*	*(2)*	*(3)*
GCdis	−2.64*** (6.06)			−3.01*** (3.44)		
KWdis		−0.18 (0.35)			0.36 (0.54)	
ECdis			0.37 (0.76)			0.08 (0.13)
HKdis		−0.76 (0.61)	−1.88* (1.93)		−2.72 (1.38)	−2.69* (1.67)
GDPdiff * GCdiff	0.06 (1.41)					
GDPdiff * KWdiff		−0.38* (1.73)				
GDPdiff * ECdiff			−0.02 (0.56)			
GDPdiff * HKdiff		−0.13 (0.93)	−0.11 (1.36)			
D90	0.50** (2.02)	0.37 (1.24)	0.45 (1.55)	−0.38 (1.09)	−0.53 (1.15)	−0.51 (1.12)
D94	0.34 (1.41)	0.38 (1.21)	0.44 (1.47)	−0.30 (0.92)	0.07 (0.18)	0.02 (0.96)
D98	0.24 (0.98)		0.48 (1.57)	−0.23 (0.75)		0.19 (0.50)
Constant	0.35 (1.66)	−0.36 (1.27)	−0.39 (1.20)	−0.77*** (2.89)	−1.38*** (3.74)	−1.34*** (3.29)
Adj R^2	0.88	0.81	0.82	0.58	0.43	0.50
No. of observations	82	60	82	80	59	80

Note: *t*-values (given within parentheses in absolute values) are based on White's method. Asterisks indicate statistical significance at different levels (in two-tailed tests): ***(1%), **(5%), *(10%).

estimations the data is simply pooled and thus not controlled for any unobserved heterogeneity with respect to country pairs. As can be seen from this table, there is fairly strong evidence that dissimilarities in GDP per capita have a negative effect on IIT as well as IIAP. Furthermore, there is some evidence that dissimilarities in secondary school enrolment ratios have a negative effect on IIT and IIAP. The estimated coefficients of the variables capturing dissimilarity in relative physical capital endowments are, however, mostly positive, although never significant.

According to the results in Table 12.3, most of the variables capturing the interaction between country size and differences in relative factor endowments do not assert a significant effect on IIT. The exception is the variable capturing the interaction between differences in GDP and differences in physical capital per worker. The estimated coefficient is negative, as expected, and significant at the 10 per cent level. This result is consistent with the view that physical capital is more important than human capital for IRS at the plant level.

As is evident from Table 12.3, the overall fit of the estimated model is fairly good in regressions of IIT. Between 80 per cent and 90 per cent of the variance in IIT is explained by the model. However, the adjusted R^2 obtained in the regressions of IIAP is considerably lower. It ranges between 0.43 and 0.58. In this sense, we are able to explain less of the observed pattern of IIAP with the predictions derived from trade theory.

Table 12.4 presents the results from random effects estimations where we exploit the panel nature of the data. In order to perform linear regressions, we have transformed Equation (12.4) and run regressions on the log of $y_{jkt}/(1 - y_{jkt})$. One problem with this procedure is that observations of the dependent variable that are zero cannot be transformed in this way. Since there are no zero observations on IIT, this only constitutes a problem in the regressions of IIAP. To simply exclude the zero observations creates selection bias. We have chosen, therefore, to set zero observations to 0.01 in these regressions.

The alternative to estimating random effects models would be to estimate fixed effects models. However, using Hausman tests, we cannot reject the hypothesis that the difference in the coefficients estimated with fixed and random effects estimations is not systematic. Since random effects estimations yield more efficient estimates, we present only the results from those estimations.

Table 12.4 reveals that there is now only one significant estimate with respect to dissimilarity in relative factor endowments – the negative estimate of the coefficient of dissimilarity in GDP per capita in the regression of IIAP. The estimated coefficients of dissimilarity in the secondary school enrolment ratios are negative in the regressions of both IIT and IIAP, but they are insignificant. The estimated coefficients of dissimilarity in the proxies for relative endowments of physical capital have different signs in different regressions.

Table 12.4   Random effects estimation of transformed logistic functions

Independent variables	Dependent variable: IIT			Dependent variable: IIAP		
	(1)	*(2)*	*(3)*	*(1)*	*(2)*	*(3)*
GCdis	−0.48 (1.11)			−2.23*** (3.25)		
KWdis		−0.71 (0.97)			0.36 (0.31)	
ECdis			1.21 (1.37)			−1.94 (1.32)
HKdis		−0.31 (0.92)	−0.20 (0.35)		−1.07 (0.91)	−0.41 (0.36)
GDPdiff *GCdiff	0.03 (1.07)					
GDPdiff *KWdiff		−0.004 (0.03)				
GDPdiff *ECdiff			0.08 (1.43)			
GDPdiff *HKdiff		−0.06 (1.36)	−0.05* (1.69)			
D90	0.49*** (4.11)	0.49*** (4.44)	−0.52 (4.36)	−0.16 (0.70)	−0.19 (0.98)	−0.29 (1.21)
D94	0.45*** (3.66)	0.45*** (3.75)	0.52*** (4.30)	0.10 (0.46)	0.20 (1.03)	0.04 (0.17)
D98	0.45*** (3.62)		0.54*** (4.13)	0.10 (0.44)		0.15 (0.56)
Constant	−0.49** (1.91)	−0.43 (1.25)	−1.04** (2.22)	−2.03*** (5.01)	−2.70*** (5.14)	−1.89** (2.52)
R^2 (within)	0.31	0.44	0.41	0.11	0.10	0.10
R^2 (between)	0.45	0.08	0.01	0.42	0.02	0.03
R^2 (overall)	0.21	0.09	0.01	0.33	0.03	0.03
No. of observations	82	60	82	80	60	81
No. of groups	21	21	21	21	21	21

Note: Estimates are based on GLS regressions. Asterisks indicate statistical significance at different levels (in two-tailed tests): ***(1%), **(5%), *(10%).

The estimated coefficients of the interaction variables are fairly similar to the ones obtained by pooling the data. However, now the only significant estimate is one of the estimated coefficients of the variable capturing the interaction between differences in GDP and differences in relative endowments of human capital. In general, the point estimates of the coefficients of the interaction variables are close to zero, and some of the estimates are positive rather than negative. This suggests that the interaction between country size and relative factor endowments does not have a strong influence on IIT. A possible interpretation of this result is that firms operating in industries where trade costs are high enough to influence location decisions tend to become multinationals by setting up plants abroad, thereby generating affiliate production rather than trade.

Although the R^2 values reported in Table 12.4 do not have the usual interpretation as the share of variation explained by the model, but instead are simply squared correlations between predicted and actual values, they still tell us something about the goodness of fit. Overall, the R^2 values are relatively low, perhaps with the exception of the two-factor model specification where GDP per capita is used as a proxy for the overall capital–labour ratio.

Turning to the results for the time dummies, there seems to be a systematic difference between the regression of IIT and IIAP. In both Tables 12.3 and 12.4, all the estimated coefficients of the time dummies in regressions of IIT have positive signs. In regressions of IIAP, on the other hand, half of the estimated coefficients have negative signs.

Table 12.5 presents the estimated change in the GL indices of IIT and IIAP over time, based on the point estimates of the coefficients of the time dummies. The figures presented in the table show the changes in the two GL indices that are unaccounted for by changes in the independent variables in the regressions. The estimated changes have been evaluated at the mean of the dependent variables in 1986. Because the estimated change varies depending on the specification of the model, we present estimates based on all regressions that include all three time dummies.[10]

Table 12.5 reveals that the estimated changes are positive and lie in the range between 0.21 and 0.27 for *IIT* (that is, the percentage share of intra-industry trade in total trade is estimated to have increased by

Table 12.5   Estimated change unexplained by included variables, 1986–98

	IIT	IIAP
Pooled data (1)	0.21	−0.21
Pooled data (3)	0.25	−0.07
Panel (1)	0.25	0.01
Panel (3)	0.27	−0.02

Note: The estimated change has been evaluated at the mean of the dependent variable in 1986.

between 21 and 27 percentage points). This evidence suggests that the change over time in IIT that is unexplained by changes in dissimilarity in relative factor endowments and changes in the interaction between country size and relative factor endowments is positive, and around 25 percentage points. For IIAP, on the other hand, the estimated change is either negative or close to zero. The changes for IIAP lie in the range between −0.21 and 0.01. This suggests that the change over time in IIAP unexplained by changes in dissimilarity in relative factor endowments is either negative or nonexistent. In any case, the estimated changes are different for IIT and IIAP, and they are different in the way that we would expect if these estimated changes capture different responses to decreases in trade costs. Both IIT and IIAP may be affected positively by, for example, an increased importance of differentiated goods in consumption. However, the result that the estimated change in IIT is greater than the estimated change in IIAP is consistent with the prediction that a reduction in trade costs would tend to reduce IIAP, but not IIT.

Concluding remarks

This study has examined determinants of intra-industry affiliate production and trade. Based on Swedish data, we have found some evidence of dissimilarity in relative factor endowments affecting the pattern of IIT and IIAP. In particular, dissimilarity in GDP per capita seems to have a negative effect on both IIT and IIAP. Furthermore, we have estimated negative effects stemming from dissimilarity in relative endowments of human capital. However, these estimated effects are not generally statistically significant. Dissimilarity in relative endowments of physical capital yields estimates with different signs in different specifications. Taken together with the fact that none of the estimates is significant, we conclude that dissimilarity in relative endowments of physical capital does not seem to have much of an effect.

Based on recent theorizing on intra-industry trade when trade is costly, we have also examined the effect of the interaction between differences in GDP and differences in relative factor endowments on IIT. However, we obtain only weak support for the hypothesis that such interaction matters.

Our results suggest that IIT and IIAP have responded differently to changes over time unaccounted for by changes in dissimilarity of relative factor endowments and the interaction between GDP and relative factor endowments. Whereas the estimated change over time is positive for IIT, it is either negative or close to zero for IIAP. One possible interpretation is that the successive lowering of trade costs among the OECD countries has tended to decrease IIAP, but not IIT, as we would expect according to theory. The tendency for a decrease in IIAP would come about through two different effects: (i) lower trade costs would lead to weaker incentives for firms to carry out horizontal FDI; and (ii) lower trade costs would make it more advantageous to carry out vertical FDI. Whether, in fact, there has been a change in the composition of FDI towards more of the vertical type and less of the horizontal type is an interesting question in this context. However, it is a question that is very difficult to answer, given the lack of information on the type of affiliate activities carried out. Nevertheless, we may note that such an interpretation would indeed be consistent with the popular notion that increased globalization has enabled firms to take better advantages of international differences in production costs by locating parts of their production abroad.

Notes

* This chapter is a revised version of a paper prepared for the conference 'Frontiers of Research on Intra-Industry Trade' in Boulder, Colorado, USA, in August 2000. I thank the participants for valuable comments and suggestions. Furthermore, I thank the Swedish Bank Tercentenary Foundation and the European Commission through the TMR project on Foreign Direct Investment for financial support.

1 Venables (1999) analyzes fragmentation of production in a perfect competition framework with positive trade costs, showing that a similar vertical production structure may arise when trade costs for intermediate inputs decrease.

2 Strictly speaking, relative market size also plays a role for IIT when trade costs are zero. In Helpman and Krugman (1985) intra-industry trade only takes place in the capital-intensive industry. If the relatively capital-abundant country is large, it may produce the whole of the capital-intensive good, which means that there will be no intra-industry trade at all. Therefore, intra-industry trade will only occur if the relatively capital-abundant country is sufficiently small.

3 Information about production is available for the foreign affiliates of Swedish multinationals, but not for the Swedish affiliates of foreign firms.

4 A general description of these data can be found in Ekholm and Hesselman (2000).

5 In our industry aggregation, the manufacturing industry is divided into nineteen industries.

6 The trade data have been supplied by Statistics Sweden.

7 Data on GDP per capita are expressed in US dollars and they have been collected from World Development Indicators (World Bank, 1998).

8 The estimate of capital per worker is defined as the cumulated depreciated sum of past gross domestic investment in producer durables, non-residential construction, and other construction (Summers and Heston, 1991,

pp. 347–54). Data on commercial energy use are reported in kg oil equivalent and have been collected from World Development Indicators (World Bank, 1998).

9 Data have been collected from UNESCO.

10 Hence, we have not calculated estimated changes based on regressions that include variables with capital per worker, since data on capital per worker were not available for 1998.

References

Brainard, S. L. (1993) 'A Simple Theory of Multinational Corporations and Trade with a Tradeoff between Proximity and Concentration', NBER Working Paper No. 4269.

Brainard, S. L. (1997) 'An Empirical Assessment of the Proximity-Concentration Trade-off between Multinational Sales and Trade', *American Economic Review*, 87: 520–44.

Dixit, A. K. and V. Norman (1980) *Theory of International Trade* (Cambridge University Press).

Dunning, J. H. (1981) 'A Note on Intra-Industry Foreign Direct Investment', *Banca Nazionale de Lavoro*, 34: 427–37.

Dunning, J. H. and G. Norman (1986) 'Intra-Industry Investment', in H. P. Gray (ed.), *Research in International Business and Finance, Vol. 5, Uncle Sam as Host*, (Greenwich, Conn. and London: JAI Press).

Ekholm, K. (1997) 'Factor Endowments and the Pattern of Affiliate Production by Multinational Firms', Research Paper 97/19, CREDIT, University of Nottingham.

Ekholm, K. (1998) 'Proximity Advantages, Scale Economies, and the Location of Production', in P. Braunerhjelm and K. Ekholm (eds), *The Geography of Multinational Firms* (Boston, Mass.: Kluwer).

Ekholm, K. and M. Hesselman (2000) 'The Foreign Operations of Swedish Manufacturing Firms: Evidence from a Survey of Swedish Multinationals 1998', Working Paper No. 540, The Research Institute of Industrial Economics, Stockholm.

Ethier, W. J. and H. Horn (1990) 'Managerial Control of International Firms and Patterns of Direct Investment', *Journal of International Economics*, 28: 25–45.

Greenaway, D., P. J. Lloyd and C. Milner (1998) 'Intra-Industry FDI and Trade Flows: New Measures of Globalisation of Production', Research Paper 98/5, Centre for Research on Globalisation and Labour Market, University of Nottingham.

Grubel H. G. and P. J. Lloyd (1975) *Intra Industry Trade: The Theory and Measurement of International Trade in Differentiated Products* (London: Macmillan).

Helpman, E. (1981) 'International Trade in the Presence of Product Differentiation, Economies of Scale, and Monopolistic Competition: A Chamberlin-Heckscher-Ohlin Approach', *Journal of International Economics*, 11: 305–40.

Helpman, E. (1984) 'A Simple Theory of International Trade with Multinational Corporations', *Journal of Political Economy*, 92: 451–71.

Helpman, E. (1985) 'Multinational Corporations and Trade Structure', *Review of Economic Studies*, 52: 443–457.

Helpman, E. and P. R. Krugman (1985) *Market Structure and Foreign Trade: Increasing Returns, Imperfect Competition, and the International Economy* (Cambridge, MA: MIT Press).

Helpman, E. (1988) 'Imperfect Competition and International Trade: Evidence from Fourteen Industrial Countries', Chapter 7 in A. M. Spence and H. A. Hazard (eds), *International Competitiveness* (Ballinger).

Horstmann, I. J. and J. R. (1992) Markusen, 'Endogenous Market Structures in International Trade (Natura Facit Saltum)', *Journal of International Economics*, 32: 109–129.

Hummels, D. and J. Levinsohn (1995) 'Monopolistic Competition and International Trade: Reconsidering the Evidence', *Quarterly Journal of Economics*, 110: 799–836.

Krugman, P. R. (1981) 'Intraindustry Specialization and the Gains from Trade', *Journal of Political Economy*, 89: 959–73.

Lancaster, K. J. (1980) 'Intra-industry Trade under Perfect Monopolistic Competition', *Journal of International Economics*, 10: 151–175.

Markusen, J. R. (1984) 'Multinationals, Multi-plant Economies, and the Gains from Trade', *Journal of International Economics*, 16: 205–26.

Markusen, J.R. (1995) 'The Boundaries of Multinational Enterprises and the Theory of International Trade', *Journal of Economic Perspectives*, 9: 169–189.

Markusen, J. R. (1998) 'Trade Versus Investment Liberalization', NBER Working Paper No. 6231.

Markusen, J. R. and K. E. Maskus (1999) 'Discriminating Among Alternative Theories of Multinational Enterprise', NBER Working Paper No. 7164.

Markusen, J. R. and A. J. Venables (1998) 'Multinational Firms and the New Trade Theory', *Journal of International Economics*, 42: 183–203.

Markusen J. and A. Venables (2000) 'The Theory of Endowment, Intra-Industry and Multinational Trade', *Journal of International Economics*, 52: 209–254.

Markusen, J. R., A. J. Venables, D. E. Konan, and K. Zhang (1996) 'A Unified Treatment of Horizontal Direct Investment, Vertical Direct Investment, and the Pattern of Trade in Goods and Services', NBER Working Paper No. 5696.

Summers, R. and A. Heston (1991) 'The Penn World Table (Mark 5): An Expanded Set of International Comparisons, 1950–1988', *The Quarterly Journal of Economics*, 106: 327–68.

Venables, A. (1999) 'Fragmentation and Multinational Production', *European Economic Review* 43: 935–945.

World Bank (1998) *World Development Indicators* 1998 (World Bank).

White, H. (1980) 'A Heteroskedasticity Consistent Covariance Matrix Estimator and a Direct Test of Heteroskedasticity', *Econometrica*, 48: 817–838.

13
Globalization and Intra-Firm Trade: Further Evidence*

Kiichiro Fukasaku and Fukunari Kimura

Introduction

Multinational enterprises (MNEs) are integrating agents in the world economy by putting the labour, capital and technology available in different countries to most productive use. According to the United Nations' *World Investment Report 2000* (United Nations, 2000), over 63 000 parent companies world-wide have established about 690 000 foreign affiliates in countries other than their own, with the amount of inward FDI stock valued at roughly US$4800 billion in 1999. These foreign affiliates are estimated to have generated total gross product of more than US$3000 billion and total employment of over 40 million in host countries. While about 90 per cent of all parent companies are located in OECD countries, more than half of all foreign affiliates are in operation in non-OECD countries, providing a major source of industrial production and employment in a number of developing host countries.[1]

MNEs are also significant – and often dominant – players in international trade by extending business networks overseas through direct investment, and providing markets for related parties beyond national boundaries. For example, in the USA, where most consistent trade data by ownership is available, about three-quarters of merchandise exports and 70 per cent of merchandise imports in 1997 were associated with either US-owned or foreign-owned MNEs and their foreign affiliates.[2] Although it is difficult to provide comparable statistics for other countries because of the paucity of relevant data, there is little doubt about the significance of MNEs in the foreign trade of many countries, both developed and developing.

One important aspect of international trade is trade between a parent company and its foreign affiliates, where products are traded internationally but stay within the ambit of a MNE.[3] This type of trade is called *intra-firm* trade as opposed to trade among unrelated parties; (also called *arm's-length* trade). It has been argued that intra-firm trade is an important part of the process of globalization – the increasing interdependence of markets and production in different countries through trade in goods and services, cross-border flows of capital, and technology transfer (Bonturi and Fukasaku, 1993; OECD, 1993). MNEs' purchasing, production and sales activities across national borders provide markets for internal transactions between a parent company and its foreign affiliates, and the sheer size of intra-firm trade testifies to the relative importance of such transactions in international trade. Earlier observations suggest, however, that globalization of corporate activities does not necessarily entail the growth of intra-firm trade (ibid.). This begs the question of why globalization brings about more intra-firm trade in certain industries than in others. It is also important to ask how intra-firm trade is likely to be affected by changes in trade policy as well as other government policies, such as corporate tax, competition, and regulation.

Globalization generates more integrated economic environment across nations and provides more room for foreign operations by firms through various transaction channels. This may enhance intra-firm trade. On the other hand, globalization reduces the cost of service links between remote locations through a substantial reduction in the cost of transportation, telecommunications, and information-exchange media.[4] This may make arm's-length trade easier and possibly result in smaller shares of intra-firm trade. We therefore cannot expect a priori that globalization will definitely increase the weight of intra-firm trade in the world. The establishment of foreign affiliates by MNEs does not necessarily accompany intra-firm trade. The relocation of production activities may simply substitute for international trade. Even where trade and FDI are complementary, generated trade does not necessarily take the form of intra-firm trade. A large part of intra-firm trade may be intra-firm, inter-process trade based on intra-firm fragmentation of production/distribution blocks.

The phenomenon of intra-firm trade has been little studied so far in international trade literature.

This is largely because of data and measurement problems inherent to analyzing this type of trade. Available international trade statistics do not distinguish between intra-firm trade and arm's-length trade, thus empirical research has to rely on firm survey data, access to which is limited to a few countries.[5]

Moreover, there is a lack of a sound analytical framework in which one can properly address the question of why firms first go abroad through direct investment rather than exporting or licensing, and then engage in intra-firm transactions as a conduit for international trade. Indeed, a recent review of international trade literature makes no mention of intra-firm trade (see Helpman, 1998). This chapter aims to present an update on this phenomenon by analyzing the available data on intra-firm trade for two major OECD countries, the USA and Japan. The chapter begins by discussing the linkages between globalization of industry and intra-firm trade in the second section.

The third section contains an empirical analysis of recent developments in intra-firm trade in the USA. The fourth section shifts attention to the case of Japan, and the results of a regression analysis of factors affecting intra-firm trade are reported, and the fifth section concludes. The nature and limitation of the data used for the third and fourth sections and are discussed briefly in the Appendix.

Globalization of industry and intra-firm trade

One way of measuring the significance of globalization of industry is to look at the relative importance of foreign affiliates in host economies. Table 13.1 summarizes information for 1996 (or the latest available year) on foreign affiliates operating in manufacturing industry in sixteen OECD countries in terms of the number of enterprises and employees as well as the value of production, exports and imports. While the available data are fragmentary and incomplete, this table indicates that in the 1990s affiliates of foreign-owned MNEs played a significant part in industrial activities in most of these countries, with the notable exception of Japan. It also appears that foreign affiliates operating in manufacturing industry are, on average, larger in size and more trade-orientated than domestic firms.

It is well documented that globalization of industry has a particular pattern of development displaying some similarities and differences across industries, as observed in major OECD countries (OECD, 1996, 1999). First, the intra-firm trade ratio varies considerably across sectors: computers, pharmaceuticals, semiconductors, and automobiles tend to have much higher shares of intra-firm trade than do other manufacturing industries (see Table 13.2).[6] At the bottom of this table are non-ferrous metals, steel, and clothing, where international transactions

Table 13.1 Significance of foreign affiliates in manufacturing industry of selected OECD countries,[a] 1996*

	(1) No. of enterprises		(2) No. of employees		(3) Production		(4) Exports		(5) Imports	
	Units	Percentage of national total	Units	Percentage of national total	US dollars (millions)	Percentage of national total	US dollars (millions)	Percentage of national total	US dollars (millions)	Percentage of national total
Canada[e]	1 816	26.4	n.a.	n.a.	193 272	50.9	75 105[b]	49.4	n.a.	n.a.
Czech Republic[f]	268	12.0	149 847[n]	15.4	8 719	24.3	n.a.	n.a.	n.a.	n.a.
Finland[c,g]	287	5.4	29 606	8.6	5 417	9.0	2 866	10.7	n.a.	n.a.
France[e]	2 787	12.6	742 663[n]	25.8	157 141	28.8	70 922	35.2	n.a.	n.a.
Germany[e]	1 454	4.0	453 000	6.9	179 226[o]	12.8	n.a.	n.a.	n.a.	n.a.
Hungary[h]	4 312	12.8	297 448	35.6	20 583[o]	62.4	10 737[p]	68.5	12.716[p]	70.2
Ireland[i]	728	15.8	106 410	47.0	38 587	66.4	34 463	83.9	8 999	75.4
Italy[b,i]	1 403	0.3	423 590[n]	8.9	114 456[o]	11.9	n.a.	n.a.	n.a.	n.a.
Japan[e]	285	0.1	86 469[n]	0.8	45 872[o]	1.2	5 994	1.5	10 342	4.0
Mexico[d,e]	1 927	n.a.	906 614	n.a.	42 320	n.a.	11 174[p]	21.5[q]	18 081[p]	27.7[q]
Netherlands[e]	844	2.6	160 487	19.0	67 038	29.7	42 957	42.4	33 907	43.2
Norway[k]	516	4.7	40 348	14.3	11 514	19.0	n.a.	n.a.	n.a.	n.a.
Sweden[l]	757	2.3	134 372[n]	19.9	34 294[o]	20.8	16 238	20.7	7 506	30.3
Turkey[k]	170	1.6	58 422	5.6	11 831	12.7	n.a.	n.a.	n.a.	n.a.
UK[e]	2 686	1.6	815 161	19.2	229 537	33.2	n.a.	n.a.	n.a.	n.a.
USA[m]	2 950	n.a.	2 213 600	11.9[q]	552 000[o]	14.9[q]	140 886[p]	22.5[q]	268 673[p]	33.8[q]

Notes: *Or latest available year

[a] 'Manufacturing industry' is defined as ISIC Rev. 3, and national currencies are converted into US dollars using period-average exchange rates.

[b] 1995.

[c] 1994.

[d]1993.

[e]Refers to majority foreign-owned firms.

[f]Refers to majority foreign-owned firms with 100 or more employees.

[g]Based on the Annual Industrial Statistics, which are establishment-level data.

[h]All foreign-owned firms with over 10 per cent of capital share.

[i]Refers to the number of all local units of multi-location enterprises (with more than 3 persons), where 50 per cent or more of the share capital is held by non-Irish residents.

[l]Refers to the number of all Italian enterprises in which a foreign person owned or controlled a direct or indirect interest of 50 per cent or more at the end of the fiscal year.

[k]Refers to majority foreign-owned establishments.

[l]Refers to majority foreign-owned non-financial firms.

[m]Refers to non-bank foreign affiliates with 10 per cent or more of the voting securities.

[n]On the full-time equivalent basis.

[o]Turnover.

[p]Refers to total merchandise trade.

[q]Estimated by the authors.

n.a. = not available.

Sources: OECD (1999), except for the data of US exports and imports, which are taken from Table A13.2 of this chapter OECD (2000); and IMF (1999).

Table 13.2   Patterns of globalization of industry, eight surveyed industries

Industries	(1) Foreign sourcing (% of total sourcing)[a]	(2) Intra-firm trade (% of total trade)[b]	(3) Affiliate sales (% of total sales)	(4) Direct investment flows (% of gfcf)[c]
Pharmaceuticals	10–30	70	40–50	50–70
Computers	20–60	50–80	50–60	30–40
Semiconductors	10–40	70	20–25	15–25
Motor vehicles	25–35	50–80	10–20	15–25
Consumer electronics	10–40	30–50	20–30	20–35
Non-ferrous metal	30–50	30	15–25	20–35
Steel	15–25	5–10	15–25	5–10
Clothing	10–40	5–10	5–15	15–20

Notes:
[a]Share of foreign sourcing in total foreign and domestic sourcing.
[b]Based on US data only.
[c]'gfcf' stands for Gross fixed capital formation.
Source: Compiled from OECD (1996), table 1.21, p. 49.

are mainly arm's-length trade, though foreign sourcing of parts and components is an important part of their production activities. Second, pharmaceuticals and computers are technology-intensive industries whose products are sold mainly to final consumers. These products are differentiated horizontally (for example, by brand name), and proximity to consumers' markets through local presence is of crucial importance to the success of business activities; hence a high ratio of intra-firm trade associated with high shares of affiliate sales and direct investment flows. Third, the basic operation of semiconductor companies – another example of technology-intensive industries – is to supply microchips to assembly companies in a variety of industries world-wide, but they do not appear to have a comparable push abroad through direct invest-ment, as with pharmaceuticals and computers. Fourth, motor vehicles and consumer electronics are assembly industries whose products are often manufactured and marketed overseas through the companies' own networks of supply and distribution, resulting in relatively higher ratios of intra-firm trade.

The stylized facts of the globalization of industry as described above indicate that the phenomenon of intra-firm trade is linked closely with that of *intra-industry* trade. Primarily, the latter concerns differenti-ated products exchanged between countries that are similar in terms of per capita income and relative factor endowments (Grubel and Lloyd, 1975). It has also been argued that economies of scale play an important role in explaining the industry pattern of intra-industry trade. In many circumstances where trade is largely of an intra-industry nature – as exemplified by trade in manufactured goods among developed countries ('North–North') – foreign direct investment followed by intra-firm trade allows a MNE to exploit internally rents associated with knowledge-based, firm-specific assets. And the potential for intra-firm trade tends to be greater in an integrated market than in a non-integrated market (Greenaway, 1987; Markusen, 1995). The predominant example of intra-industry, intra-firm trade is the USA–Canada–Mexico linked automobile trade. The cross-border trade of automotive parts and assembled cars within the North American market has been conducted between parent firms and their affiliates. Intra-firm trade is also the dominant pattern of US exports to Canada and Europe in the case of machinery and chemicals.

Another example can be seen in the case of manufactured trade among Pacific Asian economies. There was a rapid increase in intra-industry trade as a proportion of total trade over the 1990s. Such increase in intra-industry trade in Pacific Asian economies is attributable primarily to the globalization of corporate activities by US and Japanese firms, and more recently by Asian NIE firms. This involves assembly productions based on imported parts and components in different countries in East and Southeast Asia, and the establishment of these corporate networks in Pacific Asia has been associated with foreign direct investment by the USA, Japan and, more recently, the Asian NIEs (Fukasaku, 1992).[7] To the extent that international sourcing of parts and components by Northern firms takes the form of non-equity, subcontracting or commissioned-production arrangements with Southern counterparts, this trade is characterized by intra-industry trade but not intra-firm trade. Some argue that non-equity forms of corporate networking are of significant importance for the recent development of Pacific Asian economies based on outward-orientated industrialization (Oman, 1989). In fact, Japanese machinery firms have begun to form sophisticated vertical production networks across Asian countries that include their own affiliates, affiliates of their subcontractors, and firms of other nationalities. It remains to be seen how far these developments have resulted in the growth of intra-firm trade.

Developments in intra-firm trade: the case of the USA

This section reports recent developments in US intra-firm trade. For decades, the US Department of Commerce has conducted the most comprehensive surveys of foreign affiliates of US firms and US affiliates of foreign firms. Although the access to micro data is limited, the data source is suitable for analyzing the long-run trend of intra-firm trade.

Several points deserve special attention. First, intra-firm trade represents roughly 40 per cent of total merchandise trade on average since the late 1970s. Although fluctuating moderately at around 35–40 per cent, the overall intra-firm trade ratio has not changed much during the period of 1977–97 (see Table 13.3). Moreover, the relative stability of intra-firm trade ratios is in sharp contrast with a large decline in the trade of parent companies with non-affiliates relative to total merchandise trade. This has caused a secular decline in the share of the country's parent companies in total merchandise exports and imports since the late 1970s.

Second, the yearly movement of US parents' intra-firm export ratio (see column A on the right of the upper half of Table 13.3) showed a strong increase in 1982–5, when the dollar was appreciating *vis-à-vis* other major currencies, and the subsequent decline in 1985–9, when the dollar was depreciating. This might suggest that intra-firm exports were less responsive to exchange-rate movements than arm's length trade, but empirical evidence so far has been mixed.[8] Note also that the intra-firm export ratio of US affiliates of foreign parents (see Column C on the right of the upper half of Table 13.3) did not show any distinct pattern, though quantitatively small in total merchandise exports.

Third, US intra-firm exports are concentrated heavily in a small number of technology- and human-capital-intensive industries, such as machinery, transport equipment, and chemicals. These three industries taken together accounted for more than 80 per cent of total intra-firm exports of US parents in 1994. A high concentration of intra-firm trade is also observable on the import side, the first two industries alone accounting for three-quarters of total imports shipped by foreign affiliates to their US parents. On the other hand, fuels represented a large but declining share of intra-firm imports (see Table 13.4).

Fourth, intra-firm trade between the USA and other OECD countries is dominated mainly by parents' sales to their affiliates rather than the other way round (see Table 13.5)[9] This is particularly pronounced in the trade relations between foreign MNEs and their affiliates established in the USA. In 1994, sales by foreign parents to their US affiliates are three to to five times larger than the latter's sales to their parents. Such sales push to US affiliates by foreign parents is related to a high percentage of intra-firm transactions in wholesale trade, notably in the case of motor vehicles and electrical goods. In 1997, these two categories alone accounted for 35 per cent of total merchandise imports shipped to US affiliates by foreign parents. As Yamawaki (1991) argues with respect to Japanese direct investment, the success of Japanese manufacturing firms in exporting to the US markets is associated strongly with their commitments of resources to the establishment of local distribution networks. The US firms also export to

Table 13.3 US Intra-firm trade in goods, 1977–97[1]

Year	Exports shipped by US parents to foreign affiliates (billion dollars)		Exports shipped to US affiliates by foreign parents (billion dollar)	Total of (A) + (C) (billion dollars)	As percentage of total US merchandise exports			
	Total	MOFAs[2] only						
	(A)	(B)	(C)	(D)	(A)	(B)	(C)	(D)
Intra-firm exports in goods								
1977	31.3	29.3	11.7	43.0	25.4	23.8	9.5	34.9
1978	–	–	16.6	–	–	–	11.4	–
1979	–	–	22.1	–	–	–	11.8	–
1980	–	–	21.0	–	–	–	9.3	–
1981	–	–	26.9	–	–	–	11.3	–
1982	47.1	44.3	25.0	72.2	21.8	20.5	11.6	33.3
1983	49.4	45.1	22.6	72.0	24.0	21.9	11.0	35.0
1984	56.7	52.7	27.1	83.8	25.3	23.5	12.1	37.4
1985	61.9	57.6	25.9	87.8	28.3	26.3	11.8	40.1
1986	61.1	58.9	21.9	83.0	26.9	25.9	9.6	36.5
1987	66.4	65.2	19.1	85.5	26.1	25.7	7.5	33.7
1988	79.4	78.2	26.4	105.8	24.6	24.3	8.2	32.8
1989	89.4	86.1	34.3	123.7	24.6	23.7	9.4	34.0
1990	90.1	88.4	37.8	127.8	22.9	22.5	9.6	32.5
1991	97.1	95.8	42.2	139.3	23.0	22.5	10.0	33.0
1992	106.0	100.7	48.8	154.8	23.7	22.5	10.9	34.5
1993	113.8	106.8	47.4	161.1	24.5	23.0	10.2	34.7
1994	138.3	132.7	51.1	189.4	27.0	25.9	10.0	37.0
1995	152.7	147.7	57.2	209.9	26.1	25.3	9.8	35.9
1996	161.8	161.4	60.8	222.6	25.9	25.8	9.7	35.6
1997p	183.1	181.1	62.8	245.9	26.6	26.3	9.1	35.7

Year	Imports shipped to US parents by foreign affiliates (billion dollars)		Imports shipped to US affiliates by foreign parents (billion dollars)	Total of (A) + (C) (billion dollars)	As percentage of total US merchandise exports			
	Total	MOFAs[2] only						
	(A)	(B)	(C)	(D)	(A)	(B)	(C)	(D)
Intra-firm imports in goods (f.o.b)								
1977	36.3	30.9	30.9	67.1	23.9	20.4	20.4	44.3
1978	–	–	39.5	–	–	–	22.4	–
1979	–	–	45.3	–	–	–	21.5	–
1980	–	–	47.0	–	–	–	19.2	–
1981	–	–	52.2	–	–	–	20.0	–
1982	39.3	38.5	51.9	91.2	16.1	15.8	21.3	37.4
1983	43.6	41.6	54.8	98.4	16.9	16.1	21.2	38.1
1984	52.8	49.3	70.5	123.2	16.0	14.9	21.3	37.3
1985	54.0	51.8	81.7	135.8	16.1	15.4	24.3	40.3
1986	55.0	50.0	93.4	148.4	15.1	13.7	25.6	40.6
1987	60.4	55.9	108.2	168.6	14.9	13.8	26.6	41.5
1988	69.5	65.5	118.4	187.9	15.8	14.8	26.8	42.6
1989	74.7	71.3	129.9	204.7	15.8	15.1	27.5	43.3
1990	80.3	75.3	137.5	217.8	16.2	15.2	27.8	44.0
1991	83.5	77.6	132.2	215.6	17.1	15.9	27.1	44.1
1992	93.9	83.3	137.8	231.7	17.6	15.6	25.9	43.5
1993	97.1	93.2	150.8	247.9	16.7	16.1	26.0	42.7
1994	114.9	107.2	174.6	289.5	17.3	16.1	26.3	43.6
1995	122.3	118.4	191.2	313.5	16.4	15.9	25.7	42.2
1996	137.2	133.4	197.7	334.8	17.2	16.8	24.9	42.1
1997p	147.4	145.4	195.5	342.9	16.9	16.7	22.5	39.4

Notes:
[1]The data refers to non-bank US parents and affiliates.
[2]MOFAs stand for majority-owned foreign affiliates. 'p' stands for preliminary data.
Sources: See Appendix, Tables A13.1 and A13.2 .

their affiliates more than importing from their affiliates when the affiliates are located in Japan or Europe. However, when affiliates are in Canada or other countries (mainly non-OECD countries), the balance is almost even. This suggests that US parent companies also purchase upstream parts and materials from their affiliates.

In short, the hypothesis that the trend towards globalization in the 1980s and 1990s, characterized by a FDI boom, would increase the

Table 13.4 US exports and imports shipped to/by MOFAs by/to non-bank US parents, by country of affiliate and by product, 1977–94, percentages

Country of affiliate	Year	Total products	Food beverages tobacco	Crude materials	Fuels	Chemicals	Machinery (ex trans.equip.)	Road vehicles	Metal manuf.	Other manuf.
Exports										
All countries	1977	100.0	5.3	3.1	1.5	11.6	31.1	29.5	3.0	14.0
	1982	100.0	4.5	3.0	2.2	11.7	41.0	24.3	2.9	9.3
	1989	100.0	3.0	1.3	1.6	12.8	39.0	27.1	2.1	12.0
	1994	100.0	2.4	0.8	n.a.	13.2	57.4	12.3	1.5	10.6
Canada	1977	42.9	1.0	0.5	0.3	2.2	9.1	24.7	0.9	3.9
	1982	34.9	0.7	0.3	n.a.	2.0	8.3	20.0	0.6	n.a.
	1989	37.2	n.a.	n.a.	n.a.	2.6	7.3	22.2	0.6	3.0
	1994	33.6	n.a.	n.a.	0.2	2.6	18.9	7.9	0.7	2.4
Mexico	1977	2.5	0.0	0.0	0.0	0.2	0.8	1.1	0.1	0.3
	1982	4.7	0.0	0.0	n.a.	0.2	2.2	1.7	n.a.	0.4
	1989	7.1	n.a.	0.0	n.a.	0.2	2.7	3.4	0.0	0.6
	1994	10.3	n.a.	n.a.	0.0	0.4	6.7	2.4	n.a.	0.6
Europe	1977	32.3	3.5	2.3	0.3	5.2	12.1	1.0	1.2	6.4
	1982	34.2	2.9	2.2	0.7	5.2	16.4	n.a.	1.3	4.5
	1989	32.1	1.5	0.6	0.5	5.4	16.8	0.9	0.9	4.7
	1994	29.6	0.7	0.3	0.1	5.8	16.2	1.2	0.5	4.5
Japan	1977	2.4	0.0	0.1	n.a.	0.8	1.0	n.a.	0.0	0.2
	1982	3.3	0.0	0.0	0.0	0.9	1.9	n.a.	0.1	n.a.
	1989	7.1	n.a.	n.a.	n.a.	1.1	3.4	0.0	0.1	1.7
	1994	7.7	n.a.	n.a.	0.0	0.9	4.7	0.2	n.a.	1.2
Other areas	1977	19.9	0.7	0.3	n.a.	3.2	8.0	n.a.	0.8	3.3
	1982	22.8	0.8	0.4	n.a.	3.4	12.3	n.a.	n.a.	n.a.
	1989	16.5	n.a.	n.a.	n.a.	3.5	8.7	0.5	0.5	2.0
Imports										
All countries	1994	18.9	n.a.	n.a.	n.a.	3.4	10.9	0.6	n.a.	1.8
	1977	100.0	2.3	3.8	44.0	2.2	15.1	24.2	2.3	n.a.
	1982	100.0	3.1	3.8	32.3	3.5	22.1	27.4	2.7	4.4

Table 13.4 (Continued)

Country of affiliate	Year	Total products	Food beverages tobacco	Crude materials	Fuels	Chemicals	Machinery (ex trans.equip.)	Road vehicles	Metal manuf.	Other manuf.
	1989	100.0	2.2	2.0	10.2	5.0	30.9	36.9	1.8	9.6
	1994	100.0	2.6	1.1	n.a.	4.4	36.6	38.2	1.4	8.0
Canada	1977	35.5	0.6	2.1	2.9	0.6	4.3	22.2	0.7	n.a.
	1982	43.0	0.2	1.6	n.a.	n.a.	4.3	25.6	0.6	1.8
	1989	46.3	n.a.	1.1	n.a.	1.9	3.9	30.2	1.1	2.2
	1994	42.2	n.a.	0.4	0.0	1.8	5.5	27.0	0.9	n.a.
Mexico	1977	1.3	n.a.	0.0	n.a.	n.a.	0.8	n.a.	0.0	n.a.
	1982	4.0	0.0	0.0	0.0	0.1	n.a.	n.a.	n.a.	0.3
	1989	9.0	0.1	n.a.	0.0	0.1	3.7	4.5	n.a.	0.8
	1994	14.2	0.2	n.a.	0.0	n.a.	5.8	7.5	0.0	0.6
Europe	1977	10.8	0.5	n.a.	3.0	0.8	3.0	n.a.	0.7	n.a.
	1982	10.2	n.a.	0.2	n.a.	1.6	3.3	0.4	1.0	1.1
	1989	16.8	0.5	0.2	n.a.	2.2	7.7	1.7	0.5	2.8
	1994	14.8	n.a.	n.a.	0.4	2.1	6.5	n.a.	0.3	2.2
Japan	1977	1.1	0.0	n.a.	n.a.	0.0	n.a.	0.0	n.a.	n.a.
	1982	2.0	n.a.	0.0	0.0	0.0	n.a.	0.0	n.a.	0.2
	1989	2.9	0.0	0.0	0.0	0.1	2.4	0.0	0.0	0.4
	1994	2.8	n.a.	0.0	n.a.	0.1	2.0	n.a.	n.a.	0.2
Other areas	1977	51.2	n.a.	n.a.	n.a.	n.a.	n.a.	n.a.	n.a.	n.a.
	1982	40.8	n.a.	2.0	n.a.	n.a.	n.a.	n.a.	n.a.	1.1
	1989	25.0	n.a.	n.a.	n.a.	0.7	13.3	0.4	n.a.	3.4
	1994	26.0	n.a.	n.a.	n.a.	n.a.	16.9	n.a.	n.a.	n.a.

Notes: n.a.: The data in these cells are suppressed to avoid disclosure of data of individual firms.
Sources: See Appendix, Tables A 13.1 and A13.2

Table 13.5 Trade between parents and affiliates by country of parent and country of affiliate, 1989 and 1994 (in billions of dollars)

	Sales from parents to affiliates (A)		Sales from affiliates to parents (B)		Sales ratio (A)/(B)	
	1989	1994	1989	1994	1989	1994
US firms in Japan	6.1	10.2	2.0	3.0	3.1	3.4
Japanese firms in the USA	70.9	94.3	18.9	29.3	3.8	3.2
US firms in Europe	27.6	39.3	12.0	15.9	2.3	2.5
European firms in the USA	39.4	52.4	10.5	15.7	3.8	3.3
US firms in Canada	32.1	44.5	33.0	45.2	1.0	1.0
Canadian firms in the USA	7.2	7.8	1.5	1.8	4.8	4.3
US firms in other countries	20.3	38.7	24.2	43.1	0.8	0.9
Other nations' firms in the USA	12.4	20.1	3.4	4.3	3.6	4.7

Source: See Appendix, Tables A13.1 and A13.2.

relative importance of intra-firm trade in a country' foreign trade significantly does not seem to be borne out by the US experience. A possible explanation for this is that US MNEs started the globalization of their operations earlier – in the 1960s and 1970s – and that a rapid reduction in transportation and communication costs, which is by itself part of the globalization story, may have led them to change their 'internalization strategy'. Globalization seems to make arm's-length trade easier, which checks an increase in the share of intra-firm trade. Further data and analysis are needed to explain why globalization brings about more intra-firm trade in some industries than in others. This is the topic to which we turn with the Japanese micro data.

Factors affecting intra-firm trade in Japan

The Ministry of International Trade and Industry (MITI), Government of Japan conducted a comprehensive firm-level survey in the 1990s (MITI, 1996). This covered only large firms that is, firms located in Japan having more than fifty workers and capital of more than ¥30 million) having establishments in mining, manufacturing, wholesale and retail trade, or the restaurant industry. With respect to intra-firm trade, it reports each firm's sales and purchases with its related companies separately from arm's-length transactions (see the Appendix, Table A13.3). A *related company* is defined as a domestic/foreign firm in which a parent company has more than 20 per cent voting stock share. Although we cannot obtain information on the location of domestic/foreign related companies for each transaction, or the contents of it, the shares of intra-firm exports and imports to total exports and imports for each firm can be calculated. The use of such micro data then allows us to analyze in detail the relationship between intra-firm transactions and other characteristics of firms.

As can be seen in the Appendix, Table A13.3, the data include (i) both sales and purchase transactions between parent firms and their related companies located either in Japan or in foreign countries (that is, intra-firm transactions); and (ii) both sales and purchase transactions between parent firms and non-related companies (that is, arm's-length transactions). Table 13.6 reports the relative importance of these two types of transaction by industry. Note that the industry to which each firm belongs is determined on the basis of a principal activity with which the firm has the largest sales value. The shaded figures in the table indicate that domestic intra-firm transactions have a share of more than 20 per cent of domestic sales and purchases, and that foreign intra-firm transactions have a share of more than 8 per cent of foreign sales and purchases. The degree of foreign exposure as well as the importance of intra-firm transactions differs widely across industries, reflecting each industry's corporate structure and international competitiveness. Industries with high intra-firm transactions belong mainly to machinery industries (industry codes 290–320). The pattern is even clearer in case of intra-firm transactions with affiliates abroad.

Table 13.7 presents intra-firm sales and purchase ratios as well as net export ratios, to check the trade balance. The shaded figures indicate that intra-firm transaction ratios are higher than 40 per cent. Again, the divergent pattern across industries suggests that intra-firm trade is linked closely with some characteristics of industries, such as technology, the structure of firms, and industrial organization. Machinery industries have high intra-firm transaction ratios in both exports and imports. This indicates that firms develop multi-layered production/distribution networks crossing national borders. Furthermore, in many industries, intra-firm transaction ratios are higher in foreign transactions than in domestic ones. This would indicate that arm's-length transactions with firms abroad are more costly, or are accompanied by higher transaction costs, than arm's-length transactions with domestic counterparts.

Now let us investigate possible determinants of intra-firm trade. We are interested particularly in the relationship between technological

Table 13.6 Intra-firm transactions in the *Basic Survey of Business Structure and Activity* (1994 F/Y) (1)

Industry code	Industry	Share of sales by destination (%)					Share of purchases by origin (%)				
		Total	To domestic Arm's-length	To domestic Intra-firm	To foreign Arm's-length	To foreign Intra-firm	Total	From domestic Arm's-length	From domestic Intra-firm	From foreign Arm's-length	From foreign Intra-firm
	All industries in the sample	100.0	77.4	11.7	8.3	2.6	100.0	77.1	14.1	6.5	2.3
	Mining, manufacturing, and commerce	100.0	76.9	11.9	8.5	2.7	100.0	76.9	14.2	6.6	2.3
	Mining and manufacturing	100.0	69.6	18.5	7.9	4.0	100.0	70.2	22.8	5.3	1.7
50	Mining	100.0	83.4	16.2	0.4	0.0	100.0	76.6	22.4	1.0	0.0
120	Food processing	100.0	82.9	16.8	0.2	0.1	100.0	75.3	19.3	2.1	3.3
130	Beverages, tobacco, and animal feed	100.0	93.5	6.3	0.1	0.0	100.0	84.4	11.8	2.5	1.2
140	Textiles	100.0	84.9	13.7	1.2	0.1	100.0	79.8	16.1	3.7	0.4
150	Apparel	100.0	85.3	14.3	0.2	0.2	100.0	84.3	10.9	3.4	1.4
160	Wood and wood products	100.0	78.5	21.2	0.1	0.3	100.0	67.0	25.0	7.2	0.8
170	Furniture and fixtures	100.0	86.8	12.6	0.4	0.2	100.0	85.7	12.5	1.4	0.4
180	Pulp, paper, and paper products	100.0	82.6	16.2	1.1	0.0	100.0	75.8	21.4	2.1	0.8
190	Publishing and printing	100.0	91.5	7.8	0.5	0.2	100.0	90.0	9.7	0.2	0.1
200	Chemicals	100.0	75.4	17.7	5.2	1.7	100.0	74.2	18.6	4.5	2.8
210	Petroleum and coal products	100.0	79.8	17.2	3.0	0.1	100.0	28.6	10.1	52.3	9.0
220	Plastic products	100.0	84.7	13.5	1.4	0.5	100.0	84.9	13.9	0.9	0.3
230	Rubber products	100.0	56.9	31.4	6.7	5.0	100.0	74.3	17.8	5.7	2.2
240	Leather and leather products	100.0	77.1	20.9	1.7	0.2	100.0	75.2	18.6	4.7	1.4
250	Ceramics, clay, and stone products	100.0	83.9	13.1	2.3	0.7	100.0	84.0	14.3	1.2	0.5
260	Iron and steel	100.0	76.1	20.0	3.2	0.7	100.0	65.7	29.3	4.9	0.1

Table 13.6 (Continued)

Industry code	Industry	Share of sales by destination (%)					Share of purchases by origin (%)				
		Total	To domestic Arm's-length	To domestic Intra-firm	To foreign Arm's-length	To foreign Intra-firm	Total	From domestic Arm's-length	From domestic Intra-firm	From foreign Arm's-length	From foreign Intra-firm
270	Non-ferrous metal	100.0	77.2	16.0	5.4	1.4	100.0	73.1	16.7	9.6	0.6
280	Metal products	100.0	87.5	10.8	1.0	0.7	100.0	87.8	11.3	0.2	0.6
290	General machinery	100.0	67.5	14.3	12.7	5.6	100.0	81.7	14.8	2.2	1.2
291	Metal-working machinery	100.0	68.6	14.7	8.3	8.3	100.0	87.3	10.8	0.8	1.2
292	Industrial machinery	100.0	61.6	17.4	15.7	5.3	100.0	79.5	18.0	2.0	0.5
293	Office and service machinery	100.0	59.0	16.8	13.4	10.8	100.0	80.3	14.2	1.7	3.8
299	Other machinery	100.0	73.5	11.8	11.5	3.2	100.0	82.8	13.9	2.7	0.5
300	Electric machinery	100.0	56.4	21.7	14.5	7.3	100.0	64.9	28.8	4.1	2.2
301	Electric machinery for industrial use	100.0	62.2	25.4	6.1	6.3	100.0	68.2	29.3	1.2	1.3
302	Electric machinery for domestic use	100.0	54.2	11.0	34.3	0.4	100.0	84.7	7.3	7.3	0.8
303	Communication-related machinery	100.0	62.4	12.3	19.7	5.6	100.0	81.3	10.2	4.1	4.4
304	Computers and electronic apparatus	100.0	57.5	19.3	15.1	8.2	100.0	56.0	37.4	4.8	1.7
305	Electronic parts and devices	100.0	46.5	32.7	10.2	10.6	100.0	59.5	33.7	4.6	2.2
309	Other electric machinery	100.0	69.0	19.1	8.7	3.1	100.0	76.9	21.3	0.9	0.9
310	Transport equipment	100.0	52.1	26.0	13.8	8.0	100.0	66.1	31.7	1.6	0.6
311	Automobiles and parts	100.0	51.4	27.1	12.8	8.6	100.0	64.4	33.4	1.7	0.6
319	Other transport equipment	100.0	60.0	14.1	24.0	1.8	100.0	91.3	7.4	1.1	0.2
320	Precision machinery	100.0	57.2	21.6	12.5	8.8	100.0	63.6	19.5	13.9	2.9
321	Medical equipment	100.0	47.6	29.5	9.2	13.7	100.0	68.9	23.4	2.9	4.8

322	Optical equipment	100.0	41.8	37.4	9.6	11.2	100.0	78.7	17.1	2.3	1.8
323	Watches and clocks	100.0	56.8	11.7	23.5	8.0	100.0	35.5	20.9	40.1	3.4
329	Other precision machinery	100.0	73.6	13.7	8.6	4.0	100.0	77.6	16.5	4.1	1.7
340	Other manufacturing	100.0	80.9	9.4	3.9	5.9	100.0	86.8	9.1	2.8	1.4
480	Wholesale and retail trade	100.0	82.6	6.7	9.0	1.7	100.0	80.2	10.0	7.3	2.6
481	Wholesale trade	100.0	79.3	7.4	11.2	2.1	100.0	78.2	10.2	8.5	3.1
540	Retail trade	100.0	96.0	3.7	0.3	0.0	100.0	89.8	8.9	1.1	0.2
	Other industries	100.0	92.8	6.7	0.4	0.1	100.0	87.8	8.8	3.0	0.4
600	Restaurants	100.0	97.6	2.4	0.0	0.0	100.0	97.0	3.0	0.0	0.0
715	Services	100.0	88.8	10.1	0.7	0.3	100.0	82.4	9.4	6.7	1.5
900	Others	100.0	94.7	5.1	0.2	0.0	100.0	89.8	8.7	1.5	0.0

Notes: 'Related company' is defined as a firm in which a parent company has more than 20 per cent stock share; 'intra-firm transaction' is defined as a transaction between a parent company and related companies.
Source: See Appendix, Table A13.3.

Table 13.7 Intra-firm Transactions in the *Basic Survey of Business Structure and Activity* (1994 F/Y) (2)

Industry code	Industry	Intra-firm sales ratio (%)			Intra-firm purchases ratio (%)			Net export ratio $(X-M)/(X+M)$		
		Total	To domestic	To foreign	Total	From domestic	From foreign	Total	Arm's-length	Intra-firm
	All industries in the sample	14.3	13.2	23.9	16.4	15.5	25.7	0.279	0.290	0.247
	Mining, manufacturing, and commerce	14.6	13.4	23.9	16.5	15.6	25.8	0.282	0.294	0.248
	Mining and manufacturing	22.4	21.0	33.3	24.5	24.5	24.5	0.523	0.476	0.626
50	Mining	16.2	16.3	0.0	22.4	22.6	0.0	0.114	0.114	n.a.
120	Food processing	16.9	16.8	47.7	22.5	20.4	60.4	−0.805	−0.750	−0.843
130	Beverages, tobacco, and animal feed	6.4	6.4	30.0	13.1	12.3	33.1	−0.803	−0.794	−0.820
140	Textiles	13.8	13.9	9.2	16.5	16.8	9.0	−0.146	−0.147	−0.135
150	Apparel	14.4	14.3	43.6	12.3	11.4	29.9	−0.689	−0.742	−0.576
160	Wood and wood products	21.4	21.3	71.5	25.8	27.2	9.7	−0.810	−0.936	−0.126
170	Furniture and fixtures	12.8	12.7	31.5	12.9	12.7	21.7	−0.178	−0.242	0.007
180	Pulp, paper, and paper products	16.3	16.4	3.8	22.1	22.0	26.8	−0.120	0.016	−0.800
190	Publishing and printing	8.0	7.8	31.5	9.8	9.7	43.3	0.782	0.816	0.713
200	Chemicals	19.4	19.0	24.7	21.3	20.0	38.3	0.396	0.476	0.197
210	Petroleum and coal products	17.3	17.7	3.5	19.1	26.1	14.7	−0.849	−0.831	−0.962
220	Plastic products	13.9	13.7	25.0	14.2	14.1	22.3	0.507	0.494	0.548
230	Rubber products	36.3	35.5	42.5	20.0	19.3	28.3	0.529	0.445	0.660
240	Leather and leather products	21.1	21.3	12.1	20.0	19.8	22.8	−0.260	−0.199	−0.523
250	Ceramics, clay, and stone products	13.8	13.5	22.7	14.8	14.5	28.2	0.627	0.649	0.556
260	Iron and steel	20.7	20.9	17.2	29.4	30.8	2.4	0.249	0.170	0.847
270	Nonferrous metal	17.4	17.2	20.7	17.3	18.6	5.7	0.068	−0.018	0.612
280	Metal products	11.5	11.0	39.5	12.0	11.4	74.3	0.618	0.818	0.384
290	General machinery	19.8	17.5	30.5	16.0	15.3	35.5	0.812	0.825	0.785
291	Metal-working machinery	23.1	17.7	50.2	11.9	11.0	58.2	0.891	0.908	0.875

292	Industrial machinery	22.7	22.0	25.4	18.5	18.5	18.8	0.874	0.864	0.905
293	Office and service machinery	27.6	22.2	44.6	18.0	15.1	68.5	0.773	0.865	0.671
299	Other machinery	15.0	13.8	21.9	14.5	14.4	16.7	0.788	0.776	0.834
300	Electric machinery	29.0	27.8	33.5	31.0	30.7	34.6	0.723	0.727	0.715
301	Electric machinery for industrial use	31.7	29.0	51.1	30.6	30.1	52.0	0.805	0.808	0.802
302	Electric machinery for domestic use	11.4	16.9	1.2	8.0	7.9	9.7	0.863	0.874	0.267
303	Communication-related machinery	17.9	16.4	22.2	14.6	11.2	51.4	0.663	0.775	0.361
304	Computers and electronic apparatus	27.4	25.1	35.2	39.2	40.0	26.6	0.700	0.667	0.765
305	Electronic parts and devices	43.3	41.2	51.0	35.9	36.2	32.5	0.705	0.615	0.802
309	Other electric machinery	22.2	21.7	26.5	22.2	21.7	50.9	0.859	0.904	0.746
310	Transport equipment	34.1	33.3	36.9	32.3	32.4	25.7	0.870	0.849	0.908
311	Automobiles and parts	35.7	34.5	40.1	34.0	34.1	26.2	0.862	0.833	0.908
319	Other transport equipment	16.0	19.0	7.1	7.5	7.5	12.7	0.949	0.952	0.911
320	Precision machinery	30.4	27.4	41.3	22.4	23.4	17.4	0.387	0.232	0.686
321	Medical equipment	43.2	38.3	59.8	28.1	25.3	61.9	0.717	0.729	0.708
322	Optical equipment	48.6	47.2	53.9	18.9	17.9	43.3	0.787	0.744	0.826
323	Watches and clocks	19.7	17.1	25.4	24.4	37.1	7.9	0.029	-0.077	0.548
329	Other precision machinery	17.8	15.7	31.9	18.2	17.5	29.8	0.627	0.618	0.647
340	Other manufacturing	15.3	10.4	60.3	10.4	9.4	32.8	0.674	0.504	0.808
480	Wholesale and retail trade	8.3	7.5	15.7	12.6	11.1	26.2	0.126	0.191	-0.130
481	Wholesale trade	9.5	8.5	15.7	13.3	11.5	26.5	0.134	0.201	-0.127
540	Retail trade	3.7	3.7	11.4	9.1	9.0	12.5	-0.515	-0.510	-0.549
	Other industries	6.8	6.7	24.6	9.2	9.1	13.0	-0.534	-0.582	-0.271
600	Restaurants	2.4	2.4	0.0	3.0	3.0	0.0	0.344	0.344	n.a.
715	Services	10.4	10.2	30.2	10.9	10.3	18.2	-0.527	-0.582	-0.322
900	Others	5.1	5.1	10.4	8.7	8.8	0.8	-0.548	-0.583	0.568

Notes: 'Related company' is defined as a firm in which a parent company has more than 20 per cent stock share; 'intra-firm transaction' is defined as a transaction between a parent company and related companies.
Source: See Appendix, Table A 13.3.

intensity and intra-firm trade, but it does not look straightforward, as can be seen from Figure 13.1. Japan has a strong comparative advantage in R&D-intensive products, and thus R&D intensity (the ratio of R&D expenditure to total sales) and the export–sales ratio are positively correlated as shown in the upper-left diagram. Another well-established fact is that firms with high technology tend to conduct more foreign direct investment. Consistent with this is the relationship shown in the middle-left diagram, which points to a strong positive relationship between R&D intensity (RRD) and the number of manufacturing affiliates abroad. However, as is seen in the two diagrams at the bottom, the relationship between R&D intensity and intra-firm transaction ratios,

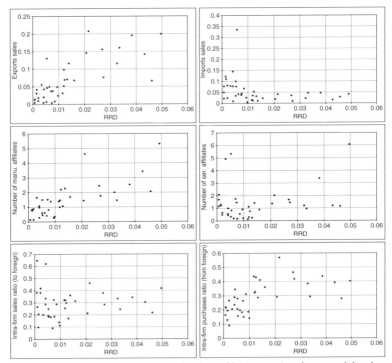

Note: The data are arithmetic averages of each variables in our micro data set and therefore do not coincide with population figures in Tables 13.6, 13.7 or Appendix A13.3.
Each dot corresponds to and industry among the industry code 050–500; and disaggregated industries in 300, 481 and 540.
Source: MITI micro data set.

Figure 13.1 Relationship between R&D intensity and other variables

both sales and purchases, is not clear at all. Having more foreign affiliates does not necessarily result in higher intra-firm transaction ratios.

To see the possible determinants of intra-firm transaction ratios, we conduct some regression analysis with the firm-level micro data. Here we do not claim any causal relationship among variables. Instead, by putting intra-firm foreign sales ratios and intra-firm foreign purchases ratios on the left-hand side, we try to detect partial correlations among variables. Table 13.8 reports the OLS regression results for the manufacturing and non-manufacturing sectors.[10] Both dependent and independent variables are for (parent) firms located in Japan. For the intra-firm sales ratios of non-manufacturing firms, the intensity of advertisement (RADV) has a positive coefficient possibly reflecting vigorous sales activities through sales affiliates by advertisement-intensive wholesale/retail firms. The intensity of R&D (RRD), on the other hand, has a positive sign in the regression of intra-firm purchases for non-manufacturing firms, which suggests that wholesale firms with relatively large R&D expenditure tend to have upstream manufacturing or wholesale activities in the form of affiliates abroad.[11] The results of regressions for manufacturing firms are much harder to interpret. Negative coefficients for capital–labour ratios (KLRATIO) and employment size (SCALE) may reflect the fact that firms with large intra-firm trade have relocated part of their production activities abroad, leaving smaller, hardcore activities for the parent companies. The negative coefficient for R&D intensity (RRD) in the intra-firm sales regression is puzzling and suggests the need to conduct more disaggregated analysis to control industry-specific characteristics.

Table 13.9 reports the regression results for four machinery industries separately. The coefficient for RRD is now positive and even significant in the regressions of general machinery (290), transport equipment (310), and precision machinery (320), which conforms to our intuition that R&D-intensive firms conduct more intra-firm trade. In the case of electrical machinery (300), however, the coefficient is significantly negative. We also conducted regression analysis for further disaggregated industries in electrical machinery (not reported here). The negative sign still prevails for RRD, but of particular significance are the negative coefficients in communication-related machinery (303), and computers and electronic apparatus (304). The electronics industry has become very competitive in recent years, and firms have started to seek vertical disintegration and specialization in preference to having fully internalized production lines. Globalization has also reduced the cost of

Table 13.8 Microdata regression results: manufacturing and non-manufacturing

Dep. var.	Manufacturing				Non-manufacturing			
	Intra-firm sales ratio (to foreign)		Intra-firm purchases ratio (from foreign)		Intra-firm sales ratio (to foreign)		Intra-firm purchases ratio (from foreign)	
Constant	0.297*** (23.856)	0.121*** (9.861)	0.352*** (20.991)	0.146*** (8.893)	0.055*** (3.981)	0.191*** (14.414)	0.082*** (6.366)	0.186*** (14.750)
KLRATIO	-0.002*** (-2.965)	-0.002*** (-4.217)	-0.002** (-2.224)	-0.001 (-1.525)	-0.001 (-1.586)	0.000* (-1.692)	0.000 (-0.937)	0.000 (-1.303)
RADV	0.313 (0.757)	0.218 (0.631)	-1.014** (-2.432)	-0.863** (-2.339)	3.940*** (6.800)	4.250*** (7.706)	0.890 (1.586)	0.623 (1.070)
RRD	-0.082 (-0.342)	-0.434** (-2.022)	0.361 (1.009)	-0.154 (-0.427)	0.179 (0.296)	0.982 (1.420)	2.312* (1.852)	4.152*** (3.280)
SCALE	-0.002 (-1.223)		-0.007*** (-3.574)		0.003 (0.870)		-0.003 (-0.649)	
MD	0.296*** (17.287)		0.382*** (17.313)		0.258*** (6.621)		0.216*** (5.262)	
SD	0.269*** (10.029)		0.145*** (4.454)		0.227*** (8.893)		0.187*** (7.357)	
M&SD	0.356*** (17.069)		0.376*** (13.548)		0.282*** (8.703)		0.309*** (8.199)	
# of Obs	2303	2303	1783	1783	917	917	1103	1103
R2	0.158	0.003	0.173	0.006	0.177	0.050	0.118	0.015
F	72.58	3.16	57.06	3.88	34.36	24.52	19.95	4.75

Notes:
KLRATIO: ratio of tangible asset to regular workers
RADV: ratio of advertisement expenditure to total sales
RRD: ratio of R&D expenditure to total sales
SCALE: the number of workers (1000 persons)
MD: manufacturing dummy takes value 1 if firm has manufacturing affiliates only and 0 otherwise
SD: service dummy takes value 1 if firm has service affiliates only and 0 otherwise
M&SD: manufacturing and service dummy takes value 1 if firm has both manufacturing and service affiliates and 0 otherwise
***, **, * means statistical significance level at 1, 5 and 10, respectively. T-value is in parenthesis.
Standard deviation is calculated by White's consistency estimator.

Table 13.9 Microdata regression results: machinery industries

Dep. var.	290 General machinery				300 Electrical machinery				310 Transport equipment				320 Precision machinery			
	Intra-firm sales ratio (to foreign)		Intra-firm purchases ratio (from foreign)		Intra-firm sales ratio (to foreign)		Intra-firm purchases ratio (from foreign)		Intra-firm sales ratio (to foreign)		Intra-firm purchases ratio (from foreign)		Intra-firm sales ratio (to foreign)		Intra-firm purchases ratio (from foreign)	
Constant	0.167*** (5.080)	0.051* (1.764)	0.023 (0.541)	0.180*** (3.770)	0.365*** (10.738)	0.164*** (4.452)	0.442*** (8.682)	0.164*** (3.131)	0.343*** (6.469)	0.067 (1.281)	0.504*** (6.646)	0.238*** (2.815)	0.119** (2.241)	0.027 (0.514)	0.229*** (2.774)	0.133 (1.427)
KLRATIO	0.006* (1.930)	0.002 (0.774)	0.003 (0.687)	0.005 (1.183)	0.010*** (3.537)	0.005** (2.084)	0.010* (1.850)	0.006 (1.184)	-0.006* (-2.094)	-0.003 (-0.983)	-0.014*** (-3.455)	-0.010** (-2.390)	0.002 (0.406)	-0.004 (-0.779)	0.004 (0.496)	-0.005 (-0.595)
RADV	-3.011 (-1.549)	-2.905 (-1.554)	-2.358 (-1.347)	-4.616** (-2.470)	-4.203 (-1.395)	-4.377 (-1.550)	0.440 (0.102)	3.342 (0.958)	-5.284 (-0.571)	0.464 (0.061)	-2.224 (-0.259)	3.434 (0.411)	1.725*** (8.385)	1.593*** (7.330)	-0.594** (-2.323)	-0.616* (-1.877)
RRD	0.507 (0.885)	0.264 (0.730)	3.289** (2.561)	4.909*** (4.199)	-1.571*** (-2.813)	-1.782*** (-3.524)	-2.005** (-2.417)	-2.108** (-2.566)	6.601*** (3.614)	5.341*** (2.981)	3.362 (1.433)	1.596 (0.661)	2.539*** (2.673)	1.766* (1.874)	1.134 (1.112)	0.414 (0.443)
SCALE	-0.002 (-0.407)		-0.011*** (-2.698)		-0.002 (-1.124)		-0.006** (-2.366)		-0.003 (-0.716)		-0.007* (-1.698)		0.056* (1.772)		0.096*** (2.806)	
MD		0.227*** (6.244)		0.358*** (6.169)		0.311*** (7.424)		0.448*** (8.038)		0.410*** (6.951)		0.385*** (4.689)		0.182** (2.411)		0.151 (1.343)
SD		0.251*** (5.200)		0.217*** (2.904)		0.392*** (6.445)		0.233*** (2.725)		0.142* (1.711)		0.065 (0.622)		0.209* (1.759)		0.047 (0.327)
M&SD		0.314*** (7.034)		0.313*** (4.206)		0.412*** (8.808)		0.467*** (7.403)		0.277*** (3.431)		0.396*** (3.981)		0.209** (2.287)		0.167 (1.280)
#of Obs	426	426	267	267	452	452	322	322	218	218	156	156	110	110	77	77
R2	0.016	0.168	0.069	0.196	0.042	0.200	0.030	0.217	0.090	0.254	0.054	0.190	0.122	0.233	0.023	0.137
F	2.30	15.21	9.47	12.35	7.66	23.25	3.03	15.07	6.95	16.02	5.13	7.18	27.71	17.27	2.31	2.92

Notes: KLRATIO: ratio of tangible asset to regular workers
RADV: ratio of advertisement expenditure to total sales
RRD: ratio of R&D expenditure to total sales
SCALE: the number of workers (1000 persons)
MD: manufacturing dummy takes value 1 if firm has manufacturing affiliates only and 0 otherwise
SD: service dummy takes value 1 if firm has service affiliates only and 0 otherwise
M&SD: manufacturing and service dummy takes value 1 if firm has both manufacturing and service affiliates and 0 otherwise
***,**,* means statistical significance level at 1, 5 and 10, respectively. T-value is in parenthesis. Standard deviation is calculated by White's consistency estimator.

international transactions, particularly for arm's-length trade. These phenomena may reflect the regression results.

In summary, empirical literature has investigated MNEs' choice of the location of their affiliates extensively, but we still do not have systematic knowledge on how their affiliates work in the whole structure of cross-border firms. We can confirm, however, that intra-firm trade has strong industry-specific or firm-specific characteristics. Particularly in the case of Japanese firms, upstream–downstream fragmentation seems to be a key to understanding the pattern of intra-firm trade.

Conclusions

To better understand the activities of firms in the era of globalization, intra-firm trade should be one of the essential topics for academic investigation. However, research in this field is still in the infant stage, both theoretically and empirically. We should probably start by accumulating more empirical knowledge about this phenomenon, even if statistical data are extremely scarce.

One of the most important findings in our study is that globalization may or may not enhance the weight of intra-firm trade in overall trade. On the one hand, globalization provides more room for firms to conduct global operations, which may result in greater intra-firm transactions. But, on the other, globalization reduces the service costs of linking remote locations together, resulting from a recent drastic decrease in the cost of international transport and telecommunications. This makes arm's-length trade easier and cheaper, which may mean a decline in the relative importance of intra-firm trade even if the absolute value of intra-firm trade increases. We observed in the case of the USA that the share of intra-firm trade to overall trade has been relatively stable over time. In the Japanese case, we found that firms with higher R&D intensity do not necessarily have higher intra-firm transaction ratios in the electronics industry.

We also found that intra-firm trade has strong industry-specific and firm-specific characteristics. Industrial patterns of intra-firm trade are largely similar to the US and Japanese cases, which suggests that whether firms wish to engage in intra-firm trade depends a great deal on the industry-specific nature of activities, such as technology, the organization of firms, and industrial organization. Furthermore, a statistical analysis of the Japanese case with micro data indicates that the determinants of intra-firm trade are highly firm-specific, depending on the characteristics of a firm's technological advantage.

Finally, our analysis suggests that intra-firm trade is largely the result of upstream–downstream fragmentation across different locations. Fragmentation sometimes takes the form of splitting a production block into several sub-blocks and locating them in the most suitable places. In other cases, a firm makes its product in one location and conducts sales activities in another. This chapter has highlighted the importance and advantage of using micro data to shed more light on an analysis of the intra-firm behaviour of MNEs.

Appendix: Data sources of intra-firm trade

International trade statistics published by national authorities do not distinguish between intra-firm trade and arm's-length trade. Data on intra-firm trade are available only through firm surveys, which involve the preparation of questionnaires by national authorities.

Among major OECD countries, the USA provides the most detailed information on intra-firm trade. The US Department of Commerce publishes data concerning related-party trade between US parents and their foreign affiliates, and between US affiliates and their foreign parents. Similarly, trade data on foreign affiliates of Japanese parents as well as majority-owned Japanese affiliates of foreign parents are available from Japan's Ministry of International Trade and Industry (MITI). A few other OECD member countries also collect and report data on intra-firm trade, but these data appear to be partial (Canada, Sweden). Given the limitations of other sources, the present study is based only on data from the US Department of Commerce and Japan's MITI.

The US Department of Commerce has published the results of four benchmark surveys (1977, 1982, 1989 and 1994) with data for foreign affiliates of US parents, as well as four benchmark surveys (1980, 1987, 1992 and 1997) with data for US affiliates of foreign parents. These data can be disaggregated into approximately thirty manufacturing sectors. The nationality of parent and affiliate companies is also available. Besides the benchmark surveys, annual survey data are also available, though these are more limited in coverage – for example, only majority-owned foreign affiliates are covered. In these surveys, the Department of Commerce provides the universe estimates on an annual basis. Tables A13.1 and A13.2 provide some of the figures related to intra-firm trade.

Japan's MITI has published the *Basic Survey of Business Structure and Activity* (MITI, 1996). This survey was first conducted in the 1991 financial year, and repeated in the 1994 financial year, and annually after that. The main purpose of the survey is to capture statistically the overall picture of Japanese corporate firms in light of their activity diversification, globalization, and strategies on R&D and information technology. The strength of this survey is the census-wide coverage of samples and the reliability of figures. It is not a sample survey but a census covering the population (the effective ratio of questionnaire returns is about 90 per cent) and collects information on an extensive set of firms' characteristics, particularly on the organization of firms and establishments' affiliates' holdings. We must, however, be careful that the survey includes only large firms. The domestic firms to be covered have more than fifty workers, the capital of more

Table A13.1 US merchandise exports and imports associated with nonbank US MNCs, 1977–97 (million dollars)

Calendar year	(1) Total US merchandise	(2) MNC-associated US [(3A) + (5)]	(3) Shipped to All US foreign affiliates: (3A) Total	of which: (3B) by US parents	(4) Shipped to US MOFAs by US parents	(5) Shipped to other foreigners by US parents	(6) US exports shipped by US parents [(3B) + (5)]
1977b	123.2	101.8	40.8	31.3	29.3	61.1	92.4
1982 b	216.4	163.4	56.7	47.1	44.3	106.7	153.8
1983	205.6	154.4	57.5	49.4	45.1	96.8	146.2
1984	224.0	169.2	66.3	56.7	52.7	102.9	159.6
1985	218.8	171.9	69.6	61.9	57.6	102.3	164.1
1986	227.2	171.1	71.1	61.1	58.9	100.1	161.2
1987	254.1	178.9	78.9	66.4	65.2	100.0	166.4
1988	322.4	215.2	94.9	79.4	78.2	120.3	199.7
1989 b	363.8	236.4	102.6	89.4	86.1	123.8	223.3
1990	393.6	241.3	106.4	90.1	88.4	134.9	224.9
1991	421.7	257.9	115.3	97.1	95.8	142.6	239.7
1992	448.2	265.9	122.0	106.0	100.7	143.9	249.9
1993	464.8	274.7	131.7	113.8	106.8	143.0	256.7
1994 b	512.6	344.5	159.5	138.3	132.7	185.1	323.3
1995	584.7	374.0	177.8	152.7	147.7	196.2	348.8
1996	625.1	405.7	194.0	161.8	161.4	211.7	373.4
1997p	688.7	434.0	215.8	183.1	181.1	218.2	401.3

Table A13.1 (continued)

Calendar year	(1) Total US merchandise	(2) MNC-associated US [(3A) + (5)]	(3) Shipped to All US foreign affiliates:		(4) Shipped to US MOFAs by US parents	(5) Shipped to other foreigners by US parents	(6) US exports shipped by US parents [(3B) + (5)]
			(3A) Total	of which: (3B) by US parents			
1977b	151.5	86.8	41.5	36.3	30.9	45.2	81.5
1982 b	244.0	120.8	51.4	39.3	38.5	69.4	108.7
1983	258.1	124.7	53.2	43.6	41.6	71.5	115.1
1984	330.7	145.9	63.0	52.8	49.3	82.9	132.3
1985	336.5	153.6	68.2	54.0	51.8	85.4	139.4
1986	365.4	147.3	65.5	55.0	50.0	81.8	136.8
1987	406.2	166.4	75.9	60.4	55.9	90.5	150.9
1988	441.0	180.9	87.3	69.5	65.5	93.6	163.1
1989 b	473.2	201.2	97.4	74.7	71.3	103.8	178.5
1990	495.3	213.4	102.2	80.3	75.3	111.2	191.5
1991	488.5	212.6	102.8	83.5	77.6	109.9	193.3
1992	532.7	217.5	106.2	93.9	83.3	111.3	205.2
1993	580.5	223.9	114.6	97.1	93.2	109.3	206.4
1994 b	663.8	256.8	134.2	114.9	107.2	122.6	237.5
1995	743.5	289.9	148.6	122.3	118.4	141.4	263.6
1996	795.3	326.2	164.8	137.2	133.4	161.4	298.6
1997p	870.6	349.9	178.7	147.4	145.4	171.2	318.6

Notes:
b. Benchmark survey years; p. Preliminary.
1. A US MNC consists of a US parent and its foreign affiliates. A US parent is a US person that owns or controls 10 per cent or more of the voting securities of an incorporated foreign business enterprise or an equivalent interest in an unincorporated foreign business enterprise. US foreign affiliates are foreign business enterprises that are so owned or controlled.

2. US exports associated with MNCs are the sum of goods shipped to US foreign affiliates by all US persons and goods shipped to other foreigners by US parents (Column 2).

3. MOFAs stand for majority-owned foreign affiliates (Column 4).

4. Intra-firm exports are defined as goods shipped by US parents to their foreign affiliates, as reported on parents' forms (Column 3B).

Sources: US Department of Commerce, *US Direct Investment Abroad* (available from: http://www.bea.doc.gov, except for 1977 and 1982 Benchmark Survey Results, which are available only on paper copies.)

Benchmark Surveys, 1977, 1982, 1989 and 1994.

Revised Estimates, 1983–88, 1990–93, and 1995–96.

Preliminary Estimates, 1997.

IMF (1999) (Column 1).

See also Bonturi and Fukasaku (1993) and Zeile (1997) for earlier estimates and data sources

Table A 13.2 US merchandise exports and imports associated with nonbank US affiliates of foreign MNCs, 1977–97 (million dollars)

Calendar year	(1) Total US merchandise exports	(2) US exports shipped by US affiliates of foreign MNCs	(3) Foreign parent group	(4) Other foreigners		
				(4A) Total	(4B) Foreign affiliates	(4C) Unaffiliated foreigners
1977	123.2	24.9	11.7	13.2	NA	NA
1978	145.8	32.2	16.6	15.6	NA	NA
1979	186.4	44.3	22.1	22.3	NA	NA
1980 b	225.6	52.2	21.0	31.2	NA	NA
1981	238.7	64.1	26.9	37.2	NA	NA
1982	216.4	60.2	25.0	35.2	NA	NA
1983	205.6	53.9	22.6	31.3	NA	NA
1984	224.0	58.2	27.1	31.1	NA	NA
1985	218.8	56.4	25.9	30.5	NA	NA
1986	227.2	49.6	21.9	27.7	NA	NA
1987 b	254.1	48.1	19.1	29.0	3.4	25.5
1988	322.4	69.5	26.4	43.1	5.9	37.2
1989	363.8	86.3	34.3	52.0	6.4	45.6
1990	393.6	92.3	37.8	54.5	7.6	47.0
1991	421.7	96.9	42.2	54.7	8.1	46.6
1992 b	448.2	103.9	48.8	55.2	9.8	45.3
1993	464.8	106.6	47.4	59.3	11.0	48.3
1994	512.6	120.7	51.1	69.5	13.7	55.8
1995	584.7	135.2	57.2	77.9	14.9	63.0
1996	625.1	140.9	60.8	80.1	14.3	65.8
1997p	688.7	140.9	62.8	78.1	13.4	64.7

Shipped by US affiliates of foreign MNCs to:

Calendar year	(1) Total US merchandise exports	(2) US exports shipped by US affiliates of foreign MNCs	(3) Foreign parent group	(4) Other foreigners		
				(4A) Total	(4B) Foreign affiliates	(4C) Unaffiliated foreigners
1977	151.5	43.9	30.9	13.0	NA	NA
1978	176.1	56.6	39.5	17.1	NA	NA
1979	210.3	63.0	45.3	17.7	NA	NA
1980 b	245.3	75.8	47.0	28.8	NA	NA
1981	261.0	82.3	52.2	30.1	NA	NA
1982	244.0	84.3	51.9	32.4	NA	NA
1983	258.1	81.5	54.8	26.7	NA	NA
1984	330.7	100.5	70.5	30.0	NA	NA
1985	336.5	113.3	81.7	31.6	NA	NA
1986	365.4	125.7	93.4	32.3	NA	NA
1987 b	406.2	143.5	108.2	35.3	1.7	33.6
1988	441.0	155.5	118.4	37.2	3.2	34.0
1989	473.2	171.8	129.9	41.9	4.3	37.6
1990	495.3	182.9	137.5	45.5	4.4	41.1
1991	488.5	178.7	132.2	46.5	4.9	41.7
1992 b	532.7	184.5	137.8	46.7	6.1	40.5
1993	580.5	200.6	150.8	49.8	8.1	41.7

Table A 13.2   (Continued)

Calendar year			Shipped by US affiliates of foreign MNCs to:			
	(1) Total US merchandise exports	*(2)* US exports shipped by US affiliates of foreign MNCs	*(3)* Foreign parent group	*(4)* Other foreigners		
				(4A) Total	*(4B) Foreign affiliates*	*(4C) Unaffiliated foreigners*
1994	663.8	232.4	174.6	57.7	11.3	46.4
1995	743.5	250.8	191.2	59.6	12.5	47.1
1996	795.3	268.7	197.7	71.0	15.5	55.5
1997p	870.6	261.5	195.5	66.0	13.2	52.7

Notes:

b. Benchmark survey years; p. Preliminary.

1. A US affiliate is a US business enterprise in which a single foreign person owns or controls 10 per cent or more of the voting securities of an incorporated foreign business enterprise or an equivalent interest in an unincorporated foreign business enterprise (Column 2).

2. A foreign parent group (FPG) consists of (1) the foreign parent, (2) any foreign person, proceeding up the foreign parent's ownership chain, that owns more than 50 per cent by the person below it, up to and including the UBO, and (3) any foreign person, proceeding down the ownership chain(s) of each of these members, that is ownded more than 50 per cent by the person above it. A foreign parent is the first person outside the United States in a US affiliate's ownership chain that has a direct investment interest in the affiliate, while an ultimate beneficial owner (UBO) is the first person, proceeding up a US affiliate's ownership chain, beginning with and including the foreign parent, that is not owned more than 50 per cent by another person (Column 3).

3. 'Foreign affiliates (Column 4B)' refers to exports to foreign business enterprises in which the US affiliate has a 10-percent-or-more ownership interest.

4. Intra-firm exports are conventionally defined as goods shipped by US affiliates of foreign MNCs to their foreign parent groups (Column 3). In a broad sense, Column 4B should also be added.

Sources: US Department of Commerce, *Foreign Direct Investment in the United States: Operations of US Affiliates* (available from: http://www.bea.doc.gov).Revised Estimates, 1977–79, 1981–86, 1988–91 and 93–96;

Benchmark Surveys, 1980, 1987 and 1992 (Final Results) and 1997 (Preliminary Results).

IMF (1999) (Column 1).

See also Bonturi and Fukasaku (1993) and Zeile (1997) for earlier estimates and data sources.

than 30 million, and have establishments in mining, manufacturing, wholesale and retail trade, or the restaurant industry. Table A13.3 presents domestic/foreign sales and purchases for the full samples of 1994 financial year survey. It provides the number of domestic/foreign affiliates, defined as firms in which a parent firm has more than 50 per cent stock share, and other information on firm characteristics such as employment size, advertisement and R&D expenditure. This paper uses the questionnaire-level data after cleaning up the samples by checking the availability of relevant variables.

Given all the complex arrangements through which firms co-operate, any empirical analysis needs to define what constitutes a *firm*. An ideal definition would involve an estimate of the level of control and ownership, but this would be practical only on a case-by-case basis. The 10 per cent ownership cut-off point is regarded in the US source as indicative of significant influence by an investor. In other words, a company is defined as an affiliate if the parent company owns 10 per cent or more of its voting stock.[12] The OECD benchmark definition of foreign direct investment recommends the same hurdle in determining whether a direct investment relationship exists. Most double-taxation agreements also use this cut-off point to determine differential withholding tax rates. Note, however, that the MITI data use different cut-off point, as described in the text.

Table A 13.3 Intra-firm trade data in the *Basic Survey of Business Structure and Activity* (1994 F/Y) (millions of yen, %)

Industry code	Industry	Number of firms in the full sample	Sales Total	To domestic To all	To rel. comp.	To foreign To all	To rel. comp.	Purchases Total	From domestic From all	From rel. comp.	From foreign From all	From rel. comp.
	All industries in the sample	25 278	584 755 777	520 940 624	68 537 806	63 815 153	15 283 503	407 976 327	372 030 060	57 501 398	35 946 267	9 228 331
	Mining, manufacturing and commerce	24 015	567 188 391	503 462 682	67 362 659	63 725 709	15 261 543	399 393 925	363 741 690	56 749 150	35 652 235	9 190 032
	Mining and manufacturing	13 784	250 708 650	220 864 622	46 293 420	29 844 028	9 946 561	132 178 320	122 832 820	30 071 891	9 345 500	2 288 749
50	Mining	53	525 414	523 460	85 145	1954	0	155 484	153 930	34 852	1554	0
120	Food processing	1325	15 004 385	14 958 399	2 519 788	45 986	21 947	7 846 935	7 421 491	1 510 575	425 444	256 897
130	Beverages, tobacco, and animal feed	222	10 514 113	10 500 734	667 524	13 379	4009	3 251 906	3 129 660	384 152	122 246	40 447
140	Textiles	480	2 609 051	2 573 759	357 898	35 292	3257	1 180 799	1 133 414	190 693	47 385	4272
150	Apparel	556	2 549 403	2 538 650	363 436	10 753	4691	1 223 389	1 164 920	133 357	58 469	17 462
160	Wood and wood products	172	3 354 959	3 343 028	710 769	11 931	8531	1 418 670	1 305 138	354 821	113 532	10 996
170	Furniture and fixtures	206	1 327 685	1 319 734	167 876	7951	2502	639 863	628 470	80 074	11 393	2468
180	Pulp, paper, and paper products	452	6 256 708	6 182 111	1 015 453	74 597	2835	3 368 775	3 273 843	720 463	94 932	25 459
190	Publishing and printing	722	7 528 569	7 475 980	585 454	52 589	16 587	2 138 147	2 131 717	206 626	6430	2783
200	Chemicals	942	24 847 728	23 129 660	4 399 025	1 718 068	424 358	10 273 321	9 529 579	1 906 491	743 742	284 847
210	Petroleum and coal products	59	9 613 933	9 319 307	1 652 024	294 626	10 216	5 877 252	2 272 373	591 988	3 604 879	530 209
220	Plastic products	639	5 146 321	5 052 348	694 336	93 973	23 459	2 571 982	2 541 269	358 716	30 713	6842
230	Rubber products	151	2 658 631	2 347 735	833 697	310 896	132 246	1 202 560	1 106 816	213 804	95 744	27 050
240	Leather and leather products	52	169 046	165 701	35 305	3345	406	92 855	87 163	17 291	5692	1295
250	Ceramics, clay, and stone products	647	6,272 368	6 089 009	823 508	183 359	41 581	2 543 152	2 501 123	363 864	42 029	11 860
260	Iron and steel	421	12 355 732	11 876 777	2 476 544	478 955	82 488	5 735 434	5 447 197	1 680 132	288 237	6840
270	Nonferrous metal	336	6 661 906	6 208 063	1 068 196	453 843	93 887	3 893 960	3 498 200	650 972	395 760	22 588
280	Metal products	987	9 343 607	9 183 074	1 006 825	160 533	63 356	4 438 068	4 400 162	502 711	37 906	28 167
290	General machinery	1 575	22 266 013	18 209 167	3 180 495	4 056 846	1 236 995	12 196 077	11 775 594	1 807 403	420 483	149 311

Table A 13.3 (continued)

Industry code	Industry	Number of firms in the full sample	Sales Total	To domestic To all	To rel. comp.	To foreign To all	To rel. comp.	Purchases Total	From domestic From all	From rel. comp.	From foreign From all	From rel. comp.
291	Metal-working machinery	281	1 365 840	1 138 621	201 447	227 219	113 978	656 074	643 009	70 529	13 065	7 601
292	Industrial machinery	379	5 227 129	4 129 294	908 425	1 097 835	278 481	2 994 444	2 920 652	539 072	73 792	13 892
293	Office and service machinery	159	4 499 871	3 412 174	756 158	1 087 697	484 610	2 530 605	2 391 599	360 459	139 006	95 268
299	Other machinery	756	11 173 173	9 529 078	1 314 465	1 644 095	359 926	6 014 954	5 820 334	837 343	194 620	32 550
300	Electric machinery	1991	50 669 545	39 586 547	10 991 231	11 082 998	3 710 692	28 303 555	26 523 334	8 148 224	1 780 221	616 620
301	Electric machinery for industrial use	411	6 522 362	5 714 091	1 654 266	808 271	413 400	3 581 069	3 493 620	1 050 280	87 449	45 454
302	Electric machinery for domestic use	217	3 772 277	2 461 041	414 921	1 311 236	16 128	1 201 053	1 104 596	87 247	96 457	9 329
303	Communication-related machinery	310	8 208 309	6 130 054	1 007 615	2 078 255	461 397	4 948 532	4 527 618	506 813	420 914	216 418
304	Computers and electronic apparatus	207	16 820 954	12 904 831	3 238 824	3 916 123	1 378 467	10 579 036	9 888 165	3 959 718	690 871	183 916
305	Electronic parts and devices	650	12 857 877	10 184 750	4 200 947	2 673 127	1 362 960	6 791 781	6 329 666	2 288 689	462 115	150 090
309	Other electric machinery	196	2 487 766	2 191 780	474 658	295 986	78 340	1 202 084	1 179 669	255 477	22 415	11 413
310	Transport equipment	1154	45 058 559	35 229 748	11 733 320	9 828 811	3 625 667	30 800 091	30 117 654	9 768 011	682 437	175 128
311	Automobiles and parts	924	41 357 233	32 485 904	11 210 678	8 871 329	3 557 827	28 847 918	28 190 328	9 623 858	657 590	171 973
319	Other transport equipment	230	3 701 326	2 743 844	522 642	957 482	67 840	1 952 173	1 927 326	144 153	24 847	3 155
320	Precision machinery	337	2 974 121	2 342 504	642 636	631 617	261 019	1 656 183	1 376 747	322 676	279 436	48 588
321	Medical equipment	72	772 678	595 527	228 095	177 151	105 874	379 717	350 480	88 707	29 237	18 086
322	Optical equipment	66	534 394	423 192	199 788	111 202	59 991	320 194	306 953	54 912	13 241	5 729
323	Watches and clocks	30	703 620	482 267	82 376	221 353	56 238	480 092	271 083	100 567	209 009	16 443
329	Other precision machinery	169	963 429	841 518	132 377	121 911	38 916	476 180	448 231	78 490	27 949	8 330
340	Other manufacturing	305	3 000 853	2 709 127	282 935	291 726	175 832	1 369 862	1 313 026	123 995	56 836	18 620
480	Wholesale and retail trade	10 231	316 479 741	282 598 060	21 069 239	33 881 681	5 314 982	267 215 605	240 908 870	26 677 259	26 306 735	6 901 283
481	Wholesale trade	6938	253 822 620	220 120 112	18 755 200	33 702 508	5 294 619	221 925 856	196 178 345	22 633 013	25 747 511	6 831 436
540	Retail trade	3293	62 657 121	62 477 948	2 314 039	179 173	20 363	45 289 749	44 730 525	4 044 246	559 224	69 847

	Other industries	1263	17 567 386	17 477 942	1 175 147	89 444	21 960	8 582 402	8 288 370	752 248	294 032	38 299
600	Restaurants	72	648 928	648 885	15 516	43		230 587	230 566	6 824	21	
715	Services	544	6 032 685	5 968 935	609 780	63 750	19 282	2 530 614	2 324 544	238 964	206 070	37 562
900	Others	647	10 885 773	10 860 122	549 851	25 651	2 678	5 821 201	5 733 260	506 460	87 941	737

Notes:

'Related company' is defined as a firm in which a parent company has more than 20 stock share.

Note that tables and figures in the text use smaller samples sets due to the data availability for some variables.

'Intra-firm transaction' is defined as a transaction between a parent company and related companies.

Source: MITI (1996), hardcopy published version.

Notes

* The earlier version of this chapter was presented as a paper at the Conference on the Frontiers of Research on Intra-Industry Trade held at the University of Colorado, Boulder on 24–26 August 2000. We would like to thank the conference participants for a number of constructive comments and suggestion. We are also grateful to Kozo Kiyota for able assistance. The MITI database was prepared and analyzed in co-operation with the Research and Statistics Department, Minister's Secretariat, Ministry of International Trade and Industry (currently called METI), Government of Japan. However, opinions expressed in this paper are those of the authors alone.

1   These statistics are taken from Tables I.1 and I.4 (United Nations, 2000).

2   The authors' own calculations based on US Department of Commerce statistics (see Appendix).

3   In principle, trade among foreign affiliates of a MNE should be included as part of intra-firm trade, though it is more difficult to gauge its magnitude statistically, given the availability of data.

4   For the concept of service links in the context of fragmentation, see Jones and Kierzkowski (1990) and Deardorff (1998).

5   The results of annual firm survey data are published regularly in the USA and Japan. In the case of European countries, there are few data available with respect to intra-firm trade. See, for example, OECD (1999) for further details.

6   The data on intra-firm trade refer to the USA only.

7   In addition, Japanese and other trading firms in East Asia are believed to be heavily involved in intra-firm trade, but this is basically of the inter-industry character. These trading firms are both intermediaries and organizers of global chains of production and marketing operations, which involve small- and medium-scale manufacturers from various industries at home and abroad.

8   See Goldsborough (1981), Julius (1990), Encarnation (1992), and Rangan and Lawrence (1993).

9   Exceptions to this rule are US affiliates established in Canada, which sell as much as they buy from their parents. Similarly, US affiliates established in other (mainly non-OECD) countries tend to sell more to their foreign parents than they buy.

10 In the following regressions, reported in Tables 13.8 and 13.9, the values of dependent variables for a number of samples are zeros. Hence, we also conducted Tobit regressions, but the results did not differ much.

11 Japanese wholesale trade firms in fact have a number of manufacturing plants abroad and conduct intra-firm imports. Kimura (2000), using the MITI data set, analyzes the discordance of parent companies' industries with industries of affiliates abroad in order to investigate vertical division of labour.

12 If the parent company owns more than 50 per cent of the voting stock, the affiliate company is considered to be a subsidiary of the parent company and is called a majority-owned foreign affiliate (MOFA) in the US data.

References

Bonturi, M. and K. Fukasaku (1993) 'Globalisation and Intra-firm Trade: An Empirical Note', *OECD Economic Studies*, 20, Spring: 145–59.

Deardorff, A. V. (1998) 'Fragmentation in Simple Trade Models', Research Seminar in International Economics, School of Public Policy, University of Michigan, Discussion Paper No. 422.

Encarnation, D. J. (1992) *Rivals Beyond Trade: America versus Japan in Global Competition* Ithaca (NY: Cornell University Press).

Fukasaku, K. (1992) 'Economic Regionalisation and Intra-industry Trade: Pacific Asian Perspectives', Technical Paper No. 53, OECD Development Centre, Paris.

Goldsborough, D. J. (1981) 'International Trade of Multinational Corporations and Its Responsiveness as Changes in Aggregate Demand and Relative Prices', *IMF Staff Papers*, 28, September: 573–99.

Greenaway, D. (1987) 'Intra-industry Trade, Intra-firm Trade and European Integration: Evidence, Gains and Policy Aspects', *Journal of Common Market Studies*, 26: 153–72.

Grubel, H. G. and P. J. Lloyd (1975) *Intra-industry Trade: The Theory and Measurement of International Trade in Differentiated Products* (London: Macmillan).

Helpman, E. (1998) 'Explaining the Structure of Foreign Trade: Where Do We Stand?', *Weltwirtschaftliches Archiv*, 134: 573–89.

IMF (1999) *International Financial Statistics Yearbook 1999* (Washington, DC: IMF).

Jones, R. W. and H. Kierzkowski (1990) 'The Role of Services in Production and International Trade: A Theoretical Framework', in R. W. Jones and A. O. Krueger (eds), *The Political Economy of International Trade: Essays in Honor of Robert E. Baldwin* (Oxford: Basil Blackwell).

Julius, D. (1990) *Global Companies and Public Policy: The Growing Challenge of Foreign Direct Investment* (London: Pinter).

Kimura, F. (2000) 'Location and Internalization Decisions: Sector Switching in Japanese Outward Foreign Direct Investment', in T. Ito and A. O. Krueger (eds), *The Role of Foreign Direct Investment in East Asian Economic Development* (Chicago, Ill.: University of Chicago Press).

Markusen, J. R. (1995) 'The Boundaries of Multinational Enterprises and the Theory of International Trade', *Journal of Economic Perspectives*, 9: 169–89.

MITI (Ministry of International Trade and Industry), Minister's Secretariat, Research and Statistics Department (1996) *Results of the Basic Survey of Business Structure and Activity, 1995. Vol. 3: Report by Subsidiary Companies* (Tokyo: Shadan Houjin Tsuusan Toukei Kyoukai).

OECD (1993) 'Intra-firm Trade', *OECD Trade Policy Issues*, No. 1 (Paris: OECD).

OECD (1996) *Globalisation of Industry: Overview and Sector Reports* (Paris: OECD).

OECD (1999) *Measuring Globalisation: The Role of Multinationals in OECD Economies* (CD-ROM) (Paris: OECD).

OECD (2000) *Main Economic Indicators*, May (Paris: OECD).

Oman, C. (1989) *New Forms of Investment in Developing Country Industries: Mining, Petrochemicals, Automobiles, Textiles and Food* (Paris: OECD Development Centre).

Rangan, S. and R. Z. Lawrence (1993) 'The Responses of U.S. Firms to Exchange Rate Fluctuations: Piercing the Corporate Veil', *Brookings Papers on Economic Activity*, 2: 341–79.

United Nations (2000) *World Investment Report 2000: Cross-border Mergers and Acquisitions and Development* (New York and Geneva: United Nations).

Yamawaki, H. (1991) 'Exports and Foreign Distribution Activities: Evidence on Japanese Firms in the United States', *Review of Economics and Statistics*, 73, May: 294–300.

Zeile, W. J. (1997) 'U.S. Intra-firm Trade in Goods', *Survey of Current Business*, February: 23–38.

14

Intra-Industry Trade in Assets

Herbert G. Grubel

The main purpose of papers presented at the Conference on the Frontiers of Research on Intra-Industry Trade is, as the name indicates, the advancement of research, with due credit given to existing publications and knowledge. My chapter considers the rather neglected aspect of intra-industry trade in assets. To the best of my knowledge, this frontier is largely unexplored, with only five published papers.[1]

When I presented a paper on the subject at a conference in Kiel in 1978, comments by participants persuaded me to adopt the title 'two-way', rather than 'intra-industry' trade in assets. I now believe that I gave in to these suggestions too readily. Much of the opposition to my original title came from several conference participants who believed that the concept of intra-industry trade generally was misguided, that it was merely a statistical artefact, and that the Heckscher–Ohlin–Samuelson model had it all covered. They did not want to see the term 'intra-industry trade' extended to explain yet another problem caused by imperfect statistical coverage. These objectors to studies of intra-industry trade have been proven wrong since then.

I was also induced to take their advice because my paper was largely a theoretical exploration. I did not have access to the kinds of data I present today. These data show that capital flows, much like trade in goods and services, involve different 'industries' such as direct investment, portfolio investment, bank loans, trade credit and a host of subcategories in each of them. As in the case of intra-industry trade in goods and services, measures of two-way flows of assets are remarkably high.

For this reason, it is important that more work is done at this frontier of research on intra-industry trade. Much more intensive and extensive studies of the empirical phenomenon are required, and these are sure to lead to useful insights into differences of the phenomenon among countries, industries, over time and at a varying levels of aggregation. At the appropriate place in this chapter I suggest some promising avenues for further research, which unfortunately I am unable to pursue myself. There is no doubt that such research will lead to extensions and refinements of the existing theories of motives for capital flows, their welfare effects, and to the study of relations with measures of global competition (such as the paper by Greenaway *et al.* 2001) and other similar economic phenomena. Importantly, the findings will be shown to have policy implications for the liberalization of capital accounts, which remains an issue hotly debated by policy-makers. I shall speculate on this issue in the last section of this chapter.

However, I do not foresee the kind of revolution of theory like that stimulated by the evidence on the importance of intra-industry trade in goods and service. Existing theories in finance can readily explain intra-industry trade in assets. For this reason, the following analysis focuses on empirical measures and presents only a rather cursory summary of relevant theory with appropriate references to the existing literature.

I trust that the empirical evidence and theory to be presented will not change the heuristically useful simplifications underlying the textbook models of international capital flows, any more than the Modern Trade Theory has replaced the Heckscher–Ohlin–Samuelson model. The Mundell–Fleming model will continue to be useful as it treats capital as a homogeneous product responsive to interest rate differentials between countries.

The empirical evidence on the magnitude of the two-way flow of capital to be presented uses the Grubel–Lloyd index as a measure of its magnitude. First I consider the capital account of Germany as a representative industrial country to indicate the relative importance of direct, portfolio and other investment, and the subcategories within these major aggregates.[2] These data provide guidance for the selection of categories of capital flows to be examined for individual countries, regional aggregates and, to a more limited degree, through time.

The chapter concludes with a brief discussion of the implications of my findings for the teaching of international finance and for assessing the effects of liberalizing capital controls.

The capital accounts in perspective

The Balance of Payments Statistics Yearbook (1999) published by the International Monetary Fund contains data on the global financial accounts of individual countries and sets of countries grouped according to some common characteristics. My statistical analysis is based on these data. Starting off with an overview of the nature of financial accounts, Table 14.1 contains those for Germany.

The table shows in rows the three major categories of capital flows in national balance of payments statistics: direct, portfolio, and other investment. The first two vertical columns give data on the *flows* of exports and imports for the year 1998. The fourth and fifth column present the *stocks* of assets and liabilities at the end of 1997. Most of the data come from national surveys of business and some international collection agencies.[3] Columns 3 and 6 are the calculated values of the GL index. I now turn to a brief discussion of the main features of these data.

Direct investment

Direct investment exports in 1998 were US$87.69 billion, while imports were only US$18.71 billion, which translates into a GL index of 0.35. It is interesting to note that the GL ratio is 0.53 for the stocks of direct investment at the end of 1997, suggesting that in 1998 Germany's involvement with inward and outward flows of direct investments was less balanced than it was in the past.

Table 14.1 Financial accounts for Germany, 1998 (billions of US$)

		Flows	1998		Stocks	1997	
		Exports ($)	Imports ($)	G–L Index	Assets ($)	Liabilities ($)	G–L Index
A	Direct investments	87.69	18.71	0.35	248.04	88.55	0.53
	Equity	61.38	7.03	0.21	248.04	88.55	0.53
	Reinvested earnings	3.41		0.00			
	Other capital	22.90	11.68	0.68			
B	Portfolio investments	146.66	145.22	1.00	490.98	752.49	0.79
	Equity securities	73.14	54.34	0.85	235.65	187.20	0.89
	Debt securities	73.52	90.88	0.89	227.48	565.29	0.57
	Money market	4.30	7.11	0.75	7.26		
	Instr. Financial derivatives	6.80		0.00			
C	Other investments	84.90	167.23	0.67	949.53	853.52	0.95
	Trade credits	−2.91	−1.26	1.40	109.93	72.17	0.79
	Loans	83.52	168.53	0.66	805.09	769.31	0.98
	Other	4.29		0.00		12.03	0.00

Source: IMF, *Balance of Payments Statistical Yearbook* (1999), Country Tables for Germany.

An examination of the components of direct investment shows that 80 per cent of direct flows take the form of equity investment; reinvested earnings and other capital make up the rest. Other capital has a GL index of 0.68. The stock figures show that equity investment has an index of 0.53, while it is zero for reinvested earnings and other capital.

Portfolio investment

Portfolio investment involves the largest category of flows in 1998 in the financial accounts. Interestingly, exports and imports of portfolio investment are virtually identical and produce a GL index of 1.0. The index is somewhat lower but still in the 0.80s for investments in equity securities and debt securities, which make up the bulk of the total.

The index for the stock of portfolio investment at the end of 1997 has a value of 0.79, less than that for the flows in 1988. This fact implies again that the pattern of 1998 flows is different from the average of past flows. The components of the stocks of equity investment exhibit similar characteristics to the flows.

Other Investment

Other investment stocks of assets at US$949 billion are larger than the stocks of direct and portfolio investment combined. The stock of liabilities is US$854 billion and just a little less than the two other categories combined. The GL ratio for the stocks of other investments is 0.95.

Loans represent 89 per cent of this category of capital flows, while other investments and trade credit total 11 per cent. For loans, the GL ratio is 0.98, the highest of all the stocks in the financial accounts.

The flow data for 1998 show that Germany borrowed nearly twice as much through loans than was loaned to foreigners, giving rise to an index of 0.66. Trade credits actually declined in 1998, even though stocks at the end of 1997 were rather high.

More information and implications

The IMF publication from which Table 14.1 was extracted contains further breakdowns of the different types of investment shown. Distinctions are made between short-term and long-term loans, and investments of banks, the monetary authority and other sectors. I have not presented these data here to keep the exposition simple, even though these breakdowns may be useful for anyone attempting to explain the causes and effects of the size of the GL indices.

The data for Germany suggest that it is most useful to consider international comparisons of intra-industry trade in assets in the following categories: direct, portfolio, and other investment. These data are presented in the following three major sections of the chapter.

Direct investment

The basic theory of foreign investment is that firms invest abroad if it is more profitable to do so than to operate a domestic enterprise for the production of a given good. The theory of comparative advantage is used to explain why foreign production is cheaper than domestic. A firm might therefore be induced to invest in Singapore because the cost of labour there is lower than it is in Canada, or the cost of transporting inputs and outputs and distribution are less. The cost of capital in the abstract in this model is assumed to favour neither of the two countries, since both can obtain capital at the same interest rate in world markets.

As is well known, this theoretical explanation is lacking in some dimensions because, while comparative advantage can explain why production takes place in one country rather than another, we need to explain why it is a Canadian and not a Singaporean entrepreneur who owns the facility. This is so especially since, realistically, it may be presumed that the Singaporean entrepreneur knows better than the Canadian his country's markets for goods, labour and political favours, knowledge which should provide him with a cost advantage.

Dunning (1993) provides an excellent summary of the theory of direct investment, which essentially is designed to provide reasons why the Canadian firm has a cost-advantage over that of a local entrepreneur.

I am drawn personally to the use of the so-called theory of internalization to increase understanding of direct foreign investment, mainly because it involves an appealing simplification in comparison with the competing so-called eclectic theory, and the political, quasi-Marxist theory offered by Stephen Hymer. The internalization theory draws heavily on analytical models of firm behaviour associated with Coase and Williamson.

These models view the firm as an organization, which uses internal production to reduce the costs and risks of doing business with independent suppliers or distributors. Inputs into the production process often involve sophisticated and frequently changing patents and product designs. Internal production reduces the cost of monitoring the suppliers using these patents and product designs. Internal production is also useful in assuring quality standards of inputs and outputs. The spillover effect of global advertising and return to it often can be captured only by an owned production facility abroad. In other words, according to internalization theory, direct foreign investment is motivated by the same factors that cause firms to buy some inputs like steel and tyres from outside suppliers while they design, assemble and market automobiles in-house.[4]

For the theory of intra-industry trade in assets it is important that firms in all countries enjoy some of these benefits from internalization through the foreign ownership of production facilities. Therefore, firms in all countries make direct investments abroad at the same time that foreign firms have such investments in their own countries. In my view, there are no unsettled questions about the causes of intra-industry trade in direct investment. The main question is the empirical significance of this phenomenon.

Before turning to this issue, it is necessary to note that direct investment differs from portfolio and other investment by providing the owners of the capital with control of the foreign operations. This control can be achieved by either direct or complete ownership of the production facility through a subsidiary or branch, or through the ownership of a controlling interest of voting shares. The data used here do not indicate whether the direct investment results from full ownership or the holding of a controlling interest.

Table 14.2 shows data on direct investment by individual industrial countries in the rest of the world, industrial and developing. The first two columns show the exports and imports during the year 1998. The third column gives the GL index. The countries are arranged in descending order of the size of that index.

The data show that the GL index ranges from the highest of 0.94 for Belgium-Luxembourg to the lowest of 0.06 for New Zealand. The countries with the largest flows that year were the USA and the UK, with indices of 0.81 and 0.77, respectively. The third largest country, Germany, had an index of only 0.35. Perhaps surprisingly, Japan, as one of the largest industrial countries, showed relatively low levels of direct investment inflows and outflows and a GL index of only 0.23. This result may be caused by Japan's economic crisis in 1998.

The index through time

Figures 14.1 and 14.2 each show the GL index for six major industrial countries between 1992 and 1998. The main conclusion arising from these data is that there are some intertemporal fluctuations in the ratios for all countries, but that there are no significant trends. The exception is the USA, which had a fairly steady rise in the ratio. Japan

Table 14.2 Direct investment, 1998 (millions of US$)

	Exports ($)	Imports ($)	GL Index
Belgium-Luxembourg	23 272	20 824	**0.94**
Sweden	22 671	19 413	**0.92**
Netherlands	39 812	33 346	**0.91**
Norway	2 521	3 597	**0.82**
United States	132 829	193 373	**0.81**
France	40 796	27 998	**0.81**
UK	106 734	67 481	**0.77**
Canada	26 411	16 515	**0.77**
Spain	18 509	11 392	**0.76**
Portugal	2 947	1 783	**0.75**
Finland	19 392	10 793	**0.72**
Iceland	73	150	**0.65**
Austria	2 759	6 034	**0.63**
Australia	2 464	6 255	**0.57**
Switzerland	14 226	5 488	**0.56**
Ireland	1 118	2 920	**0.55**
Germany	87 693	18 712	**0.35**
Italy	12 407	2 635	**0.35**
Japan	24 625	3 268	**0.23**
Denmark	260	6 373	**0.08**
New Zealand	77	2 657	**0.06**

Source: IMF, *Balance of Payments Statistical Yearbook* (1999), Aggregated Presentations, Section B, Direct Investment and Other Long-term Capital.

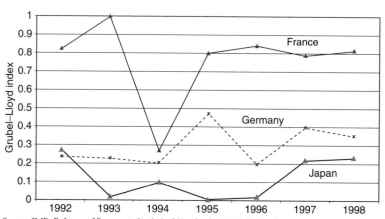

Source: IMF, *Balance of Payments Statistical Yearbook* (1999), Individual Country Tables.

Figure 14.1 Direct investment: Japan, France, Germany

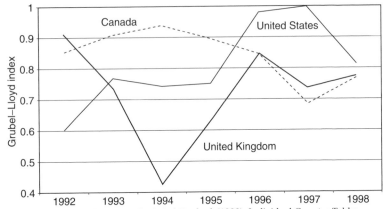

Source: IMF, *Balance of Payments Statistical Yearbook* (1999), Individual Country Tables.

Figure 14.2   Direct investment: Canada, US and UK

and Germany's ratios fluctuate around a level that is low relative to that of the other six countries.

The figures invite extension into earlier years and the introduction of other variables to explain the variations – variables such as trade imbalances, economic growth and, of course, interest rates relative to a global norm. It would also be interesting to investigate bilateral flows rather than the global flows of direct investment among sending and receiving countries.

Major regions

Table 14.3 presents the direct investment flow data aggregated for all the industrial countries and regional groupings of developing countries for the years 1992–8.

Let us first consider only the dollar values of these flows. The large flows by industrial countries do not come as a surprise to most people. What may surprise some readers is that all the regional aggregates of developing countries have some, albeit relatively small, amounts of exports of direct investment. After all, these countries are known to suffer from a relative scarcity of capital and are engaged in relatively low levels of research, marketing and other activities giving rise to benefits from internalization. Further investigation of this phenomenon is required. I suspect that such studies will require data on bilateral flows between countries, and that they may reveal that, for example, most of the direct investment out of African countries comes from South Africa.

Table 14.3   Direct investment by major regions 1992–8 (in millions of US$)

| | Industrial countries | | Developing countries of | | | | | |
| | | | Africa | | Asia | | Western hemisphere | |
	Exports	Imports	Exports	Imports	Exports	Imports	Exports	Imports
1992	186 785	119 826	2 290	2 601	8 194	25 486	1 916	14 973
1993	212 656	146 175	498	2 931	10 404	45 280	2 760	13 733
1994	246 412	142 737	1 456	4 323	11 367	55 939	3 468	23 289
1995	312 385	206 501	2 654	5 012	14 551	62 497	4 036	29 853
1996	339 734	222 476	1 167	5 111	17 113	71 840	3 230	43 537
1997	411 234	272 086	2 434	9 132	15 882	79 158	7 554	65 002
1998	585 519	458 348	1 733	5 561	14 298	71 421	8 389	70 338

Source: IMF, *Balanced of Payments Statistics Yearbook* (1999), Aggregated Presentations, Section B, Direct Investment and Other Long-term Capital.

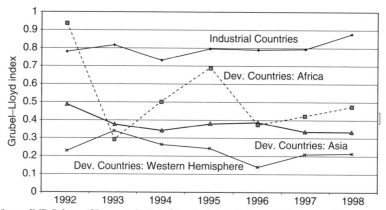

Source: IMF, *Balance of Payments Statistical Yearbook* (1999), Aggregated Presentation, Section B, Direct Investment and Other Long-term Capital.

Figure 14.3   Direct investment by regions

Figure 14.3 shows through time the GL index for the groups of countries listed in Table 14.3. The GL index is at 0.8, with minimal fluctuations and a slight upward trend for the industrial countries. This stability is probably attributable to the large size of the flows and the contribution of many countries, which are likely to have had often offsetting increases and decreases in their direct investment flows. The developing countries of the western hemisphere have an index of only 0.2, with a slight downward trend. The index for the developing countries of Africa is the second highest, and rather unstable. The index for the developing countries of Asia is very stable at around 0.35. The Asian currency crisis of the 1990s is not reflected in either the index or the size of the in- and outflows of direct investment shown in Table 14.3.

Portfolio investment

Portfolio investment is made up of investment in equities, bonds and notes. The simple textbook model has these flows motivated by simple interest rate differentials. However, the highly developed portfolio theory has long ago overshadowed this simple model by adding the argument that wealth-holders choose assets on the basis of returns as well as risk.

In Grubel (1968) I applied portfolio theory to document the extent to which international diversification gives rise to welfare gains for wealth-holders. Using data from the stock markets of eleven countries, I estimated the means, variance and correlation matrix of monthly returns, adjusted for exchange rate changes, over about ten years. A computer program was used to simulate the risk–return frontier of an efficient portfolio based on the characteristics of these assets.

The results of my calculations were that an American investor who exploited the imperfect correlation of returns from investments in different countries would have enjoyed considerably higher returns for any given risk than was available through investment in the US stock market alone. Alternatively, for any given return, international diversification reduced the risk of portfolios relative to that of investments drawn only from the US market. One interesting implication of the model was that a country with low interest rates could become a net importer of capital. This event takes place if that country's growth in wealth is so large that the maintenance of portfolio balance requires the import of more assets than are leaving the country.

Most important for the theory of intra-industry trade in portfolio assets is that wealth-holders in country A hold assets issued in country B while, at the same time, the wealth-holders of country B hold assets issued in country A. By doing so, the welfare of the residents in both countries is increased.

This is not the place to consider the limitations of this analysis. Let me just mention that my estimates were based on *ex post* data, while investors must make decisions involving an unknown future. Another criticism pointed to the fact that multinational enterprises with diversified operations in principle offer the same benefits of more stable earnings than do diversified portfolios. Therefore, investors need not buy foreign assets but can restrict themselves to the purchase of such domestic enterprises with diversified foreign operations.

The data on the magnitude of foreign portfolio assets in all countries presented in Table 14.4 suggests that these objections to my analysis have not been very important. Intra-industry trade in portfolio securities is a significant phenomenon.

Table 14.4 Portfolio investment flows, 1998 (in millions of US$)

Country/region	Equity securities			Bonds and notes		
	Assets ($)	Liabilities ($)	GL Index	Assets ($)	Liabilities ($)	GL Index
USA	77 753	43 808	0.72	25 064	223 020	0.20
Canada	10 242	9 070	0.94	4 686	8 009	0.74
Australia	1 380	10 211	0.24	580	(7 167)	n.a.
Japan	13 998	16 115	0.93	60 144	(19 367)	n.a.
New Zealand	986	85	0.16	557	(619)	n.a.
Austria	5 209	992	0.32	6 529	15 316	0.60
Belgium-Luxembourg	27 226	58 624	0.63	52 549	(5 996)	n.a.
Finland	2 099	9 068	0.38	1 828	(3 703)	n.a.
France	24 318	15 775	0.79	62 724	46 319	0.85
Germany	73 137	54 339	0.85	62 426	83 764	0.85
Italy	26 570	14 423	0.70	82 493	67 371	0.90
Netherlands	12 152	650	0.10	25 298	13 535	0.70
Norway	9 417	136	0.03	1 063	6 105	0.30
Portugal	891	2 138	0.59	4 956	5 108	0.98
Spain	10 123	10 256	0.99	31 738	8 501	0.42
Sweden	7 427	(328)	n.a.	9 721	703	0.13
Switzerland	2 529	8 633	0.45	12 277	1 615	0.23
UK	4 526	61 781	0.14	49 257	(5 373)	n.a.
All industrial countries	309 349	315 705	0.99	505 500	434 245	0.92
All developing countries	19 004	13 817	0.84	10 437	40 863	0.41
Africa	4 796	8 792	0.71	1 051	1 032	0.99
Asia	12 592	3 223	0.41	6 831	(2 178)	n.a.
Europe	(299)	3 992	n.a.	2 754	5 388	0.68
Middle East	(2)	355	n.a.	(1 487)	1 282	n.a.
Western hemisphere	1 917	(2 544)	n.a.	1 306	35 340	0.07
International organizations				37 046	40 382	0.96

Note: Figures in parentheses indicate that the flows of assets or liabilities in 1998 were negative, therefore the GL Index could not be calculated.
Source: IMF, *Balance of Payments Statistical Yearbook (1999)*, Aggregated Presentations, Section B Direct Investment and Other Long-term Capital.

Three points are worth making about the data in Table 14.4. First, the flows of portfolio investments among industrial countries in 1998 were very large. Combined exports and imports of equities alone amounted to US$625 billion, while those for bonds and notes were US$940 billion. In comparison, the flows of developing countries were relative modest. Second, the GL index values for all regions are very high. Those for all industrial countries are 0.99 for equities and 0.92 for bonds and notes. But even developing countries have high indices for equity securities of 0.84, while for bonds and notes they were a more modest 0.41. For international organizations, the bonds and notes index is 0.96, indicating that they act as intermediaries, floating their own bond obligations, which they lend out as bonds to borrowing countries. The indices for individual countries are considered in Table 14.5.

Third, in the case of some countries, the annual flows were negative. For example, the UK experienced a reduction in its liabilities (foreigners

Table 14.5   Portfolio investment – Equities, GL Index and ranking 1998

Country/region		Rank order		
	GL Index	GL	$x - m$	$x + m$
Spain	0.99	1	12	11
Canada	0.94	2	10	10
Japan	0.93	3	14	8
Germany	0.85	4	2	4
All developing countries	0.84	5	8	9
France	0.79	6	7	12
USA	0.72	7	1	5
Africa	0.71	8	15	7
Italy	0.70	9	3	14
Belgium-Luxembourg	0.63	10	19	2
Portugal	0.59	11	13	18
Switzerland	0.45	12	16	17
Asia	0.41	13	5	1
Finland	0.38	14	17	13
Austria	0.32	15	9	19
Australia	0.24	16	18	6
New Zealand	0.16	17	11	20
UK	0.14	18	20	3
Netherlands	0.10	19	4	15
Norway	0.03	20	6	16

Source: IMF, *Balance of Payments Statistical Yearbook (1999)*, Aggregated Presentations, Section B, Direct Investment and Other Long-term Capital.

extending credit to agents in the UK) in the form of bonds and notes, while at the same time it increased the volume of bonds and notes sold to foreign agents. Under such conditions, it is not possible to calculate the GL index. Such cases are identified in the table with the letters n.a. In the following tables, countries with such conditions are omitted.

Let me now turn to Table 14.5, which gives data for all countries and regions for which a complete set is available. The second column shows the GL index for each in descending order. The following two columns are the rank in which each country is found according to the size of its net equity flows $(X - M)$ and total flows $(X + M)$. I use this table to engage in some very preliminary and tentative testing of hypotheses about the causes of intra-industry trade in portfolio assets, going beyond the risk diversification model.

Thus, I hypothesize that a country's GL index column is an increasing function of the size of its exports, plus imports shown in the fourth column. The argument is that the absolute size of a country's capital flows reflects the absolute size of its capital market and the extent to which it is integrated into world capital markets. Both of these characteristics are presumed to reflect financial opportunities and the freedom of the markets from regulation and control, which are conducive to the purchase of foreign equities by its own citizens and the purchase of its national equities by foreigners. On the other hand, the rank correlation between net capital flows, positive or negative, should be related inversely to the index, since by definition it reflects the imbalance of net purchases and net sales of equities by domestic and foreign wealth-holders, respectively.

Figure 14.4 shows the scatter diagram between the GL index and the total flows. The correlation coefficient (R-squared) for these data is 0.09. The sign on the beta coefficient is positive and has a t-value of 1.32. On the other hand, the correlation between net capital flows and the GL index is virtually nil, and the sign on the beta coefficient is positive. Using both the total and net flows in a multiple regression improves the result on the variable for gross flow only very marginally. I conclude that there is some support for my hypothesis that the larger countries are, and the more open their capital markets, the greater the degree of intra-industry trade in equities.

I have made a duplicate of Table 14.5 for the portfolio investments in the form of bonds and notes, but to save space, I have not reproduced it here. The correlation in the ranks of countries in this table between the GL index and exports minus imports is also very low and statistically insignificant. On the other hand, the regression between the index and

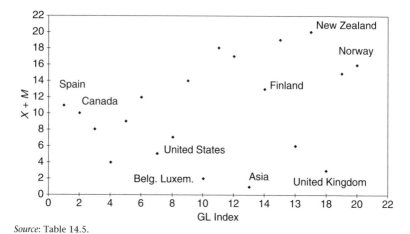

Figure 14.4   Equities rank order: *GL Index* v. $X + M$

the sum of exports and imports shows an R-square of 0.18 and a t-value on the beta coefficient of 1.9. However, the sign on the coefficient is negative. This implies that the index is smaller when countries' total trade in bonds and notes are larger. I have no explanation for this result and its contrast with the result for portfolio investment in equities, and welcome suggestions for further study.

Other investments

Other investments consist predominantly of 'loans', 'trade credits', 'currency and deposits' and 'other assets'. Through a cursory study of the data I have found some interesting differences between the data of Germany and the USA, which are probably due to the use of different statistical classifications and surveys. Thus about 90 per cent of Germany's trade in these categories of assets is undertaken through loans by banks. In the case of the USA, currency and deposits by banks make up a similarly large proportion of the trade in 'other investments'.

Pending further study of the nature of this 'other investment', I assume that it involves the activities of banks of one country operating in other countries. The existence of such multinational banking can be explained through the extension of the theory of direct investment to financial intermediaries. I published a paper (Grubel, 1983) for this purpose and showed the rapid growth in the extent to which banks have penetrated each other's geographical territories. I also theorize about the causes and welfare effects of this growth in international banking.

One motive has been to service direct foreign investment and tourists visiting from the countries in which the banks have their headquarters. There is also the risk-diversification argument. However, the bulk of the activity is attributed to the fact that foreign banks in most countries are not subject to the host or home countries' reserve requirements. These requirements represent a tax on banking, which is small relative to other forms of taxation, but large given the razor-thin margins of lending and borrowing in money markets and loans to large ultimate borrowers, particularly in the case of short-term funds. The depositors and borrowers from banks in foreign countries are often firms headquartered in the banks' home countries. These firms are forced into this diversion of business location by the existence of the regulatory tax.

The most interesting issue for the purposes of this chapter is the empirical magnitude of the phenomenon that country A's banks borrow and lend in country B directly and through subsidiaries there, while country B's banks engage in analogous activities. Table 14.6 presents this information.

Table 14.6   Other investments, flows 1998 (in million of US$)

Country/region	Assets ($)	Liabilities ($)	GL Index	X − M ($)	X + M ($)
Ireland	37 539	41 133	0.95	(3 594)	78 672
International organisations	62 132	54 383	0.93	7 749	116 515
Netherlands	57 688	67 657	0.92	(9 969)	125 345
USA	50 387	42 434	0.91	7 953	92 821
Switzerland	59 724	43 324	0.84	16 400	103 048
Middle East	20 484	29 019	0.83	(8 535)	49 503
Europe	20 298	30 796	0.79	(10 498)	51 094
All industrial countries*	292	497	0.74	(204)	789
Austria	810	1 381	0.74	(571)	2 191
All developing countries	91 679	51 626	0.72	40 053	143 305
Western hemisphere	15 186	7 801	0.68	7 385	22 987
Spain	22 482	43 802	0.68	(21 320)	66 284
Germany	84 898	167 229	0.67	(82 331)	252 127
Italy	21 232	9 816	0.63	11 416	31 048
Portugal	5 866	13 289	0.61	(7 423)	19 155
UK	24 837	71 493	0.52	(46 656)	96 330
Norway	1 591	4 939	0.49	(3 348)	6 530
Africa	3 213	11 808	0.43	(8 595)	15 021
Denmark	1 867	8 485	0.36	(6 618)	10 352

Table 14.6   (Continued)

Country/region	Assets ($)	Liabilities ($)	GL Index	X – M ($)	X + M ($)
Sweden	5 901	32 015	**0.31**	(26 114)	37 916
Finland	261	5 157	**0.10**	(4 896)	5 418
Australia	371	8 592	**0.08**	(8 221)	8 963
Canada	(12 256)	7 355	n.a.	(19 611)	(4 901)
Japan	(37 944)	(93 329)	n.a.	55 385	(131 273)
New Zealand	(1 175)	1 697	n.a.	(2 872)	522
Belgium-Luxemburg	(6 121)	16 713	n.a.	(22 834)	10 592
France	(25 935)	7 002	n.a.	(32 937)	(18 933)
Greece	(980)	(1 845)	n.a.	865	(2 825)
Iceland	(52)	805	n.a.	(857)	753
Asia	32 497	(27 772)	n.a.	60 269	4 725

Note: Figures in parentheses are negative.* The figures for 'All industrial countries' are in billions of dollars.

Source: IMF, *Balance of Payments Statistical Yearbook* (1999), Aggregated Presentations, Section C, Other Short-term Capital.

The countries in Table 14.6 are again arranged in descending order by size of the GL index. I have also included for each country the net and gross flows. The following facts are worth noting. First, out of the twenty-two ranked countries and regions, four have GL indices above 0.9 and six below 0.5. Second, the countries/region with the highest indexes are Ireland, the Netherlands, the USA, Switzerland and the Middle East. These countries/region have relatively liberal regulatory regimes for banks. This fact lends some support to the analysis of the causes of such lending presented in the preceding paragraph.

Third, Germany has made by far the largest value of loans, with over US$252 billion in 1998 and a net negative balance of US$82 billion. Germany's index is a respectable 0.67 in spite of the large imbalance. Third, the Netherlands and Switzerland have the second and third highest level of exports and imports of loans, respectively. Since they are also in the top group of countries by index size, there is some supporting evidence for the fact that countries with favourable regulatory regimes attract both large imports and exports of loans.

Summary and conclusions

The capital accounts of countries involve the export and import of assets in different categories, the most important of which are portfolio investments, direct investments, and loans. Each category of this trade in assets is in the main carried out by firms that offer different services and appeal to different customers. They can therefore reasonably be considered to make up different industries. As result, intra-industry trade exists, not only in goods and services but also in assets.

This chapter has shown that this intra-industry trade in assets is substantial, especially in portfolio investments. This finding suggests that models, which give rise to this phenomenon, can enrich the theory of international capital flows. In this chapter I have drawn on some earlier papers to present simple models capable of this task. Much more work needs to be done to link the evidence on intra-industry trade to such models.

However, it is unlikely that the intra-industry trade in assets will give rise to anything approaching the importance of the New Trade Theory, which developed in part in response to evidence on the importance of intra-industry trade in goods and services. Theories of finance and direct investment are sophisticated enough to handle the phenomenon. One of the most important implications of the existence of intra-industry trade has been for free trade policy. The lowering of trade barriers does not lead to the destruction and growth of major industries predicted by the Heckscher–Ohlin–Samuelson model. Instead the production of differentiated goods by each industry is rationalized and brings with it gains in productivity much in excess of that implied by traditional theory. Importantly, such adjustments are also less costly for the factors of production than is implied by classical and neoclassical trade theory.

By analogy, the liberalization of capital markets may be expected to bring lower adjustment costs and greater welfare gains than is implied by the simple models of finance. Deregulation will increase simultaneously the exports and imports of assets by all industries trading on capital accounts, and the liberalization will be accompanied by the increased foreign presence of banks and other financial intermediaries.

Small and developing countries in particular can expect to retain their financial intermediaries, which might expand abroad. Foreign intermediaries are likely to invest in the liberalized capital markets. In other words, the financial sectors of these countries will not be wiped out and dominated by foreign business, as is feared by those who rely on the traditional models of capital flows. It is not too late to introduce these ideas into the stalled negotiations about the liberalization of capital accounts in many countries of the world still plagued by them.

Notes

1 The only relevant previous studies are Grubel (1968) (1979) Dunning (1981), Dunning and Norman (1981), and Greenway *et al.* (2001)
2 Official reserves are included in the financial accounts. They reflect government rather than private market decisions and are therefore excluded from my analysis.
3 Readers are referred to the *Balance of Payments Statistical Yearbook* (1999) for more precise information about definitions, valuation principles and the sources of the data used in this chapter.
4 The recent reductions in the cost of information brought about by the electronics revolution have changed considerably the costs of monitoring, and have resulted in ever more outsourcing of supplies in the automobile industry. Outside suppliers may soon be producing entire chassis to the assemblers of automobiles.

References

Dunning, J. H. (1981) 'A Note on Intra-Industry Foreign Direct Investment', *Banca Nazionale del Lavoro Quarterly Review*, 139: 427–37

Dunning, J. H. (1993) *Multinational Enterprises and the Global Economy* (New York: Addison-Wesley).

Dunning, J. H. and G. Norman (1981) 'Intra-Industry Investment', in *Research in International Business and Finance*, 5, (Greenwich, Conn.: JAI Press).

Greenaway, D., P. J. Lloyd and C. Milner, (2001) 'New Concepts and Measures of the Globalisation of Production' *Economics Letters*, Vol. 73, pp 57–63.

Grubel, H. G. (1979) 'Towards a Theory of Two-way Trade in Capital Assets' in H. Giersch, editor, *On the Economics of Intra-industry Trade* (Tuebingen: J.C.B. Mohr)

Grubel, H. G. (1968) 'Internationally Diversified Portfolios: Welfare Gains and Capital Flows', *American Economic Review*, lvii (5): 1299–314.

Grubel, H. G. (1983) 'The New International Banking', *Banca Nazionale del Lavoro Quarterly Review*, 146: 263–84.

International Monetary Fund (1999) *Balance of Payments Statistical Yearbook* (Washington, DC: International Monetary Fund.)

Author Index

Abd-El-Rahmann, K. S., 138
Anderson, S., 59
Annicchiarico, B., 122
Aquino, A., 21–2, 114
Armington, P., 17
Azhar, A. K., 124–5, 127, 137

Balassa, B., 22, 88, 90, 91, 168, 169
Bauwens, L., 90, 168, 169
Bergstrand, J. H., 22
Bernard, A. B., 34
Bernhofen, D. M., 56, 57, 59
Bhagwati, J. N., 52
Boone, L., 147
Brainard, S. L., 220
Brander, J., 54–5
Brülhart, M., 120, 123–4, 127, 167

Campa, J., 82–3
Carr, D., 219
Celi, G., 81
Chen, S., 80

Davis, D., 26–7, 53, 54, 91, 92, 181
Dixit, A. K., 15, 16, 162
Dixon, P. B., 117–18, 123
Drèze, J., 109
Dunning, J. H., 277
Durkin, J. T., 191

Ekholm, K., 221
Elliott, R. J. R., 124–5, 127, 191
Emerson, M., 147
Ethier, W. J., 69, 72
European Commission, 134–5

Falvey, R. E, 15, 16, 68, 168, 169
Feenstra, R. C. J. R., 57–8, 80
Finger, J. M., 13–14, 23
Flam, H., 189, 195
Fontagné, L., 138
Frankel, J. A., 147
Freudenberg, M., 138

Fukasaku, K., 243

Goldberg, L., 82–3
Görg, H., 81
Gray, H. P., 14, 25
Greenaway, D., 22, 23, 116–17, 119,
    122, 139, 180, 191, 221, 225, 274
Grossman, G. M., 15, 16, 68, 162
Grubel, H. G., 17–21, 50, 67, 68, 69, 83,
    113, 172, 243, 282, 286
Gullstrand, J., 191

Hafeez, Z., 56, 57
Hamilton, C., 110, 114, 117, 118, 119,
    137, 167, 168
Helpman, E., 16, 19, 51, 52, 68, 134,
    168, 180, 182, 183, 189, 194, 195,
    222, 239
Hine, R., 139, 187
Hummels, D., 89, 185, 194, 228

Ishii, J., 34

Jensen, J. B., 34
Jones, R., 68, 70, 72

Kierzkowski, H., 68, 70, 72, 159
Kniest, P., 110, 114, 117, 118, 119, 137,
    167, 168
Krugman, P. R., 14, 15, 35, 45, 52, 53,
    55, 68, 111, 134, 146, 168, 180,
    182, 194
Krygier, M., 191

Lancaster, K., 14, 15, 16, 68, 169
Lee, H.-H., 22–3, 169
Lee, Y.-Y., 22–3, 169
Levinsohn, J., 90, 185, 194, 228
Lipsey, R. E., 13
Lloyd, P. J., 16, 17–21, 50, 67, 68, 69,
    83, 113, 120–1, 172, 243
Loertscher, R., 90, 91
Lovely, M. E, 137

Markusen, J. R., 218, 220, 221, 222
Maskus, K. E., 218, 221
McDowell, M., 121
Menon, J., 117–18, 123
Milner, C., 22, 23, 139, 180, 187, 191

Nelson, D. R., 137

Oliveras, J., 120
Oman, C., 243

Pagoulatos, E., 91

Quintieri, B., 122

Rauch, J. E., 91, 92
Rayment, P. B. W., 14
Rose, A. K., 33, 147

Sharma, P., 80
Sorensen, R., 91

Stone, J., 169

Tang, L., 56–7, 159
Terra, I., 120
Thom, R., 121
Toh, K., 91
Trefler, D., 27

Vanek, J., 25–6
Venables, T., 35
Verdoorn, P. J., 109

Weiss, L. W., 91
Weinstein, D. E., 26–7, 54
Wolter, F., 90, 91

Yamawaki, H., 246
Yeats, A. J., 72
Yi, K. M., 34

Zhu, S. C., 27

Subject Index

adjustment costs, 109, 110, 111–12,
   127, 131
aggregate trade imbalance
   adjustment for, in IIT for goods and
      services, 172–5
   adjustments for, in IIT measure, 21–4
aggregation of international trade
      statistics, 2, 13–17, 113
   choice of aggregation level, 24–5
aggregation theory, 16
aircraft industry, US–Canadian
      production sharing, 78–9
Annicchiarico–Quintieri index, 122
apparel industry, fragmentation of
      production, 77–8
Aquino index, 21–2, 114
Armington assumption, 17
arm's-length trade, 7, 238, 242, 249
   Japan, 249, 251–3
Asian countries, bilateral intra-
      industry trade, 193
attributes, prices of, 137–8
automobile industry
   intra-firm trade, 239, 242, 243
   intra-industry trade, 4, 76–7
Azhar–Elliott measure, 124–5

banking sector, 286–7
   investment flows, 287–8
base year weighted percentage growth
      of IIT, 117
base year weighted percentage growth
      of net trade, 117
'beach economy'
   factor endowments, 99
   geography, industrial location and
      IIT, 100–4
Bertrand–Nash competition, 56
bilateral trade
   Asian countries, 192–3
   between EU and China, 151–2
   between USA and Germany, for
      homogeneous petrochemicals, 56

European Union, 138–9, 148–51
   intensity of, as measured by GL
      index, 55, 56
   in manufactured goods, vertical and
      horizontal IIT relative importance,
      UK, 188, 189
   in manufactures, vertical and
      horizontal IIT shares, USA, 187–8
   and per capita income differences,
      184
   trade types, 5, 131, 132
   unit values, 5, 131, 132, 136
biological model of intra-industry
      trade, 52–3
bonds and notes, see portfolio
      investment
Brander model, 54–5
   and intensity of intra-industry trade,
      56, 57, 64
   and international anti-trust policy, 55
   and product homogeneity, 58
Brülhart index, 120, 123–4, 167, 168

C–H–O model see Chamberlin–
      Heckscher–Ohlin model
Canada
   fragmentation of production studies,
      80–1
   input share, manufacturing
      industries, 82–3
   production sharing with USA, 78–9,
      243
Canada–US Free Trade agreement, 73
capital accounts, 274–7, 288–9
   direct investment, 275–6, 277–82
   other investment, 276, 286–8
   portfolio investment, 276, 282–6
capital-intensive techniques, and
      higher-quality commodities, 68
capital markets, liberalization of, 289
Caribbean Basin Economic Recovery
      Act (CBERA) countries, and
      apparel industry, 77–8

categorical aggregation, 2, 13–17, 24–5, 113, 165
cge modelling, 16, 17
Chamberlin–Heckscher–Ohlin model, 6, 180–95
cross-sectional test summary, USA–OECD trade, 185, 186
and horizontal differentiation, 184–5, 194; country-specific effects and panel estimation, 185–6, 187; direct measurement of factor composition, 185; measurement of horizontal IIT, 186–9
implications for adjustment and policy, 191–4
panel equation tests, USA–OECD trade, 185–6, 187
relative importance of vertical and horizontal IIT in UK's bilateral trade in manufactured goods, 188, 189
shares of horizontal and vertical IIT in USA's bilateral trade in manufactures, 187–8
traditional view: evidence, 183–4; theory, 182–3
and vertical differentiation, 189–91, 195
China, bilateral trade with EU, 151–2
colour television industry, and fragmentation of production, 4, 73–6, 84
commodities, higher-quality, and intra-industry trade, 68
Common Market, 132
comparative advantage
European Union, 148, 153
and IIT in homogeneous products, 50–4
and inter-industry trade, 51, 181
and international fragmentation of production, 71–2
test of, 25–6
computer industry, intra-firm trade, 239, 242
constant returns to scale, and IIT in homogeneous products, 52–3
Cournot–Nash equilibrium, 56, 59, 61

demand specifications, in intra-industry trade models, 68–9
differentiated products, *see* product differentiation
direct investment, 275–6, 277–82
by major regions, 280–2
GL index through time, 278–80
industrial countries, 278, 279
theory of, 277–8
see also foreign direct investment
dissimilarity in relative factor endowments, 7
distance, and relative intra-industry trade, 4–5
Dixit–Grossman model, 15, 16, 27, 28
Dixit–Stiglitz 'love-of-variety' formulation, 68–9, 72
Dixit–Stiglitz–Krugman model, 3, 33, 34
and non-traded goods, 34–5
Dixon–Menon measures, 117–18, 127
domestic anti-trust authorities, 63

eclectic theory, 277
economies of scale
and intra-industry trade, 51
and non-traded goods, 44–5
economy-wide measure of intra-industry trade, 18
elasticity of substitution, and barrier to trade, 38
empirical studies, of IIT, 5–6, 21–4
empirical tests
technology differences in, 26, 27
test of comparative advantage, 25–6
equities, *see* portfolio investment
Europe
Monetary Union, 132, 146–7
production sharing, 81
Single Market effects, 147, 152
structural asymmetries, 147
trade flows, 81–2, 138–9
European integration, 132–6, 152
European trade patterns, 5, 131–2
characteristics, 138–9
economic policy concerns, 132–6
European Union (EU)
bilateral trade with China and Hong Kong, 151–2

comparative advantage, 148, 153
contribution of industries to trade
  balance, 151
and increased inter-industry
  specialization, 146–7, 148
market segment positioning by
  member states, 147–52
members' trade by price-quality
  range, 148–51
qualitative division of labour, 148–
  51, 153
trade patterns: empirical evidence,
  139–43; one-way trade, 139–40,
  141, 142, 152; two-way trade in
  horizontal differentiation, 140,
  141, 142; two-way trade in
  vertically differentiated goods,
  140, 141, 142, 143
trade types: in bilateral intra-EU
  trade, 145; determinants, 143–7;
  evolution in trade by EU country,
  144
Eurostat classification
  of products, 138–9
  of trade in services, 6, 159, 172, 176–
  7
export share, change in
  with economies of scale, 44–5
  with trade liberalization, 43–4

factor content of international trade,
  2–3, 25–8
  fragmentation effects, 27–8
  intra-industry trade role, 26–7, 54
  and trade in intermediate inputs,
  27–8
factor endowments
  distributions, effect on inter-
    industry specialization, 52
  effect on relative intra-industry
    trade, 89, 97–100
  predictions, and trade liberalization,
    50
  see also relative factor endowments
factor-market adjustments, 5, 109,
  110, 127, 193
Falvey model, 15, 16, 27
Falvey–Kierkowski model, 191
FDI, *see* foreign direct investment (FDI)

final commodities, in intra-industry
  trade, 68–9
first-differentiated GL indices, 115–16
Flam–Helpman model, 189–91, 195
foreign affiliates, significance in
  manufacturing industry, OECD
  countries, 239, 240–1
Foreign Affiliates Trade Statistics
  (FATS), 161–2
foreign direct investment (FDI)
  and activities by MNEs, 220–1
  determinants of IIAP and IIT
    according to trade theory, 221–4
  empirical results, 210–18
  general equilibrium model of trade
    and affiliate activity, 202–10
  horizontal, 220, 221–2
  and IIT, 7, 199–218
  IIT and IIAS indices, 200–2
  and intra-firm trade, 243
  knowledge-capital model, 220, 221,
    222
  'real' side of, 200
  theory, 6, 199, 221–4
  vertical, 220, 221, 222
  see also intra-industry affiliate
    production; intra-industry
    affiliate sales
fragmentation of production
  aircraft industry, 78–9
  apparel industry, 77–8
  automobile industry, 76–7
  colour television industry, 73–6
  and concept of increasing returns,
    70, 72
  important studies, 80–3
  international fragmentation of
    vertical production chains, 71–2
  and intra-industry trade, 1, 4, 27–8,
    69–84
  production blocks and service links,
    70–1
  semiconductor industry, 79
  Thom–McDowell index and MIIT, 121
  USA, Mexico and Canada, 73–9

General Agreement on Trade in
  Services (GATS), 159–60
  service trade definition, 160–1

general equilibrium models, 1, 111
  incorporation of H–O and non-H-O
    sources into, 180
  of trade and affiliate activity, 202–10
geography of intra-industry trade, 4–5,
    87–104
  empirical findings, 88–95
  industrial location effects,
    monopolistic competition, 100–4
  reference case, 92–5
  transport costs and demand
    elasticities, 95–7
Germany
  bilateral trade with USA,
    petrochemicals, 56
  financial accounts, 275–7
  price-quality range in bilateral trade,
    150, 151
GL index, *see* Grubel–Lloyd index
    (measure)
globalization
  and intra-firm trade, 7–8, 237–69
  patterns of globalization of industry,
    239, 242
  significance of in host economies,
    239, 240–1
gravity-type equation, strategic trade
    model, 57–8
Greenaway–Hine–Milner–Elliott
    measure, 116–17
Grubel–Lloyd index (measure), 1, 2, 6,
    7, 17–20, 87, 110, 112–13, 183
  adjustment for overall trade
    imbalance, 2, 21–4, 114
  aircraft, USA–Canada, 79
  automobiles, USA–Mexico, 77
  banking sector, 286–8
  basis of, 136–7
  categorical aggregation, 2, 13–17,
    24–5, 113, 165
  changes in, for affiliate sales and
    total trade, 202, 203
  direct investment: by regions, 281–2;
    industrial countries, 278–80
  and direction of trade, 57
  and effect of changes over time, 114–
    16, 137
  financial accounts for Germany,
    275–7

and the geography of IIT trade, 95
IIAP between Sweden and OECD
    countries, 225–6
IIT between Sweden and OECD
    countries, 225, 227
IIT with investment liberalization,
    207, 209, 210
IIT with investment and trade
    liberalization, 207, 209
IIT with no liberalization, 205, 206,
    209
IIT with trade liberalization, 206,
    209, 210
intra-European trade, 140
for intra-industry affiliate
    production, 20, 223–4
and intra-industry affiliate sales
    (IIAS) indices, 200–2
manufacturing sector, 201–2
of marginal IIT, 120, 127
matching proportions, 19–20
portfolio investment, 283–5
for RIIT under monopolistic
    competition, 100–2
scale invariance, 114
semiconductors, USA–Canada, 79
services sector, OECD countries,
    163–6
static nature, 114
televisions, USA–Mexico, 76
to measure intensity of bilateral IIT,
    55, 56, 57

H–O model, *see* Heckscher–Ohlin
    model
Hamilton–Kniest index, 118–19
Heckscher–Ohlin model, 14, 16, 17,
    26, 27, 191, 273, 274, 289
  boundaries between two industries,
    51–2
  factor endowment predictions, and
    trade liberalization patterns, EEC,
    50
  incorporation into general
    equilibrium framework, 180
  monopolistic competition trade
    perspective, 51
  multi–country, 53
  notion of industry, 51

with several countries and large
    numbers of commodities, 70
two-commodity version, 70
Heckscher–Ohlin–Vanek framework,
    54
Helpman–Lancaster model, 16, 27
homogeneous products, intra-industry
    trade in, 3–4, 49–64, 131
horizontal foreign direct investment,
    220, 221–2
and IIAP, 223, 228
horizontally differentiated products, 1,
    3, 6, 16–17, 33–46, 68, 69, 139, 180
economies of scale and non-traded
    goods, 44–5
European trade patterns, 140, 141,
    142
IIT with non-traded goods, 39–44
IIT and robustness of C–H–O model,
    184–9
intra-industry specialization, 180,
    181, 194
model, 35–6, 46
standard results without non-traded
    goods, 36–9
Hummels–Levinsohn model, 185, 194

IIAP, *see* intra-industry affiliate
    production
IIAS, *see* intra-industry affiliate sales
IMF *Balance of Payments Manual*
    (BMP5), service trade definition,
    160, 161
import share
Canada, UK and Japan, 82–3
manufacturing industries, 82–3
United States, 73, 74–5, 77–8, 80,
    243–8, 261–6
index of similarity, 20
industries
definitions, 15
industrial organization view, 51
notion of, literature views, 51–2
integrated equilibrium framework, 52,
    53
inter-industry specialization in
    homogeneous goods, 180, 194
inter-industry trade, 18, 19, 116, 124,
    131, 135

and comparative advantage, 51
Europe, 132, 133, 134
see also marginal inter-industry trade
intermediate inputs
factor content of international trade,
    27–8
in intra-industry trade, 69
internalization theory, 277–8
international anti-trust policy, 4
and Brander model, 55
and product homogeneity, 59, 62–3
international banking, 286–8
international collusion, 4, 62–3
international fragmentation of
    production
and comparative advantage, 71–2
vertical production chains, 71
international passenger air transport,
    163
International Standard Industrial
    Classification, 225
international telephone industry,
    intra-industry trade, 56–7, 159
international trade, 2
factor content of, 2–3, 25–8
as inter-industry trade, 52
and international economic
    specialization, 55
lower tariff effects, 33
Ricardian model, 53
vertical specialization in production
    effects, 34
international trade statistics,
    aggregation into exports and
    imports, 13
intra-European trade, empirical
    evidence, 139–43, 153
intra-firm trade
close link with IIT, 242–3
data sources, 261–9
and globalization, 7–8, 237–69
Japan, 7, 243, 249–60, 261, 266–9
United States, 7, 243, 244–9, 261,
    262–6
intra-industry affiliate activity
general equilibrium model, 202–4
horizontal firms, 204
implications for relationship between
    IIT and IIAS indices, 205–10

intra-industry activity (*cont.*)
national firms, 204
vertical firms, 204–5
intra-industry affiliate employment,
Sweden, 225
intra-industry affiliate production
(IIAP), 7, 200, 218, 221
definition, 223
and degree of similarity in relative
factor environments, 223
determinants of IIAP and IIT
according to trade theory, 221–4
estimated change unexplained by
included variables, IIT and IIAP,
232–3
GL indices, Sweden–OECD
countries, 225–6
and horizontal FDI, 223, 228
IIT indices, 221, 223
non-linear estimations of logistic
functions, 229–30
random effects estimation of
transformed logistic functions,
230–2
and relative factor endowments,
224–34
relative market size effects, 224
results, 228–33
Swedish data and methods, 224–8
intra-industry affiliate sales (IIAS), 218
logit regressions, 212–14, 225
ratio to intra-industry trade OLS
regressions, 216–18
intra-industry affiliate sales (IIAS)
indices, 6, 210
empirical results, 210–18
with full liberalization, 209–10
and GL index, 200–2
with investment liberalization, 208,
209
with investment liberalization,
countries twice as big, 208, 209
intra-industry affiliate trade, 161–2
intra-industry specialization, 53, 180
European Union, 146–7, 148
and factor endowment distributions,
52
in horizontally differentiated goods,
180, 181, 194

intra-industry trade
biological model, 52–3
and the C–H–O model, 180–95
concept, 1, 51
definition, 18, 51, 113
empirical studies, 5–6, 21–4
Europe, 132–4
in the factor content of international
trade, 2–3, 25–8, 54
and foreign direct investment (FDI),
7, 199–218
geography of, 4–5, 87–104
as statistical phenomenon, 13–14
strategic, *see* strategic intra-industry
trade
intra-industry trade in assets, 8, 273–89
capital accounts in perspective, 274–7
direct investment, 275–6, 277–82
other investments, 276, 286–8
portfolio investment, 276, 282–6
intra-industry trade expansion,
measure of, 109–27
intra-industry trade in homogeneous
products, 3–4, 49–64, 131
and comparative advantage, 50–4
and constant returns to scale, 52–3
explanations for occurrence of, 54
lessons learned from empirical and
theoretical work, 63–4
product homogeneity and volume of
intra-industry trade, 58–9
strategic IIT, 54–63
intra-industry trade in horizontally
differentiated products, *see*
horizontally differentiated
products
intra-industry trade index, *see* Grubel–
Lloyd index (measure)
intra-industry trade logit regressions,
214–16
intra-industry trade measures, 1, 2, 13
adjusting for the trade imbalance,
21–4
changes over time, 114–18, 137
choice of level of aggregation, 24–5
choice of statistic, 17–21
see also Grubel–Lloyd index
(measure); quasi-dynamic
measures

intra-industry trade models, 3–5, 14–15
  categorization according to
    specialization, 53–4
  consistent aggregation application,
    2, 16–17
  with economies of scale, 15
  with horizontal differentiation, 1, 3,
    6, 16, 33–46
  with two industries and numbers of
    factors, 15–17
intra-industry trade in services, 2, 5–6,
    23, 56–7, 159–77
  adjustment for aggregate trade
    imbalances, 172–5
  by industry, 167
  combined with IIT in goods, 171–5
  cross-country analysis, 168–71
  determinants, 170–1
  future research directions, 175–6
  influence of trade orientation, 169,
    171
  measurement, 163–8
  OECD countries: 1-digit and 2-digit
    industry comparison, 165–6;
    1-digit industries, 163–5
  relationship to country's level of
    trade barriers, 169
  relationship to country's per capita
    income, 168–9, 171
  relationship to country's size, 169
intra-industry trade in vertically
    differentiated products, *see*
    vertically differentiated products
intra-industry variation among factor
    intensities, 14
investment liberalization
  countries twice as big, and IIAS
    index, 208, 209
  and IIAS index, 208, 209
  and IIT index, 207, 209, 210
  trade liberalization, and IIT index,
    207, 209
inward processing trade (IPT), USA
    imports from Europe, 81
Italy, price-quality range in bilateral
    trade, 150, 151

Japan
  exports to USA, 246

import share, 83
intra-firm trade, 7, 243, 249–60;
  by industry, 250, 251–5; data,
  249–50, 261, 266–9; determinants,
  250, 256–7; machinery industries,
  microdata regression results,
  257, 259; manufacturing and
  non-manufacturing, microdata
  regression results, 257, 258
  relationship between R&D intensity
    and other variables, 256–7
Jones specific factor model, 16, 17

knowledge-capital model of FDI, 220,
    221, 222
Krugman monopolistic competition
    trade model, 51, 53, 55, 58, 180

labour market adjustment costs,
    111–12, 127
Law of Comparative Advantage, 15
liberalized capital markets, 289
long-term trends in intra-industry
    trade, 5, 131–53

manufactured goods
  bilateral trade: UK, 188, 189; USA,
    187–8
  world trade growth, 3, 33, 45
manufacturing industries
  fragmentation, 82–3
  intra-firm trade, 239, 242, 243, 257,
    258
  intra-industry trade, 57, 201–2
marginal inter-industry trade, 118
marginal intra-industry trade, 5, 21,
    110, 114, 137
  matched trade changes, 118;
    extensions to MIIT index, 120–2;
    GL style measure of MIIT, 120;
    Hamilton–Kniest index, 118–19;
    unscaled MIIT measures, 122–3
  and sectoral performance, 123–5
  in services: by industry, 167, 168;
    OECD countries, 165, 168
  which measure is best?, 125–6
market power, 55

market segment positioning by member
    states, European Union, 147–52
market size
    IIT and relative factor endowments,
        224–8
    and laws of gravity, 57–8
market structure, differentiation of
    products and determinants of
    trade, 136
measure of similarity, 20
Mexico
    apparel industry, and industry
        fragmentation, 77–8
    automobile industry, and industry
        fragmentation, 76–7
    colour television industry, and
        industry fragmentation, 73–6, 84
model building, 16–17
Monetary Union, Europe, 132, 146–7
monopolistic competition trade
    model, 51, 53, 55, 58, 180, 191–2
    FDI and relative factor endowments,
        222–3
    relative intra-industry trade, 100–4
multi-country Heckscher–Ohlin–
    Samuelson model, 53
multinational enterprises (MNEs)
    and FDI, 8, 220–1
    IIAP and factor endowments, 220–34
    and intra-firm trade, 7–8, 237–69
    Japan, and intra-firm trade, 249–60
    significance of, 237–8
    size and value of, 237
    United States, and intra-firm trade,
        244–9
Mundell–Fleming model, 274

NAFTA, 73, 74
neoclassical trade theory, 51, 52, 55, 110
new trade theory, 51, 52, 111, 134,
    136, 137, 200, 289
non-disruptive trade expansion,
    measure of, 109–27
non-tariff barriers, 92
non-traded goods
    demand-side versus supply-side
        asymmetry, 35
    domestic market and export market
        analyses, 39–41

and economies of scale, 44–5
    intra-industry trade with, 39–44
    share of trade with, 42–4
    standard model without, 36–9
    switch to traded goods, 3, 34–5
    trade liberalization with, 41–2, 44
    trade liberalization without, 37–9
North–North trade, 6, 183, 194, 195,
    243
    in a H–O setting, 181
    patterns of inter- and intra-industry
        trade, 27
North–South trade, 6, 68, 183, 194, 195

OECD–Eurostat classification of trade
    in services, 6, 159, 172, 176–7
oligopolistic industries, trade
    liberalization, 59
one-sector industrial organization
    models, 51
one-way trade, 139
    European Union, 140, 141, 142, 152
other investments (banking sector),
    276, 286–8
outward processing trade (OPT),
    Europe, 81–2

Pacific Asian economies,
    manufactured trade, 243
petrochemical industry, intra-industry
    trade, 56
pharmaceuticals industry, intra-firm
    trade, 239, 242
portfolio investment, 276, 282–6
    bonds and notes, GL index, 285–6
    by industrial countries, 283–4
    criticisms, 282–3
    equities, GL index and rankings,
        284–5
    equities rank order, 285, 286
post-Second World War, world
    manufactured trade growth rate,
    3, 33, 45
price–quality range, EU members,
    148–51
product differentiation
    and Brander model, 58
    horizontal, 3, 6, 16, 33–46, 68, 69,
        139

and international collusion, 4
market demand for differentiated
products, 67, 68
strategic intra-industry trade, 57
vertical, 4, 6, 16–17, 69, 131
product homogeneity
and profitability of international
trade, policy implications, 59–63
two-country model of international
trade, 59; equilibrium analysis,
61–2; firms, 60–1; goods and
consumers, specification of, 60;
and international collusion, 62–3
and volume of IIT, 58–9
production factors, transferability
among products, 112
products, Eurostat classification, 138–9

qualitative division of labour, Europe,
148–51, 153
quality ladders, 68
quasi-dynamic measures, 114–15
Dixon–Menon measures, 117–18
first-differentiated GL indices, 115–
16
Greenaway–Hine–Milner–Elliott
measure, 116–17

'racetrack economy'
factor endowments, 97–9
and RIIT measures, 92–5, 100
transport costs and demand
elasticities, 95–7
reciprocal dumping, 55
relative factor endowments
dissimilarity in, 7, 220, 224–34
and FDI under monopolistic
competition, 222–3
and horizontal FDI, 222
and IIAP, 224–34
and IIT and market size, 224–8
relative intra-industry trade, decline
with distance, 4–5, 87–104
cross-section studies, 88–9, 90
empirical findings, 88; country
studies, 88–90; industry studies,
90; reference case, 92–5; trade
costs, 90–2
factor endowment effects, 89, 97–100

inverse relationship, 88–9
monopolistic competition, 100–4
signs on factor endowments and
country size, 89–90
transport costs and demand
elasticities, 95–7

sectoral performance, and MIIT, 123–5
semiconductor industry
intra-firm trade, 239, 242
US–Canadian production sharing,
79
services trade, *see* trade in services
share of trade with non-traded goods,
42–4
Single Market effects, Europe, 146, 147,
152
smooth adjustment hypothesis (SAH),
109, 110–12, 194
South–North trade, 194
South–South trade, 6, 181, 183, 194
spatial pattern of trade, forces
affecting, 87–104
Standard International Trade
Classification (SITC), 13, 14, 24,
150, 172
Revision 2, 72
static IIT, 110, 112–14
see also Grubel–Lloyd index
(measure)
Stolper–Samuelson mechanism, 132,
134
strategic intra-industry trade, 3–4, 54–
64
entry barriers and product
differentiation, 57–8
explaining intensity of IIT, 55, 56–7
market size and laws of gravity, 57–8
product homogeneity and
profitability of international trade,
59–63
product homogeneity and volume of
IIT, 58–9
strategic trade policies, 55
Sweden, intra-industry affiliate
employment, 225
Sweden–OECD countries
GL indices of IIAP, 226–7
GL indices of IIT, 227

tariff decline, and growth of
   international trade, 33
technology matrices, 54
telecommunications industry, 163
television industry, intra-industry
   trade, 4, 73–6, 84
Thom–McDowell index, 121–2
trade balance, contribution of
   industries to, Europe, 151
trade costs, measurement, 90–2
trade flows
   Europe, 81–2, 138–9
   incorporating local sales of foreign
      affiliates, 120–1
   measurement, 109–10
   structure, 110
trade imbalance
   adjustment for, in IIT for goods and
      services, 172–5
   adjustment for, in IIT measure, 21–4
   effect on GL index, 169
   'equilibrium' and 'non-equilibrium'
      multilateral imbalances, 23, 114
   equiproportionate adjustment, 22
   factors, OECD countries, 174–5
   regressing the unadjusted index,
      22–3
trade liberalization, 3, 45, 110–11
   effect on share of trade in total
      output, 42–4
   and change in share of exports,
      43–4
   EEC patterns at odds with factor
      endowment predictions of
      Heckscher–Ohlin model, 50
   effect on change from non-traded to
      traded goods, 34–5
   and elasticity of substitution, 38
   factor-market adjustment to, 5
   IIT index with, 206, 209, 210
   IIT index without, 205, 206, 209
   investment liberalization, and IIT
      index, 207, 209
   with non-traded goods, 41–2, 44
   in oligopolistic industries, 59
   without non-traded goods, 37–9
trade orientation, and IIT in services,
   169, 171
trade overlap, 14, 137

trade patterns, 109
   Europe: characteristics, 138–9; and
      economic policy concerns, 132–6
   European Union, 139–43
trade in services
   'BMP5' definition, 160–1
   characteristics of, 162–3
   choice of definition to use, 162
   GATS definition based on modes,
      160–1
   nature of, 159–60
   OECD–Eurostat classification, 6,
      159, 172, 176–7
   problem of collecting statistics, 161
   proposed use of FATS, 161–2
   share of, OECD countries, 163, 164
   see also intra-industry trade in services
trade theory, 109, 112
   advent of, 50–1
   empirical tests, test of comparative
      advantage, 25–6
   and European integration, 132, 133
   Grubel–Lloyd measure application, 19
   see also neoclassical trade theory;
      new trade theory
trade types, 5, 131, 132
   determinants in EU, 143–7
   measuring, 136–9
   share of, EU trade, 140–2
transport costs
   cross-industry variation, 96
   and demand elasticities, 95–7
   distance, and cross-industry
      differences, 96–7
   and industrial location, under
      monopolistic competition, 100,
      102–3
   measurement, 91
transportation services, intra-industry
   trade, 159
two-way trade in assets, *see* intra-
   industry trade in assets
two-way trade in similar, horizontally
   differentiated products, *see*
   horizontally differentiated
   products
two-way trade in vertically
   differentiated products, *see*
   vertically differentiated products

United Kingdom
  bilateral trade, manufactured goods,
    188, 189
  import share, 82
unit values, interpretation of
    differences in, 5, 131, 132, 136,
    137–8, 140
United States
  affiliate production statistics, 161–2
  apparel industry, and fragmentation
    of production, 77–8
  automobile industry, and
    fragmentation of production, 76–
    7, 243
  colour television industry, and
    fragmentation of production, 73–
    6, 84
  exports of goods, 34, 243; intra-firm
    trade, 243, 244–8, 261, 262–6
  fragmentation of production studies,
    80; imports of goods, 73, 74–5, 77–
    8, 80; intra-firm trade, 243, 244–8,
    261, 262–6
  intra-firm trade, 7, 243, 244–9;
    importance of in a country's
    foreign trade, 246, 249; with other
    OECD countries, 244, 246, 249

production sharing with Canada,
    78–9, 243
US Production Sharing Provision of
    Harmonized Tariff Schedule (HTS
    PSP), 73, 77, 78, 80

vertical foreign direct investment, 220,
    221, 222, 223
vertical specialization in production,
    effects on international trade, 34
vertically differentiated products, 1, 4,
    6, 16–17, 69, 131, 139, 181
  and C–H–O model, 189–91, 195
  cross-section and panel testing,
    USA–OECD trade, 191, 192
  European trade patterns, 132, 135,
    140, 141, 142, 143
  factors affecting, 138

wage flexibility, impediments to, 111,
    112
world manufactured trade, growth
    rate, 3, 33, 45